Nova Scotia,
New Brunswick &
Prince Edward Island

DATE DUE

Demco

PLAN YOUR TRIP

NOVA SCOTIA P40

NEW BRUNSWICK P102

ON THE ROAD

Contents

SPECIAL FEATURES

Welcome to Nova Scotia, New Brunswick & Prince Edward Island

Fashioned by the mighty Atlantic, these down-home Canadian provinces call you 'deary,' and offer you hot seafood chowder as whales breach in the distance.

Water World

'Water everywhere,' you think, as you scan the horizon from the windy clifftop. Then you see it on the water: a fine spray emanating from what appears to be a log. The log morphs into two giant tail flukes arching up, water cascading from their scalloped edges, before they slap down and upwell a fan of water. Seconds later the slick curve of a whale body roll-slides on the inky ocean surface.

It's a freeze-frame moment – one of many to experience in Atlantic Canada. Such flashes might occur as you whiz past a lupine-fringed, sienna-colored beach on your bike in Prince Edward Island, fly-fish the legendary rivers of New Brunswick, watch icebergs float by in Newfoundland, or mount a tidal bore wave in a dinghy in Nova Scotia.

Light the Way

Welcome to what's perhaps the lighthouse capital of the world. Follow paved or small dirt tracks to points where waves crash against granite shores amid windswept surroundings. If you're lucky, the picture-perfect beacon will house a museum and offer access to the top so that you can enjoy the view. Let your imagination wander over the centuries to picture the ships kept safe from icy waters by these Maritime lifesavers.

A Foot-tapping Good Time

Here's a culture defined by fiddle playing and wearing out the dancing shoes. Maritimers are well-practiced in the art of partying and like nothing more than to share the good times with all who visit; if these come-one-come-all get-togethers don't make you tap your feet, check your pulse. Outdoor music and food festivals fill up the summer calendar, as the good times expand with the sunshine. Everyone is in on the festivities – Acadian and Scottish each have their own distinct music – and you're all invited, so be there by six.

Shellfish Bliss

Gear up for some serious crustacean battles by wearing a bib and not worrying about getting butter in your hair. Lobster, scallops, crab, mussels and oysters form one of the best bounties the sea has to offer. Confused about how to get the meat out of that crustacean leg? These thoughtful Canadians often supply you with instructions on the placemat for how to master the beast with your supplied utensils. Part surgeon, part warrior, part gourmand, the experience of eating these critters is almost as good as the taste.

Why I Love Nova Scotia, New Brunswick & Prince Edward Island

By Celeste Brash, Author

The first time I visited the Maritimes I was adopted by an elderly couple. I had been dining alone at a restaurant (as Lonely Planet authors do) and they invited me to sit with them. By dinner's end they'd invited me to stay. While these Canadian provinces hold natural wonders to rival anywhere in the world – the Fundy tides, endless coastline of wild rose, pink- and white-sand beaches, forested mountain trails and more – the people are so real and kind that it's hard to say goodbye.

For more about our authors, see page 288

Above: Peggy's Cove (p56), Nova Scotia

Nova Scotia, New Brunswick & PEI

ELEVATION

2000m
1000m
750m
500m
300m
200m
100m
0

Iceberg Alley
Watch 15,000-year-old
chunks of ice float by (p197)

Belle
Isle

Mary's
Harbour

Cartwright

Paradise
River

**Port Hope
Simpson**

Rigolet

Lake
Melville

North West
River

Happy Valley-
Goose Bay

International
Military Base

Cape
Harrison

Hamilton Inlet

Makkovik

Hopedale

Postville

Nipishish
Lake

Davis Inlet

Labrador
Sea

Nain

Mistastin
Lake

Harp
Lake

Fraser River

Hebron

**Kaumajet
Mountains**

**Mont d'Iberville
(1652m)**

Torngat Mountains

LABRADOR

Churchill
Falls

Churchill River

500

Smallwood
Reservoir

Atikonak
Lake

Schefferville

Esker

500

Labrador
City
Wabush

Lake
Joseph

Ashuanipi
Lake

Ungava
Bay

QUÉBEC

Lac
Caniapiscau

200 km
100 miles

Nova Scotia, New Brunswick & Prince Edward Island's
Top 10

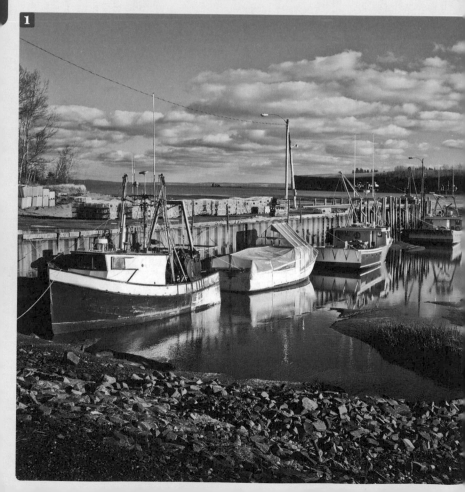

Bay of Fundy Tides

1 The Bay of Fundy (p115) is home to the highest tides in the world. Boats look hopelessly beached on mud flats and piers look ridiculously lofty at low tide. Then, when one billion tonnes of water flow back into the bay, boats bob up to 15m above where they were six hours earlier – it's surreal. Get right into the tidal action by rafting the tidal bore, or relax with a whale-watching cruise, on which you might see blue whales or the rare fin whale.

Peggy's Cove

2 It's on all the postcards and is clogged with tour buses throughout summer, yet Peggy (p56) enchants all who visit. The lighthouse, the blue-grey sea and the tiny sheltered bay scattered with crab traps and Popeye-esque boat docks are all straight out of a sailor's yarn. To get beyond the snapshot take time to meander and experience a glimpse of life in a very, very small Maritime village. It's surprising Disney hasn't made a film here yet.

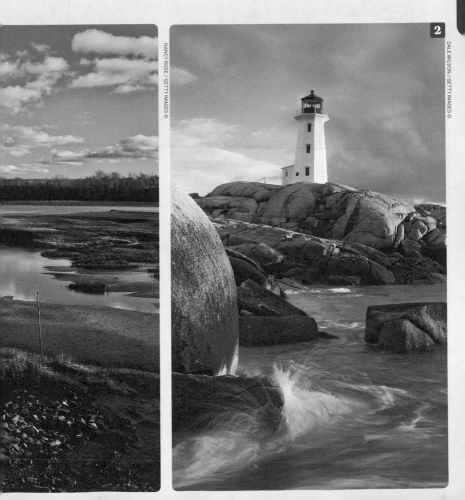

NANCY ROSE / GETTY IMAGES ©

DALE WILSON / GETTY IMAGES ©

2

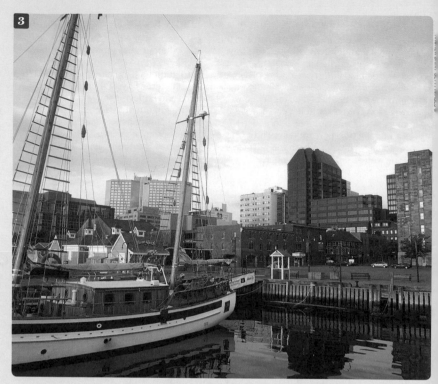

Wandering the Halifax Waterfront

3 When the fog is in the tall ships, piers and harbor take on the air of an eerie pirate-movie set. A foghorn blows and you can almost imagine the cold, dingy scene of yesteryear. Then the sun comes out and everything turns festive: street buskers, laughter peeling from outdoor pub seating and kids with ice-cream cones fill the waterfront while container ships and sailboats chug across the sparkling bay. Hop on the Dartmouth ferry to get a view back to shore of Halifax's boxy downtown (p44).

Scottish & Acadian Music

4 Long cold winters have been endured for centuries with the help of lively fiddle playing and dancing. Call it a ceilidh, kitchen party or concert, but don't miss the chance to experience something that brings joy to much of this part of the world (p233). Listen to bagpipes or watch young fiddle virtuosos play while the oldies get up and step dance. Music is practiced indoors all winter to be let loose to party in summer at community halls, pubs, parks and festivals. Bagpipe player, Citadel Hill National Historic Site (p45)

The Viking Trail

5 The Viking Trail (p200), aka Rte 430, connects Newfoundland's two World Heritage sites on the northern peninsula. Gros Morne National Park, with its fjordlike lakes and geological oddities rests at its base, while the sublime, 1000-year-old Viking settlement at L'Anse aux Meadows – Leif Eriksson's pad – stares out from the peninsula's tip. The road is an attraction in its own right, holding close to the sea as it heads resolutely north past the ancient burial grounds of Port au Choix and the ferry jump-off to big bad Labrador. Gros Morne National Park (p200)

EMILY RIDDELL / GETTY IMAGES ©

Lobster Suppers

6 Slapping on a bib was never so much fun. Join the crowds of hungry revelers attacking their plate-sized, orange-red crustacean with forks, pickers and nutcrackers. Get covered in lobster juice; dunk each mouthful in butter and enjoy. Don't forget to leave room for the feast's common accompaniments: mussels, chowder, fresh biscuits, salad and strawberry shortcake for dessert. You can get the lobster supper experience (p244) at restaurants but the best, cheapest and most fun meals are at local churches and town halls.

Cape Breton Highlands National Park

7 Circuitous roads wind along evergreen ridgelines and dramatic coastal cliffs, eagles soar above, whales spout in the distance and moose can be seen along the roadside. Tackle this national park (p88) as a drive or a cycle but be sure to buckle up your hiking boots at least once to explore the trails that lead past streams, waterfalls and wildflowers to ever more stunning vistas. On the coast, paddle a kayak or take a whale-watching tour to look for minke whales, seabirds and seals.

6

ROBERT RUSHTON / GETTY IMAGES ©

ANDREW PEACOCK / GETTY IMAGES ©

Floating Iceberg Alley

8 They shimmer from white to electric blue as they float down the grey-black Atlantic (p197). It's a wonder that these icebergs have broken away from their Greenland home to create such a show, but even more amazing is that some of the ice is more than 15,000 years old. While icebergs have been floating around here for centuries, they are doing so at an ever-increasing rate. For an unusual treat cool down a summer drink with the world's most ancient ice cubes.

Green Gables

9 Let the stories of your childhood come alive at the real-life sites that provided the backdrop to the beloved *Anne of Green Gables* series (p163). All over Prince Edward Island you'll find kitsch gift shops, little girls dressed up in red polyester 'Anne' braids, and antiques and old-time memorabilia, as well as places that understandably inspired names such as the 'Lake of Shining Waters' and 'White Way of Delight.'

House of Green Gables (p163), Cavendish

Grand Manan Island

10 From windy, jagged cliffs and marshland, to spruce forests and sloping points with storybook lighthouses, Grand Manan (p122) has incredible natural diversity along its 30km length. There are dozens of trails to wander and coves to explore but no fast-food restaurants or traffic. The silence is broken only by the rhythmic ocean surf. You feel about a million nautical miles away from anything not windswept, rugged or overwhelmingly natural. To get out of a peaceful stupor, go kayaking, cycling, whale watching or birding. Swallowtail Lighthouse (p122)

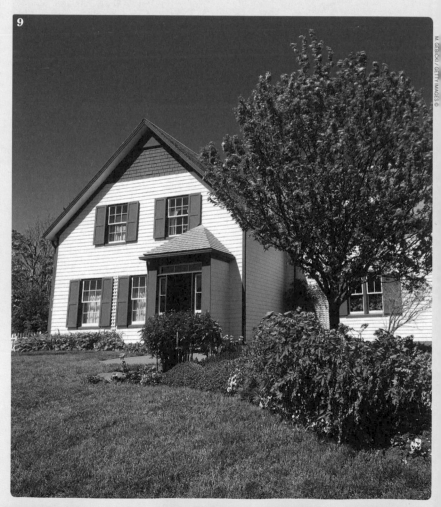

9

M GEBICKI / GETTY IMAGES ©

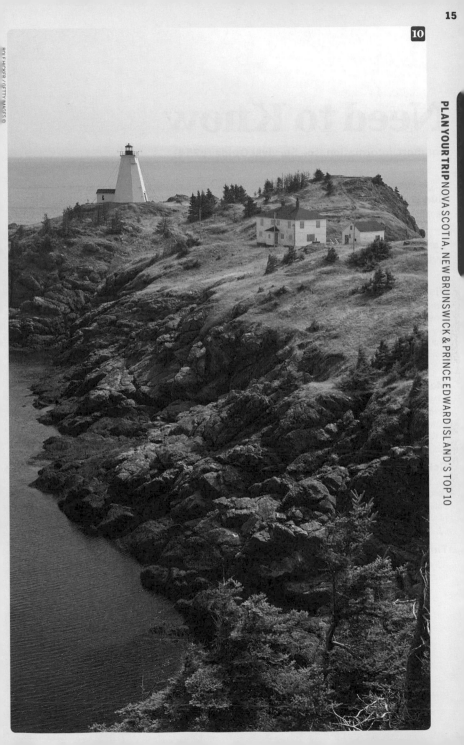

Need to Know

For more information, see Survival Guide (p254)

Currency
Canadian dollar ($)

Language
English and French

Visas
Generally not required for stays of up to 180 days; some nationalities require a temporary resident visa.

Money
ATMs widely available. Credit cards accepted in most hotels and restaurants.

Cell Phones
Local SIM cards can be used in unlocked GSM 850/1900 compatible phones.

Time
Atlantic (GMT minus four hours)

When to Go

Mild summers, cold winters
Cold climate

L'Anse aux Meadows National Historic Site
GO Jun–Sep

St John's
GO Dec–Apr

Charlottetown
GO Jun–Sep

Cape Breton Island
GO Jun–Oct

Grand Manan Island
GO Jun–Sep

Annapolis Valley
GO May–Sep

High Season
(Jul & Aug)

➡ Sunshine and warm weather prevail.

➡ The whole region plunges into festival mode, with theater, music and food extravaganzas.

➡ Attractions and visitor information centers keep longer summer hours.

Shoulder
(May–Jun & Sep–Oct)

➡ Wildflowers bloom in the spring and leaves turn gold and red in the fall.

➡ Temperatures are cool but comfortable.

➡ Some lodgings and restaurants shut.

Low Season
(Nov–Apr)

➡ Few lodgings and attractions outside the big cities and ski resorts remain open.

➡ Darkness and cold take over.

➡ Christmas festivals liven up December and January.

Websites

Nova Scotia Tourism (www.novascotia.com)

Tourism New Brunswick (www.tourismnewbrunswick.ca)

Tourism Prince Edward Island (www.tourismpei.com)

Newfoundland & Labrador Tourism (www.newfoundland-labrador.com)

Parks Canada (www.pc.gc.ca)

Lonely Planet (www.lonely-planet.com/canada)

Important Numbers

Nova Scotia and Prince Edward Island's area code is ☑902, New Brunswick is ☑506, and Newfoundland and Labrador is ☑709. Many accommodations have toll-free numbers that are free to dial from Canada and the USA. For local calls you need to use the area code but not the country code.

Country Code	☑1
International access code	☑011
Emergency	☑911
Directory assistance	☑411

Exchange Rates

Australia	A$1	C$0.94
Europe	€1	C$1.03
Japan	¥100	C$1.25
New Zealand	NZ$1	C$0.82
UK	UK£1	C$1.58
US	US$1	C$1.03

For current exchange rates see www.xe.com.

Daily Costs

**Budget:
Less than $100**

➡ Dorm bed: $25–40

➡ Campsite: $20–35

➡ Self-cater meals from markets and supermarkets

**Midrange:
$100–250**

➡ B&B or room in a midrange hotel: $90–180

➡ Restaurant meal: from $20 plus drinks

➡ Rental car: $25–70 per day

➡ Attraction admissions: $5–15

**Top End:
More than $250**

➡ Four-star hotel room or luxury B&B: from $180

➡ Three-course meal in a top restaurant: from $40 plus drinks

➡ Sea kayaking or canoe day tour: $55–150

Opening Hours

Opening hours may vary throughout the year and from place to place. We've provided high season opening hours in cities and larger towns; hours may decrease outside the summer season and in rural areas.

Banks 8am-5pm Mon-Fri; varies branch to branch

Restaurants breakfast 7:30-10:30am; lunch 11am-2pm; dinner 5:30-9pm

Cafes 6:30am-5pm

Bars 6pm-2am

Shops 10am-5pm

Arriving

Halifax Stanfield International Airport The Metro Express runs every 30 to 60 minutes between 5:45am and 12:15am. Taxis take 30 minutes to downtown ($56).

St John's International Airport It's a 10-minute taxi ride to downtown ($25 plus $3 for each additional passenger).

Land Border Crossings Canadian Border Services Agency (p267) Posts updated wait times hourly; usually less than 30 minutes.

Getting Around

Public transportation is available in cities and between larger towns but most visitors rent a car.

Car Good-value rentals are available in Nova Scotia and New Brunswick. Prince Edward Island and Newfoundland have fewer vehicles available and higher prices.

Train Clean, economical and reliable **VIA Rail** (p267) connects Halifax to Montreal via New Brunswick.

Bus Better coverage than trains; places not serviced by buses usually have private shuttle services for similar fares, more cramped seating and door-to-door service.

Keep in Mind

Remember the large scale of Canada's Atlantic provinces: distances can be large and travel times slow. Consider exploring just one or two regions in depth.

Blackflies and mosquitoes can be a major annoyance in the summer. Bring insect repellent and cover up, especially in northern and woodsy regions.

Book ahead for transportation and accommodation in summer.

For much more on **getting around**, see p268

If You Like...

Seafood

Sweet Atlantic lobsters are ubiquitous and other underwater delicacies such as Digby scallops and Malpeque oysters are world famous for their quality.

Lobster suppers A Maritime seafood feast found mostly in Nova Scotia and Prince Edward Island (PEI), best taken in churches and town halls. (p244)

Lobster Pound & Moore Takes lobster suppers into gourmet territory, plus serves the best lobster ravioli on the planet. (p96)

Water Prince Corner Shop Scarf a scallop burger or get a lobster to eat there or to go. (p151)

Norseman Restaurant & Art Gallery Put on rubber boots to handpick your lobster right on the shore. (p206)

Wine & Spirit Tasting

Hard to believe, but Nova Scotia's Annapolis Valley has the same latitude as Bordeaux, France. Other areas produce harder stuff: whiskey, vodka and good old-fashioned moonshine.

Annapolis Valley & Bear River regions Wineries are popping up everywhere through these two adjacent areas perfect for touring. (p67; p71)

Glenora Inn & Distillery Canada's only single malt whiskey is produced here; tour the distillery and take a swig of the spirits. (p88)

Rossignol Estate Winery Specializes in fruit wines including an award-winning (and delicious) blackberry meade. (p154)

Prince Edward Distillery One makes fine potato vodka and the other makes Canada's first legal moonshine so potent it evaporates on the tongue. (p155)

Auk Island Winery Try fruit wines made with iceberg water and local fruit. (p196)

Historic Sites

Leif Eriksson was probably the first European to set foot in the Americas in Newfoundland, marking the beginning of this region's rich European history. Folks get into it too, dressing up in period garb and acting the part, bringing the sites to life.

Louisbourg The mother of this region's historical sites – the size and authenticity of the re-created sites make you feel like you time-warped to the 18th century. (p97)

L'Anse aux Meadows National Historical Site Seriously, this is where the Vikings landed? Yup and it's just as cool as you hoped it would be. (p205)

King's Landing Historical Settlement Woo hoo! It's a re-created 19th-century Loyalist village including pub food and children's programs. (p110)

Canadian Museum of Immigration at Pier 21 More than one million immigrants landed here to start their lives anew in Canada or the USA. Prepare to be moved by true heartwarming stories and maybe find the names of your ancestors. (p45)

Lighthouses

When most people envision the Atlantic and Maritime provinces, there's a lighthouse in the image somewhere. A drive to any coastal spit will usually turn up a red-and-white beacon just waiting to be photographed.

Peggy's Cove The quintessential Maritime image: a red-and-white storybook lighthouse on rolling granite backed by the cold Atlantic. (p57)

(Above) Harvesting grapes, Rossignol Estate Winery (p154), Prince Edward Island
(Below) North Rustico (p162), Prince Edward Island

Cape Enrage Watch the rise and fall of the Fundy tides from this windswept, 150-year-old beacon. (p132)

Long Point Spot icebergs in May and June from the 360-degree view in this 1876 lighthouse. (p196)

Swallowtail Lighthouse White-washed perfection on a grassy bluff where you can watch seals raiding ancient fish traps. (p122)

Point Amour Lighthouse Provincial Historic Site The tallest lighthouse in Atlantic Canada also has a small maritime history museum. (p216)

Point Prim PEI's prettiest beacon with views over the island; climb up and try the hand-pump fog horn. (p154)

Hiking & Walking

This is a forested region with so many fantastic hiking possibilities that we can hardly list them all. From coastal jaunts to deep woods, mountains, lakes and valleys, you'll be looking out for birdlife and moose.

Cape Breton Highlands National Park Winding roads to ocean vistas perfect for spotting whales, moose or eagles. (p90)

Fundy National Park See the highest rise and fall of the tides from forested bliss. (p130)

Mt Carleton Start out in French cowboy country to discover rugged hiking and quiet lakes. (p114)

East Coast Trail Part easy walking, part tough wilderness trail, often with free guided hikes. (p176)

Cape Split There's no better place to hike along the Fundy tidal shore, then reward yourself afterwards with a glass of red. (p74)

Kayaking & Canoeing

Perhaps the most Canadian of sports and a spectacular way to experience this region from a watery perspective. From mellow lake paddles to high action in the waves past spouting whales, the water is a huge part of what makes these provinces tick.

Eastern Shore Nova Scotia's forgotten coast is studded with islands and calm bays, perfect for paddling, all beautiful even in dense fog. (p98)

Mt Carleton Gorgeous canoeing through a string of wilderness lakes surrounded by tree-clad mountains. (p114)

North Rustico Scoot off from the red-sand beach and burn the calories you'll replenish at a lobster supper that night. (p162)

Chiputneticook Lakes Take a four-day camping and canoeing trip through this spectacular wilderness lake area. (p114)

Whale Watching

Thar she blows! Humpbacks and minke are the most common whales you'll spot in this region but lucky souls will see elusive blue whales and the endangered fin whale, two of the largest creatures on Earth.

Digby Neck Get way out into the Bay of Fundy for your best chances to see blue and fin whales. (p69)

Pleasant Bay You'll find plenty of folks leading tours up here and you'll probably see eagles soaring close to shore too. (p91)

Fundy Isles The whales are here but you'll surely also get to see plenty of seals and bird life including puffins. (p119)

Witless Bay Ecological Reserve Just when you thought your dreams had been realized with whale, seal and puffin sightings, an iceberg floats by. Yeah, this place has it all. (p184)

Music

Whether it's Scottish, folk or rock, music rings everywhere in this corner of Canada. Ceilidhs, kitchen parties and some awesome festivals liven up the summer and extend into the fall.

Ceilidh Trail Nonstop kitchen parties and ceilidhs await along this highway; finish up in Chéticamp for a taste of Acadian rhythms. (p87)

Halifax It's got one of the highest rates of bars per capita in the world and nearly every one of them swells with live music. You'll find everything here, but this is your best stop for modern and hip sounds. (p44)

Stan Rogers Folk Festival It ain't Glastonbury but even the most seasoned festival-goers rave about the intimate vibe and quality of music here that ranges from bluegrass to Celtic. (p100)

Cavendish Beach Festival Camp on the beach and enjoy the best modern country music scattered with some rock and folk acts. Big names show up at this one. (p22)

Acadian Culture

No, they aren't Québecois, these French speakers have their own unique culture with a soulful brand of fiddle music, their own tricolor flag and a delicious cuisine specializing in delicately spiced meat pies.

Northeastern New Brunswick Staunchly Acadian and sporting one of the region's best historical sites, the Acadian Historic Village. (p140)

Chéticamp, Nova Scotia Probably the best place to get into the culture via summer music, theater performances and Acadian restaurants. (p89)

West Pubnico, Nova Scotia Out of the way but so friendly with its own historical re-creation, Le Village Historique Acadien. (p66)

French Shore, Nova Scotia Less touristed than Chéticamp, find nightly concerts in summer and roadside eateries serving rappie pie (a hearty casserole thickened with potato juice; p207).

Région Évangeline, PEI Small but with a punch: this was the first region where the Acadian flag was ever unfurled. (p167)

Month by Month

February

This is not a popular month to visit this part of Canada unless you're looking for deep snow and hard ice. Expect a warm welcome during one of the coldest months of the year.

🏃 Skiing

Atlantic Canada's best skiing is at Marble Mountain in Corner Brook, Newfoundland, open from December to April. It's challenging terrain but lift lines are short and the snow is plentiful.

🏃 World Pond Hockey Tournament, Plaster Rock, New Brunswick

Hockey purists, don't miss this event. All proceeds go toward building an arena for the folks of Tobique Valley, but until then the ponds are cleared and more than 120 teams come to shoot pucks around the ice.

April

The land is usually thawing by April and trees are sprouting new leaves, but if you visit you'll be enjoying it all with very few other people around.

✨ Mi-Carême

Mid-Lent, usually in March or April, is marked in the Acadian town of Chéticamp by getting in disguise and visiting neighborhood homes to see if anyone can guess who they are. Meanwhile music, feasts and entertainment are found around town.

June

Dodge the crowds by showing up in June when the weather can be sunny but brisk. In some areas many tourist-oriented attractions may still be shut or keep low-season hours.

🏃 Whale Watching

Whales begin to be seen in the Bay of Fundy and off the coast of Newfoundland this month, then hang around to feed until around October or November. Meanwhile, on Nova Scotia's South Shore the season runs from July to October.

🏃 Drifting Icebergs

Spring and early summer are the best times to see some of the tens of thousands of icebergs that break off in Greenland to sail down the coast of Newfoundland's 'Iceberg Alley.' The iceberg-tracking site www.icebergfinder.com can help you plan where to go and what times of year are best to visit.

☆ Acadian Concerts

In late June you'll start to find summer Acadian concerts and kitchen parties along the Nova Scotia coast between Yarmouth and Digby. More are scheduled through July, and by August you can find a performance most nights of the week.

July

Summer starts to heat up, festivals bring music and food to the streets and all outdoor activities are a go. Yet early in the month things can still be relatively uncrowded.

✖ Lobster Suppers

During the summer lobster season (that changes depending on the region), tasty crustaceans get boiled up en masse and served to hungry crowds with all-you-can-eat fixings and pie for dessert.

☆ Ceilidhs

Cape Breton is the capital of these foot-tapping Scottish music performances where most people in the small communities participate, show up as audience and get up and dance. While found year-round, you can find them nightly in July and August.

🎪 Canada Day

Canada's national holiday is celebrated throughout the region with parades, fireworks, music and picnics. Many businesses shut in observance so make sure you have plans and a picnic packed before the big day, 1 July.

🎪 Cavendish Beach Festival

Some of the biggest names in country music go to Cavendish, Prince Edward Island (PEI), to play beachside while campers get their party on. This is one of the largest outdoor music festivals in North America and the island swells with people.

🎪 Indian River Festival

As an antidote to Cavendish partying, this festival from the end of June into October showcases classical, jazz and world music in an acoustically sublime St Mary's Church. The French Gothic architecture complements the beautiful music in a wonderful summer experience.

👁 Peak of Lupine Season

Lupine usually begin blooming in June but by July they cover hillsides, colorfully border the highways and decorate home fronts. Purple is the dominant color but you'll also see scatterings of pink lupine, especially in PEI.

🎪 Halifax Pride Week

Halifax booms with events for Pride Week, the largest this side of Montréal. Don't miss the annual, highly entertaining Dykes vs Divas Softball game, the Queer Acts Theatre Festival, dance party and the extravagant parade.

🎪 Tall Ships

It's magical watching tall ships sail through Halifax Harbour. Unfortunately, the Tall Ship Festival isn't a yearly event so check www.my-waterfont.ca for the schedule. However, there are always a few ships docked along the waterfront.

🎪 Bastille Day

Celebrate the 14 July French national holiday with *bona fide* French nationals in St Pierre. The town comes alive with music, food stalls and family-oriented games for nonstop fun. Stop in for a few éclairs while you're there as well.

August

High season is in full swing by August when the weather is at its sunniest, everything is open for extended hours and festivals are going on everywhere.

🎪 Stan Rogers Folk Festival

The tiny remote seaside town of Canso swells with visitors once a year for what many claim is one of the best music festivals in the Maritimes. It's a mellow scene with camping, easy-going people and amazing live performances.

🎪 Halifax International Busker Festival

Comics, mimics, daredevils and more from Canada and around the world perform on several outdoor stages over 11 days. This is the oldest festival of its kind in Canada. The audience usually exceeds 500,000 people.

✖ Bakeapple Season

Called 'cloudberries' throughout much of the rest of the world, this rare and delectable berry is in full season by mid-August – then it's tossed liberally into pies and jam.

✖ Digby Scallop Days

Celebrating Digby's massive scallop fleet, this five-day festival in early August lets you try out different styles of preparation. Alongside it are parades, dances, car shows and even a kids' pie-eating contest.

⚜ Miramichi Folksong Festival

Another superlative event, this is North America's oldest folk-fest set along its winding, namesake river in New Brunswick. Expect a low-key family vibe set to the tune of fiddlers and singers with all the old folks getting up to boogie.

⚜ Royal St John's Regatta

Newfoundland keeps up the action with this rowing regatta, claimed to be the oldest sporting event in North America, on Quidi Vidi Lake. St John's becomes a ghost town as thousands head to watch and enjoy the sunshine.

September

Summer gets extended for a slew of music festivals, while the harvest of food and wine is enjoyed to the fullest. Temperatures become more brisk but the sun still makes regular appearances.

⚜ PEI Fall Flavours

Called 'the biggest kitchen party in Canada,' here you get your hands juicy with interactive culinary demos, gorge on the best seafood in the world and enjoy two chowder championships. Meanwhile there's live music, a widely regarded oyster-shucking contest and chef challenges.

⚜ Atlantic Film Festival

Atlantic Canada and Canada's best films plus some gems from around the world get screened at this intimate yet internationally recognized festival in Halifax. Of course, this is Nova Scotia so there are plenty of music performances scheduled alongside.

⚜ Canadian Deep Roots Festival

Enjoy live folk and rock to Mi'kmaw (aboriginal peoples), Acadian and other unique music all with Canadian roots, in the fun university town of Wolfville. Workshops are available with some of the artists.

⚜ Nova Scotia Fall Wine Festival

There's no better moment to enjoy Nova Scotia's wines than at this event where you can meet wine makers and enjoy their vintages paired with meals prepared by renowned chefs.

October

Ah, the colors of fall. As the world turns from green to red and the temperatures start to really drop, there are still plenty of music events plus Canadian Thanksgiving to keep you warm.

◉ Fall Foliage

One of nature's most spectacular shows of color begins late September and peaks in October. Panoramas are filled with brick reds, rust, gold and copper that eventually turn brown before dropping to the ground.

⚜ Thanksgiving

Unlike the US, Canadian Thanksgiving is celebrated on the first Monday in October in thanks of the harvest, not of aboriginal hospitality. Families tend to eat their big meal over the weekend and a few fall festivals surround the big day.

⚜ Celtic Colours

Big names in Nova Scotian music make it to this music festival that runs for nine days. Expect appearances from the rest of the Celtic music world as well, as the fall colors reach their peak.

December

⚜ Christmas

The festivities begin in November with Christmas parades and festivals of light that then move into Father Christmas greetings and Christmas markets. The big day is of course on 25 December when most families get together for holiday supper.

Itineraries

1 WEEK Essential Nova Scotia

Soak up some music and culture in **Halifax** (p44) then travel to nearby **Peggy's Cove** (p56). Jostle for position to snap the most photographed lighthouse in the world, or have a more subdued experience picnicking in equally pretty **Prospect** (p57). Don't forget your sunscreen in **Mahone Bay** (p58), where the sun shines on great craft shopping and sea kayaking. Move on slightly south to **Lunenburg** (p60), a World Heritage site known for its colorful boxy buildings and *Bluenose* schooner where you could easily wander for a day or two. The **Kejimkujik Seaside Adjunct** (p64) provides miles of unspoiled white beaches (and maybe seals), while its big brother **Kejimkujik National Park** (p63) lies inland and is a prime place to float a canoe and drift through the woods. Cross the province to **Annapolis Royal** (p71) to stay at a heritage bed and breakfast, explore its fort by day and graveyard by night. The next day visit the wineries around **Wolfville** (p74) and the **Grand Pré National Historic site** (p75), before stopping to down a meal at a fine restaurant. Lastly explore the Fundy coast by hiking around **Scots Bay** (p74) or go to **Maitland** (p77) to get right in and raft the tidal bore.

Cabot & Viking Trails

3 WEEKS

Spend a couple of days in **Halifax** (p44) enjoying lively bars and a nonstop music scene, then hit the road up the Atlantic Coast. Stop for a chilly surf at **Lawrencetown Beach** (p56) or a hike through pine forest to a spectacular white-sand beach at **Taylor Head Provincial Park** (p100). Visit the historical village at **Sherbrooke** (p100) then either cut up Hwy 7 for a shortcut to Cape Breton Island or, with an extra day or two, continue on the coast to the sheltered picture-perfect hamlet of **Guysborough** (p99). Just after arriving on Cape Breton from the causeway, veer left toward Hwy 30 and stop in at one of the many ceilidh music gatherings along this route. Hook up with the Cabot Trail, at **Chéticamp** (p89), a deeply Acadian town. Next you can watch whales or chant with monks at the Tibetan monastery in **Pleasant Bay** (p91), and look for moose and nesting bald eagles in **Cape Breton Highlands National Park** (p90). Get your art fix at the studios along the **St Ann's Loop** (p93) before heading over to **Baddeck** (p94) to learn everything you ever wanted to know about Alexander Graham Bell at the town's fabulous museum. From here take a jaunt east to **Louisbourg** (p97) to visit the massive, windy restored French Fort complete with costumed thespians and activities to bring you back to the 18th century. Stop at the Miner's Museum in **Glace Bay** (p97) before arriving in industrial North Sydney for the ferry to Newfoundland.

It's a six-hour sail over the sometimes rough swell of the Cabot Strait to **Port aux Basques** (p211). Alight and drive north to **Gros Morne National Park** (p200), rich with mountain hikes, sea-kayak tours, fjords and weird rock formations. Take the Viking Trail from here to its awe-inspiring endpoint: **L'Anse aux Meadows National Historic Site** (p205), North America's first settlement. Leif Eriksson and his Viking pals homesteaded the place 1000 years ago, and it probably looked much the same then as it does now. After coming all this way, you too will feel like an Atlantic explorer.

2 WEEKS Bay of Fundy Tidal Tour

Experience the dramatic Fundy tides and its wildlife on this loop that could be tackled from Maine, USA. Cross the bridge to **Campobello Island** (p120), the childhood home of 32nd US president Franklin D Roosevelt, from Lubec, Maine, then visit the Roosevelt's home that's now a fascinating museum. The next day take the car ferry to fisher-funky **Deer Island** (p119) to check out Old Sow, the world's second-largest natural tidal whirlpool, before boarding another ferry that shuttles you to the mainland. Drive north to gritty yet cosmopolitan **Saint John** (p124), to fill up on fine dining, and warm up your hiking boots at **Irving Nature Park** (p126) the following day to see hundreds of birds and possibly seals. Spend the next few days really breaking your boots in throughout **Fundy National Park** (p130) and its extensive coastal trails. Continue north to **Cape Enrage** (p132) to take a tour of the lighthouse, sea kayak, or rappel down the rock cliffs that meet the rise and fall of the powerful tides. Move on to a day trip to the bizarre **Hopewell Rocks** (p132) formations, a must-see, but expect hundreds of visitors.

Now it's time to change provinces. Drive across the border to Nova Scotia and down to **Joggins** (p82) to see the Unesco World Heritage fossil cliffs. Continue along driftwood-strewn Chignecto Bay to stop for lunch in **Advocate Harbour** (p81), then move onto **Parrsboro** (p80) to look for semiprecious stones on the beach and stay the night. Enjoy the views of the Cobequid Bay tides, which can change up to a foot per minute, until you reach **Maitland** (p77) where you can get into inflatable dinghies for an exhilarating rafting adventure on the tidal bore. Get your hiking boots on again around **Scots Bay** (p74) where you'll be rewarded with some of the best views of the tides on this entire route. Reward your physical exertion with a day and night in **Digby** (p70) where you can dine on succulent scallops and explore **Digby Neck** (p69), home to the region's most spectacular whale watching and even more hiking trails. From Digby, take the car ferry back to Saint John, New Brunswick, to complete the loop.

Foodie Loop

Eat and drink your way through **Halifax** (p44), then take the car ferry to **Wood Islands** (p154), Prince Edward Island (PEI). Spend your first day in Canada's cutest province exploring the east; stop at **Rossignol Estate Winery** (p154), quirky distilleries and stroll on gorgeous **Basin Head Beach** (p156). Dine in **St Peter's** (p157) before basing yourself in **Charlottetown** (p147) for the next few days as you explore the central part of the province. Learn about *Anne of Green Gables* in **Cavendish** (p163), gorge on lobster in **New Glasgow** (p161), oysters in **Malpeque** (p165) and enjoy Charlottetown itself by dining at Lot 30.

Spend a night or two in **Summerside** (p165) to explore western PEI with a drive up the scenic west coast through Acadian villages to lighthouse vistas. Gape at the giant windmills of **North Cape** (p168) before looping back on the east coast, stopping to learn about Mi'kmaq culture on lovely **Lennox Island** (p168).

Take the **Confederation Bridge** (p147) to drive back to Halifax via the wine region around **Tatamagouche** (p83) or head down the Fundy Coast to **Parrsboro** (p80) as described in the Bay of Fundy Tidal Tour.

Maritime Drive-Through

Short on time but want to see as much as possible? Enjoy **Halifax** (p44) for a day before swinging down to snap a few photos at **Peggy's Cove** (p57), then stop for the night in World Heritage–listed **Lunenburg** (p60) and spoil yourself with dinner at Fleur de Sel. The next day cross via Bridgewater up Hwy 8 stopping for a day hike or a paddle in **Kejimkujik National Park** (p63), then stay in **Annapolis Royal** (p71) and take the town's famous nighttime graveyard tour. Take a short drive to **Digby** (p70), perhaps enjoying a scallop lunch, then take the ferry to **Saint John** (p124), New Brunswick. Stay or camp in **Fundy National Park** (p130) or in adorable **St Martins** (p129), spending the next day hiking and continuing up the Fundy Coast to view the tides at **Cape Enrage** (p132) and **Hopewell Rocks** (p132). The next day drive across the **Confederation Bridge** (p147) into Prince Edward Island (PEI) and **Charlottetown** (p147). Explore Anne's Land around **Cavendish** (p163), have a lobster supper then take a tour of PEI's east coast the following day before taking the car ferry back to Nova Scotia. From here it takes an hour and 45 minutes to drive back to Halifax.

Outdoor Activities

Atlantic Canada does a good job of harnessing its cliffy, marine-mammaled terrain for outdoor adventures. Visitors can now get out in the sun (or rain or fog) to hike, kayak, whale watch or even surf. The season is short for most activities (May to October in a good year), but you'll find plenty of tour operators eager to help. It's also easy to arrange independent adventures.

On the Water

Best Places to Whale Watch

Twillingate Island, Newfoundland

Digby Neck, Nova Scotia

Grand Manan Island, New Brunswick

Pleasant Bay, Nova Scotia

Witless Bay Ecological Reserve, Newfoundland

Best Paddling Locations

Eastern and south shores, Nova Scotia

Cape Breton, Nova Scotia

Fundy Isles, New Brunswick

Eastern Fundy shore, New Brunswick

Cartwright, Labrador

Witless Bay, Newfoundland

North Rustico, Prince Edward Island

Kayaking & Canoeing

Atlantic Canada is chock-full of possibilities to get out on the water, be it a lazy canoe trip or a battle with rolling white water. Sea kayaking has exploded here, with myriad places to paddle. A unique activity in the region is tidal-bore rafting, where you harness the blasting force of the famous Fundy tides.

National and provincial parks are excellent places to start if you've never dipped an oar. Maps and equipment rentals are usually available from the park information centers, where the staff can also give route recommendations.

Canoeing doesn't have the cachet of sea kayaking in the region, but there are still some lovely opportunities. The sport is best suited to inland lakes and rivers, so it's no shocker that Kejimkujik National Park ranks high on the list. It's a good place to paddle into the backcountry and camp. In New Brunswick, canoeing in untouched, moose- and bear-trodden Mt Carleton Provincial Park is sweet, while those who wish to remain closer to city life can push off from Fredericton and paddle through the Saint John River. Canoeing in Newfoundland centers on the region's Terra Nova National Park (p195).

Whale Watching

The region's most precious gift to visitors is whale watching. The thrill of spotting a whale's spout followed by its giant tail flukes arching and descending is unbeatable.

More than 22 species of whale and porpoise lurk offshore throughout Atlantic Canada, drawn to the rich fishy feeding waters. The standout species include the leaping and diving humpback whale, the highly endangered North Atlantic right whale and the largest leviathan of all, the mighty blue whale.

Whale-watch boat operators are ubiquitous and will bring you close to the creatures. Popular tour areas include Cape Breton, Nova Scotia's Cabot Trail coastline, especially around Pleasant Bay.

The most common sightings here are humpback, minke and pilot whales. In New Brunswick, there is excellent whale watching along the eastern Fundy Shore and around the Fundy Isles; right whales and blue whales are viewable. Newfoundland pretty much has whales swimming all around its shores, with humpback and minke commonly seen; tour operators cluster around Witless Bay Ecological Reserve and Twillingate.

Some tours get you closer to the action in Zodiacs while other tours are conducted on big, relatively comfortable ferry-like motorboats. Look for smaller tours such as Ocean Explorations Whale

Cruises (p69) on Digby Neck, which are led by marine biologists. Many tours focus on more than just whales and will take you to see seals, puffins or other seabirds as well.

Standard trips last about two hours and cost around $55 to $80 per adult. The sighting success rate is often posted and you should ask if there's any sort of money-back guarantee if you do not see whales. Remember, you're heading out on open sea for many of these tours, so be prepared for a wavy ride. If you're at all prone to seasickness, medicate beforehand. It's also cold out there, so take a jacket or sweater. The season varies by location but usually is in July and August.

And while whale-watch tours are great, never underestimate what you can see from shore, especially from places such as Cape Breton's Cabot Trail and throughout Newfoundland's Avalon Peninsula. Seeing the faraway spout of a whale from a cliff top while a bald eagle soars overhead is a true Maritime experience.

TYING KNOTS

Unleash your inner sailor (or fisher or rock climber) by learning to tie a half hitch, bowline and others with *Knots and Splices* (2006) by Cyrus Day and Colin Jarman. Also helpful for budding escape artists.

SEA KAYAKING

If there's any one activity that is Atlantic Canada's specialty, it's sea kayaking. It's everywhere; it's absolutely the best way to see the remarkable coastlines and you'll often be kayaking alongside whales, seals and a huge amount of bird life.

Most companies cater to beginners, so no need to feel unworthy if you've never kayaked before. Conversely, advanced paddlers can rent crafts and head out on their own. It can be very rough out there due to volatile weather, high winds and strong currents, so know your limits. The Canadian government publishes an excellent resource titled *Sea Kayaking Safety Guide*, available via download from **Transport Canada** (www.tc.gc.ca/BoatingSafety/pubs/kayak/menu.htm). It details each province's weather and kayaking terrain, and also provides trip-planning tips.

Trips range from paddling around icebergs in Newfoundland to navigating protected inlets ringed by forest on uninhabited isles along the Eastern Shore of Nova Scotia. If you're a beginner the best place to start are calm waters where your boat won't get jostled around by waves or currents. Some companies make multiday trips, including camping in places you couldn't get to otherwise.

PLAN YOUR TRIP OUTDOOR ACTIVITIES

STRAP ON YOUR HIKING BOOTS

Nova Scotia
Nova Scotia holds so much variety of terrain and well-tended backcountry that you'll be spoilt with options.

➡ **Cape Breton Highlands National Park** (p90) offers exquisite hiking over dramatic coastline; the Skyline Trail is the most popular path, but it's hard to go wrong with any of them.

➡ **Cape Split** is one of the best hikes to view the Fundy tides plus pastoral to wilderness scenery.

➡ **Taylor Head Provincial Park** (p100) occupies a slender sprig of land on the eastern shore and has trails traversing forest and beach.

New Brunswick
Rugged, forested New Brunswick holds an unlistable number of hiking options ranging from mountains and river valleys to the dramatic Fundy coastline.

➡ **Fundy National Park** (p130) and **Fundy Trail Parkway** (p132) have a variety of paths along the wooded coastline.

➡ **Mt Carleton Provincial Park** offers adventurous hikes over mountain peaks to river valleys and lakes. Expect to see wildlife but few humans.

➡ **Grand Manan Island** shines as the provincial jewel for seaside-themed mellow hikes. Cliffs, marshes and lighthouses are all on the paths.

Newfoundland
Remnants of old walking paths that used to connect local communities and provided escape routes inland from pirates now make for fantastic hiking since most clutch the shoreline and often provide whale views.

➡ **East Coast Trail** (p184) is on the Avalon Peninsula.

➡ **Skerwink Trail** (p189) is on the Bonavista Peninsula.

➡ **Gros Morne National Park** (p200) is renowned for its vistas.

Prince Edward Island
This region is very flat, so there are far less hiking opportunities than the other provinces. That said, there are plenty of beaches to stroll. **Prince Edward Island National Park** (p158) is the best choice if you feel the need to use your feet.

Hiking

Trails – from gentle jaunts around an interpretive path to breath-sapping slogs up a mountain – crisscross the area's national and provincial parks. And hiking – aside from being low-cost – is the most enjoyable way to absorb the region.

The hiking season runs from May to October, with optimal conditions from July onward, when the trails have dried out. Maps are available at park information centers, although for extended hikes you may need topographic maps.

And don't forget that Canada is also home to one of the most ambitious paths ever conceived, the **Trans Canada Trail** (www.tctrail.ca), an 18,078km-long ribbon from Cape Spear in Newfoundland that runs all the way across the country to Victoria, British Columbia. It's still a work in progress, but trails in the provinces sometimes coincide with it.

Birdwatching

No need to be a binocular-toting ornithologist to get into the scene here. Birds swarm the region, and whether you're a birder or not, you'll find it tough to resist the charm of a funny-looking puffin or common murre.

Seabirds are the top draw. Many whale-watch tours also take visitors to seabird colonies as whales and birds share a taste for the same fish they will often lurk in the same areas. So you'll be able to feast your eyes upon razorbills, kittiwakes, arctic terns, and yes, puffins and murres. The colonies can be up to one million strong, their shrieks deafening and their smell, well, not so fresh. Still, it's an amazing sight to behold.

Also impressive to watch are the Arctic-nesting shorebirds that migrate south through the Bay of Fundy. Each year millions of tiny sandpipers refuel in the rich mudflats exposed by the world's highest tides. The prime time is mid-August, and the prime places are around Windsor and Grand Pré in Nova Scotia's Annapolis Valley.

The *Sibley Field Guide to Birds of Eastern North America* (2003) by David Sibley makes an excellent, illustrated and portable companion for birdwatchers.

Cycling & Mountain Biking

Cycling is where PEI shines. Several years ago, the province converted a defunct 357km railway bed into a cycling route called the **Confederation Trail** (www.tourismpei.com/pei-cycling), and it landed PEI on the map as an international cycling destination. The trail runs along the length of the island, with feeder paths down to most towns. Good services and facilities line it, many provided in reconditioned train stations. This easy service availability, combined with compact distances and flat terrain, make cycling here doable even for those with limited experience. The seaside stretch from St Peter's to Mt Stewart is particularly inspiring.

New Brunswick is working hard to do something similar, and you'll find finished but as yet unconnected sections of the **New Brunswick Trail** (www.nbtrail.com) around the province. Rewarding rides include the Fundy Trail Parkway along coastal wilderness, and paths through the backcountry in Kouchibouguac National Park.

In Nova Scotia the area around Lunenburg and Mahone Bay is a cyclist's dream with few hills, sweet ocean views and little vehicle traffic. Cape Breton Highlands National Park (p90) certainly has the scenery going for it, but it's tough riding due to the hilliness and traffic – not a good place for beginners.

Rugged terrain, high winds, poor road conditions and long stretches of road between towns make Newfoundland a difficult cycling destination. If you want to give it a try, Gros Morne National Park (p200) and CA Pippy Park (p176) in St John's are options.

For a more urban experience, you can rent bikes and explore Halifax's waterfront with even more wind in your hair.

Fishing

Fly-fishing in this region is downright mythical. Avid anglers get all slack-jawed and weak-kneed when names such as 'Miramichi' and 'Margaree' are invoked. No, these aren't beautiful women, but rather places to cast a line for Atlantic salmon and trout (speckled and brown, among the many).

FISHING RULES & LICENSES

Staff at any tourist office will have the most current information about fishing regulations and outfitters. Each province also produces its own 'angler's guide' booklet that includes licensing rules. License prices vary by province and by species fished; a seven-day license costs anywhere from $30 to $90. Check with each province's environmental or natural resources department for further information:

Newfoundland & Labrador (☑709-637-2409; www.env.gov.nl.ca)

New Brunswick (☑506-453-2440; www.gnb.ca)

Nova Scotia (☑902-426-5433; www.gov.ns.ca/fish)

Prince Edward Island (☑902-368-6080; www.gov.pe.ca)

MARINE CONDITIONS

Kayakers, fisherfolk and anyone else sailing out to sea can check www. buoyweather.com for marine conditions all around Atlantic Canada.

On the tranquil Miramichi River in New Brunswick, everyone from Prince Charles to Dick Cheney to Marilyn Monroe has reeled one in. The Humber River in Newfoundland and Pinware River in Labrador Straits are known for salmon fishing. If the latter isn't remote enough, Labrador offers several fly-in lodges that host the likes of George Bush Sr.

These places all have experienced ups and downs with overfishing, poaching and unknown causes (perhaps climate change) affecting stocks, but they seem to be at sustainable levels presently.

Deep sea fishing is huge around North Rustico in PEI where you can sign on with any of a fleet of fishing boats, often captained by bearded seamen who come from long generations of plying these oceans. There are plenty of other opportunities to cast a line for the big one – try boats around Lunenberg and along the Cabot Trail in Nova Scotia.

And finally, lobster fishing provides a unique experience, one that kids will love. Haul up crustacean-filled pots in Lunenburg in Nova Scotia. Then grab a bucket and a shovel to go clamming in PEI.

Board Sports

Surfing seems an unusual sport for Atlantic Canada – too damn cold, right? Think again. People do surf here and not only is it cold, it's bloody freezing, since the best waves break in winter. Luckily, the ideal time for beginners is summer when the waves are smaller and the water is at least a little bit warmer.

The place to partake of the madness is Lawrencetown Beach on Nova Scotia's eastern shore. L-town, as it's called, faces due south and picks up stormy weather from hundreds of kilometers away; this results in exceptional wrapping waves, especially plentiful in the colder months. So bundle up in your 7mm wetsuit, try not to freeze your ass off in the 0°C water, and join the line-up. People do surf at warmer times of the year, too. Board rentals cost about \$30 per day, lessons about \$80. Kejimkujik Seaside Adjunct provides additional waves and the prices are similar.

Perhaps even more radical than surfing is kite-surfing, in which you cruise in, over and out of waves using some cool equipment. Shippagan in northeastern New Brunswick is a good place to try it. Lawrencetown Beach in Nova Scotia is a great place to watch a spectacular show of kite surfers flying along and over waves.

A new stand up paddle (SUP) option is now available in calm Malpeque Bay in PEI, a perfect spot for beginners. Work up an appetite thinking of all those yummy oysters growing beneath you.

Check www.wavewatch.com for wave forecasts for the region.

Skiing & Snowboarding

Atlantic Canada's best skiing and snowboarding take place at Newfoundland's Marble Mountain (p208) outside Corner Brook. It may not have the height of Whistler or other top resorts, but it's lower cost with far fewer queues, so you get more time on the slopes.

Marble has 35 trails, four lifts, a 488m vertical drop and annual snowfall of 4.8m.

ADVENTURES IN SNOW-KITING

This will impress the friends at the next beer-up: tell them you went snow-kiting in Newfoundland. Of course, it will entail actually going to Newfoundland – in winter – but you'll be going to Corner Brook, near the renowned ski resort of Marble Mountain, so you won't feel too out of place.

Snow-kiting is sort of a windsurfing-meets-snowboarding endeavor, and the patient folks at My Newfoundland Adventures (p208) teach you how to do it, no experience required. Just bring some very, very warm clothes for the half-day intro lesson (\$175) and off you'll zip across the tundra. (OK, it's not really tundra, but it's cold enough to be!)

There are snowboarding and tubing parks, as well as night skiing on Friday. The region caters to cross-country skiers at Blow-Me-Down Cross Country Ski Park (p208), about 10 minutes from the mountain.

Serious cross-country skiers will want to head far north to where the Canadian national team trains in Labrador West. The Wapusakatto Mountains (p220) let loose with good, cold, dry snow from late October to late April, a much longer season than elsewhere in the region – or anywhere in Canada.

Wentworth is the favorite spot in Nova Scotia, although it's small with 815 vertical feet and 20 runs. See www.skiwentworth.ca for more details about the slopes. The park also offers cross-country skiing and snow shoeing.

New Brunswick has three ski parks, the biggest being **Poley Mountain** (www.poley-mountain.com) near Sussex, with more than 100 acres of ski-able terrain and 10 night skiing trails.

For further information contact the **Canadian Ski Council** (☎905-212-9040; www.canadianskicouncil.org).

Other Winter Sports

Windsor, Nova Scotia, claims to be the birthplace of hockey so, as you'd expect, there are plenty of ice-skating areas around the region, although not many cater to visitors. You're best bet for gliding across the ice is at the new Emera Oval in downtown Halifax where even skate lending is free of charge.

Dog sledding, snow mobiling and ice climbing are all available with My Newfoundland Adventures (p208) in Newfoundland. A half-day sled ride is a whopping (but many say worth it) $400.

PLAN YOUR TRIP OUTDOOR ACTIVITIES

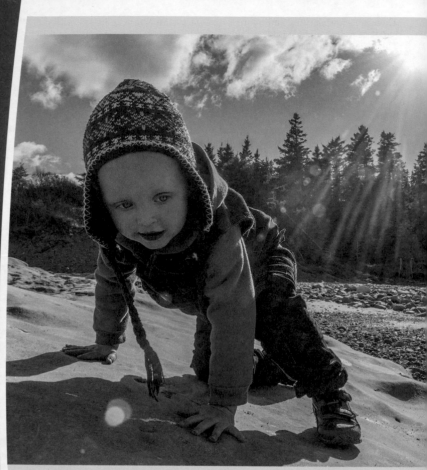
Climbing on rocks, Nova Scotia (p40)

Plan Your Trip

Travel with Children

These Canadian provinces were made for kids. As if seeing moose, eagles and whales or running around in the snow or on the beach all day wasn't fun enough, everywhere you turn those crafty Canadians have cooked up some hands-on learning experience, living history lesson or child-oriented theater.

Where to go in the Maritime's Playground

Halifax, Nova Scotia

Cartoon-like tugboat rides, cycling, kayaking, a free year-round skating area, parks and family-friendly festivals galore through summer.

Prince Edward Island's Beaches

Sandy stretches of white or pink sand with lightly lapping, bearably cool waves.

Fundy National Park, New Brunswick

Low-tide flats to putter around, trails to waterfalls, lakes to swim in.

St John's, Newfoundland

Nearby whale-watching tours.

Nova Scotia, New Brunswick & Prince Edward Island for Kids

Between learning about pirates on antique sailing vessels, playing on low-key beaches and climbing to the top of lighthouses, it's impossible to make a bad decision about where to take your kids in these provinces. Canada caters better to families than nearly anywhere else in the world and the mix of coast with forest, easy to manage cities and lakes galore make this region a top choice in the country. The food isn't daunting, people are exceptionally friendly and there's a prevalent sense of peace and welcome.

Museums, Monuments & Lighthouses

Halifax, Saint John and St John's all have science museums that specialize in hands-on activities to get all ages involved, while at historic sites strewn across the region costumed thespians get you right into the period and often have demonstrations of everything from blacksmithing to cooking. At some of these places there are also puppet or theatrical performances for children and other events such as hayrides. Teens often enjoy these sites as well, since they are large, diverse and great for exploration.

Lighthouses seem to be perched on every headland and you can climb up to the top of many, usually for a small fee. If you're lucky there'll be a hand pump horn to set off.

Outdoor Activities

Endless coastlines, fresh air, wildlife, snow, sand, rivers, lakes and mountains make almost any outdoor activity you may be yearning for entirely possible. Prince Edward Island's mostly flat Confederation Trail traverses the island and can be picked up from almost any point, while the coastline of the Prince Edward Island National Park has dedicated cycling lanes that run along the beaches. The Halifax waterfront is also a great place for family bike rentals. Canoeing is a Canadian activity *par excellence*, available in lakes in Nova Scotia and New Brunswick while most sea-kayaking outfits throughout the region cater to families. Skiing and snowboarding are available at small family-friendly slopes in winter.

But perhaps the most exciting thing to do with all the surrounding seas is to set sail, either to explore and feel the wind in your hair or to look for the many species of whale thriving in the Bay of Fundy, Cabot Straight and the mighty Atlantic Ocean.

Eating Out

Fast food is ubiquitous in Canada so healthy eaters may find that the biggest hurdle is finding food that's not fried. Cabins and family suites often have kitchens so you can self-cater and in cities you'll find options fit for any type of diet.

Most budget to midrange restaurants offer booster seats and servers almost always love children. As an alternative to kid's menus you can often ask for half portions of mains on the adult menu.

Children's Highlights

A History Lesson

➡ **European Colonization** L'Anse aux Meadows (p205; Newfoundland), Louisbourg (p97; Nova Scotia), King's Landing Historic Settlement (p110; New Brunswick)

➡ **Fossils** Joggins Fossil Centre (p82; Nova Scotia)

➡ **First Nation** Lennox Island (p168; PEI), Port au Choix National Historic Site (p204; Newfoundland)

➡ **Pirates & the Titanic** Halifax Waterfront, Maritime Museum of the Atlantic (p45; Halifax), Titanic Burial Grounds (p45; Halifax)

Out in Nature

➡ **Whale and Sealife Watching** Brier Island (p69; Nova Scotia), Witless Bay Ecological Reserve (p184; Newfoundland), Grand Manan Island (p122; New Brunswick)

➡ **Wild Waters** Rafting the Fundy tidal bore (p78; Nova Scotia), Sea kayaking (p101; Nova Scotia), Clamming at Point Prim (p154; PEI)

➡ **Beaches** Prince Edward Island National Park (p158; PEI), Kejimkujik Seaside Adjunct (p64; Nova Scotia), Parlee Beach Provincial Park (p137; New Brunswick; www.gnb. ca/0354/)

➡ **Forests & Lakes** Anchors Above Zipline Adventure (p85; Nova Scotia), Kejimkujik National Park (p63; Nova Scotia), Mt Carleton (p112; New Brunswick)

Theme Park Delight

➡ **Upper Clements Park** (www. upperclementsparks.com) Wild rides, zip lines and a wildlife park near Annapolis Royal, Nova Scotia

➡ **Magic Mountain Water Park** (www. magicmountain.ca) Steep and fast slides to lazy floats make this great for all ages in Moncton, New Brunswick

➡ **Avonlea** (p163) Brings the *Anne of Green Gables* books to life in PEI

➡ **Ross Farm Museum** (www.museum.gov. ns.ca/rfm/) Re-creates 1800s' farm life including hands-on animal experiences and sleigh rides in winter (Nova Scotia)

Anne of Green Gables actor, Prince Edward Island (p143)

Planning

Children who are traveling to Canada without both parents need authorization from the nonaccompanying parent.

Once in Canada kids receive a wide range of discounts on attraction admissions and transportation fares. Usually kids aged six to 17 are half price; younger children are free. Ask about 'family' admissions if your posse consists of two adults and two or more kids.

Kids often stay for free in hotels and motels. B&Bs are not so gracious, and may even refuse to accept pint-sized patrons. Ask when booking. Most restaurants other than fine-dining establishments will usually offer you booster seats and anything else you might need as soon as you steer your family through the door. Children's menus are widely available as well.

Baby food, infant formula, milk, disposable diapers (nappies) and the like are widely available in drugstores and supermarkets. Breastfeeding in public is legal. In all vehicles, children under 18kg must be restrained in safety seats.

Most tourist offices can lead you to resources for children's programs, childcare facilities and pediatricians.

Regions at a Glance

Yaar! This is the Canada for enjoying steel-colored seascapes and salt air with a big bowl of chowder and a pint of ale to wash it down. Everything here revolves around the cold Atlantic Ocean, from today's whale-watching adventures and lobster feasts to the history of Vikings and pirates. While tied together by geography and history each province has its own personality, from the iceberg-clad desolation of Newfoundland to the forested inland rivers and lakes of New Brunswick, the storybook farmlands of Prince Edward Island (PEI) and the never-ending coastal and cultural variations of Nova Scotia. Wherever you choose to go, you'll never be far from the sound of waves crashing on a beach or a simple supper of fresh fish.

Nova Scotia

Culture
Activities
History

Cultural Mishmash

Tartan shops, French-speaking villages and aboriginal communities are all within kilometers of each other. Throw in some African Nova Scotians and Pier 21, Canada's entry point for more than a million immigrants, and you have the definition of a cultural melting pot.

Coves, Cliffs & Tides

Coastal coves between evergreen islets are bird and marine-mammal habitats that beg you to go paddling. On the Fundy Coast the highest tides in the world constantly change the landscape. Cape Breton Island's coastal cliffs are home to moose and nesting bald eagles.

Time Warp

Nova Scotians don't just preserve their historical vestiges, they get in period costume and do old-time activities from sewing to blacksmithing, re-creating the scene as it might have been hundreds of years ago.

p40

New Brunswick

**Activities
Fishing
Wildlife**

You in a Canoe

From the tranquil Chiputneticook Lakes to the quicksilver Tobique River, New Brunswick is tops for canoeing, the most Canadian of activities. You can even meet artisans who still make canoes the old-fashioned way – a dying art.

Tie Your Flies

Baseball stars and captains of industry used to come to New Brunswick to cast their fly rods into the province's salmon- and trout-choked rivers. Why not do the same?

Puffin Lovin'

Whether you're a hardcore birdwatcher or just want to be able to tell your friends you saw a moose, New Brunswick's got plenty of animal action to go around. Your best bet: observing rare Atlantic puffins on desolate Machias Seal Island.

p102

Prince Edward Island

**Culture
Cuisine
Beaches**

It's All about Anne

Personified by Anne Shirley, LM Montgomery's red-headed star of the *Anne of Green Gables* series, Prince Edward Island (PEI) is as pretty as it's portrayed in the books. Red dirt and sands mimic Anne's hair, while white picket fences and fields of wildflowers paint the real-life backdrop.

Lobster Suppers, Oysters & Potatoes

Vying with Idaho as potato capital of the Americas, you'll pass vine-covered hills to reach town halls serving fisher-sized suppers of PEI's second most famous food, lobster. Then hit coves of sunlit fishing boats pulling up succulent Malpeque oysters.

White & Pink Beaches

PEI has sienna beach flats topped by red-and-white lighthouses, cream-colored road-eating dunes and stretches of white sands that 'sing' when you walk on them.

p143

Newfoundland & Labrador

**Seascapes
Culture
History**

Great Big Sea

'There's one,' someone shouts, and sure enough a barnacled humpback steams through the water. Or maybe they're referring to the icebergs. Whether you're along shore, out in a boat or by your window, Newfoundland's sea delivers.

Strange Brew

The peculiar brogue is vaguely Irish, the slang indecipherable enough to merit its own dictionary, plates arrive with cod tongues, bakeapple jam and figgy duff (sweet pudding made with raisins and molasses), while towns have names such as Dildo and Jerry's Nose. This region is so offbeat it even has its own time zone: a *half* hour ahead of the mainland.

Viking Vestiges

They've taken a low-key approach at L'Anse aux Meadows, Leif Eriksson's 1000-year-old settlement, but the forlorn sweep of land is more powerful that way. You can feel the Vikings' isolation.

p169

On the Road

Newfoundland
& Labrador
p169

Prince Edward
Island
p143

New
Brunswick
p102

Nova Scotia
p40

Nova Scotia

Includes ➡

Best Places to Eat

➡ Fleur de Sel (p62)

➡ Front & Central (p75)

➡ Wild Caraway (p82)

➡ Lobster Pound & Moore (p96)

➡ Lobster suppers (at town halls and churches)

Best Places to Stay

➡ Waverley Inn (p50)

➡ Desbarres Manor (p99)

➡ Lightkeeper's Kitchen & Guest House (p81)

➡ Cranberry Cove Inn (p98)

➡ Digby Backpackers Hostel (p70)

Why Go?

If provinces were mother Canada's children, Nova Scotia would be the cute kid who charms the world with her lupine-studded fields, gingerbread-like houses, picture-perfect lighthouses and lightly lapping waves on sandy shores. But then you put her in a hockey rink or perhaps a fishing boat in a strong gale and another side comes out. Good looks aside, this near island and her residents are tough, resourceful and bad ass; most enjoy a drink, a song, a dance and a new face to share it with. If it's nature you're seeking, it's easy to discover empty coastal beach trails and wilderness paths through mixed forest to vistas with briny breezes. For something more cosmopolitan, head to Halifax for world-class dining and a rocking music scene.

When to Go
Halifax

Jun–Aug Wild-flowers carpet the country while whales come close to feed.

Sep & Oct Trees aflame with golds and reds provide a backdrop to fall music festivals.

Aug–Nov Put on a thick wetsuit, hood and booties to surf icy hurri-cane swells.

History

From time immemorial, the Mi'kmaq First Nation lived throughout present-day Nova Scotia. When the French established the first European settlement at Port Royal (today's Annapolis Royal) in 1605, Grand Chief Membertou offered them hospitality and became a frequent guest of Samuel de Champlain.

That close relationship with the French led to considerable suspicions by the British after they gained control of Nova Scotia, and rewards were offered for Mi'kmaw scalps. Starting in 1755, most French-speaking Acadians were deported to Louisiana (where they became Cajuns) and elsewhere for refusing to swear allegiance to the British Crown.

Nova Scotia was repopulated by some 35,000 United Empire Loyalists retreating from the American Revolution, including a small number of African slaves owned by Loyalists and also freed black Loyalists. New England planters settled other communities and, starting in 1773, waves of Highland Scots arrived in northern Nova Scotia and Cape Breton Island.

Most Nova Scotians trace their ancestry to the British Isles, as a look at the lengthy 'Mac' and 'Mc' sections of the phone book easily confirms. Acadians who managed to return from Louisiana after 1764 found their lands in the Annapolis Valley occupied. They settled instead along the French Shore between Yarmouth and Digby and, on Cape Breton Island, around Chéticamp and on Isle Madame. Today Acadians make up some 18% of the population, though not as many actually speak French. African Nova Scotians make up about 4% of the population. There are approximately 20,000 Mi'kmaq in 18 different communities concentrated around Truro and Bras d'Or Lake on Cape Breton Island.

Local Culture

With nearly 8000km of coastline, Nova Scotia has a culture that revolves around the sea. Historically, it has been a hard-working region of coal mines and fisheries. The current culture is still very blue collar but, with the decline of the primary industries, many young Nova Scotians are forced to leave their province in search of work.

Perhaps because of the long winters and hard-working days, an enormous number of Nova Scotians play music. Family get-togethers, particularly Acadian and Scottish, consist of strumming, fiddling, foot-tapping and dancing.

NOVA SCOTIA FAST FACTS

➡ Population: 921,727

➡ Area: 55,491 sq km

➡ Capital: Halifax

➡ Quirky fact: Has the only tidal power plant in the western hemisphere

❶ Getting There & Away

AIR

Most flights go to/from Halifax, but there's also an international airport in Sydney on Cape Breton Island. Airlines include **Air Canada** (www.aircanada.com), **Westjet** (www.westjet.com), **United** (www.united.ca), **Delta** (www.delta.com) and **Iceland Air** (www.icelandair.ca). There are multiple flights daily between Halifax and cities such as Toronto, Montréal, Ottawa, Saint John, Moncton and Boston (Massachusetts). In summer and fall there are direct flights to London and Iceland.

BUS

Maritime Bus (p267) provides a bus service through the Maritimes and connects with **Orleans Express** (www.orleansexpress.com) buses from Québec. From Halifax, destinations include Charlottetown ($58.25, 5½ hours, two daily) and Moncton ($49, four hours, three daily).

Contactable through Maritime Bus, several shuttles service the rest of the province.

BOAT
New Brunswick

Bay Ferries (☑ 888-249-7245; www.bayferries.com; adult/child/car/bicycle $43/28/81/10) has a three-hour trip from Saint John in New Brunswick to Digby. Off-season discounts and various packages are available.

Newfoundland

Marine Atlantic (☑ 800-341-7981; www.marine-atlantic.ca) operates ferries year-round to Port aux Basques in Newfoundland from North Sydney (adult/child/car $42/20/109). Daytime crossings take between five and six hours, and overnight crossings take about seven hours. Cabins and reclining chairs cost extra.

In summer, you can opt for a 14-hour ferry ride (adult/child/car $112/54/225) to Argentia on Newfoundland's east coast. Reservations are required for either trip.

Nova Scotia Highlights

① People-watch along the waterfront and take in an unforgettable meal in **Halifax** (p44).

② Sample French soldiers' rations or a general's feast c1744 at **Louisbourg National Historic Site** (p97).

③ Crash through the waves of the tidal bore at **Maitland** (p77).

④ Experience the misty peace of kayaking through the deserted islands and protected coves around **Tangier** (p101).

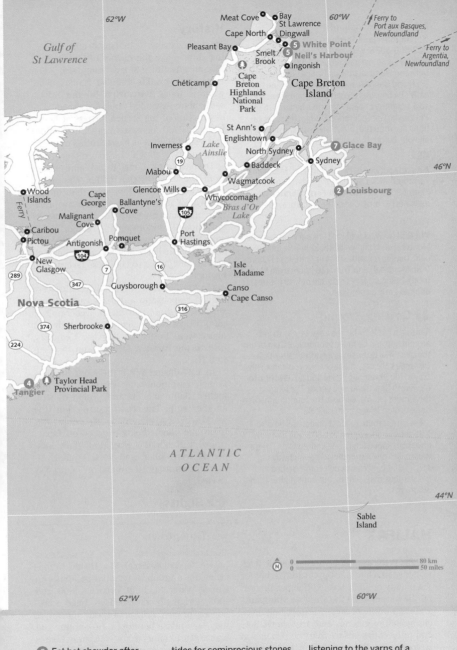

Gulf of St Lawrence

Meat Cove · Bay
St Lawrence
Cape North · Dingwall
Pleasant Bay · ⑤ **White Point**
Smelt · ⑤ **Neil's Harbour**
Brook
⓪ · Ingonish
Cape
Breton
Highlands
National
Park
Chéticamp · **Cape Breton Island**

St Ann's
Englishtown ·
Inverness · *Lake Ainslie* · North Sydney · ⑦ **Glace Bay**
(19) · Sydney
Mabou · Baddeck
Glencoe Mills · Wagmatcook
I·105 · Whycocomagh · *Bras d'Or Lake* · ② **Louisbourg**
Wood Islands
Cape George · Ballantyne's Cove · Port Hastings
Malignant Cove · Pomquet · Isle Madame
Caribou · Antigonish
Pictou · **I·104**
New Glasgow · (7) · (16) · Canso
(289) · (347) · Guysborough · Cape Canso
Nova Scotia · (316)
(374) · Sherbrooke
(224)
④ ⓪ Taylor Head Provincial Park
Tangier

Ferry to Port aux Basques, Newfoundland
Ferry to Argentia, Newfoundland

46°N
44°N

ATLANTIC OCEAN

Sable Island

Ⓝ 0 —————— 80 km
0 —————— 50 miles

62°W · 60°W

⑤ Eat hot chowder after looking for eagles and whales from **White Point** to **Neil's Harbour** (p93).

⑥ Search the sand flats exposed by extreme Fundy tides for semiprecious stones around **Parrsboro** (p80).

⑦ Voyage under the ocean floor to the coal mines of **Glace Bay** (p97) while listening to the yarns of a retired miner.

Prince Edward Island

Northumberland Ferries (☑ 888-249-7245, 902-566-3838; www.peiferry.com; adult/child $17/free, car incl passengers $68) cruises between Wood Islands on Prince Edward Island (PEI) and Caribou, near Pictou, up to nine times daily (1¼ hours). You only pay when leaving PEI, so it's slightly cheaper to arrive by ferry then exit PEI via the Confederation Bridge. No reservations are required, but it's wise to show up half an hour before the sailing.

USA

A nightly service between Portland, Maine and Yarmouth, Nova Scotia is expected to begin in May of 2014 with **NS-USA Ferry Service** (www.nsusaferry.com). Check the website for details.

TRAIN

VIA Rail (www.viarail.ca) runs services between Montréal and Halifax ($145, 21 hours, daily except Tuesdays), with stops in Amherst (17 hours from Montréal) and Truro (18 hours from Montréal). Discount fares may sell out, so it's best to book as early as possible.

❶ Getting Around

Renting a car is by far the easiest way to get around and can be more economical than taking the bus. Shuttle buses are another alternative. Distances are very manageable; you can easily stay in the Annapolis Valley and do day trips to the South Shore and vice versa. The longest drive most people will do is the four-hour haul to Cape Breton Island from Halifax.

The direct route to most places will be on a 100-series highway (eg 101, 102, 103), which have high speed limits and limited exits. There is usually a corresponding older highway (eg 1, 2, 3) that passes through communities and has varying speed limits, but none higher than 80km/h.

HALIFAX

POP 390,096

Halifax is the kind of town that people flock to, not so much for the opportunities, but for the quality of life it has to offer. Sea breezes off the harbor keep the air clean, and parks and trees nestle between heritage buildings, cosmopolitan eateries and arty shops. Several universities ensure that the population is young and the bars and nightclubs full. Stroll the historic waterfront, catch some live music and enjoy the best of what the Maritimes have to offer. In summer, never-ending festivals ignite the party ambience that much more.

History

Pirates, warring colonialists and exploding ships make the history of Halifax read like an adventure story. From 1749, when Edward Cornwallis founded Halifax along what is today Barrington St, the British settlement expanded and flourished. The destruction of the French fortress at Louisbourg in 1760 increased British dominance and sealed Halifax as Nova Scotia's most important city.

Despite being home to two universities from the early 1800s, Halifax was still a rough and ready sailors' nest that, during the War of 1812, became a center for privateer black-market trade. As piracy lost its government endorsement, Halifax sailed smoothly into a mercantile era, and the city streets, particularly Market and Brunswick Sts, became home to countless taverns and brothels.

On April 14, 1912, three Halifax ships were sent in response to a distress call: the 'unsinkable' *Titanic* had hit an iceberg. Over 1500 people were killed in the tragedy and many were buried at Fairview Cemetery, next to the Fairview Overpass on the Bedford Hwy.

In 1917 during WWI, the *Mont Blanc*, a French munitions ship carrying TNT and highly flammable benzol, collided with another ship. The 'Halifax Explosion,' the world's biggest man-made explosion prior to atomic bombs being dropped on Japan, ripped through the city. More than 1900 people were killed and 9000 injured. Almost the entire northern end of Halifax was leveled.

◉ Sights

◎ Downtown

Historic Properties   NOTABLE BUILDING
(www.historicproperties.ca) The Historic Properties are a group of restored buildings on Upper Water St, built between 1800 and 1905. Originally designed as huge warehouses for easy storage of goods and cargo, they now house boutiques, restaurants and bars and are connected by waterfront boardwalks. Artisans, merchants and buskers do business around the buildings in the summer. The 1814 **Privateers Warehouse** is the area's oldest stone building. The privateers were government sanctioned and sponsored pirates who stored their booty here. Among

the other vintage buildings are the wooden **Old Red Store**, once used for shipping operations and as a sail loft, and **Simon's Warehouse**, built in 1854.

Alexander Keith's Nova Scotia Brewery   BREWERY
(🖉902-455-1474; www.keiths.ca; Brewery Market, 1496 Lower Water St; adult/child $16/8; ⊘11am-8pm Mon-Thu, to 9pm Fri & Sat, noon-4pm Sun) A tour of this brewery takes you to 19th-century Halifax via costumed thespians, quality brew and dark corridors. Finish your hour-long tour with a party in the basement pub with beer on tap and ale-inspired yarns. Note that you'll need your ID. Kids are kept happy with lemonade.

Maritime Museum of the Atlantic   MUSEUM
(🖉902-424-7490; http://maritimemuseum.novascotia.ca/; 1675 Lower Water St; adult/child $9.25/5; ⊘9:30am-5pm Wed-Mon, to 8pm Tue) Part of this fun waterfront museum used to be a chandlery, where all the gear needed to outfit a vessel was sold. You can smell the charred ropes, cured to protect them from saltwater. There's a wildly popular display on the *Titanic* and another on the Halifax Explosion. The 3D film about the *Titanic* costs $5. Outside at the dock you can explore the CSS *Acadia,* a retired hydrographic vessel from England.

The last WWII corvette **HMCS Sackville** (adult/child $3/2; ⊘10am-5pm) is docked nearby and staffed by the Canadian navy.

Canadian Museum of Immigration at Pier 21   MUSEUM
(🖉902-425-7770; www.pier21.ca; 1055 Marginal Rd; adult/child $8.60/5; ⊘9:30am-5:30pm) Named by CBC (Canadian Broadcasting Company) as one of the Seven Wonders of Canada, Pier 21 was to Canada what Ellis Island was to the USA. Between 1928 and 1971 over a million immigrants entered Canada through Pier 21. Their stories and the historical context that led them to abandon their homelands are presented in this museum.

Researchers fanned out across Canada to get firsthand testimonials from immigrants who passed through Pier 21. These moving videos are shown in screening rooms off a railcar – bring your hankie. The museum became a national museum in 2012 and, with the new funding that brings, expansion and upgrades are expected.

Citadel Hill National Historic Site   HISTORIC SITE
(🖉902-426-5080; off Sackville St; adult/child $11.70/5.80; ⊘9am-6pm) Canada's most visited national historic site, the huge and arguably spooky Citadel, is a star-shaped fort atop Halifax' central hill. Construction began in 1749 with the founding of Halifax; this version of the Citadel is the fourth, built from 1818 to 1861. Guided tours explain the fort's shape and history. The grounds inside the fort are open year-round, with free admission when the exhibits are closed.

Art Gallery of Nova Scotia   GALLERY
(🖉902-424-7542; www.artgalleryofnovascotia.ca; 1723 Hollis St; adult/child $12/5; ⊘10am-5pm Wed, Fri & Sat, to 9pm Thu, noon-5pm Sun) Don't miss the permanent, tear-jerking Maud Lewis Painted House exhibit that includes the 3m-by-4m house that Lewis lived in most of her adult life. The main exhibit in the lower hall changes regularly, featuring anything from ancient art to the avant-garde. Free tours are given at 2pm Sunday year-round and daily during July and August.

Halifax Public Gardens   GARDENS
At the corner of Spring Garden Rd and South Park St, these are considered the finest Victorian city gardens in North America. Oldies bands perform off-key concerts in the gazebo on Sunday afternoons in summer, tai chi practitioners go through their paces, and anyone who brings checkers can play on outside tables.

Titanic Burial Grounds   HISTORIC SITE
When the *Titanic* sank, the bodies not buried at sea were brought to Halifax. Today there are 19 graves at **Mt Olivet Catholic Cemetery** (7076 Mumford Rd), 10 in the **Baron de Hirsch Jewish Cemetery** at the north end of Windsor St, and 121 in the adjacent **Fairview Lawn Cemetery**; 40 graves are still unidentified. J Dawson, whose name was the basis for Leonardo DiCaprio's character in the film *Titanic,* is buried at Fairview Cemetery.

Anna Leonowens Gallery   GALLERY
(🖉902-494-8184; http://nscad.ca; 1891 Granville St; ⊘11am-5pm Tue-Fri, noon-4pm Sat, show openings 5:30-7:30pm Mon) **FREE** Off the pedestrian area on Granville St, this gallery shows work by students and faculty of the Nova Scotia College of Art & Design. The gallery is named for the founder of the college, who

Halifax

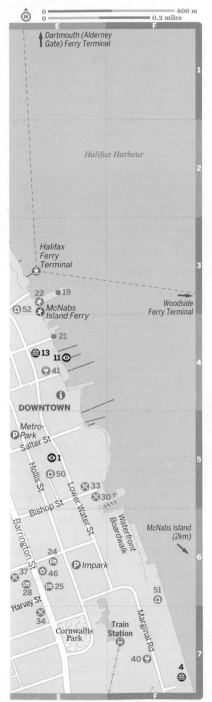

was immortalized in *The King and I* for her relationship with the king of Siam.

St Paul's Church   CHURCH
(☑ 902-429-2240; 1749 Argyle St; ☺ 9am-4pm Mon-Fri) Established in 1749 with the founding of Halifax, Anglican St Paul's Church once served parishioners from Newfoundland to Ontario. Across the square, Halifax' **City Hall** is a true gem of Victorian architecture.

St Mary's Cathedral Basilica   CHURCH
(☑ 902-423-4116; 1508 Barrington St; ☺ free tours 10am & 2pm Jul-Sep) You can't miss this cathedral which purportedly has the largest free-standing spire in North America.

Old Town Clock   NOTABLE BUILDING
At the top of George St, at Citadel Hill, the Old Town Clock has been keeping time for 200 years. The inner workings arrived in Halifax from London in 1803, after being ordered by Prince Edward, the Duke of Kent.

◉ North End

The North End has been a distinct neighborhood for almost as long as Halifax has existed. In the early 1750s the 'North Suburbs' area became popular and subsequently grew because of its larger building lots.

Africville Heritage Trust Museum   MUSEUM
(www.africvillemuseum.org, 5705 Africville Rd; adult/child $3.30/2; ☺ 10am-4pm Tue-Sun) Learn the story of Africville, an African Nova Scotian part of town that was destroyed in the 1960s. Poignantly, the museum is housed in a replica of the Seaview United Baptist Church that was once the center of the community. If Eddie Carver is around, he'll have some stories to tell you.

Maritime Command Museum   MUSEUM
(☑ 902-427-0550, ext 6725; 2725 Gottingen St; ☺ 9:30am-3:30pm Mon-Fri) FREE The admiral of the British navy for all of North America was based in Halifax until 1819 and threw grand parties at Admiralty House, now the Maritime Command Museum. Apart from the beautiful Georgian architecture, the museum is worth a visit for its eclectic collections: cigarette lighters, silverware and ship's bells, to name a few.

St George's Round Church   CHURCH
(☑ 902-423-1059; www.roundchurch.ca; 2222 Brunswick St) St George's Round Church was built in 1800 and is a rare circular Palladian

Halifax

church with a main rotunda 18m in diameter. Tours are by arrangement.

Cornwallis Street Baptist Church CHURCH
(5457 Cornwallis St) The Cornwallis Street Baptist Church has been serving African Nova Scotians since the 1830s. Walk by on Sunday morning and hear the gospel music flow through its walls.

Little Dutch Church CHURCH
(2405 Brunswick St) Tours of the 1756 Little Dutch Church, the second-oldest building in Halifax, can be arranged through St George's Round Church (p47).

◎ Outside the Center

Point Pleasant Park PARK
Some 39km of nature trails, picnic spots and the **Prince of Wales Martello Tower** (a round 18th-century defensive structure)

are all found within this 75-hectare sanctuary, just 1.5km south of the city center. Trails around the perimeter of the park offer views of McNabs Island, the open ocean and the North West Arm. Bus 9 along Barrington St goes to Point Pleasant, and there's ample free parking off Point Pleasant Dr.

McNabs Island ISLAND
(www.mcnabsisland.ca) Fine sand and cobblestone shorelines, salt marshes, abandoned military fortifications and forests paint the scenery of this 400-hectare island in Halifax harbor. Staff of the **McNabs Island Ferry** (☎ 902-465-4563; www.mcnabsisland.com; Government Wharf; round-trip adult/child $20/10; ⊙ 24hr) will provide you with a map and an orientation to 30km of roads and trails on the island. For camping reservations contact the **Department of Natural Resources** (☎ 902-861-2560). The ferry runs from Fish-

erman's Cove in Eastern Passage, a short drive through Dartmouth.

🏃 Activities

Cycling

Cycling is a great way to see sites on the outskirts of Halifax. You can take bikes on the ferries to Dartmouth or cycle over the MacDonald Bridge. There are usually a few places renting out bikes by Bishop's Landing (at the end of Bishop St) along the waterfront for $9 per hour or $15 for a half day from mid-June through August.

Otherwise, **Pedal & Sea Adventures** (☑ 877-772-5699, 902-857-9319; www.pedalandseaadventures.com; bicycle rental per day/week from $35/140) will deliver the bike to you, complete with helmet, lock and repair kit. It also leads good-value self-guided tours; five-day trips including lodging and meals cost from $1099.

Hiking

There are both short and long hikes surprisingly close to downtown. **Hemlock Ravine** is an 80-hectare wooded area that has five trails, suitable for all levels. To get there, take the Bedford Hwy from central Halifax then turn left at Kent Ave; there's parking and a map of the trail at the end of this road. See www.novatrails.com for more detailed trail descriptions and directions to other trailheads. There's also hiking in Point Pleasant Park and on McNabs Island.

☞ Tours

Check whether the two-masted schooner *Bluenose II* (p60) is in town for a harbor tour.

Tall Ship Silva   BOAT TOUR
(☑ 902-429-9463; www.tallshipsilva.com; Queen's Wharf, Prince St; cruises adult/child $22/15; ⊙ noon, 2pm, 4pm, 6pm & 10:30pm daily May-Oct) Lend a hand or sit back and relax while taking a 1½-hour daytime cruise or a two-hour evening party cruise on Halifax' square-masted tall ship.

East Coast Balloon
Adventures   SCENIC FLIGHTS
(☑ 902-306-0095; www.eastcoastballoonadventures.com; 45min flights per person $250) Float from Halifax over the patchwork fields of Annapolis Valley at sunrise or sunset for the ultimate, peaceful views of this stunning province. Only available for ages eight and upwards.

HALIFAX HIGHLIGHTS

➡ Peruse crafts and snack on fresh delights at Halifax Seaport Farmers Market (p54).

➡ Enjoy a breezy budget cruise on the Dartmouth ferry (p55).

➡ Learn all about the Halifax Explosion and the *Titanic* at the Maritime Museum of the Atlantic (p45).

➡ Citadel Hill National Historic Site (p45), for history and a view.

➡ Live music at a variety of pubs and other venues (p53).

Bluenose Sidecar Tours   DRIVING TOUR
(☑ 902-579-7433; www.bluenosesidecartours.com; tours $74-189) Enjoy free and breezy views from fun, old-school motorcycle sidecars on tours around Halifax or to Peggy's Cove, Lunenburg and the South Shore.

Tattle Tours   WALKING TOUR
(☑ 902-494-0525; www.tattletours.ca; per person $10; ⊙ 7:30pm Wed-Sun) Lively two-hour tours depart from the Old Town Clock and are filled with local gossip, pirate tales and ghost stories. Walking tours are also available on demand – ask at any visitors information center (p54).

Salty Bear Adventure Travel   BUS TOUR
(☑ 902-224-1313; www.saltybear.ca; tours from $299) A sociable backpacker's choice for touring the province.

Great EARTH Expeditions   ECOTOUR
(☑ 902-223-2409; www.greatearthexpeditions.com; half-/full-day tours from $75/100) Half- and full-day ecotours led from Halifax can include hiking, kayaking or historical themes, including a tour to McNabs Island in Halifax Harbour. Longer four-day tours up the Cabot Trail and through Kejimkujik are also on offer.

Murphy's Cable Wharf   BOAT TOUR
(☑ 902-420-1015; www.mtcw.ca; 1751 Lower Water St) This tourism giant runs a range of tours on Halifax Harbour, from deep-sea fishing and two-hour scenic cruises to the popular 55-minute Harbour Hopper Tours (adult/child $30/17) on an amphibious bus.

LOCAL KNOWLEDGE

FREE SKATING ON THE COMMON

The Emera Oval (www.halifax.ca/skate-hrm; ⊙ 7am-late) FREE on the Halifax Common serves as a speed-skating rink in winter and morphs into an inline-skating rink in summer. Skates, helmets and sledges (for use on the outside lane only) are free to borrow and there are even free lessons. Check the website and bring a valid ID.

✯✯ Festivals & Events

Halifax is most vibrant during its jovial festivals. Check out volunteering opportunities through festival websites.

Nova Scotia Multicultural Festival CULTURE
(www.mans.ns.ca; ⊙ late Jun) Performers, artisans, chefs and more entertain, promote and explore the province's multiculturalism at this huge festival.

Nova Scotia Tattoo CULTURE
(www.nstattoo.ca; tickets $27-65; ⊙ early Jul) The world's 'largest annual indoor show' is a military-style event with lots of marching bands.

Atlantic Jazz Festival MUSIC
(www.jazzeast.com; evening tickets $15-30; ⊙ mid-Jul) A full week of free outdoor jazz concerts each afternoon, plus evening performances ranging from world music to classic jazz trios.

Halifax International Busker Festival PERFORMING ARTS
(www.buskers.ca; ⊙ early Aug) Comics, mimes, daredevils and musicians from all over the world perform along the Halifax waterfront.

Atlantic Fringe Festival THEATER
(www.atlanticfringe.com; ⊙ mid-Sep) Offbeat and experimental theater from both emerging and established artists.

Atlantic Film Festival FILM
(www.atlanticfilm.com; tickets $10-15; ⊙ mid-Sep) Ten days of great flicks from the Atlantic region and around the world.

Halifax Pop Explosion MUSIC
(www.halifaxpopexplosion.com; wristbands $50; ⊙ mid-Oct) Some 130 concerts are spread out over 12 clubs during a five-day period and include hip-hop, punk, indie rock and folk.

A wristband gets you into as many shows as you can manage to see.

🛏 Sleeping

Halifax Backpackers Hostel HOSTEL $
(☑ 902-431-3170, 888-431-3170; www.halifax-backpackers.com; 2193 Gottingen St; dm/d/ste $20/57.50/80; 🛜) Coed dorms at this hip, 36-bed North End hostel hold no more than six beds. It draws a funky young crowd and everyone congregates at the downstairs cafe to swill strong coffee, eat cheap breakfasts and mingle with the eclectic local regulars. City buses stop right in front, but be warned: it's a slightly rough-edged neighborhood.

HI Nova Scotia HOSTEL $
(☑ 902-422-3863; www.hihostels.ca; 1253 Barrington St; HI member/nonmember dm $26/30, r $57; 🛜) Expect a dark and dormy night and a bright and cheery do-it-yourself breakfast at this exceptionally central, 75-bed hostel set in a Victorian house. The staff are friendly, and the shared kitchen is lively. Reserve ahead in summer.

Dalhousie University HOSTEL $
(☑ 902-494-8840; www.dal.ca/dept/summer-accommodations.html; s/d $48.50/75; ⊙ May-Aug; 🛜🚭) Dorm rooms with shared bathrooms are nearly sterile (read: no posters or beer bottles). Most people stay at Howe Hall (6230 Coburg St), which is adjacent to all the included university amenities and is a short walk to the Spring Garden Rd area.

★ Waverley Inn INN $$
(☑ 902-423-9346, 800-565-9346; www.waverley-inn.com; 1266 Barrington St; d incl breakfast $135-235; 🛜@🛜) Every room here is furnished uniquely and nearly theatrically with antiques and dramatic linens. Both Oscar Wilde and PT Barnum once stayed here and probably would again today if they were still living. The downtown location can't be beat.

Fresh Start B&B B&B $$
(☑ 888-453-6616, 902-453-6616; www.bbcanada.com/2262.html; 2720 Gottingen St; r $110-130; @🛜) Run by two retired nurses, this majestic yet lived-in-feeling Victorian is in a gay-friendly part of the North End. Rooms with en-suite bathrooms are the best value.

Marigold B&B B&B $$
(☑ 902-423-4798; www.marigoldbedandbreak-fast.com; 6318 Norwood St; s/d $75/85) Feel at home in this artist's nest full of bright floral paintings and fluffy cats. It's in a tree-lined

residential area in the North End with easy public transport access.

Pebble Bed & Breakfast   B&B $$$
(☑888-303-5056, 902-423-3369; www.thepebble.ca; 1839 Armview Tce; r $175-225; 🕾 🏠) Bathroom aficionados will find heaven at this luxurious B&B. The tub and shower are in a giant room that leads to a terrace overlooking a leafy garden. The bedrooms are equally generous with plush, high beds and a modern-meets-antique decor. Irish owner Elizabeth O'Carroll grew up with a pub-owning family and brings lively, joyous energy from the Emerald Isle to her home in a posh, waterside residential area.

Halliburton   INN $$$
(☑902-420-0658; www.thehalliburton.com; 5184 Morris St; r $159-350; 🏠 @ 🕾) Pure, soothing class without all that Victorian hullabaloo can be found at this exceedingly comfortable and well-serviced historic hotel right in downtown.

Lord Nelson Hotel   HOTEL $$$
(☑902-423-5130, 800-565-2020; www.lordnelsonhotel.com; 1515 S Park St; d $130-360; 🏠 @ 🕾) When rock stars such as the Rolling Stones come to Halifax, they stay here. It's an elegant yet not stuffy 1920s building right across from Halifax Public Gardens. Rates drop dramatically in the off-season.

Prince George Hotel   HOTEL $$$
(☑800-565-1567, 902-425-1986; www.princegeorgehotel.com; 1725 Market St; d $160-350; 🏠 @ 🏊 🏠) A suave and debonair gem, central Prince George has all the details covered. Garden patios are a great place to take a drink or a meal, or even work, as an alternative to indoor meeting areas. Parking is $15.

🍴 Eating

Bars and pubs often serve very good food; kitchens close around 10pm.

Heartwood Vegetarian Cuisine
& Bakery   VEGETARIAN $
(☑902-425-2808; 6250 Quinpool Rd; light meals from $5; ⊘10am-8pm Mon-Sat; 🖋) Try the local organic salad bar or amazing baked goods, along with a cup of fair-trade coffee.

Annie's Place Café   BREAKFAST $
(1592B Queen St; breakfasts $3-8; ⊘7am-3pm Mon-Fri, to 2pm Sat) A slice of small town in the heart of Halifax, Annie welcomes you in

and cooks up a hearty breakfast, including freshly baked bread and homemade chai. You'll have a whole new set of friends by the time you leave.

Just Us! Coffee Roaster's Co-Op   CAFE $
(1715 Barrington St; ⊘7am-5:30pm Mon-Thu, to 9pm Fri & Sat; 🕾) This bright yet cozy cafe serves up fair-trade, house-roasted coffee and baked goods made from locally sourced ingredients. It has free wi-fi and a central location; there's also a **second branch** (5896 Spring Garden Rd) nearby.

★Edna   MODERN CANADIAN $$
(www.ednarestaurant.com; 2053 Gottingen St; mains $14-22; ⊘from 5pm Tue-Sun) Everything here is delicious, from the Southern fried rock hen to the filled-with-everything-good-from-the-sea Atlantic bouillabaisse. You can dine at a big wooden table where guests from everywhere chat and mingle, at the bar for a little less socializing or at a regular old table for two. It's a unique, vivacious, food-and-drink-loving atmosphere.

HALIFAX FOR CHILDREN

Discovery Centre (☑902-492-4422; www.discoverycentre.ns.ca; 1593 Barrington St; adult/child $8.50/6; ⊘10am-5pm Mon-Sat, 1-5pm Sun) Hands-on exhibits, live shows and movies make science fun for all ages. In 2014 the center will change locations to a modern new venue on the waterfront.

Museum of Natural History (☑902-424-7353; http://naturalhistory.novascotia.ca/; 1747 Summer St; adult/child $5.75/3.75; ⊘9am-5pm Mon, Tue & Thu-Sat, to 8pm Wed, noon-5pm Sun) Daily summer programs introduce children to Gus the toad and demonstrate the cooking of bugs. Exhibits on history and the natural world will keep parents engaged, too.

Theodore Too Big Harbour Tours (☑902-492-8847; www.mtcw.ca/theodoretugboat; 1751 Lower Water St; adult/child $20/15; ⊘11am, 12:30pm, 2pm, 3:30pm & 5pm daily Jun-Sep) One-hour tours on this funny-looking cartoon-character boat of book and television fame are particularly good for children under six.

★**Bicycle Thief**   MODERN CANADIAN **$$**
(☑902-425-7993; 1475 Lower Water St; lunch mains $14-18, dinner mains $15-29; ☉11.30am-late Mon-Fri, 5:30pm-late Sat) Named for the 1948 classic Italian film, this shabby-chic waterfront restaurant has won similar critical acclaim by local foodies – and with good reason. Start with regional oysters or polenta with wild mushroom ragout, then continue with dishes like pistachio-honey roasted salmon or pancetta wrapped pork tenderloin. The wine and cocktail list is several pages longer than the food menu.

Brooklyn Warehouse   CANADIAN **$$**
(☑902-446-8181; www.brooklynwarehouse.ca; 2795 Windsor St; lunch mains $8-15, dinner mains around $20; ☉11:30am-10pm Mon-Sat; ☑) This North End hot spot is loaded with vegetarian and vegan options – the eggplant moussaka stack is excellent. It has a huge beer and cocktail menu, and an atmosphere that feels like a modern, hip version of *Cheers* – but with way better food.

Morris East   ITALIAN **$$**
(☑902-444-7663; www.morriseast.com; 5212 Morris St; pizzas $14-17; ☉11:30am-2:30pm Tue-Sat & 5-10pm Tue-Sun) At this cosmopolitan cafe, you'll find creative wood-fired pizzas on your choice of white, whole-wheat or gluten-free dough; try the peach, rosemary aioli and prosciutto pizza. They also have snazzy cocktails, like basil, lime and vodka punch.

Epicurious Morcels   FUSION **$$**
(☑902-455-0955; Hydrostone Market, 5529 Young St; mains around $12; ☉11:30am-8pm Tue-Thu, 10:30am-8pm Fri & Sat, 10:30am-2:30pm Sun) The specialties are smoked salmon, gravlax (dill-cured salmon) and unusual but extremely tasty homemade soups. The rest of the internationally inspired menu is also fantastic.

Hamachi Steak House Bar & Grill   JAPANESE, FUSION **$$**
(☑902-425-1600; 1477 Lower Water St; teppanyaki $11-26; ☉11:30am-10pm Mon-Sat, 4-10pm Sun) Watch the show grill-side, while your chef slices, dices and sets the stove aflame to cook up the meats, seafood and veggies that make a crowd-pleasing Japanese teppanyaki. For a less theatrical experience, grab a table and enjoy the teppanyaki, sushi or Alberta steaks quietly, with a beautiful view of the harbor.

Wooden Monkey   CANADIAN **$$**
(☑902-444-3844; 1707 Grafton St; mains $14-23; ☉11am-10pm; ☑) ⏻ This dark, cozy nook with outdoor sidewalk seating on sunny days adamantly supports local organics and is a fab place to get superb gluten-free and vegan meals, as well as humane meat dishes.

Henry House   PUB **$$**
(1222 Barrington St; mains $11-20; ☉11:30am-midnight) Yeah, it's a pub, but the fish cakes are consistently rated the best in town and the bread pudding is legendary. Nosh all this with a frothy pint in a dimly lit and distinctly English-feeling basement or outside on the deck when the sun's out.

Chives Canadian Bistro   CANADIAN **$$$**
(☑902-420-9626; 1537 Barrington St; mains $17-35; ☉5-9:30pm) The menu changes with what's seasonably available and uses mostly local ingredients. The food is fine dining, while the low-lit cozy ambience is upscale casual.

Da Maurizio   ITALIAN **$$$**
(☑902-423-0859; 1496 Lower Water St; mains $28-34; ☉5-10pm Mon-Sat) Many locals cite this as their favorite Halifax restaurant. The ambience is as fine as the cuisine; exposed brick and clean lines bring out all the flavors of this heritage brewery building. Reservations are strongly recommended.

🍷 Drinking & Nightlife

Halifax rivals Saint John's, Newfoundland, for the most drinking holes per capita. The biggest concentration of attractive bars is on Argyle St, where temporary street-side patios expand the sidewalk each summer. Pubs and bars close at 2am (a few hours earlier on Sunday).

Lower Deck   PUB
(☑902-422-1501; 1869 Lower Water St) A first stop for a real Nova Scotian knee-slapping good time. Think pints in frothy glasses, everyone singing, and live music all spilling out over the sidewalks on summer nights. When someone yells 'sociable!' it's time to raise your glass.

Economy Shoe Shop   PUB
(☑902-423-8845; 1663 Argyle St) This has been the 'it' place to drink and people-watch in Halifax for well over a decade. On weekend nights, actors and journalists figure heavily in the crush. It's a pleasant place for afternoon drinks and the kitchen dishes out tapas until last call at 1:45am.

Middle Spoon   COCKTAIL BAR

(www.themiddlespoon.ca; 1559 Barrington St; cocktails around $11; ⊙ 4-11pm Mon-Thu, to 1am Fri & Sat) What could be better than a place that serves only beer, wine, creative cocktails and decadent desserts? How about one with a super secret – should we even be writing this? It has a speakeasy-inspired lounge downstairs that serves even better cocktails. Get the password by clicking on the >: symbol on the website and don't tell.

Garrison Brewing Company   BREWERY

(1149 Marginal Rd; ⊙ 10am-8pm Sun-Thu, to 10pm Fri & Sat) Not much beats a $2 taster glass of craft beer on a sunny patio except maybe five varieties of tasters, which is how many the brewery serves on tap each day. Other bottled beers are sold in the shop but, because they're not legally a bar (and Canada has complicated liquor laws), you can't drink them on the premises.Brewery tours are available by reservation.

Onyx   COCKTAIL BAR

(☑ 902-428-5680; 5680 Spring Garden Rd) A sultry place for a chic cocktail, the Onyx has a backlit white onyx bar that serves a huge selection of fine wines, single malt whiskeys and nine signature fresh-fruit mojitos, among other options. Imbibe small plates of Asian-French cuisine made with local ingredients.

☆ Entertainment

Check out *Coast* (www.thecoast.ca) to see what's on. A free weekly publication available around town, it's the essential guide for music, theater, film and events.

Live Music

Halifax seems to be fueled by music, with folk, hip-hop, alternative, country and rock gigs around town every weekend. Cover charge depends on the band.

Carelton   LIVE MUSIC

(☑ 902-422-6335; 1685 Argyle St) Catch acoustic sets, then enjoy the reasonable meals including a late-night menu.

Seahorse Tavern   LIVE MUSIC

(☑ 902-423-7200; 1665 Argyle St) The place to see punk, indie and metal bands.

Bearly's House of Blues & Ribs   LIVE MUSIC

(☑ 902-423-2526; 1269 Barrington St; cover $3) The best blues musicians in Atlantic Canada play here at incredibly low cover charges. Wednesday karaoke nights draw a crowd and some fine singers.

Theater

The two professional theaters in and around Halifax – Neptune Theatre and Eastern Front Theatre in Dartmouth – take a break in summer, with their last shows typically playing in May. However, Shakespeare by the Sea provides diversion through the summer.

Neptune Theatre   THEATER

(☑ 902-429-7070; www.neptunetheatre.com; 1593 Argyle St) This downtown theater presents musicals and well-known plays on its main stage (from $35), and edgier stuff in the studio (from $15).

Shakespeare by the Sea   THEATER

(☑ 902-422-0295; www.shakespearebythesea.ca; Point Pleasant Park; suggested donation $15; ⊙ Jun-Sep) Fine performances of the Bard's works at the Cambridge Battery, an old

---

GAY & LESBIAN HALIFAX

Halifax has a thumping and thriving gay and lesbian scene, with most of the nightlife action concentrated around Gottingen St. In the city center, **Reflections Cabaret** (☑ 902-422-2957; 5184 Sackville St) is a wild disco that attracts a mixed crowd. It opens at 4pm, but the action really starts after 10pm (it stays open until 3am).

Lesbian travelers can stop by **Venus Envy** (☑ 902-422-0004; 1598 Barrington St; ⊙ 10am-6pm Mon-Wed & Sat, to 7pm Thu & Fri, noon-5pm Sun) to network, browse books and check out fun toys. Squeaky clean **Seadog's Sauna & Spa** (☑ 902-444-3647; www. seadogs.ca; 2199 Gottingen St; ⊙ 4pm-1am Mon-Thu, from 4pm Fri through 1am Mon) is the largest private men's club east of Québec City and has all the spa fixings. The same folks have opened **Menz Bar** (2182 Gottingen St; ⊙ 3pm-2am), which offers its own Menz Pale Ale on tap.

Halifax Pride Week (www.halifaxpride.com) takes place every year around mid-July. Don't miss the Dykes versus Divas softball game that usually kicks off the week.

fortification in the middle of Point Pleasant Park. Check the website for details.

Sports

Halifax Metro Centre STADIUM
(☑902-451-1221; 5284 Duke St; tickets $15) Halifax Mooseheads junior hockey team plays here.

🛍 Shopping

Halifax has some truly quirky shops to discover in the city center between Spring Garden Rd and Duke St.

★Halifax Seaport Farmers Market MARKET
(www.halifaxfarmersmarket.com; Marginal Rd; ⊙10am-5pm Tue-Sun) The old Halifax Brewery Farmers Market was so popular this larger edifice was built to expand the fun. Find over 250 vendors selling everything from artisanal soaps to fresh carrots and baked goods. The market is biggest on Friday, Saturday and Sunday, but it's a great lunch stop anytime it's open.

Halifax Farmers Brewery Market MARKET
(☑902-492-4043; 1496 Lower Water St; ⊙7am-1pm Sat) North America's oldest farmers market, in the 1820s Keith's Brewery Building, has been overshadowed by the Seaport Market, but it's still worth checking this place out for the beautiful old building and longtime artisan vendors.

Nova Scotian Crystal ARTS & CRAFTS
(☑888-977-2797; 5080 George St; ⊙9am-6pm Mon-Fri, 10am-5pm Sat & Sun) It's as much of a show as a place to shop. Watch glass blowers form beautiful crystal glasses and vases, then pick the ones you want in the classy adjacent shop.

ℹ Orientation

The downtown area, three universities and older residential neighborhoods are contained on a compact peninsula cut off from mainland Halifax by an inlet called the North West Arm. Almost all sights of interest to visitors are concentrated in this area, making walking the best way to get around. Point Pleasant Park is at the extreme southern end of the peninsula, and the lively North End neighborhood – home to African Nova Scotians, art-school students and most of Halifax' gay bars – stretches from the midpoint to the northern extreme.

Two bridges span the harbor, connecting Halifax to Dartmouth and leading to highways north (for the airport) and east. The MacDonald Bridge at the eastern end of North St is closest to downtown. The airport is 40km northeast of town on Hwy 102.

ℹ Information

INTERNET ACCESS

Many cafes, restaurants and public spaces have wi-fi. The new **Halifax Central Library** (Spring Garden Rd; ⊙10am-9pm Tue-Thu, to 5pm Fri & Sat, 2-5pm Sun) has free wi-fi and computers on a first-come, first-served basis.

MEDICAL SERVICES

Family Focus (☑902-420-2038; 5991 Spring Garden Rd; consultation $65; ⊙8:30am-9pm Mon-Fri, 11am-5pm Sat & Sun) Walk-in or same-day appointments.

Halifax Infirmary (☑902-473-7605, 902-473-3383; 1796 Summer St; ⊙24hr) For emergencies.

MONEY

Bank branches cluster around Barrington and Duke Sts.

POST

Lawton's Drugs (☑902-429-0088; 5675 Spring Garden Rd; ⊙8am-9pm Mon-Fri, to 6pm Sat, noon-5pm Sun) Post office inside.

Main Post Office (☑902-494-4670; 1680 Bedford Row; ⊙7:30am-5:15pm Mon-Fri) Pick up mail sent to General Delivery, Halifax, NS B3J 2L3.

TOURIST INFORMATION

Check out posters for performances and events on the bulletin boards just inside the door of the Spring Garden Road Memorial Library.

Tourism Nova Scotia (☑902-425-5781, 800-565-0000; www.novascotia.com) Operates visitors information centers in Halifax and other locations within Nova Scotia province, plus a free booking service for accommodations, which is useful when rooms are scarce in midsummer. It publishes the *Doers & Dreamers Guide* that lists places to stay, attractions and tour operators.

Visitors Information Centre (VIC) Halifax International Airport (☑902-873-1223; ⊙9am-9pm); Waterfront (☑902-424-4248; 1655 Lower Water St; ⊙8:30am-8pm).

USEFUL WEBSITES

Destination Halifax (www.halifaxinfo.com) Halifax' official tourism site has information on everything from events to package bookings.

Halifax Regional Municipality (www.halifax.ca) Info on everything from bus schedules to recreation programs.

❶ Getting There & Away

AIR

Most air services in Nova Scotia go to/from Halifax and there are multiple daily flights to Toronto, Calgary and Vancouver.

BUS

The only province-wide (and beyond) bus company is **Maritime Bus** (www.maritimebus.com), which services the main highways from Kentville to Halifax and up to Truro. From Truro the routes fork: towards North Sydney in one direction and towards Amherst and onto New Brunswick in the other.

Private shuttle buses compete with the major bus companies. Shuttles usually pick you up and drop you off from your hotel; with fewer stops, they travel faster, but the trade-off is a more cramped ride. They also tend to go out of business or change names frequently, so check online or ask around. Some of the more reliable companies include the following:

Cloud Nine Shuttle (☑902-742-3992, 888-805-3335; www.thecloudnineshuttle.com) Does the Yarmouth–Halifax route ($75, 3½ hours), stopping along the South Shore; airport pickup or drop-off is an extra $5.

Kathleen's Shuttle & Tours (☑903-834-2024; www.digbytoursandshuttle.webs.com) Halifax airport to Digby and Annapolis areas for around $65.

PEI Express Shuttle (☑902-462-8177, 877-877-1771; www.peishuttle.com) Goes to Charlottetown (PEI; $69), with early morning pickups.

TRAIN

One of the few examples of monumental Canadian train station architecture left in the Maritimes is found at 1161 Hollis St. Options with **VIA Rail** (www.viarail.ca) include overnight service to Montréal (21 hours, daily except Tuesdays).

❶ Getting Around

TO/FROM THE AIRPORT

Halifax International Airport is 40km northeast of town on Hwy 102 toward Truro. The cheapest way to get there is by Metro Transit public bus 320, which runs half-hourly to hourly between 5am and midnight from the Metro X bus stop on Albemarle St between Duke and Cogswell Sts. If you arrive in the middle of the night, as many flights do, your only choice is a taxi, which costs $56 to downtown Halifax. There are often not enough taxis, so it's prudent to reserve one in advance. Try **Halifax Airport Taxi** (☑902-999-2434; www.halifaxairportlimotaxi.com), which has 24-hour airport service.

CAR & MOTORCYCLE

Pedestrians almost always have the right-of-way in Halifax, so watch out for cars stopping suddenly!

Outside the downtown core, you can usually find free on-street parking for up to two hours. Otherwise, try private **Impark** (1245 Hollis St; per 1/12hr $1.50/8) or the municipally owned **Metro-Park** (☑902-830-1711; 1557 Granville St; per 1/12hr $2.25/15). Halifax' parking meters are enforced from 8am to 6pm Monday to Friday.

All the major national rental chains are represented at the airport and in downtown Halifax. Some will let you pick up in town and drop off at the airport free of charge.

PUBLIC TRANSPORTATION

Metro Transit (☑902-490-6600; www.halifax.ca/metrotransit; one-way fare $3.25) runs the city bus system and the ferries to Dartmouth. Maps and schedules are available at the ferry terminals and at the information booth in Scotia Sq mall.

Bus 7 cuts through downtown and North End Halifax via Robie St and Gottingen St, passing both hostels. Bus 1 travels along Spring Garden Rd, Barrington St, and the south part of Gottingen St before crossing the bridge to Dartmouth. **Fred** is a free city bus that loops around downtown every 30 minutes in the summer.

Taking the **ferry to Dartmouth** (one-way fare $2.25; every 15 to 30 minutes from 6am to 11:30pm) from the Halifax Ferry Terminal is a nice way of getting on the water, even if it's just for 12 minutes. Woodside, where another ferry goes in peak periods, is a good place to start a bike ride to Eastern Passage or Lawrencetown.

AROUND HALIFAX

Dartmouth

Founded in 1750, one year after Halifax, Dartmouth is Halifax' counterpart just across the harbor. It is more residential than Halifax, and the downtown area lacks the capital's charm and bustle, but it can make a pleasant base, since getting to Halifax by bus or ferry is so easy.

It's definitely worth a day trip just for the short cruise across the harbor on the ferry, the oldest saltwater ferry system in North America. Alderney Gate houses Dartmouth's ferry terminal.

Dartmouth Heritage Museum (☑902-464-2300; www.dartmouthheritagemuseum.ns.ca; 26 Newcastle St; admission $3; ☺10am-5pm

Tue-Sun mid-Jun–Aug, 1:30-5pm Wed-Sat Sep–mid-Jun) displays an eclectic collection in Evergreen House, the former home of folklorist Helen Creighton, who traversed the province in the early 20th century recording stories and songs. Tickets include same-day admission to the 1786 Quaker House (59 Ochterloney St; ☺10am-5pm Tue-Sun Jun-Aug), the oldest house in the Halifax area, which was built by Quaker whalers from Nantucket who fled the American Revolution.

Shubie Campground (☎800-440-8450, 902-435-8328; www.shubiecampground.com; Jaybee Dr, off Waverley Rd; campsites from $33.50), the only campground accessible from Halifax on public transportation, is privately run and municipally owned. Facilities include showers and a laundry.

Haligonians head to Dartmouth just for the massive buttery chocolate croissants at Two If By Sea (66 Ochterloney St; chocolate croissants $3; ☺7am-6pm Mon-Fri, 8am-5pm Sat & Sun). But be warned, they are usually sold out by about 1pm. Even sans pastries, it's a hip place to stop for coffee and people-watching on a sunny day, with a distinctly Dartmouth atmosphere.

Eastern Shore Beaches

When downtown dwellers venture over the bridge to Dartmouth on a hot summer's day, it's most likely en route to a beach. There are beautiful, long, white-sand beaches all along the Eastern Shore, and although the water never gets very warm, brave souls venture in for a swim or a surf, particularly if the fog stays offshore.

The closest – and therefore busiest – of the Eastern Shore beaches, Rainbow Haven, is 1km long. It has washrooms, showers, a canteen and a boardwalk with wheelchair access to the beach. Lifeguards supervise a sizable swimming area.

The most popular destination for surfers, cobblestone Lawrencetown Beach faces directly south and often gets big waves compliments of hurricanes or tropical storms hundreds of kilometers away. It boasts a supervised swimming area, washrooms and a canteen. To surf, learn to surf or just enjoy the view, stay at Lawrencetown Beach House (☎902-827-2345; www.lawrencetownbeachhouse.com; dm/d $28/75), a comfy hostel with 10 beds and three private rooms. It's beautifully nestled in the beach grass above one of the only stretches of real sand and often books up months before summer even begins, so plan in advance. There are several places in the area to rent surfboards (around $15 per day) and wet suits (also $15 per day). Surf lessons are around $75 for 1½ hours including equipment; try Dacane Sports (☎902-431-7873; http://dacanesurfshop.com), Nova Scotia Surf School (www.ecsurfschool.com) or the all-women-run One Life Surf School (☎902-880-7873; www.onelifesurf.com).

With more than 3km of white sand backed by beach grass, Martinique is the longest beach in Nova Scotia and one of the prettiest in the area. Even if you find the water too cold for a swim, it's a beautiful place to walk, watch birds or play Frisbee.

DON'T MISS

FISHERMAN'S COVE

If you're heading up the Eastern Shore from Dartmouth or Halifax, detour onto Hwy 322 to Fisherman's Cove in Eastern Passage, a Popeye-esque fishing port with some of the region's best seafood samplings. Wharf Wraps (104 Government Wharf Rd; fish & chips $12; ☺10am-6pm Jun-Sep) has an outdoor seating area and deservedly famous (and huge) portions of fish and chips, or head next door to the Fish Basket (100 Government Wharf Rd; ☺9am-6pm) for fish and lobster by the pound or a delicious fresh lobster sandwich ($8) for the road.

Sambro

Just 18km south of Halifax, Crystal Crescent Beach is on the outskirts of the fishing village of Sambro. There are actually three beaches here in distinct coves; the third one out, toward the southwest, is clothing optional and gay friendly. An 8.5km hiking trail begins just inland and heads through barrens, bogs and boulders to Pennant Point; to get to the trailhead, take Herring Cove Rd from the traffic circle in Halifax all the way to Sambro, then follow the signs.

Peggy's Cove

Peggy's Cove is one of the most visited fishing towns in Canada and for a good reason: the rolling granite cove highlighted by a perfect red-and-white lighthouse exudes a dreamy seaside calm, even through the parading tour buses. Most visitors hop off their air-con bus, snap a few pictures, then get right back on the bus. If you stick around, you'll find it surprisingly easy to chat with the friendly locals (there are only 45 of them) and settle into fishing-village pace. At 43km west of Halifax on Hwy 333, it makes a mellow day trip from the city.

It's best to visit before 10am in the summer, as tour buses arrive in the middle of the day and create one of the province's worst traffic jams.

◉ Sights

Peggy's Cove Lighthouse   NOTABLE BUILDING
(◷9:30am-5:30pm May-Oct) The highlight of the cove is this picture-perfect lighthouse, which for many years was a working post office. Meander around the granite landscape that undulates much like the icy sea beyond.

DeGarthe Gallery   GALLERY
(☑902-823-2256; admission $2; ◷on demand) See paintings by local artist William deGarthe (1907–83), who sculpted the magnificent 30m-high *Fishermen's Monument* into a rock face in front of the gallery.

⌂ Sleeping & Eating

Wayside Camping Park   CAMPGROUND $
(☑902-823-2271; www.waysidecampground.com; 10295 Hwy 333, Glen Margaret; campsites/RV sites $25/35; ◷May-Oct; ☎☷) About 10km north of Peggy's Cove and 36km from Halifax, this camping park has lots of shady sites on a hill. It gets crowded in midsummer.

Peggy's Cove Bed & Breakfast   B&B $$
(☑902-823-2265, 877-725-8732; www.peggyscove-bb.com; 17 Church Rd; r $120-145; ◷Apr-Oct) The only place to stay in the cove itself, this B&B has an enviable position with one of the best views in Nova Scotia, overlooking the fishing docks and the lighthouse; it was once home to artist William deGarthe. You'll definitely need advance reservations.

Oceanstone Inn & Cottages   INN $$
(☑866-823-2160, 902-823-2160; www.oceanstone. ns.ca; 8650 Peggy's Cove Rd, Indian Harbour; r $95-145, cottages $185-365; @☎☷) Whimsically decorated cottages are a stone's throw from the beach and just a short drive from Peggy's Cove. Guests can use paddleboats to venture to small islands. Rhubarb, the inn's dining

room, is considered one of the best seafood restaurants in the region.

Dee Dee's   ICE CREAM $
(◷noon-6pm May-Sep) On hot days, explore the area licking a delicious homemade-with-local-ingredients ice-cream cone from Dee Dee's, near the tourist information center.

☆ Entertainment

Old Red Schoolhouse   THEATER
(☑902-823-2099; www.beales.ns.ca; 126 Peggy's Point Rd; suggested donation $10) This performance venue puts on comedies and music performances through the high season. A few shows per season are serviced by shuttle vans that offer round-trips to Halifax hotels. Check the website for details.

❶ Information

There's a free parking area with washrooms and a **tourist information office** (☑902-823-2253; 109 Peggy's Cove Rd; ◷9am-7pm May-Oct) as you enter the village. Free 45-minute walking tours are led from the tourist office daily from mid-June through August.

SOUTH SHORE

This is Nova Scotia's most visited coastline and it's here you'll find all those quintessential lighthouses, protected forested coves with white beaches, and plenty of fishing villages turned tourist towns. The area from Halifax to Lunenburg is cottage country for the city's elite and is quite popular with day-tripping tourists and locals. Hwy 3 – labeled the 'Lighthouse Route' by tourism officials –

can be slow as a result. Take this scenic route if you're not pressed for time and want to check out antique shops or artisans' wares en route. Travel times can be halved by taking Hwy 103 directly to the closest exit for your destination.

Chester

Established in 1759, the tiny town of Chester has today become a choice spot for well-to-do Americans and Haligonians to have a summer home. It's had a colorful history as the haunt of pirates and Prohibition-era bathtub-gin smugglers and it keeps its color today via the many artists' studios about town. There's a large regatta in the tranquil harbor in mid-August.

◉ Sights & Activities

Lordly House Museum   MUSEUM
(☑902-275-3842; 133 Central St; ⊘10am-4pm Tue-Sat Jun-Sep) FREE A fine example of Georgian architecture from 1806, the Lordly House Museum has three period rooms illustrating 19th-century upper-class life and Chester history. The museum is also an artists' studio.

Tancook Island   ISLAND
This island (population 190) is a 45-minute ferry ride from Chester's government wharf (round-trip $5.50, four services daily Monday to Friday, two daily on weekends). Walking trails crisscross the island. Settled by Germans and French Huguenots in the early 19th century, the island is famous for its sauerkraut. The last ferry from Chester each day overnights in Tancook Island.

🛏 Sleeping & Eating

Graves Island Provincial Park CAMPGROUND $
(☑902-275-4425; www.parks.gov.ns.ca; campsites $24) An island in Mahone Bay connected by a causeway to the mainland has 64 wooded and open campsites. RVs usually park in the middle of the area, but some shady, isolated tent sites are tucked away on the flanks of the central plateau. It's 3km northeast of Chester off Hwy 3.

Mecklenburgh Inn B&B   B&B $$
(☑902-275-4638; www.mecklenburghinn.ca; 78 Queen St; r $115-155; ⊘May-Jan; 🛜) This casual four-room inn, built in 1890, has a breezy 2nd-floor veranda. Some rooms have private adjacent balconies; most have private bath-

rooms. The owner is a cordon-bleu chef, so expect an excellent breakfast.

Kiwi Café   CAFE $
(☑902-275-1492; 19 Pleasant St; lunch mains $9-14; ⊘8am-4pm Sun-Wed, to 8pm Thu-Sat; 🛜 ⧉) A New Zealand chef prepares excellent soups, salads, sandwiches and baked goods that you can eat in or take away in recyclable containers. The walls are painted kiwi green and there's beer, wine and a relaxed atmosphere.

Rope Loft   PUB $$
(☑902-275-3430; 36 Water St; mains around $15; ⊘11:30am-11pm) You couldn't find a better setting than this bay-side pub. Hearty pub food is served indoors or out.

☆ Entertainment

Chester Playhouse   THEATER
(☑902-275-3933; www.chesterplayhouse.ca; 22 Pleasant St; tickets around $25) This older theater space has great acoustics for live performances. Plays or dinner theater are presented most nights in July and August, with occasional concerts during spring and fall.

❶ Information

Tourist Office (☑902-275-4616; Hwy 3; ⊘9:30am-5:30pm) In the old train depot near the Chester turnoff.

Mahone Bay

The sun shines more often here than anywhere else along the coast. With more than 100 islands only 100km from Halifax, it's a great base for exploring this section of the South Shore. Take out a kayak or a bike or simply stroll down Main St, which skirts the harbor and is scattered with shops selling antiques, quilts, pottery and works by local painters.

◉ Sights & Activities

Mahone Bay's skyline is dotted with three magnificent old churches along the seafront that draw in many keen photographers and host live music (tickets cost $20) in the summer.

Mahone Bay Settlers' Museum   MUSEUM
(☑902-624-6263; 578 Main St; ⊘10am-5pm Tue-Sun Jun-mid-Oct) FREE Exhibits on local architecture and the settlement of the area by 'Foreign Protestants' in 1754.

You can rent boats at **Paddle South Kayaks** (617 Main St; 1hr/daily rentals from $30/70; ⊘9am-8pm Jun-Oct) or bikes at **Sweet Rides Cycling** (523 Main St; half-/full-day rentals $20/30; ⊘10am-5pm Mon-Sat, noon-5pm Sun).

👉 Tours

South Shore Boat Tours BOAT TOUR
(✍902-543-5107; www.southshoreboattours.com; ⊘Jul & Aug) Offers boatbuilding and nature tours (1¾ hours, adults $35).

✨ Festivals & Events

Mahone Bay Pirate Festival & Regatta REGATTA
(http://mahonebayregatta.wordpress.com) On the weekend prior to the first Monday in August, this pirate-themed festival includes lots of costumed thespians and ends with the dramatic burning of a model ship out on the bay.

Great Scarecrow Festival & Antiques Fair CULTURE
(⊘1st weekend Oct) Locals make outlandish scarecrows and carved pumpkins to display them outside their homes. Meanwhile, a popular antique fair rages on.

🛏 Sleeping & Eating

Kip & Kaboodle Backpackers Hostel HOSTEL $
(✍902-531-5494, 866-549-4522; www.kiwikaboodle.com; Hwy 3; dm $30; ⊘Apr-Oct; 🌐) This friendly nine-bed hostel is superbly located, 3km from the attractions of Mahone Bay

and 7km from Lunenburg. Owners offer town pickup, as well as economical tours, a shuttle service, BBQs and bonfires, and excellent area tips. There is also bike rental and one private room.

Fisherman's Daughter B&B $$
(✍902-624-0483; www.fishermans-daughter.com; 97 Edgewater St; r $115-145; 🌐🐾) Set on the bay by the three beautiful churches, this very old house (1840) has been meticulously remodeled for comfort, while retaining all the charm. Two rooms have views through sharply pitched Gothic-style windows and all four rooms have good-sized attached bathrooms. It has all the friendly service you'd want from a top B&B.

Three Thistles B&B B&B $$
(✍902-624-0517; www.three-thistles.com; 389 W Main St; r $100-150; 🌐) 🐾 Owner Ama Phyllis uses environmentally conscious cleaning agents and cooks with organic foods. Rooms are sparkling and clean and there's a back garden that stretches to a wooded area.

LaHave Bakery DELI $
(cnr Edgewater & Main Sts; sandwiches from $4; ⊘9am-6pm; 🐾) This bakery is famous for its hearty bread. Sandwiches are made on thick slabs of it.

⭐**Mateus Bistro** MODERN CANADIAN $$$
(✍902-531 3711; 533 Main St; mains $22-35; ⊘5-9pm Mon, Thu & Fri, 10am-9pm Sat & Sun) Tucked into a little gallery with an outdoor patio, this place may miss the sea views but once you hit the cocktails, wine and food, you'll

---

A PIRATE'S TREASURE

Oak Island, near Mahone Bay, is home to a so-called 'money pit' that has cost over $2 million in excavation expenses and six lives. There is still not a shred of information about what the pit is or what might be buried there.

The mystery began in 1795 when three inhabitants of the island came across a depression in the ground. Knowing that pirates had once frequented the area, they decided to dig and see what they could find. Just over half a meter down, they hit a layer of neatly placed flagstone; another 2.5m turned up one oak platform, then another. After digging to 9m, the men temporarily gave up but returned eight years later with the Onslow Company, a professional crew.

The Onslow excavation made it down 27.5m; when the crew returned the next morning, the shaft had flooded and they were forced to halt the digging. A year later, the company returned to dig 33.5m down in a parallel shaft, which also flooded. It was confirmed in 1850 that the pit was booby-trapped via five box drains at Smith Cove, 150m from the pit. The beach was found to be artificial.

Ever since, people have come to seek their fortune from far and wide at the 'money pit.' Only a few links of gold chain, some parchment, a cement vault and an inscribed stone have been found.

likely not care. The European-inspired menu changes with what's fresh locally, from oysters and Fundy scallops to duck and a rainbow of veggies.

🛍 Shopping

Amos Pewter ARTS & CRAFTS
(☑800-565-3369; www.amospewter.com; 589 Main St; ⊗9am-7pm Mon-Sat, 10am-7pm Sun) Watch demonstrations in the art of pewter making, then buy wares at the attached store.

ⓘ Information

Biscuit Eater Booktrader & Cafe (☑902-624-2665; 16 Orchard St; internet per hr $5; ⊗9am-5pm Wed-Sat, 11am-5pm Sun; 🛜) The best place to check email, with a fair-trade coffee and a light organic meal. Free wi-fi.

Mahone Bay (www.mahonebay.com) Links to restaurants and accommodations.

Visitors Information Centre (VIC; ☑902-624-6151; 165 Edgewater St; ⊗9am-7pm May-Oct) Has do-it-yourself walking-tour brochures.

Lunenburg

The largest of the South Shore fishing villages is historic Lunenburg, the region's only Unesco World Heritage site and the first British settlement outside Halifax. The town is at its most picturesque viewed from the sea around sunset, when the boxy, brightly painted old buildings literally glow behind the ship-filled port. Look for the distinctive 'Lunenburg Bump,' a five-sided dormer window on the 2nd floor overhanging the 1st floor.

Lunenburg was settled largely by Germans, Swiss and Protestant French, who were first recruited by the British as a workforce for Halifax, then later became fishermen. Today Nova Scotia has been hard hit by dwindling fish stocks, but Lunenburg's burgeoning tourism trade has helped shore up the local economy.

◉ Sights & Activities

Fisheries Museum of the Atlantic MUSEUM
(☑902-634-4794; http://fisheriesmuseum.nova-scotia.ca; 68 Bluenose Dr; adult/child $10/3; ⊗9:30am-5pm) The knowledgeable staff at the Fisheries Museum of the Atlantic includes a number of retired fisherfolk who can give firsthand explanations of the fishing industry. A cute aquarium on the 1st floor lets you get eye-to-eye with halibut, a

6kg lobster and other sea creatures. Film screenings and talks are scheduled throughout the day.

Knaut-Rhuland House MUSEUM
(☑902-634-3498; 125 Pelham St; admission $3; ⊗11am-5pm Tue-Sat, 1-5pm Sun Jun-Sep) Knaut-Rhuland House is considered the finest example of Georgian architecture in the province. This 1793 house has costumed guides who point out its features.

Ironworks Distillery DISTILLERY
(www.ironworksdistillery.com; 2 Kempt St; ⊗noon-5pm Wed-Mon) Tastings are free but good luck getting out of this old ironworks building without buying a bottle of something amazing. Local ingredients craft a changing selection of liquors, a strong apple brandy, apple vodkas and a very quaffable black spiced rum.

Bike Barn CYCLING
(☑902-634-3426; www.bikelunenburg.com; 579 Blue Rocks Rd; bicycle rental per day $25) About 2km east of town, the Bike Barn rents bikes. On a small peninsula, this area is a cyclist's dream, with few hills, great ocean views and little vehicle traffic. Owners Merrill and Al will gladly help you plan your trip.

Pleasant Paddling KAYAKING
(www.pleasantpaddling.com; 221 The Point Rd; kayak rental 2hr/day $30/70, half-/full-day tours $65/110) The knowledgeable folks at this beautiful place to paddle offer rentals and tours in double or single kayaks.

⌗ Tours

Numerous fishing, sailing and whale-watching tours depart from the wharf adjacent to the Fisheries Museum on Bluenose Dr. Book on the dock or at the visitor information center (p62).

Bluenose II SAILING
(☑800-763-1963, 902-634-1963; www.bluenose.novascotia.ca; 2hr cruise adult/child $20/10) This classic replica of the *Bluenose* racing schooner is sometimes in Halifax and sometimes in Lunenburg. The boat was getting worked on in 2013 but should reopen in 2014. Check the website for details.

Lunenburg Town Walking Tours WALKING TOUR
(☑902-634-3848) Enthusiastic and very experienced Sheila Allen leads leisurely tours during the day or spooky lantern-lit ones at night; call for more information.

Lunenburg

Trot in Time TOUR
(adult/child $20/8; ⊙ Jun–mid-Oct) Take a half-hour tour of town in a horse-drawn cart. Leaves from outside the Fisheries Museum of the Atlantic.

🎺 Festivals & Events

Boxwood Festival MUSIC
(www.boxwood.org; festival pass $50; ⊙ late Jul) Flautists and pipers from around the world put on stellar public concerts.

Lunenburg Folk Harbour Festival MUSIC
(☑ 902-634-3180; www.folkharbour.com; ⊙ Aug) Singer-songwriters from Canada and beyond, plus traditional music and gospel.

Nova Scotia Folk Art Festival ARTS
(www.nsfolkartfestival.com; ⊙ 1st Sun Aug) Buffet dinner, artist talks and then a big art show and sale.

🛏 Sleeping

Make reservations as far ahead as possible, especially during summer festivals. Kip & Kaboodle Backpackers Hostel (p59), 7km north of town, is the best budget option.

Board of Trade Campground CAMPGROUND $
(☑ 902-634-3656, 902-634-8100; lbt@aliantzinc.ca; 11 Blockhouse Hill Rd; campsites/RV sites

$23/30; @) This campground, beside the visitor information center, has great views and a lot of gravel RV sites. Grassy tent sites are closely packed together and lack shade.

Sail Inn B&B B&B $$
(☑ 877-247-7075, 902-634-3537; www.sailinn.ca; 99 Montague St; r $100-140; 🛜) Rooms have a

view over the waterfront and are bright, airy and modern with an antique twist. You get a free sail on the owner's 15m ketch with your stay. Don't miss checking out the old well on the ground floor that's been turned into a lighted fish pond.

1775 Solomon House B&B   B&B $$
(☑ 902-634-3477; www.bbcanada.com/5511.html; 69 Townsend St; r $110-130; 🛜) A wonderfully antique place with undulating wooden floors and low door jams (watch your head), this B&B has the nicest and most helpful owner ever. Rooms are cozy amid the aging walls and you'll be talking about the breakfasts for the rest of your trip. The only drawback is the minuscule bathrooms.

Lennox Tavern B&B   B&B $$
(☑ 888-379-7605, 902-634-4043; www.lennoxinn. com; 69 Fox St; r $85-140; 🛜) This place feels authentically old, with electric candles lighting the halls and massive plank-wood floors. The inn is the oldest in Canada and you get to eat breakfast in what was once the tavern.

✖ Eating

Try some offbeat Lunenburg specialties. Solomon Gundy is pickled herring with onions. Lunenburg pudding – pork and spices cooked in the intestines of a pig – goes well with Scotch and water.

Salt Shaker Deli   DELI $
(☑ 902-640-3434; 124 Montague St; meals $8-15; ⊙ 11am-9pm Tue-Sat, to 3pm Sun) With a clean-cut modern atmosphere, a waterfront deck and amazing food, it's no wonder this new deli-restaurant is always packed. Try the thin-crust pizzas or a pound of mussels cooked to the style of your choosing.

Magnolia's Grill   DINER $
(☑ 902-634-3287; 128 Montague St; mains $8-16; ⊙ lunch & dinner) Try one of the many soups of the day at this diner-style locals' favorite. Seafood, including Solomon Gundy, and an extensive wine list are available.

★ Fleur de Sel   FRENCH $$$
(☑ 902-640-2121; 53 Montague St; mains $22-38; ⊙ 11am-2pm & 5-10pm; ♪) This is by far the most elegant eating option in the region. French-inspired seafood, meat and vegetarian dishes made from organic produce are served in the classic, bright dining area. For one of the best culinary treats ever, indulge in the $90 several-course tasting menu.

Make that treat even better by adding a $58 wine pairing.

The restaurant now also offers a suite that includes exquisite meal packages.

☆ Entertainment

Lunenburg Opera House   THEATER
(☑ 902-634-4010; 290 Lincoln St; tickets $5-25) This recently refurbished old 400-seat theater is rumored to have a resident ghost. Built as an Odd Fellows hall in 1907, it's now a favorite venue for rock and folk musicians. Check the posters in the window for what's coming up.

❶ Information

Explore Lunenburg (www.explorelunenburg. ca) Local history and tourism information.
Lunenburg Public Library (☑ 902-634-8008; 19 Pelham St; ⊙ 10am-6pm Tue, Wed & Fri, to 8pm Thu, to 5pm Sat) Free internet access.
Visitors Information Centre (VIC; ☑ 902-634-8100, 888-615-8305; 11 Blockhouse Hill Rd; ⊙ 9am-8pm May-Oct) Walking-tour maps and help with accommodations.

❶ Getting There & Away

At the time of writing, there were no public buses. Your best bet from Halifax is with **Kiwi Kaboodle** (☑ 902-531-5494; www.novascotia-toursandtravel.com), who run shuttles for $35.

Liverpool

There is plenty to do in Liverpool and it's well situated for exploring several gorgeous beaches, as well as Kejimkujik National Park (68km north) and its Seaside Adjunct (15km southwest). That said, it lacks the seaside quaintness of the villages to its north.

◉ Sights

Rossignol Cultural Centre   MUSEUM
(☑ 902-354-3067; www.rossignolculturalcentre. com; 205 Church St; adult/child $5/3; ⊙ 10am-5:30pm Mon-Sat) Local character Sherman Hines' most fabulous endeavor is a must-see for anyone who enjoys the offbeat. There are halls of taxidermy animals, cases of gorgeous aboriginal beadwork, walls of Hines' beautiful photography (including from his Mongolian adventures) and a room dedicated to outhouses around the world.

If you love it so much you don't want to leave, an authentic Mongolian yurt (with en-suite bathroom) is for rent adjacent to the museum for a $100 per night donation.

Admission to the museum includes entry to the **Sherman Hines Museum of Photography** (☑902-354-2667; www.shermanhinesphotographymuseum.com; 219 Main St; ⊙10am-5:30pm Mon-Sat).

Perkins House Museum   MUSEUM
(☑902-354-4058; http://perkinshouse.novascotia.ca; 105 Main St; adult/child $4/2; ⊙9:30am-5:30pm Mon-Sat, 1-5:30pm Sun Jun-Oct) Perkins House Museum displays articles and furniture from the colonial period. Built in 1766, it's the oldest house belonging to the Nova Scotia Museum.

Queen's County Museum   MUSEUM
(☑902-354-4058; www.queenscountymuseum.com; 109 Main St; admission $4; ⊙9:30am-5:30pm Mon-Sat, 1-5:30pm Sun) This museum has First Nations artifacts and materials relating to town history, as well as some writings by early citizens.

Fort Point   LIGHTHOUSE
(☑902-354-5260; 21 Fort Lane; ⊙10am-6pm May-Oct) **FREE** At Fort Point a cairn marks the site where Frenchman Samuel de Champlain landed in 1604. You can blow the hand-pumped foghorn in the lighthouse at the end of Main St.

Hank Snow Home Town Museum   MUSEUM
(☑902-354-4675; www.hanksnow.com; 148 Bristol Ave; admission $3; ⊙9am-5pm Mon-Sat, noon-5pm Sun) This museum sheds light on Nova Scotia's status as a northern Nashville. In the old train station, it captures the history of Snow, Wilf Carter and other crooners and yodelers.

✪ Festivals & Events

Privateer Days   HISTORY
(www.privateerdays.com; ⊙early Jul) A celebration of piracy and history.

⌂ Sleeping & Eating

Geranium House   B&B $
(☑902-354-4484; 87 Milton Rd; r $60) This B&B on a large wooded property next to the Mersey River has three rooms with shared bathroom, ideal for cyclists and families.

Lane's Privateer Inn   INN $$
(☑902-354-3456, 800-794-3332; www.lanesprivateerinn.com; 27 Bristol Ave; r incl breakfast $95-150, mains $9-25; ⊙dining room 7am-10pm; ☞) Originally the home of a swashbuckling privateer, this 200-year-old inn now looks more 1980s than anything else, but it's a clean and pleas-

ant place to stay. It's the center of action in summer, with live music on weekends and special events like wine tastings. There's also a dining room that serves the best food in town.

☆ Entertainment

Astor Theatre   THEATER
(☑902-354-5250; www.astortheatre.ns.ca; 59 Gorham St) The Astor is the oldest continuously operating performance venue in the province. Built in 1902 as the Liverpool Opera House, it presents films, plays and live music.

ⓘ Information

Located near the river bridge, the **tourist office** (☑902-354-5421; 28 Henry Hensey Dr; ⊙9:30am-5:30pm May-Oct) has a walking-tour pamphlet.

Kejimkujik National Park

Less than 20% of Kejimkujik's 381-sq-km wilderness is accessible by car; the rest is reached either on foot or by canoe. Birdwatchers can hope to see plenty of water fowl, barred owls and pileated woodpeckers, while wildlife ranges from porcupines to black bear. On a less joyful note, biting insects are rampant; watch out for mosquitoes the size of hummingbirds and eel-like leeches in the lakes.

🏃 Activities

The main hiking loop is a 60km trek that begins at the east end of George Lake and ends at the Big Dam Lake trailhead. A shorter loop, ideal for an overnight trek, is the 26km Channel Lake Trail that begins and ends at Big Dam Lake. September to early October is prime hiking time; the bugs in the spring would drive you mad. More than a dozen lakes are connected by a system of portages, allowing canoe trips of up to seven days. A topographical map ($10) may be required for ambitious multiday trips.

Rent canoes and other equipment in the park at **Jakes Landing** (☑902-682-2289; ⊙8am-9pm Jun-Sep). One-/24-hour hire of a double kayak, canoe or rowboat is $8/35; kayak or bike, $7/30. One-week hire for any of these is $125. It's open during the off-season by appointment.

🛏 Sleeping & Eating

Forty-five backcountry campsites ($24.50 per night including firewood) are scattered among the lakes of Kejimkujik. You must book them in advance by contacting the park's visitors center. There's a 14-day maximum; you can't stay more than two nights at any site.

Caledonia Country Hostel HOSTEL **$**
(☏902-682-3266, 877-223-0232; www.caledonia-countryhostel.com; 9960 Hwy 8, Caledonia; dm/d $25/60; 🐾) In the heart of Caledonia – the only town near the park that has an internet cafe, a VIC, a gas station and a grocery store – this spotless hostel has beds on the 2nd floor of an adorable Victorian-style home. Cozy nooks with TV, books, old-style upholstered chairs and country linens abound. The owners also have tours and shuttle services available.

Raven Haven Hostel & Family Park HOSTEL, CAMPGROUND **$**
(☏902-532-7320; www.hihostels.ca; 2239 Virginia Rd, off Hwy 8, South Milford; dm HI member/nonmember $22/24, campsites/RV sites $20/24, cabins $72; ☉Jun-Aug) This HI hostel and campground are 25km south of Annapolis Royal and 27km north of the national park. The four-bed hostel is in a cabin near the white-sand beach and rustic two-bedroom cabins have equipped kitchens but no linens. There are 15 campsites, but the camping in the park is better. Canoes and paddleboats can be rented.

Jeremy's Bay Campground CAMPGROUND **$**
(☏877-737-3783; campsites/RV sites $25.50/29.40) Of the 360 campsites within the park, 30% are assigned on a first-come, first-served basis. There is only one shower area for the whole camp, so be prepared to wait for a stall. It costs from $10 to reserve a site.

Mersey River Chalets CABIN **$$**
(☏902-682-2447, 877-667-2583; www.mersey-riverchalets.ns.ca; tepees $90, cabins $170-250; 🐾) Comfy cabins have pine floors, wood-burning stoves and very private porches complete with barbecue; rooms in the lodge have private decks with lake views; and cozy tepees have fully equipped kitchens. Free canoes and kayaks are available for guests.

M&W Restaurant & Variety Store DINER **$**
(☏902-682-2189; Hwy 8; mains $4-12; ☉9am-8pm May-Oct) Only 500m from the park entrance, this place serves 'hungry camper' breakfasts ($6), as well as lunch and dinner. It's also a general store stocked with camping supplies, including firewood, and a Laundromat.

❶ Information

Get an entry permit and reserve backcountry sites at the **visitors center** (☏902-682-2772, 800-414-6765; www.parkscanada.gc.ca/keji; Hwy 8; park entrance adult/child $5.80/2.90; ☉8:30am-8pm).

Seaside Adjunct (Kejimkujik National Park)

The 'Keji Adjunct' protects angelic landscapes of rolling low brush, wildflowers, white sandy coves and the granite outcrops spreading between Port Joli and Port Mouton Bay. The only access from Hwy 103 is along a 6.5km gravel road. From the parking lot, two mostly flat trails lead to the coast. **Harbour Rocks Trail** (5.2km return) follows an old cart road through mixed forest to a beach where seals are often seen. A loop trail around **Port Joli Head** is 8.7km.

The Port Joli Basin contains **Point Joli Migratory Bird Sanctuary** with waterfowl and shorebirds in great numbers; *Nova Scotia Birding on the Lighthouse Route* is an excellent resource available at the visitor information centers. It's only easily accessible by kayak. The **Rossignol Surf Shop** (☏902-683-2550; www.surfnovascotia.com; White Point Beach Resort) in nearby White Point rents kayaks (half-/full-day rental $30/45), surfboards and bodyboards ($20/40), and offers kayak tours ($65/110) and surfing lessons ($75).

Thomas Raddall Provincial Park (☏902-683-2664; www.parks.gov.ns.ca; campsites $24; ☉May-Oct), across Port Joli Harbour from Keji Adjunct, has large, private campsites, eight of which are walk-in. The forested campground extends out onto awesome beaches.

Port Mouton International Hostel (☏902-947-3140; www.wqccda.com/PMhostel; 8100 Hwy 3; dm $30; 🐾), only five minutes from Keji Adjunct, is run on a volunteer basis by the community in a former school. There are 30 beds plus one private room, a good kitchen and a washer and dryer. Call in advance or, if you arrive between 10am and 5pm, you can usually check in at the crafts store next door.

Shelburne

Shelburne's historic waterfront area bobs with sailboats and has 17 pre-1800 homes – it feels like a historical recreation but it's real. The wonderfully maintained, low-in-the-earth buildings once housed Loyalists who retreated here from the American Revolution. In 1783 Shelburne was the largest community in British North America, with 16,000 residents, many from the New York aristocracy, who exploited the labor of Black Loyalists living in nearby Birchtown. Shelburne's history is celebrated with **Founders' Days** during the last weekend of July.

⊙ Sights & Activities

Shelburne has started organizing a slew of activities from mid-June to mid-August, including daily demonstrations around town by folks in period costumes of old-style cooking, sewing, music, military exercises, carving and more; schedules change daily but start around 1pm. Check at the visitor information center for more information.

There's a **trail** for hiking or biking the 6km to Birchtown across from Spencer's Garden Centre at the far south end of Main St. Pick up an excellent self-guided walking-tour map at the visitor information center.

Admission to the following museums is $4, but you can buy a pass that covers all four for $10.

Ross-Thomson House   MUSEUM
(☑ 902-875-3141; http://rossthomson.novascotia.ca; 9 Charlotte Lane; ⊙ 9:30am-5:30pm Jun-Oct)

Built in 1784, Ross-Thomson House belonged to well-to-do Loyalist merchants who arrived in Shelburne from Cape Cod. Furniture, paintings and original goods from the store are on display. The house is surrounded by authentic period gardens. Admission is free on Sunday mornings.

Shelburne County Museum   MUSEUM
(☑ 902-875-3219; www.historicshelburne.com; cnr Maiden Lane & Dock St; ⊙ 9:30am-5:30pm) A Loyalist house (c 1787) is now the Shelburne County Museum. It has a collection of Loyalist furnishings, displays on the history of the local fishery and a small collection of Mi'kmaw artifacts.

Muir-Cox Shipyard   MUSEUM
(☑ 902-875-1114; www.historicshelburne.com/muircox.htm; 18 Dock St; ⊙ 9:30am-5:30pm) The Muir-Cox Shipyard has been in almost continuous operation since 1820, turning out barks, yachts and fishing boats. It's still active year-round, but the interpretive center is seasonal.

Dory Shop Museum   MUSEUM
(☑ 902-875-3219; http://doryshop.novascotia.ca; 11 Dock St; ⊙ 9:30am-5:30pm Jun-Sep) Shelburne dories (small open boats once used for fishing from a mother schooner) are still made to order at the Dory Shop Museum for use as lifeboats.

🛏 Sleeping & Eating

Water Street Lighthouse B&B   B&B $
(☑ 902-875-2331; www.shelburnelighthouse.com; 263 Water St; r $60-80; 🕾) Not really luxurious,

---

BLACK LOYALIST BIRCHTOWN

Just as Shelburne was once the largest settlement in British North America, so Birchtown was once the largest settlement of freed African slaves in North America. After the American Revolution, about 3500 Black Loyalists were rewarded by the British with land for settlements near Shelburne, Halifax, Digby and Guysborough. Nine years later, in 1792, after barely surviving harsh winters and unequal treatment, 1200 of them boarded 15 ships bound for Sierra Leone, in West Africa, where they founded Freetown. An additional 2000 from the USA settled in the Maritimes after the War of 1812, and others came from the Caribbean in the 1890s to work in the Cape Breton Island coal mines.

The future was no brighter. Underfunded, segregated schools existed until the 1950s. Birchtown's **Black Loyalist Heritage Society Historical Site & Museum** (☑ 902-875-1381, 888-354-0722; www.blackloyalist.com; 104 Birchtown Rd; admission $3; ⊙ 11am-6pm Tue-Fri, noon-6pm Sat, to 5pm Sun) includes a museum and a walking trail that leads to a 'pit house,' which archaeologists think was once a temporary shelter. There is also a **trail** for hiking or cycling the 6km to Shelburne.

A self-guided tour of African heritage in Nova Scotia is available online (www.gov.ns.ca/nsarm/virtual/africanns).

but comfy and friendly, this is a great B&B to shack up your bike for the night. A lighthouse theme runs through the house.

Islands Provincial Park CAMPGROUND $
(☑ 902-875-4304; www.parks.gov.ns.ca; off Hwy 3; campsites $20) Across the harbor from Shelburne are 65 campsites in mature forest and a beach for swimming.

★Cooper's Inn B&B B&B $$
(☑ 902-875-4656, 800-688-2011; www.thecoopersinn.com; 36 Dock St; r $100-185; ☞) Part of this waterfront building dates to 1784 and was brought here from Boston. Now it's a relatively modern but still charmingly heritage-style inn with six rooms and a flower-filled garden, where you can drink your complimentary bottle of Jost wine at sunset.

Bean Dock CAFE $
(☑ 902-875-1302; sandwiches from $5; ☺ 10am-4pm Mon, Tue & Thu-Sat, to 8pm Wed) Snuggle over to a wood table overlooking the bay for coffee, grilled sandwiches and light mains, from fish cakes to sun-dried-tomato pasta salad. The giant Adirondack chair out front is worth chatting about.

★Charlotte Lane MODERN CANADIAN $$$
(☑ 902-875-3314; 13 Charlotte Lane; mains $16-35; ☺ 11:30am-2:30pm & 5-8pm Tue-Sat) People drive from Halifax to eat here, and rave about it; evening reservations are highly recommended. Swiss chef Roland Glauser is constantly revising an extensive annotated wine list to accompany his ever-changing menu of local seafood, meat and pasta dishes.

❶ Information

Visitors Information Center (VIC; ☑ 902-875-4547; 31 Dock St; ☺ 8am-8pm May-Sep) Has copies of a self-guided historic-district walking tour.

Barrington to West Pubnico

At Barrington you can choose to take the fast, not-very-scenic Hwy 103 to Yarmouth or meander along about 100km of interesting coastline via Hwy 3. It's worth taking a detour to **Cape Sable Island** (not to be confused with Sable Island), a puddle-flat appendage that is Nova Scotia's southernmost point. Many of the island's windy, white-sand beaches are designated as 'important bird areas,' and a few are piping plover nesting grounds. The whole island tends to get banked in fog, which might explain why its lighthouse is 31.1m tall, the tallest in Nova Scotia.

Not to be confused with all the other nearby Pubnicos, West Pubnico is an old Acadian community. **Le Village Historique Acadien** (☑ 902-762-2530; Old Church Rd; adult/child $6/2; ☺ 9am-5pm Jun-Oct) re-creates an Acadian village, with a blacksmith shop, a timber-frame house and a fish store.

Yarmouth

Yarmouth is the biggest town in southern Nova Scotia, due mostly to the ferry that linked the province to Bar Harbor (Maine) since the 1950s. Sadly, the ferry service stopped in 2010, although the area has been fighting to get it back ever since. Without the ferry, Yarmouth has had a tough time. The only really pretty area is out beyond town around the lighthouse but, like anywhere in the province, stay awhile and the people will win you over.

◎ Sights & Activities

First settled by New Englanders from Massachusetts in 1761, Yarmouth reached its peak of growth and prosperity in the 1870s. The Collins Heritage Conservation District protects many fine Victorian homes built around that time. Check at the visitor information center (p67) for a self-guided walking tour.

Yarmouth Light NOTABLE BUILDING
(☑ 902-742-1433; Hwy 304; ☺ 9am-9pm) **FREE**
Yarmouth Light is at the end of Cape Forchu, left on Hwy 304 from Main St. The lighthouse affords spectacular views and there's a tearoom below. Stop at **Stanley Lobster Pound** (Hwy 304; ☺ 11am-7pm Mon-Sat, 2-7pm Sun), where you can get a fresh-cooked lobster at market-value price to take and eat on the beach.

Art Gallery of Nova Scotia GALLERY
(☑ 902-749-2248; www.artgalleryofnovascotia.ca; 341 Main St; adult/child $12/7; ☺ 10am-5pm) Practical Yarmouth is the unexpected home to the refreshingly cosmopolitan Art Gallery of Nova Scotia. The new three-storey building has well-selected works from mostly Maritime artists.

Yarmouth County Museum   MUSEUM

(☑902-742-5539; http://yarmouthcountymu-seum.ednet.ns.ca; 22 Collins St; adult/student $5/2; ⊘9am-5pm Mon-Sat, 2-5pm Sun) This museum, in a former church, contains five period rooms related to the sea. The ticket includes **Pelton-Fuller House** (⊘9am-5pm Mon-Sat Jun-Oct) next door, which is filled with period artwork, glassware and furniture.

🛏 Sleeping & Eating

Lakelawn B&B Motel   MOTEL $

(☑902-742-3588; www.lakelawnmotel.com; 641 Main St; r $59-99; 🛜🐾) This place is as cute and service oriented as motels come. Rooms are clean and basic; the owner Mathew is a well of local info; and some of the better meals in town are available in the country-style dining area. Go even classier in the four B&B-style rooms in the central Victorian house.

★MacKinnon-Cann House

Historic Inn   INN $$

(☑902-742-0042; www.mackinnoncanninn.com; 27 Willow St; r $140-185; 🛜) Each of the six rooms represents a decade from the Victorian 1900s to the groovy '60s, depicting the decade at its most stylish, while managing to stay calming and comfortable. Two rooms can be joined to create a family suite.

Rudder's Brew Pub   PUB $$

(☑902-742-7311; 96 Water St; pub menu $8-14, dinner mains $14-32; ⊘11am-late) The 300 seats at this waterfront pub and restaurant fill fast. A mean ale is brewed on-site and there's a wide-ranging menu. Drinks are poured until the wee hours on busy summer nights.

ℹ Information

Visitors Information Centre (VIC; ☑902-742-5033; 228 Main St; ⊘7:30am-9pm May-Oct) Also has a money-exchange counter.
Yarmouth Public Library (☑902-742-2486; 405 Main St; ⊘10am-8pm Mon-Thu, to 5pm Fri, to 4pm Sat, 1-4pm Sun) Free internet access.

ℹ Getting There & Away

Cloud Nine Shuttle (p55) runs to Halifax.
A nightly ferry service to Portland, Maine is expected to begin in May 2014 with **NS-USA Ferry Service** (www.nsusaferry.com). Check the website for details.

ANNAPOLIS VALLEY & FRENCH SHORE

Heading up the French Shore, you'll be regularly waved to by the Stella Maris, the single-starred, tricolored Acadian flag. Admire the many elaborate Catholic churches, stop at a roadside eatery to sample Acadian rappie pie (a type of meat pie topped with grated pastelike potato from which all the starch has been drawn) and take a walk along a fine-sand beach. If you stay longer, don't miss the chance to sample the region's foot-tapping music performances that take place frequently in summer.

Continuing northeast, the Annapolis Valley was the main breadbasket for colonial Canada and still produces much of Nova Scotia's fresh produce, especially apples. Recently, wineries have taken advantage of the sandy soil. Make sure to get to the Fundy coast at Annapolis Royal and eastwards for tidal vistas over patchwork farmland, red sands and undulating hills.

Cape St Mary to Meteghan

A long, wide arc of fine sand, just 900m off Hwy 1, **Mavilette Beach** is great for collecting seashells, and the marsh behind it is good for birdwatching. At the southern edge of Meteghan, the largest community on the French Shore, **Smuggler's Cove Provincial Park** is named for its popularity with 19th-century pirates. A hundred wooden stairs take you down to a rocky beach and a good cave for hiding treasure. There are picnic sites containing barbecue pits at the top of the stairs, with a view across St Mary's Bay to Brier Island.

Stop for lunch at **La Cuisine Robicheau** (9651 Hwy 1, Saulnierville; mains $8-29; ⊘8am-9pm Tue-Sun), which serves this area's most *haute* Acadian cuisine. The rappie pie, seafood lasagna and chocolate pie may make you exclaim *'sacré bleu!'* they're so good and affordable. There's often live music at suppertime during summer.

À la Maison d'Amitié B&B (☑902-645-2601; www.houseoffriendship.ca; 169 Baseline Rd; r $140-175; 🛜) is perched dramatically on a cliff close to the beach on six private hectares. The huge, American-style home has cathedral ceilings and sky-high windows with views on all sides.

Church Point to St Bernard

The villages of Church Point, Grosses-Coques, Belliveau Cove and St Bernard, on the mainland directly across St Mary's Bay from Digby Neck, make up the heart of the French Shore. This is where Acadians settled when, after trekking back to Nova Scotia following deportation, they found their homesteads in the Annapolis Valley already occupied. Now linked by Hwy 1 – pretty much the only road in town – these are small fishing communities.

🅞 Sights & Activities

Rendez-Vous de la Baie   CULTURAL BUILDING
(www.rendezvousdelabaie.com; Université Ste-Anne, Church Point; ⊘ 7am-7pm Mon-Fri, 9am-5pm Sat & Sun) If there's one essential stop along this coast, this is it. Learn about Acadian history and culture at the museum; check out local art at the gallery; watch musical performances and more at the theater; and get tourist tips at the information center – and all this is under one roof. The center also runs Acadian-themed tours of the area for $50 per person including lunch.

Église Ste-Marie   CHURCH
(☑ 902-769-2808; Hwy 1; admission incl guide $2; ⊘ 9am-5pm May-Oct) The town of Church Point, also commonly known as Pointe de l'Église, takes its name from Église Ste-Marie, which towers over the town. Built between 1903 and 1905, the church is said to be the tallest wooden church in North America. An informative guide will show you around. Adjacent is the **Université Ste-Anne**, the only French university in the province and a center for Acadian culture, with 300 students.

Belliveau Beach   BEACH
Belliveau Beach, near the southern end of Belliveau, is reached by turning right onto Major's Point. The beach is made up of masses of sea-polished stones broken only by small clumps of incredibly hardy fir trees. Just behind the beach, a cemetery and monument recall the struggles of the early Acadian settlers of the French Shore.

St Bernard Church   CHURCH
(☑ 902-837-5637; Hwy 1; ⊘ tours Jun-Sep) St Bernard is known for its church, a huge granite structure built by locals who added one row of blocks each year between 1910 and 1942. It has incredible acoustics, which are showcased each summer through the **Musique St-Bernard** (www.musiquesaintbernard.ca; adult/child $15/5) concert series.

Hinterland Adventures & Gear   KAYAKING
(☑ 902-837-4092; www.kayakingnovascotia.com; 54 Gates Lane, Weymouth; kayak rentals per 1hr/day $7/40, half-/full-day tours $45/115) Running tours for over 15 years, this respected kayaking and canoeing outfit specializes in paddling tours of St Mary's Bay and the Sissiboo River.

✸ Festivals & Events

Festival Acadien de Clare   CULTURE
(www.festivalacadiendeclare.ca; ⊘ late Jul) The oldest of the annual Acadian cultural festivals, Festival Acadien de Clare is held at Church Point.

Théâtre Marc-Lescarbot   THEATER
(☑ 902-769-2114; adult/child $25/15) In July and August, the musical *Évangéline*, based on Henry Wadsworth Longfellow's romantic poem about the Acadian deportation, is presented at the Théâtre Marc-Lescarbot at Church Point. Performances are given in English on Saturday; in French with English headset translation on Tuesday and Friday; and outdoors in French on Wednesday.

🛏 Sleeping & Eating

Several Acadian-style eateries have opened up along this stretch, so you'll be spoiled for choice.

DON'T MISS

LIVING WHARVES

Between mid-June and the end of September, the Acadian coast, from Dennis Point to Belliveau Cove and five points between, invites you to get a hands-on appreciation for what this area is all about: fishing. Each day of the week, one of the seven wharves opens up for visitors from 1pm to 4pm. During this time, active and retired fisherfolk tell yarns about their sea adventures and let you try your hand at a few odd jobs. More than anything, it's a great place to meet locals, hear stories and get closer to the salty lifestyle of Nova Scotia's south. More information is available at www.livingwharves.com.

Barn at the Point   B&B $
(www.thebarnatthepoint.ca; 63 Lighthouse Rd,
Gilbert's Cove; r $75-100; 🛜) Quietly situated
on 90 acres near Gilbert's Cove Lighthouse,
only 20 minutes from Digby, this afford-
able retreat offers the relaxation of rural
forest, the thrill of the coast and the convenience of town. The on-site cafe gets rave
reviews and serves the owners' own special
blend of coffee.

Roadside Grill   ACADIAN $
(☑902-837-5047; 3334 Hwy 1; meals $7-15;
⊗8am-9pm) At this pleasantly old-fashioned
and long-running local restaurant in Belliveau Cove, try the steamed clams or the
rappie pie. It also rents out three small
cabins (singles/doubles $60/80) with ca-
ble TV and microwaves. There's live Acadian music Tuesday nights from 5:30pm to
7:30pm June through August.

Digby Neck

Craning out to take a peek into the Bay
of Fundy, Digby Neck is a giraffe's length
strip of land that's a haven for whale- and
seabird-watchers. At the far western end of
the appendage are Long and Brier Islands,
connected by ferry with the rest of the
peninsula.

Plankton stirred up by the strong Fundy
tides attracts finback, minke and humpback whales and this is the best place in
the world to see the endangered North
Atlantic right whale. Blue whales, the
world's largest animal, are also sighted on
occasion, plus you're almost certain to see
plenty of seals.

Bring plenty of warm clothing (regardless of how hot a day it seems), sunblock
and binoculars; motion-sickness pills are
highly recommended.

❶ Getting There & Away

Two ferries connect Long and Brier Islands to
the rest of Digby Neck. The *Petit Passage* ferry
leaves East Ferry (on Digby Neck) 25 minutes
after the hour and Tiverton (on Long Island) on
the hour; ferries are timed so that if you drive
directly from Tiverton to Freeport (18km)
there is no wait for the *Grand Passage* ferry to
Westport (on Brier Island). Both ferries operate
hourly, 24 hours a day, year-round. Round-trip
passage on each ferry is $5.50 for a car and all
passengers. Pedestrians ride free.

Long Island

Most people head straight to Brier Island,
but Long Island has better deals on whale-
watching, as well as a livelier community. At
the northeastern edge of Long Island, **Tiverton** is an active fishing community.

The **Island Museum** (☑902-839-2853;
3083 Hwy 217; ⊗9:30am-7:30pm Jun-Oct) FREE,
2km west of the Tiverton ferry dock, has exhibits on local history and a tourist information desk.

One of the best whale-watching tours in
the province is found just near the Tiverton
ferry dock. **Ocean Explorations Whale
Cruises** (☑877-654-2341, 902-839-2417; www.
oceanexplorations.ca; half-day tours adult/child
$59/40; ⊗Jun-Oct), led by biologist Tom
Goodwin, has the adventurous approach
of getting you down low to whale level in a
Zodiac. Shimmy into an orange coastguard-
approved flotation suit and hold on tight!
Goodwin has been leading whale-watching
tours since 1980 and donates part of his proceeds to wildlife conservation and environmental education organizations. Discounts
are given for groups of three or more; tour
times depend on weather and demand.

A 4km round-trip trail to the **Balancing
Rock** starts 2km southwest of the museum.
The trail features rope railings, boardwalks
and an extensive series of steps down a
rock bluff to the bay. At the time of writing, a longer but easier-to-walk trail was in
the works as an alternate route. At the end
there's a viewing platform where you can
see a 7m-high stone column perched pre-
cariously just above the pounding surf of St
Mary's Bay.

Near the center of Long Island, **Central
Grove Provincial Park** has a 2km-long hiking trail to the Bay of Fundy.

At the southwestern end of Long Island,
Freeport is central for exploring both Brier
and Long Islands.

Lavena's Catch Café (☑902-839-2517;
15 Hwy 217; mains $5-15; ⊗11:30am-8pm) is a
country-style cafe directly above the wharf
at Freeport; it's the perfect spot to enjoy a
sunset and you might even see a whale from
the balcony. There's occasional live music in
the evenings.

Brier Island

Westport was the home of Joshua Slocum,
the first man to sail solo around the world,
and is the only community on Brier Island.

It's a quaint little fishing village and a good base to explore the numerous excellent, if rugged and windy, hiking trails around the island; don't miss a trip to the West Lighthouse. Columnar basalt rocks are seen all along the coast and agates can be found on the beaches.

The **Brier Island Backpackers Hostel** (☑ 902-839-2273; www.brierislandhostel.com; 223 Water St; dm/ ste $20/100; ☜) is a tiny, spotless place about 1.5km to the left as you come off the ferry. The common room and kitchen area has big windows with views over the water. There's a general store, gas station and basic **cafe** (mains $5-8; ☺ 8am-9pm Mon-Sat, 10am-8pm Sun) next door, owned by the same people. You can book excellent whale-watching tours (2½ to five hours, depending on where the whales are) with eco-conscious **Brier Island Whale & Seabird Cruises** (☑ 800-656-3660, 902-839-2995; www. brierislandwhalewatch.com; adult/child $49/27; ☺ Jun-Oct).

Atop cliffs 1km east of Westport, **Brier Island Lodge** (☑ 800-662-8355, 902-839-2300; www.brierisland.com; r $90-140; ☜☒) has four rooms, some with ocean views. Its **restaurant** (mains $8-29) is the best dining option, with views on two sides, perfect service and fabulously fresh seafood. Boxed lunches are available.

Digby

Known for its scallops, mild climate and daily ferry to Saint John, New Brunswick, Digby (www.digby.ca) is nestled in a protected inlet off the Bay of Fundy. Settled by United Empire Loyalists in 1783, it's now home to the largest fleet of scallop boats in the world.

Digby has been a tourist mecca for more than a century, and although the town itself doesn't offer the architectural charm of starlets such as Lunenburg or Annapolis Royal, it's a pleasant and convenient base from which to explore Digby Neck, the French Shore and some beautiful, lesser-known hiking trails in the area (hint: get out to Point Prim). If you're here in passing, the best things to do are to stroll the waterfront, watch the scallop draggers come and go, and eat as much of their catch as your belly can hold.

If you're in town mid-August, reserve even more space in your gut for the delicious **Digby Scallop Days** (www.digbyscallopdays. com) festival. Another of the year's highlights is the **Wharf Rat Rally** (www.wharfratrally.com) at the end of August, where at last count 30,000 bikers buzz in for motorcycle-oriented contests, tours and general mingling.

The only real sight in town is the **Admiral Digby Museum** (☑ 902-245-6322; www. admuseum.ns.ca; 95 Montague Row; admission by donation; ☺ 9am-5pm Mon-Sat), a mid-19th century Georgian home which contains exhibits of the town's marine history and early settlement.

🛏 Sleeping & Eating

⭐**Digby Backpackers Hostel**　　　HOSTEL $
(☑ 902-245-4573; www.digbyhostel.com; 168 Queen St; dm/r $28/65; ☜) Arguably the nicest hostel in Nova Scotia; Saskia and Claude keep the solid four-bed dorm rooms spotless and often spontaneously take the whole hostel out to see the sunset or throw barbecues. The heritage house has plenty of communal areas, including a deck, and there's a lively vibe. Internet access, a light breakfast and towels are included in the price.

Bayside Inn B&B　　　B&B $$
(☑ 888-754-0555, 902-245-2247; www.baysideinn. ca; 115 Montague Row; r $64-108; ☜) In continuous operation since the late 1800s, the historic 11-room Bayside is Digby's oldest inn. Centrally located in town, it has views over the scallop fleet and Fundy tides. The cheaper rooms have shared bathrooms.

Digby Pines Golf Resort & Spa　　　HOTEL $$$
(☑ 902-245-2511, 800-667-4637; www.digbypines. ca; 103 Shore Rd; r $160-442; ☺ May-Oct; ☜☒☒) At the posh Pines, you almost expect Jay Gatsby to come up and slap you on the back with a hearty 'old sport.' Rooms are elegantly furnished with dark woods and lush beds, but are small for the price. The family-friendly grounds include a golf course, a spa, a good restaurant, walking trails and a playground.

Boardwalk Café　　　CAFE $
(☑ 902-245-5497; 40 Water St; lunch mains $8-15; ☺ 11am-2pm & 5-8pm Mon-Fri, noon-3pm Sat) This little waterfront cafe serves delicious light mains, such as chicken rappie pie and shrimp jambalaya. Dinner is a more upscale experience, with mains around $18.

⭐**Mag Pye's**　　　CAFE $$
(Water St; lunch mains around $12; ☺ breakfast & lunch daily, dinner Thu-Sat in summer) Furnished like a posh granny's house, this comfortable-as-your-own-living-room cafe sells delicious

baked goods, coffee, breakfasts, and the best lunches in town. Dinners are even more special, with $30 set menus including starters like scallop ceviche, mains that often involve more of the local catch and amazing bakery desserts.

ℹ Information

Visitors Information Centre (VIC; ☎902-245-2201; Shore Rd; ⊙8:30am-8:30pm May-Oct) A large provincial tourist office, 2km from the ferry wharf, with hundreds of brochures.
Western Counties Regional Library (☎902-245-2163; 84 Warwick St; ⊙12:30-5pm & 6-8pm Tue-Thu, 10am-5pm Fri, 10am-2pm Sat) Free internet access.

ℹ Getting There & Away

Kathleen's Shuttle & Tours (p55) and a few other shuttle companies run to Halifax airport for $65 per person. Digby is also the port for Bay Ferries (p41) boats to New Brunswick.

Bear River

This country haven for offbeat artists is only minutes from the coast but enjoys inland, fogless temperatures. There's a strong Mi'kmaq presence mixed in with Scottish roots, giving Bear River a unique vibe. Some buildings near the river are on stilts, while other historic homes nestle on the steep hills of the valley. A few wineries are starting to pop up just out of town.

◉ Sights & Activities

Bear River Vineyards   WINERY
(☎902-467-4156; www.wine.travel; 133 Chute Rd) 🐾 All estate-produced, award-winning wines made at this adorable little winery use solar energy, biodiesel, wind power and the natural slope of the property. Stop by to take a free tour and tasting (July to September) or stay longer at friendly hosts Chris and Peggy's one-room B&B ($130 per night) to enjoy wine-making workshops and retreats.

Annapolis Highland Vineyards   WINERY
(☎902-467-0917; www.novascotiawines.com; 2635 Clementsvale Rd; ⊙10am-5pm Mon-Sat, noon-5pm Sun) Don't miss the gold-medal White Wedding dessert wine if you come in for a free tasting at this rather commercial winery. Delicious fruit wines are available.

Bear River First Nation   FIRST NATION
Bear River First Nation is a five-minute drive from the heart of town: turn left after cross-

ing the bridge, then take a left where the road forks. In a beautiful building, with a wigwam-shaped foyer, the **Heritage & Cultural Centre** (☎902-467-0301; 194 Reservation Rd; admission $3) offers demonstrations of traditional crafts and hands-on workshops, but unfortunately it's rarely open.

A 1km trail starts behind the center and highlights plants with traditional medicinal uses.

✕ Eating

Bear River Cafe   CAFE $
(☎902-467-3008; 1870 Clementsvale Rd; mains $7-14; ⊙10am-5pm Tue-Sun) Stop in to chat with locals, drink a cup of coffee over a slice of pie, and enjoy the view of Bear River.

🛍 Shopping

Flight of Fancy   SOUVENIRS
(☎902-467-4171; Main St; ⊙9am-7pm Mon-Sat, 11am-7pm Sun) This exquisitely curated craft store and gallery has work by more than 200 artists and craftspeople. If you want to buy just one unique treasure to take away from Nova Scotia, this is a good place to find it.

Bear Town Baskets   SOUVENIRS
(☎902-467-3060; 44 Maple Ave, Bear River First Nation; ⊙10am-10pm) Baskets sold here are made by a retired chief of the Bear River First Nation, who is often there working away and is always happy to welcome visitors. Follow the signs to the studio in his front yard where he makes traditional ash baskets.

Annapolis Royal & Around

The community's efforts of village restoration have made this one of the most delightful places to visit in the region. In fact, Annapolis Royal is one of the only well-trodden towns of its size in Nova Scotia without a Tim Hortons (a ubiquitous fast-food franchise).

The site was Canada's first permanent European settlement. Formerly called Port Royal, it was founded by French explorer Samuel de Champlain in 1605. As the British and French battled, the settlement often changed hands. In 1710 the British had a decisive victory and changed the town's name to Annapolis Royal in honor of Queen Anne.

◉ Sights & Activities

Most sights are on or near long, curving St George St. A waterfront boardwalk behind King's Theatre on St George St provides views of the village of Granville Ferry across the Annapolis River.

Fort Anne National Historic Site
HISTORIC SITE

(☑902-532-2397;www.parkscanada.gc.ca/fortanne; Upper St George St; adult/child $4/2; ☺9am-5:30pm) This historic site in the town center preserves the memory of the early Acadian settlement, plus the remains of the 1635 French fort. Entry to the extensive grounds is free, but you'll also want to visit the museum, where artifacts are contained in various period rooms. An extraordinary four-panel tapestry, crafted in needlepoint by more than 100 volunteers, depicts 400 years of history.

Annapolis Royal Historic Gardens
GARDENS

(☑902-532-7018; www.historicgardens.com; 441 St George St; adult/student $10/8.50; ☺9am-8pm May-Oct) Gorgeous Annapolis Royal Historic Gardens covers a rambling 6.5 hectares with various themed gardens, such as an Acadian kitchen garden one might have seen in the late 1600s and an innovative modern one. Munch on blueberries, ogle the vegetables and look for frogs. The **Secret Garden Café** offers lunches and German-style baked goods.

Port Royal National Historic Site
HISTORIC SITE

(☑902-532-2898; 53 Historic Lane; adult/child $4/2; ☺9am-6pm) Some 14km northwest of Annapolis Royal, Port Royal National Historic Site is the actual location of the first permanent European settlement north of Florida. The site is a replica of de Champlain's 1605 fur-trading habitation, where costumed workers help tell the story of this early settlement.

Tidal Power Project
MUSEUM

(☑902-532-5454; ☺10am-6pm) **FREE** A hydroelectric prototype at the Annapolis River Causeway, Tidal Power has been harnessing power from the Bay of Fundy tides since 1984. An interpretive center includes models, exhibits and a video.

★Tour Annapolis Royal
WALKING TOUR

(www.tourannapolisroyal.com; Fort Anne National Historic Site; ☺9:30pm Tue-Sun) Runs several history-oriented tours. The best is where an undertaker-garbed guide leads a creepy tour (adult/child $7/3) of the Fort Anne graveyard. Everyone carries a lantern to wind through the headstones and discover the town's history through stories of those who've passed. Proceeds go to the Annapolis Royal Historical Society.

Delap's Cove Wilderness Trail
HIKING

Over the North Mountain from Annapolis Royal, Delap's Cove Wilderness Trail lets you get out on the Fundy shore. It consists of two loop trails connected by an old inland road that used to serve a Black Loyalist community, now just old foundations and apple trees in the woods. Both the loop trails are 9km return.

🛏 Sleeping & Eating

Many of the B&Bs, such as the Queen Anne, are open for elegant lunches and dinners.

Croft House B&B
B&B $

(☑902-532-0584; www.crofthouse.ca; 51 Riverview Lane; r $55-85; 🛜🐾) This farmhouse stands on about 40 hectares of land, about a five-minute drive from Annapolis Royal across the river. One of the enthusiastic owners is a chef, and he whips up a fine breakfast with organic ingredients.

Dunromin Campground
CAMPGROUND $

(☑902-532-2808; www.dunromincampground.ca; Hwy 1, Granville Ferry; campsites/RV sites $28/42, tepees/caravans $53/58, cabins $65-120; ☺May-Oct; 🛜🐾) This offbeat campground has some secluded riverside sites, as well as nifty options such as a tepee for up to six people and a gypsy caravan. You can rent canoes for $10 per hour.

★Queen Anne B&B
B&B $$

(☑902-532-7850, 877-536-0403; www.queenanneinn.ns.ca; 494 St George St; r $99-200, carriage house $239; ☺May-Nov; 🛜) Arguably the most elegant property in Annapolis Royal, this B&B is the perfect balance of period decor and subtle grace. It's so beautiful, with the Tiffany lamp replicas, manicured grounds and sweeping staircases, that it might seem stuffy were it not for the friendly owners, who make you feel like you could (almost) kick your feet up on the antique coffee table.

★Bailey House B&B
B&B $$

(☑902-532-1285, 877-532-1285; www.baileyhouse.ca; 150 Lower St George St; r $100-250; 🛜) The only B&B on the waterfront, Bailey House is also the oldest inn and one of the best in the area. The friendly owners have managed to keep the vintage charm (anyone over 6ft might hit their head on the doorways!), while adding all the necessary modern comforts and conveniences.

Ye Olde Pub PUB **$**
(☑902-532-2244; 9-11 Church St; mains $5-15; ☺11am-11pm Mon-Sat, noon-8pm Sun) On sunny days, eat gourmet pub fare on the outdoor terrace; when it's cooler, slip into the dark and cozy old bar. Try the marinated scallop appetizer.

Cafe Compose EUROPEAN **$$**
(St George St; lunch $9-15, dinner $16-26; ☺lunch & dinner; 🛜) This cafe is Austrian-German run, so you can finish your meal of European-style meats and seafood with a strudel or linzer torte. Reflections off the water light up the mustard-yellow interior. Dine on the outdoor garden patio to get even closer to the beach.

☆ Entertainment

King's Theatre THEATER
(☑902-532-7704; www.kingstheatre.ca; 209 St George St; movies $8, live shows $14-25) Right on the waterfront, this nonprofit theater presents musicals, dramas and concerts most evenings in July and August, and occasionally during the rest of the year. Hollywood films are screened on most weekends and independent films most Tuesdays year-round.

🛍 Shopping

Farmers & Traders Market MARKET
(cnr St George & Church Sts; ☺10am-3pm Wed, 8am-noon Sat) Annapolis Royal's thriving community of artists and artisans offer their wares alongside local farmers at this popular market. There's live entertainment most Saturday mornings.

ℹ Information

Annapolis Royal (www.annapolisroyal.com) Links to history, festivals and everything else.
Visitors Information Centre (VIC; ☑902-532-5769; 209 St George St; ☺10am-6pm May-Oct) At the Tidal Power Project; pick up a historic walking tour pamphlet.

ℹ Getting There & Away

Nelson's Shuttle (☑902-532-0441; www.nelsonsshuttle.com) Runs to/from Halifax and the Halifax airport for $60.

ℹ KINGS TRANSIT

The local **Kings Transit** (☑888-546-4442, 902-628-7310; www.kingstransit.ns.ca) bus line runs every other hour from 6am to around 7pm from Weymouth (just north of Church Point) to Bridgetown (just north of Annapolis Royal), stopping in every little town along the way. Tickets cost around $3.50 depending on the distance traveled.

Kentville

Kentville is the county seat for this area, with a number of government offices and stately old homes.

During the colorful spring bloom of the valley, the **Annapolis Valley Apple Blossom Festival** (www.appleblossom.com) in early June brings folks together with concerts, a parade, barbecues and art shows.

At the eastern end of town, the **Agriculture Research Station** (☑902-678-1093; off Hwy 1; ☺8:30am-4:30pm) **FREE** includes a museum on the area's farming history and the apple industry in particular. Guided museum tours are offered during summer.

Local artifacts, history and an art gallery can be seen at the **Old King's County Museum** (☑902-678-6237; 37 Cornwallis Ave; ☺9am-4pm Mon-Sat) **FREE**.

North of Highway 1

The North Mountain, which ends at the dramatic Cape Blomidon, defines one edge of the Annapolis Valley. On the other side of the mountain are fishing communities on the Bay of Fundy. The valley floor between Hwy 1 and the North Mountain is crisscrossed with small highways lined with farms and orchards. It's a great place to get out your road map – or throw it away – and explore. To start the adventure, turn north on Hwy 358 just west of Wolfville (at exit 11 off Hwy 101). The quaint, historic town of Canning is en route to Scots Bay, where Hwy 358 ends and a dramatic hiking trail leads to views of the Minas Basin and the Bay of Fundy.

Port Williams

Only a blink away from Wolfville on Hwy 358 is **Tin Pan** (☑902-691-0020; 978 Main St;

mains $3-11; ⊘ breakfast, lunch & dinner Mon-Sat), a favorite for motorcyclists who congregate here Saturday mornings for hearty breakfasts.

Prescott House Museum (☑ 902-542-3984; http://prescotthouse.novascotia.ca; 1633 Starr's Point Rd; adult/student $4/2.75; ⊘ 10am-5pm Mon-Sat, 1-5pm Sun Jun-Oct), c 1814, is one of the finest examples of Georgian architecture in Nova Scotia and is the former home of the horticulturalist who introduced many of the apple varieties grown in the Annapolis Valley. To get here, turn right on Starr's Point Rd at the flashing light in Port Williams, 2km north of Hwy 1, and follow it for 3.25km.

Canning

From November to March, hundreds of **bald eagles** – a photographer's and nature lover's dream – gather in the Canning area, attracted by local chicken farms. Just west of Canning on Hwy 221, Blomidon Estate Winery (p76) offers tastings and free tours. Further along Hwy 358, stop at the **Look-Off**. About 200m above the Annapolis Valley, this is the best view of its rows of fruit trees and picturesque farmhouses.

Art Can Gallery & Café (☑ 902-582-7071; www.artcan.com; 9850 Main St; mains $10-14; ⊘ 10am-5pm Tue-Thu, to 10pm Fri & Sat, to 4pm Sun) is an art-store-cum-cafe. Enjoy fair-trade coffee and delicious baked goods with views over the valley. Check the website for the availability of art classes and workshops.

Scots Bay

The hike to the end of **Cape Split** starts in Scots Bay. This is one of the most popular hiking trails in Nova Scotia. It's about 14km return, taking three to five hours, with little elevation change through a tunnel of forest. The hike ends in a dramatic, often windy clearing on cliffs high above the Bay of Fundy, where seabirds nest and squawk. Wander down to the rocky outcrop at the vertiginous end of the trail to see the tides creating waves called tidal rips that flow through a cluster of rock pinnacles.

Take time before or after the hike to look for agates along the beach at Scots Bay.

Blomidon Provincial Park (☑ 902-582-7319; www.parks.gov.ns.ca; off Hwy 358; campsites $24) is on the opposite side of Cape Blomidon from Scots Bay. There are a number of routes to get here from Hwy 358, all well

signed. One route begins 15km south of Scots Bay and involves driving 10km along the Minas Basin. The campground is set atop high cliffs that overlook the basin. There's a beach and picnic area at the foot of the hill and a 14km system of hiking trails within the park.

Hall's Harbour

Further southeast on the Bay of Fundy, **Hall's Harbour** is a great spot to spend an afternoon hiking along the beach and in the surrounding hills. It's also one of the best places in Nova Scotia to eat lobster.

Pick your own lobster at **Hall's Harbour Lobster Pound** (☑ 902-679-5299; ⊘ noon-8pm May-Oct). The prices are determined by the market, but this is definitely a somewhat gentrified seafood shack and prices rival those of the restaurants in Wolfville. Still, it's arguably more fun to eat lobster closer to the source.

To get to Hall's Harbour, take any route west from Hwy 358 until you hit Hwy 359, then take it over the North Mountain.

Wolfville

Wolfville has a perfect blend of old college-town culture, small-town homeyness, and the fine food and drink scene that's grown around the surrounding wine industry. The students and faculty of Acadia University make up about 50% of the town's 7000-plus residents. Just outside town, you'll find Acadian dikes, scenic drives and some of the best hiking along the Fundy Coast. It's considered one of the most livable and diverse towns in the province; some 12% of the residents have moved here from outside Canada.

⊙ Sights & Activities

Waterfront Park   PARK
(cnr Gaspereau Ave & Front St) Waterfront Park offers a stunning view of the tidal mudflats, Minas Basin and the red cliffs of Cape Blomidon. Displays explain the tides, dikes, flora and fauna, and history of the area. This is an easy spot to start a walk or cycle on top of the dikes.

Randall House Museum   MUSEUM
(☑ 902-542-9775; 171 Main St; admission by donation; ⊘ 10am-5pm Mon-Sat, 2-5pm Sun Jun-Sep) Randall House Museum relates the history

of the New England planters and colonists who replaced the expelled Acadians.

Rent bikes at **Valley Stove & Cycle** (✆902-542-7280; 234 Main St; half-/full-day bicycle rental $25/30).

✖️ Festivals & Events

Canadian Deep Roots Festival   MUSIC (www.deeprootsmusic.ca) If you're in town in early fall, rock out to modern roots music at the annual Canadian Deep Roots Festival.

🛏️ Sleeping & Eating

★ Garden House B&B   B&B $$

(✆902-542-1703; www.gardenhouse.ca; 220 Main St; r $65-110; 🛜) This antique house retains its old-time feel in the most comfortable way. Creaky floors, a rustic breakfast table decorated with wildflowers, and that everyone is encouraged to take off their shoes creates a lived-in vibe you instantly feel a part of. Bathrooms are shared.

Blomidon Inn   INN $$

(✆902-542-2291, 800-565-2291; www.theblomidon.net; 195 Main St; d $120-160, ste $160-269; ❄️@🛜) Lofty Victorian architecture and old-world extravagance make this a very upper-crust-feeling inn. On 2.5 hectares of perfectly maintained gardens, the rooms are just as well groomed. Check the website for package deals.

Gingerbread House Inn   INN $$

(✆902-542-1458; www.gingerbreadhouse.ca; 8 Robie Tufts Dr; d $125-135, ste $145-215; 🛜🛁) The exterior of this unique B&B is like a big pink birthday cake with lacy white edging. Rooms, several of which have a hot tub, are like your own candlelit spa.

★ Front & Central   FUSION $$

(✆866-542-0588; 117 Front St; small plates $8-15; ⊙lunch Thu-Sun, dinner Tue-Sun) Choose creative small plates, from a delicious vegetarian 'faux pho' to scallops with a maple glazed pork belly. Share the plates, mix and match and have fun with it. Light eaters may find one is enough, while big appetites may devour four or more. Whatever you choose, waitstaff will pair it with the perfect wine.

Privet House   FUSION $$

(✆902-542-7525; 268 Main St; lunch mains $11-18, dinner mains $19-36; ⊙11:30am-9pm) The finest dining in town serves up aged Atlantic beef, local seafood and game (ingredients are all

Canadian) prepared with everything from European to Indian and Thai influences. The tablecloths are white; the wine list is long and the service is excellent.

Coffee Merchant & Library Pub   CAFE, PUB

(✆902-542-4315; 472 Main St; ⊙11:30am-midnight Mon-Sat) Downstairs, the cafe serves up good fair-trade coffee and baked goods. Upstairs, you can get a pint and a square meal at the cozy pub.

ℹ️ Information

Tourist Office (✆902-542-7000; 11 Willow Ave; ⊙9am-9pm May-Oct) A very helpful office at the east end of Main St.

Wolfville (www.wolfville.info) Information on Wolfville, Acadia University and exploring Nova Scotia.

Wolfville Memorial Library (✆902-542-5760; 21 Elm Ave; ⊙11am-5pm Tue-Sat, 6:30-8:30pm Tue-Thu, 1-5pm Sun) Free internet access.

ℹ️ Getting There & Away

Maritime Bus (www.maritimebus.com) stops at Acadia University in front of Wheelock Hall off Highland Ave. **Kings Transit** (✆888-546-4442, 902-678-7310; www.kingstransit.ns.ca) buses run between Cornwallis (southwest of Annapolis Royal) and Wolfville and stop at 209 Main St.

Grand Pré

Grand Pré feels like the bucolic fringe of Wolfville. Today it's a very small English-speaking town, but in the 1750s, it was the site of one of the most tragic but compelling stories in eastern Canada's history, the Acadian deportation. Learn all about it at the Grand Pré National Historic Site.

◉ Sights

Grand Pré National Historic Site   HISTORIC SITE

(✆902-542-3631; 2205 Grand Pré Rd; adult/child $8.50/4.20; ⊙9am-6pm May-Oct) At the Grand Pré National Historic Site, a modern interpretive center explains the historical context for the deportation from Acadian, Mi'kmaw and British perspectives and traces the many routes Acadians took from, and back to, the Maritimes. In 2012, the landscapes of this area became a Unesco World Heritage site.

Beside the center, a serene **park** contains gardens and an Acadian-style stone church.

WOLFVILLE REGION WINE TOUR

The wine-making tradition in Nova Scotia goes back to the early 1600s and it's possible that this was the first place in North America where wine grapes were grown. Today wineries are springing up everywhere. There are six distinct wine-growing regions in the province, although most wineries are found in the Annapolis Valley and on the Malagash Peninsula.

L'Acadie Blanc, a French hybrid grape, grows particularly well in Nova Scotia and has become the province's signature grape. It makes a medium-bodied, citrusy white wine that pairs well with scallops or smoked salmon. New York Muscat also grows well and is often used for dry white and ice wines. Most wineries make a blend of local varieties called Tidal Bay, an appellation specific to the region.

This tour of our favorite wineries starts at Blomidon Estate Winery in Canning, north of Hwy 1. From here go into downtown Wolfville and turn inland on Gaspereau Dr across from Tim Hortons. Follow the signs to the next three vineyards. Then, once you've left Luckett's, take a right when you reach the bottom of the hill, then take the first left, which will bring you back to Hwy 101 almost directly in front of Domaine de Grand Pré.

If you don't want to drive, hop on the **Wolfville Magic Winery Bus** (☑902-542-4093; www.wolfvillemagicwinerybus.ca; hop-on, hop-off bus passes $10; ☺10:30am-5:30pm Sat & Sun) that runs from September through mid-October.

Blomidon Estate Winery (☑902-582-7565; www.blomidonwine.com; 10318 Hwy 221; tastings $4; ☺10am & 6pm Jun-Sep) The friendly and laid-back winemaker comes out to chat to those tasting wines. The sparkling wines and Tidal Bay are probably the best, but the oaky red is worth a try. It's worth the trip just for the pretty drive to Canning.

There's also a bust of American poet Henry Wadsworth Longfellow, who chronicled the Acadian saga in *Evangeline: A Tale of Acadie,* and a statue of his fictional Evangeline, now a romantic symbol of her people.

Beyond the park, you can see the farmland created when the Acadians built dikes along the shoreline as they had done in northwest France for generations. There are 12 sq km below sea level here, protected by just over 9km of dike.

🛏 Sleeping & Eating

Olde Lantern Inn & Vineyard INN $$
(☑902-542-1389, 877-965-3845; www.oldlanterninn.com; 11575 Hwy 1; r $100-155; 🛜) Clean lines, a friendly welcome and attention to every comfort makes this a great place to stay. The vineyard grounds overlook Minas Basin, where you can watch the rise and fall of the Fundy tides and gaze over the Grand Pré Unesco landscape.

★**Le Caveau** EUROPEAN $$
(☑902-542-1753; 11611 Hwy 1; mains $16-32; ☺lunch & dinner) Considered to be the finest Northern European–style restaurant in the province, this Swiss restaurant is on the grounds of Domaine de Grand Pré. The beautiful outdoor patio is paved with fieldstones and shaded with grapevines.

🛍 Shopping

Tangled Garden FOOD, DRINK
(☑902-542-9811; 11827 Hwy 1; ☺10am-6pm) Impossible to classify, this is probably the best-smelling shopping experience in Nova Scotia. Buy a bottle of herb-infused vinegar or jelly to take away, or stroll the gardens and meditative labyrinth while licking herb-flavored ice cream.

Windsor

Windsor was once the only British stronghold in this region, but today it's just a graying little town eking out an existence between the highway and the Avon River. Windsor is a place to enjoy bluegrass music – think lots of fast banjo picking. Avon River Park hosts two bluegrass festivals, one in June and one in July, and is a hangout for aficionados all summer long. The **tourist office** (☑902-798-2690; 31 Colonial Rd; ☺8:30am-6:30pm daily Jul & Aug, Sat & Sun Jun, Sep & Oct) is just off exit 6 from Hwy 101. The dike beside the tourist office offers a view of the tidal river flats.

Gaspereau Vineyards (☎902-542-1455; www.gaspereauwine.com; 2239 White Rock Rd; ◷10am-5pm May-Oct, tours noon, 2pm & 4pm) This is one of the province's best-known wineries, with award-winning ice wine. Definitely also try the Estate Riesling. The tasting room in a big red barn is posh on the inside and the staff is extra friendly.

L'Acadie Vineyards (☎902-542-8463; www.lacadievineyards.ca; 310 Slayter Rd; cottages $150; ◷10am-5pm May-Oct) Overlooking Gaspereau Valley, this geothermally powered winery grows certified-organic grapes to make traditional-method sparkling and dried-grape wines. You can also stay in one of three country-style two-bedroom, kitchen-equipped cottages, which, of course, include a free bottle of wine.

Luckett Vineyards (www.luckettvineyards.com; 1293 Grand Pré Rd, Wolfville; tastings $7, lunch mains $9-15; ◷10am-5pm May-Oct) This is one of the best destination wineries in the region, with palatial views over the vines and hillsides down to the Bay of Fundy cliffs. After sampling the red, white, fruit and dessert wines, and the particularly good ice wine, chill on the patio and dine on gourmet sandwiches, soups and salads at lunch or, in summer, on fine set meals at dinner. There's also an old British phone box in the vineyards, from where you can make free calls to anywhere in Canada!

Domaine de Grand Pré (☎902-542-1753; http://grandprewines.ns.ca; 11611 Hwy 1; tours $9; ◷10am-6pm, tours 11am, 3pm & 5pm) A great destination winery and one of the best known in the province, it has a delicious spicy muscat and a nice sparkling Champlain Brut. The tours take about 45 minutes or you can do tastings and stroll through the vines by yourself. Le Caveau Restaurant has been named one of the 20 best winery restaurants in the world by *Wine Access* magazine.

While in town, check out **Haliburton House** (☎902-798-2915; 414 Clifton Ave; adult/student $3.60/2.55; ◷10am-5pm Mon-Sat, 1-5pm Sun), once home to Judge Thomas Chandler Haliburton (1796–1865), writer of the Sam Slick stories. Many of Haliburton's expressions, such as 'quick as a wink' and 'city slicker,' are still used.

Stay the night at the **Clockmaker's Inn** (☎866-778-3600, 902-792-2573; www.the-clockmakersinn.com; 1399 King St; d $99-179; ☎), a French-château-style mansion with curved bay windows, lots of stained glass and sweeping hardwood staircases. It's gay friendly and afternoon tea is served daily, as is breakfast.

CENTRAL NOVA SCOTIA

Hiking, rafting and rockhounding are the activities of choice around this mildly touristed region. For those traveling overland from the rest of Canada, this is your first taster of Nova Scotia – do not let it pass you by on bleak Hwy 104.

Called the 'Glooscap Trail' in provincial tourism literature, the area is named for the figure in Mi'kmaw legend who created the unique geography of the Bay of Fundy region. Unfortunately, stories and representations of Glooscap are easier to come across than genuine acknowledgments of present-day Mi'kmaq people.

Shubenacadie

Shubenacadie, or simply 'Shube,' is best known for the **Shubenacadie Provincial Wildlife Park** (☎902-758-2040; https://wildlifepark.novascotia.ca; 149 Creighton Rd; adult/child $4.50/2; ◷9am-6:30pm), the place to commune with Nova Scotia's wildlife. You can hand-feed the deer and, if you're lucky, pet a moose. The animals were either born in captivity or once kept as 'pets' and, as a result, cannot be released into the wild – they live in large enclosures. Turn off Hwy 102 at exit 11 and follow Hwy 2 to the park entrance.

Maitland

Tiny Maitland is the place to go rafting on the white water that is created by the outflow of the Shubenacadie River meeting the blasting force of the incoming Fundy tides. It's also one of the oldest towns in Canada.

Wave heights are dependent on the phases of the moon; get information from your rafting company about the tides for your chosen day since your experience (either mild or exhilarating) will be dictated by this. Outboard-powered Zodiacs plunge right through the white water for the two to three hours that the rapids exist. Prepare to get very, very wet – no experience is needed.

⚡ Activities

Shubenacadie River Runners RAFTING
(☏902-261-2770, 800-856-5061; www.tidalbore-rafting.com; 8681 Hwy 215; half-day $60-70) The biggest rafting company is organized and professional in every way. Prices depend on how big the tide and waves are.

Shubenacadie River Adventures RAFTING
(☏902-261-2222, 800-878-8687; www.shubie.com; 10061 Hwy 15; rafting per day incl lunch adult/child $85/80) Besides the exciting tidal bore rafting day trips, mellow half-day river tours ($65) are also on offer.

🛏 Sleeping

There are a handful of places to sleep in Maitland, but the few eating options have unpredictable opening hours. Bring your own food or a full belly.

Tidal Life Guesthouse B&B $$
(☏902-261-2583; www.thetidallife.ca; 9568 Cedar St; dm $35, r $90-120; ☺May-Oct; ☏☀) This

---

THE POWER OF THE BORE

The **tidal bore** phenomenon occurs when the first surge of the extreme Bay of Fundy tides flows upriver at high tide. Sometimes the advancing wave is only a ripple but, with the right phase of the moon, it can be a meter or so in height, giving the impression that the river is flowing backwards. You'll have to sit awhile to see the changes in the tide, but a good place to watch is from the lookout on Tidal Bore Rd, off Hwy 236 just west of exit 14 from Hwy 102 on the northwest side of Truro. Staff in the adjacent Palliser Motel **gift shop** (☏902-893-8951) can advise when the next tidal bore will arrive. There's another viewpoint in Moncton, New Brunswick.

---

backpackers-B&B hybrid in an old beauty of a house has grand airy rooms and large windows overlooking grassy fields. Artistically designed communal spaces are everywhere, including a hammock on the back porch. All options include a big healthy breakfast and bathrooms are shared. The drawback is that it can be hard to get in touch with the place, so contact them early.

Cresthaven by the Sea B&B $$
(☏902-261-2001, 866-870-2001; www.cresthavenbythesea.com; r $140-150; ☏) Stay here for what is possibly the best view over the Fundy tides. The immaculate white Victorian house sits on a bluff right over the point where the Shubenacadie River meets the bay. All the rooms have river views and the lower ones are wheelchair accessible.

Truro

Several major highways converge here, along with a VIA Rail line, so it's no wonder Truro is known as the hub of Nova Scotia. While the town does look somewhat like an aging shopping mall, it's exceptionally well serviced and can make a good stop to pick up that nagging item you need or just stock up on food.

◉ Sights

Victoria Park PARK
(Park St, off Brunswick St) Escape Truro's busy streets at Victoria Park, 400 hectares of green space in the very center of town, including a deep gorge and two waterfalls. The park attracts dozens of bird species.

⭐ Festivals & Events

Millbrook Annual Powwow CULTURE
(☏902-897-9199; www.millbrookfirstnation.net; ☺2nd weekend Aug) The best time to visit Truro is when Millbrook First Nation hosts its annual powwow. Campsites and showers are available; drugs and alcohol are prohibited.

🛏 Sleeping & Eating

Baker's Chest B&B B&B $$
(☏902-893-4824, 877-822-5655; www.bakers-chest.ca; 53 Farnham Rd; r/ste $100/120; ☏☀) This newly restored classic older home has contemporary decor, a fitness room, a pool and a hot tub. The famous tearoom is open from noon to 2pm on weekdays and

is an adorable stop for soups, snacks and, of course, a nice cup of tea.

Wooden Hog CANADIAN **$$**
(📞902-895-0779; 627 Prince St; lunch mains $8, dinner mains $11-17; ⊗9am-4pm Mon, to 9pm Tue-Fri, 11am-9pm Sat) Named for the huge, sculpted Harley that hangs off the back wall, this popular restaurant cooks up local and Mexican specialties, plus decadent desserts.

ℹ️ Information

Tourist Office (📞902-893-2922; Victoria Sq, cnr Prince & Commercial Sts; ⊗8:30am-7:30pm May-Oct) This place offers internet access and a terrific guide to the tree sculptures around town. The trees were carved after the region was affected by Dutch elm disease more than 30 years ago.

ℹ️ Getting There & Away

Maritime Bus stops en route to Amherst and Halifax.

Economy to Five Islands

Hwy 2 hugs the shore of the Minas Basin, the northeast arm of the Bay of Fundy, and Economy is the first sizable community that you'll arrive at. There's great **hiking** and several interesting sites around Economy.

◉ Sights & Activities

Cobequid Interpretation
Centre MUSEUM, HIKING
(📞902-647-2600; 3248 Hwy 2, near River Phillip Rd; by donation; ⊗9am-4:30pm Jun-Sep) Stop here for good exhibits on the area's ecology and history. Climb a WWII observation tower for a bird's-eye view of the surrounding area and pick up hiking information from the staff.

The nearby **Thomas Cove Coastal Trail** is actually two 3.5km loops with great views across the Minas Basin and the Cobequid Mountains. They begin down Economy Point Rd, 500m east of the Cobequid Interpretation Centre. Follow the signs to a parking area.

Economy Falls HIKING
The most challenging hikes in the area are around Economy Falls. The **Devil's Bend Trail** begins 7km up River Phillip Rd toward the Cobequid Mountains. Turn right and park; the 6.5km (one-way) trail follows the river to the falls.

The **Kenomee Canyon Trail** begins further up River Phillip Rd, at the top of the falls. A 20km loop, it takes you up the river to its headwaters in a protected wilderness area. Several streams have to be forded. There are designated campsites, making this a good two-day adventurous trek.

Five Islands Provincial Park HIKING
(📞902-254-2980; http://parks.gov.ns.ca) Just 7km west of Economy, there are several hikes in Five Islands Provincial Park. The 4.5km **Red Head Trail** is well developed, with lookouts, benches and great views.

🛏️ Sleeping & Eating

Several takeaway stands selling fried clams pop up along the highway near Five Islands Provincial Park in the summer.

Mo's at Five Islands HOSTEL, CAFE **$**
(📞902-254-8088; www.mosatfiveislands.com; 951 Hwy 2, Five Islands; dm/r $28/65, light meals from $4; ⊗May-Sep; 🔊🍴) You can usually count on an interesting crowd at this spotless hostel and the large homey cafe out front. The owner also owns one of the five islands (of the eponymous town) and holds a running race each year from the mainland to the island when the tide goes out high enough – the race and the hostel are named after Moses and his parting of the Red Sea.

Four Seasons Retreat RESORT **$$**
(📞902-647-2628, 888-373-0339; www.fourseasonsretreat.ns.ca; 320 Cove Rd, Upper Economy; 1-/2-bedroom cottages $109/225; 🔊🌊🍴) Fully equipped cottages are surrounded by trees and face the Minas Basin. In summer, there's a hot tub near the pool; in winter – or on a chilly night – there are woodstoves.

High Tide B&B B&B **$$**
(📞902-647-2788; www.hightidebb.com; 2240 Hwy 2, Lower Economy; d $85-95; 🔊) This friendly, modern bungalow has great views. Janet, one of the owners, will have you down on the beach for a clam boil in no time.

That Dutchman's Farm CAFE **$**
(📞902-647-2751; www.thatdutchmansfarm.com; 112 Brown Rd, Upper Economy; lunch $8; ⊗11am-5pm Jul & Aug) The yummy cafe here offers sandwiches, soups and plates of the eccentric farmer's own Gouda. You can tour the farm for a small fee.

Parrsboro

Rock hounds come from far and wide to forage the shores of Parrsboro, the largest of the towns along the Minas Basin. The Fundy Geological Museum has wonderful exhibits and good programs that take you to the beach areas known as Nova Scotia's 'Jurassic Park.' For more serious rock lovers, the annual **Gem & Mineral Show** is in mid-August.

◎ Sights

Fundy Geological Museum   MUSEUM
(☑902-254-3814;   http://fundygeological.novascotia.ca; 162 Two Islands Rd; adult/child $8/4.50; ◎9:30am-5:30pm) This award-winning museum got a $1 million makeover in 2010 and uses interactive exhibits to help its visitors 'time travel' to when the fossils littering Parrsboro's beaches were alive. You can see a lab where dinosaur bones are being cleaned and assembled.

Beach tours are included in the admission price and focus on minerals or fossils. Times, length and frequency are dependent on the tides.

Partridge Island   ISLAND
Steeped in history, Partridge Island is the most popular shoreline to search for gems, semiprecious stones and fossils. Connected to the mainland by an isthmus, the island is 4km south of town on Whitehall Rd. From the end of the beach, a 3km **hiking trail** with explanatory panels climbs to the top of the island for superb views of Cape Blomidon and Cape Split.

Ottawa House Museum   MUSEUM
(☑902-254-2376;   www.ottawahousemuseum.ca; 1155 Whitehall Rd; admission $2; ◎10am-6pm) Just before the beach is Ottawa House Museum, a 21-room mansion that was once the summer home of Sir Charles Tupper (1821–1915), who served as both premier of Nova Scotia and prime minister of Canada. The museum has exhibits on shipbuilding, rum-running and the former settlement on Partridge Island.

⊨ Sleeping & Eating

Riverview Cottages   COTTAGES $
(☑902-254-2388;   www.riverviewcottages.ca; 3575 Eastern Ave; cottages $60-100; ◎May-Nov; ☜☗) These rustic, country-cute, completely equipped cottages are a steal. You can canoe and fish on the bordering river and there's a big lawn perfect for a barbecue.

Mad Hatter Hostel   HOSTEL $
(☑902-254-3167; madhatterhostel@hotmail.com; 16 Prince St; dm/s/d $20/35/50; ☜) More like a few rooms and beds upstairs in an inviting home, this 'hostel' offers a ton of hospitality, kitchen use and a great location right in town.

Evangeline's Tower B&B   B&B $$
(☑902-254-3383,   866-338-6937;   www.evangelinestower.ca; 322 Main St; d $70-150; ☜☗) This elegantly decorated 1890s Victorian home has three rooms; two can be combined into a two-room suite for families. The generous, home-cooked breakfasts are delicious and cyclists are welcome.

LOCAL KNOWLEDGE

RODD & HELEN TYSON: GEOLOGISTS & MINERAL DEALERS

Rodd Tyson is considered one of the most successful mineral dealers in Canada. He and his wife Helen moved to Parrsboro several years ago and opened a small shop that displays some of their finest pieces.

Why Parrsboro? The tides and rains are moving things all the time, so on any given day we could still potentially find something suitable for our own private collection in one of several places.

Where to Go Partridge Island is the easiest place to go. Just remember to wear good footwear, be careful of the cliffs and be vigilant about checking the tides, so you don't get stuck somewhere.

What to Look For You're looking for color. Stilbite is amber-gold; chabazite is orange; agates have banded colors and patterns; and jasper is a deep brick red or forest green. You won't find much amethyst here, no matter what anyone tells you, unless it's pretty pale. It's illegal to take fossils.

Harbour View Restaurant CANADIAN $$
(145 Pier Rd; mains $9-16; ⊗7am-8pm) Hang out with the local fishers devouring Parrsboro's best I-worked-hard-all-day portions of fish and chips, chowder, homemade pies and more. It's right on the water, but the set-up blocks most of the view.

☆ Entertainment

Ship's Company Theatre THEATER
(⊠800-565-7469, 902-254-3000; www.shipscompany.com; 18 Lower Main St; tickets $12-28; ⊗Jul-Sep) This innovative theater company performs new Canadian and Maritime works 'on board' the MV *Kipawo,* the last of the Minas Basin ferries, now integrated into a new theater. There's high-quality theater for kids, improv comedy, readings and concerts.

🛍 Shopping

Parrsboro Rock & Mineral Shop ROCKS & MINERALS
(⊠902-254-2981; 39 Whitehall Rd; ⊗9am-9pm Mon-Sat, to 5pm Sun May-Nov) Browse the collection of prehistoric reptile fossils and semiprecious stones from Parrsboro and around the world. There's even a one-of-a-kind fossilized footprint of the world's smallest dinosaur, found by the proprietor, Eldon George. If Eldon is there, don't miss the chance to chat with him – he's one of Parrsboro's favorite characters.

Tysons' Fine Minerals ROCKS & MINERALS
(⊠902-254-2376; 249 Whitehall Rd; ⊗from 10am) This place is more like a museum than a shop, with some of the most sparkling, massive and colorful minerals on display you're likely to see anywhere. Sometimes Helen takes visitors in to see the Tysons' private collection, which is even more breathtaking.

ℹ Information

Tourist Office (⊠902-254-3266; Fundy Geological Museum, 162 Two Islands Rd; ⊗10am-7pm Jun-Oct) Tide information and free internet access.

Cape d'Or

This spectacular cape of sheer cliffs was misnamed Cape d'Or (Cape of Gold) by Samuel de Champlain in 1604 – the glittering veins he saw in the cliffs were actually made of copper. Mining took place between 1897 and 1905 and removed the sparkle.

★**Lightkeeper's Kitchen & Guest House** (⊠902-670-0534; www.capedor.ca; s/d $85/125; ⊗May-Oct; 🅿🐾), an original light-

WORTH A TRIP

AGE OF SAIL HERITAGE CENTRE

Stop for tea, baked goods and a tour at the **Age of Sail Heritage Centre** (⊠902-348-2030; Rte 209; adult $3; ⊗10am-6pm Jun-Sep) in Port Greville, about 20km to the west of Parrsboro on Rte 209. It captures the area's ship-building heritage. The site also includes a restored 1857 Methodist church and a working blacksmith shop.

house keeper's residence, is now a laid-back four-room guesthouse at what is perhaps one of the most perfect spots in Nova Scotia (even more so when the sun's out). Take the side road off Hwy 209 to Cape d'Or, then hike down the dirt trail. Its cosmopolitan **restaurant** (lunch mains $9-16, dinner mains $22-28; ⊗noon-7pm; 🍴) pumps out low-volume techno music and serves original seafood, meat and vegetarian creations.

Cape Chignecto Provincial Park & Advocate Harbour

The **Cape Chignecto Coastal Trail** is a rugged 60km loop with backcountry – nay, old-growth – campsites. Allow four days and three nights for the hike. The **Mill Brook Canyon Trail** (15km return) and the hike to **Refugee Cove** (20km return) are other challenging overnight hikes. There are some easier hikes and more are being developed – the newest is the **Eatonville Trail** (5.6km return) that begins at a new 'Phase 2' entrance to the park about 15km north of the main entrance. Some hikers have tried to avoid the ups and downs of the trails by taking shortcuts along the beach at low tide and have been cut off by Bay of Fundy tides. Get a tide table and follow advice from park staff to avoid being trapped on the cliffs.

Park visitors must register and leave an itinerary at the **visitors center** (⊠902-392-2085; www.capechignecto.net; 1108 West Advocate Rd; day/annual hiking permits $5/25, campsites $24; ⊗8am-7pm Mon-Thu, to 8pm Fri & Sat). Camping in the backcountry requires reservations. In addition to 51 wilderness campsites at six points along the coastal trail and 27 walk-in sites near the visitors center, there is also a bunkhouse ($55, up to four people) and a wilderness cabin ($55, up to four people).

Advocate Harbour is the nearest town, about 2km southeast of the park entrance. It's a breathtaking place with a 5km-long beach piled high with driftwood that changes dramatically with the tides. Behind the beach, salt marshes reclaimed with dikes by the Acadians are now replete with birds.

Kayak through Cape Chignecto Provincial Park with **Nova Shores Adventures** (☑866-638-4118; www.novashores.com; Hwy 33, Advocate Harbour; 1-/2-day tours $95/350; 🐾). You'll often see seals and bears. Overnight tours include accommodations and food.

★**Wild Caraway Restaurant & Cafe** (☑902-392-2889; www.wildcaraway.com; 3721 Hwy 209; lunch mains $6-15, dinner mains $18-24; ⊘11am-8pm Thu-Mon; 🐾) is inviting, cozy, overlooks the harbor, and is the best place to eat along this coast. Try the ploughman's lunch with house-smoked pork and cheese from local That Dutchman's Farm, or dine on applewood-smoked mackerel or a selection of seasonal specials. There are also two charming B&B rooms ($90) upstairs in this beautiful Victorian home.

Joggins

Between Amherst and Advocate Harbour on Chignecto Bay, Joggins is famous for its Unesco World Heritage fossil cliffs, said to be the best place on Earth to see what life was like over 300 million years ago in the late Carboniferous period. The wealth of fossils in the 15km of seaside cliffs are preserved in their original setting and include rare land species. The state-of-the- art **Joggins Fossil Centre** (www.jogginsfossilcliffs.net; 100 Main St; admission from $10.50; ⊘9:30am-5:30pm May-Nov) is the place to start your visit and explains through displays and film what you can see in the cliffs below. Ticket price includes a half-hour tour, but you can also opt for a ticket including a two- ($25) or four-hour ($55) tour. The best time to visit the cliffs is at low tide when all of the beaches can be accessed – otherwise you'll be cut off from some of the more interesting sites by high water. Tours leave on an irregular schedule, depending on the tides; you can reserve in advance on the website.

Amherst

Amherst is the geographic center of the Maritimes and a junction for travelers to Nova Scotia, PEI and New Brunswick. There's little reason to dawdle here, as you're just a short drive from either the Bay of Fundy shore or the Northumberland Strait (between Nova Scotia and PEI). The historic downtown does have some stately buildings and there's birdwatching at the 490-hectare **Amherst Point Migratory Bird Sanctuary** nearby (off exit 3 from the Trans-Canada Hwy). The massive **visitors information center** (VIC; ☑902-667-8429; ⊘8:30am-8pm) is at exit 1 off Hwy 104, just as you cross the border from New Brunswick.

Maritime Bus has bus services to Halifax that leave from the Circle K at 213 S Aubion St. The Trans-Canada Hwy east of Amherst charges a toll of $4. It's an incentive to use scenic Hwy 2 through Parrsboro instead of dull – but fast – Hwy 104. The Sunrise Trail (Hwy 6) through Pugwash and Tatamagouche to Pictou also avoids the toll.

SUNRISE TRAIL

It's claimed that the Northumberland Strait between Nova Scotia's north shore and PEI has some of the warmest waters north of the US Carolinas, with water temperatures averaging slightly over 20°C during summer. It's a prime area for beachhopping, cycling and exploring friendly countryside towns.

Wallace

Wallace is perfect territory for birding and beachcombing. The tourist information center is at the **Wallace Museum** (☑902-257-2191; Hwy 6; ⊘9am-5pm Mon-Sat, 1-4pm Sun), where collections of baskets woven by the Mi'kmaq, period dresses and shipbuilding memorabilia are displayed.

Wallace Bay Wildlife Bird Sanctuary (1km north of Hwy 6 on Aboiteau Rd) protects 585 hectares, including tidal and freshwater wetlands. In the spring, keep your eyes peeled for bald eagles nesting near the parking lot, which is on the left just before the causeway.

Wentworth

The Wentworth Valley is a detour off the shore, 25km south of Wallace via Hwy 307, and is particularly pretty in fall when the deciduous trees change color. The 24-bed, cabin-like **Wentworth Hostel** (☑902-548-2379; www.hihostels.ca; 249 Wentworth Station Rd; HI member/nonmember dm $25/30, r $45/50; ☎) is 1.3km west of Hwy 4 on Valley Rd, then straight up steep, dirt Wentworth Station Rd. The rambling farmhouse, built in 1866, has been used as a hostel for half a century. It's central enough to be a base for both the Sunrise Trail and much of the Minas Basin shore. Trails for hiking and mountain biking start just outside the door. It gets particularly booked up in winter for the cross-country and downhill skiing nearby.

Tatamagouche

The Malagash Peninsula, which juts out into protected Tatamagouche Bay, is a low-key, bucolic loop for a drive or bike ride. Stop at the local winery for tastings, explore beaches galore or take a peek in some interesting museums found just inland. Tatamagouche is the largest town on the Northumberland Shore coast west of Pictou and makes a great base for exploring.

◎ Sights

Jost Winery   WINERY
(☑902-257-2636; www.jostwine.com; off Hwy 6, Malagash; ◉tours noon & 3pm Jun-Sep) Take a free tour of the scenically located Jost Winery. While regular wine is free to taste, the ice wine costs $5. If you want to try all three ice wine varieties, ask to have three small glasses for the price of one large one. Winery signs direct you about 5km off Hwy 6.

Balmoral Grist Mill   HISTORIC SITE
(☑902-657-3016; 660 Matheson Brook Rd; adult/child $3/2; ◉9:30am-5:30pm Mon-Sat, 1-5:30pm Sun) In a gorgeous setting on the stream that once provided it with power, the Balmoral Grist Mill still grinds wheat in summer. From Tatamagouche, turn south on Hwy 311 (at the east edge of town) and then east on Hwy 256.

Sutherland Steam Mill   HISTORIC SITE
(☑902-657-3365; off Hwy 326, Denmark; adult/child $3/2; ◉9:30am-5:30pm Mon-Sat, 1-5:30pm Sun) Built in 1894, the Sutherland Steam Mill produced lumber, carriages, wagons and windows until 1958. To get here from Hwy 256, drive east, and then north on Hwy 326.

Blue Sea Beach   BEACH
Blue Sea Beach on the Malagash Peninsula has warm water and fine sand, and a marsh area just inland that's ideal for birdwatching. There are picnic tables and shelters to change in.

Rushton's Beach   BEACH
Small cottages crowd around Rushton's Beach, just east of Tatamagouche in Brule. It's worth a visit to look for seals (turn left at the end of the boardwalk and walk toward the end of the beach) and birdlife in the adjoining salt marsh.

✯ Festivals & Events

Oktoberfest   BEER
(☑902-657-2380; tickets $10-20; ◉Sep) The wildly popular Oktoberfest is held the last weekend in September – yes, September.

⊨ Sleeping & Eating

Train Station Inn   INN $$
(☑902-657-3222, 888-724-5233; www.trainstation.ca; 21 Station Rd; carriages $99-179; ◉May-Nov; ☎⚒) It's a museum, it's a kooky gift shop, it's a restaurant, it's a hotel and...it's a stationary train. Each unique carriage suite is an eight-year-old boy's dream decorated with period train posters, toy trains and locomotive books.

The dreamer behind the inn, James LeFresne, grew up across the tracks and saved the train station from demolition when he was just 18. Dine on delicious seafood, meat and salads in the c 1928 dining car or have a blueberry pancake breakfast in the station house. Free self-guided tours are available from the gift shop.

Sugar Moon Farm   CANADIAN $$
(☑902-657-3348, 866-816-2753; www.sugarmoon.ca; Alex Macdonald Rd, off Hwy 311, Earltown; mains $10-30; ◉9am-5pm Thu-Mon Jul & Aug, Sat & Sun Sep-Jun) The food – simple, delicious pancakes and locally made sausages served with maple syrup – is the highlight of this working maple farm and woodlot. Check online for special happenings.

🛍 Shopping

Lismore Sheep Farm
SOUVENIRS
(☑ 902-351-2889; 1389 Louisville Rd, off Hwy 6; ⊘ 9am-5pm) A working farm with more than 300 sheep, this is a fun destination even if you don't buy a rug, blanket or socks. From May to October, the barn is open for visitors to pat the lambs and learn all about producing wool.

❶ Information

Fraser Cultural Centre (☑ 902-657-3285; 362 Main St; ⊘ 10am-5pm Mon-Fri, to 4pm Sat, 11am-3pm Sun Jun-Sep) Has tourist information, internet access and local history displays.

Pictou

Many people stop in Pictou for a side trip or as a stopover via the ferry from PEI, but it's also an enjoyable base for exploring Northumberland Strait. Water St, the main street, is lined with interesting shops and beautiful old stone buildings but, unfortunately, the sea views are blighted by a giant smoking mill in the distance. The town is known as the 'Birthplace of New Scotland' because the first Scottish immigrants to Nova Scotia landed here in 1773.

◎ Sights & Activities

You can picnic and swim at Caribou/Munroes Island Provincial Park.

Hector
SHIP
(admission $7.50; ⊘ 9am-7pm Jun-Oct) A replica of the ship *Hector* that carried the first 200 Highland Scots to Nova Scotia is tied up for viewing. Descend into the large hull crammed with bunks to get a feel of how challenging the crossing was. The ticket includes admission to **Hector Heritage Quay** (☑ 902-485-4371; 33 Caladh Ave; adult/student $5/2; ⊘ 9am-5pm Mon-Sat, noon-5pm Sun May-Sep), which has an interpretive center, a re-created blacksmith shop, a collection of shipbuilding artifacts and displays about the *Hector* and its passengers.

Northumberland Fisheries Museum
MUSEUM
(☑ 902-485-4972; 71 Front St; admission $5; ⊘ 10am-6pm Mon-Sat) In the old train station, this museum explores the area's fishing heritage. Exhibits include strange sea creatures and the spiffy *Silver Bullet,* an early-1930s lobster boat.

✹ Festivals & Events

Pictou Landing First Nation Powwow
CULTURE
(☑ 902-752-4912; ⊘ 1st weekend Jun) Across the Pictou Harbour (a 25-minute drive through New Glasgow), this annual powwow features sunrise ceremonies, drumming and craft demonstrations. Camping and food are available on-site; it's strictly alcohol and drug free.

Lobster Carnival
FOOD
(☑ 902-485-5150; www.townofpictou.ca; ⊘ mid-Jul) Begun in 1934 as the Carnival of the Fisherfolk, this four-day event now offers free entertainment, boat races and lots of chances to feast on lobster.

Hector Festival
MUSIC
(☑ 902-485-8848; www.decostecentre.ca; ⊘ mid-Aug) Free daily outdoor concerts, Highland dancing and piping competitions, and a *Hector* landing reenactment.

🛏 Sleeping & Eating

Pictou is no culinary center, but there are some excellent dining options 20km away in New Glasgow. Plenty of pub-food and fish-and-chip-style joints line the waterfront and main drags.

Caribou/Munroes Island Provincial Park
CAMPGROUND $
(☑ 902-485-6134; www.parks.gov.ns.ca; 2119 Three Brooks Rd; campsites $24) Less than 5km from Pictou, this park is set on a gorgeous beach. Sites 1 to 22 abut the day-use area and are less private; sites 78 to 95 are gravel and suited for RVs. The rest are wooded and private.

Pictou Lodge
HOTEL $$
(☑ 888-662-7484, 902-485-4322; www.pictoulodge.com; 172 Lodge Rd, off Braeshore Rd; r/cottages from $109/159; 🗟🗙🐾) This atmospheric 1920s resort is on more than 60 hectares of wooded land between Caribou/Munroes Island Provincial Park and Pictou. Beautifully renovated ocean-side log cabins have original stone fireplaces. Motel rooms are also available. There's a life-sized checkerboard, paddleboats, a private beach and the best restaurant in town.

Willow House Inn
B&B $$
(☑ 902-485-5740; www.willowhouseinn.com; 11 Willow St; r with shared/private bathroom $60/120; 🗟🐾) This historic c 1840 home is a labyrinth of staircases and cozy, antique rooms.

The owners whip up great breakfasts, as well as conversation and tips for what to do around town.

Customs House Inn INN $$
(☑902-485-4546; www.customshouseinn.ca; 38 Depot St; r incl breakfast $80-170; 🛜) The tall stone walls here are at once imposingly chic and reassuringly solid. The chunky antique decor is as sturdy and elegant as the walls and many rooms have waterfront views. You'll be left pretty much to your own devices, including at the continental breakfast in the basement, which can be a nice break after days of B&B chitchat.

Carver's Coffeehouse & Studio CAFE $
(☑902-382-3332; 41 Coleraine St; light meals around $8; ☺8am-9pm) This bright and inviting cafe used to be the carving studio for Keith Matheson, who did the detail work on the *Hector*. Nowadays it's a mellow stop for soup, sandwiches, coffee and pastries.

☆ Entertainment

deCoste Centre MUSIC, THEATER
(☑902-485-8848; www.decostecentre.ca; 91 Water St; tickets about $18; ☺box office 11:30am-5pm Mon-Fri, 1-5pm Sat & Sun) Opposite the waterfront, this impressive performing arts center stages a range of live shows. Experience some top-notch Scottish music during a summer series of ceilidhs (*kay*-lees; adult/child $15/7) at 2pm from Tuesday to Thursday.

❶ Information

Pictou Public Library (☑902-485-5021; 40 Water St; ☺noon-9pm Tue & Thu, to 5pm Wed, 10am-5pm Fri & Sat) Free internet access.
Town of Pictou (www.townofpictou.ca) Links to sights and festivals.
Visitors Information Centre (VIC; ☑902-485-6213; Pictou Rotary; ☺8am-9:30pm May-Dec) A large information center situated northwest of town to meet travelers arriving from the PEI ferry.

❶ Getting There & Away

Northumberland Ferries (p269) to PEI leave from a terminal a few kilometers from Pictou.

New Glasgow

The largest town on the Northumberland Shore, New Glasgow has always been an industrial center; the first mine opened in

neighboring Stellarton in 1807. Still, it's a pleasant town with plenty of aging architecture, a river running through the center and some good places to eat. The few major local attractions are in Stellarton, a 5km drive south.

⊙ Sights & Activities

Crombie Art Gallery GALLERY
(☑902-755-4440; 1780 Abercrombie Rd; ☺tours hourly 9-11am & 1-4pm Wed Jul & Aug) **FREE** In the personal residence of the founder of the Sobeys supermarket chain, this private gallery has an excellent collection of 19th- and early-20th-century Canadian art, including works by Cornelius Krieghoff and the Group of Seven.

Museum of Industry MUSEUM
(☑902-755-5425; http://museumofindustry.nova-scotia.ca; Hwy 104 at exit 24; adult/child $7/3; ☺9am-5pm Mon-Sat, 10am-5pm Sun; ♿) This is a wonderful place for kids. There's a hands-on water-power exhibit and an assembly line to try to keep up with.

Anchors Above Zipline Adventure ZIP LINE
(www.anchorsabovezipline.ca; 464 McGrath Mountain Rd, French River; 1 ride $30; ☺10am-5pm) Nova Scotia's only zip line is found off Hwy 104 (exit 27) on the way to Antigonish. Two lines total 600m (2000ft) and dangle 75m (250ft) up in the trees. The first is a bit slower and lets you get the hang of it, while the second drops down about 60m (190ft) and goes quite fast!

✗ Eating

The Bistro MODERN CANADIAN $$
(☑902-752-4988; 216 Archimedes St; mains $19-32; ☺from 5pm Tue-Sat) The only constant on the menu is creativity in spicing and sauces. The menu changes daily according to what's available and in summer everything is organic. Try the Thai grilled salmon, or pork tenderloin with black-mission-fig butter. Enjoy the local art on display that's also for sale.

Hebel's INTERNATIONAL $$$
(☑902-695-5955; 71 Stellarton Rd; lunch mains $9-14, dinner mains $22-36; ☺11:30am-2pm Tue-Fri, 5-9pm Tue-Sat) Flavors from all over the world are mingled with fresh Nova Scotian ingredients at this bright and homey, fire-warmed spot in an elegant Victorian. Choices may include anything from seafood creole or beef stroganoff to miso-glazed salmon on Japanese noodles.

Antigonish

Beautiful beaches and hiking possibilities north of town could easily keep you busy for a couple of days, but Antigonish town is lively enough and has some great places to eat. Catholic Scots settled and established St Francis Xavier University and today the university still dominates the ambience of the town. Antigonish is known for the Highland Games held each July since 1861.

◉ Sights & Activities

St Francis Xavier University NOTABLE BUILDING
The attractive campus of 125-year-old St Francis Xavier University is behind the Romanesque **St Ninian's Cathedral** (120 St Ninian St; ⊙7:30am-8pm). The **Hall of the Clans** is on the 3rd floor of the old wing of the Angus L MacDonald Library, just beyond the St Ninian's Cathedral parking lot. In the hall, crests of all the Scottish clans that settled this area are displayed. Those clans gather each July for the Antigonish Highland Games.

Antigonish Landing HIKING, CYCLING
A 4km hiking and cycling trail to the nature reserve at Antigonish Landing begins just across the train tracks from the museum, then 400m up Adam St. The landing's estuary is a good birdwatching area where you might see eagles, ducks and ospreys.

⁂ Festivals & Events

Antigonish Highland Games CULTURE
(www.antigonishhighlandgames.ca; ⊙mid-Jul) An extravaganza of dancing, pipe playing, and heavy-lifting events involving hewn logs and iron balls.

Evolve MUSIC
(www.evolvefestival.com; ⊙late Jul) Five stages of funk, bluegrass, hip-hop and more, plus workshops on everything from puppetry to media literacy.

⌂ Sleeping & Eating

Shebby's Tourist Home B&B $$
(Antigonish Highland Heart; ☑902-863-1858, 800-863-1858; www.bbcanada.com/3241.html; 135 Main St; r $90-110; ⊙May-Oct; ☎) Smiling Shebby, the friendly owner of this c 1854 house, brightens her centrally located home with special touches such as rag dolls on the beds.

★ **Gabrieau's Bistro** MODERN CANADIAN $$
(☑902-863-1925; 350 Main St; lunch mains $8-16, dinner mains $16-32; ⊙10am-9pm Mon-Fri, 4-9:30pm Sat; ☑) Dine on any of a number of imaginative vegetarian dishes, salads, meats and seafood for lunch or dinner. Locals credit chef Mark Gabrieau for setting the culinary high-water mark in Antigonish. The Thai shrimp and lobster risotto is divine.

ℹ Information

Antigonish Public Library (☑902-863-4276; 274 Main St; ⊙10am-9pm Tue & Thu, to 5pm Wed, Fri & Sat) Free internet access. Enter off College St.

Visitors Information Centre (VIC; ☑902-863-4921; 56 West St; ⊙10am-8pm Jun-Sep) Brochures, free local calls and free internet access. It's in the Antigonish Mall parking lot at the junction of Hwys 104 and 7.

ℹ Getting There & Away

Maritime Bus services stop at Bloomfield Centre at St Francis Xavier University.

Pomquet

About 16km east of Antigonish, this tiny Acadian community is on a stunning **beach** with 13 dunes that keep growing; waves dump the equivalent of more than 4000 truckloads of sand on the beach each year. Many bird species frequent the salt marshes behind the dunes.

Cape George

It's a pleasant day cruising this 72km route that loops up Hwy 245 from Antigonish to Malignant Cove and around Cape George. It's been dubbed a 'mini Cabot Trail' but really the two routes are quite different; Cape George is much less mountainous and forested and has more beaches.

From a well-marked picnic area close to **Cape George Point Lighthouse**, a 1km walk leads to the lighthouse itself. It's automated and not that big, but there are lovely views to Cape Breton Island and PEI. Signs at the picnic area point to longer hikes through forests and coastal areas, including one 32km loop.

You can also start exploring these trails from the wharf at **Ballantyne's Cove**, one of the prettiest communities in Nova Scotia. To walk from the wharf to the lighthouse and back again is an 8km trip. Also stop in at the **Ballantyne's Cove Tuna Interpretive Centre** (☎902-863-8162; 57 Ballantyne's Cove Wharf Rd; ☻10am-7:30pm Jul-Sep) **FREE** for displays on both the fish and the fishery. A fish-and-chip van parks nearby.

CAPE BRETON ISLAND

Floating over the rest of Nova Scotia like an island halo, Cape Breton is a heavenly, forested realm of bald eagles, migrating whales, palpable history and foot-tapping music. Starting up the Ceilidh Trail along the western coastline, Celtic music vibrates through the pubs and community centers, eventually reaching the Cabot Trail where more-eclectic Acadian-style tunes ring out around Chéticamp.

The 300km Cabot Trail continues around Cape Breton Highlands National Park. It winds and climbs around and over coastal mountains, with heart-stopping ocean views at every turn, moose on the roads (watch out!) and plenty of trails to stop and hike.

Take a side trip to Glace Bay to learn firsthand about the region's coal-mining history; Fortress Louisbourg in the east, to get a taste of 18th-century military life; or the Highland Village Museum in Iona, to get some visuals of what life was like for early Scottish immigrants. The region around Bras d'Or Lake offers opportunities to explore the past and present of the Mi'kmaq First Nation and in Baddeck you can learn everything you ever wanted to know about Alexander Graham Bell.

Most tourists visit in July and August, and many restaurants, accommodations and VICs are only open from mid-June through September. **Celtic Colours** (www.celtic-colours.com; ☻Oct), a wonderful roving music festival that attracts top musicians from Scotland, Spain and other countries with Celtic connections, helps extend the season into the fall, a superb time to visit.

Port Hastings & Port Hawkesbury

Cape Breton Island ceased to be a true island when the Canso Causeway was built across the Strait of Canso in 1955. A big and busy **visitors information center** (VIC; ☎902-625-4201; 96 Hwy 4; ☻9am-8pm) is on your right as you drive onto Cape Breton Island. This is definitely worth a stop: there are few other information centers on Cape Breton, especially outside of July and August; the staff is very well informed; and one wall is covered with posters advertising square dances and ceilidhs.

If you need lunch or a kick of caffeine, stop in at **Haven Coffee Bar** (3 Water St, Port Hawkesbury; sandwiches $6.75; ☻8am-5pm Mon-Fri). They bake their own bread, brew a fine cup of joe and provide a cozy place to enjoy it all on the waterfront, although there's not much of a view.

Ceilidh Trail

Take a hard left immediately after leaving the Port Hastings VIC to get on the Ceilidh Trail (Hwy 19), which snakes along the western coast of the island. Then put on your dancing shoes: this area was settled by Scots with fiddles in hand and is renowned for its ceilidh music performances, square dances and parties.

For a great introduction to local culture, visit the **Celtic Music Interpretive Centre** (☎902-787-2708; www.celticmusiccentre.com; 5473 Hwy 19, Judique; admission $12; ☻9am-5pm Mon-Fri Jun-Aug). Half-hour tours (which can be self-guided if you arrive when no guides are available) include a fiddle lesson and a dance step or two. Square dances are advertised around the admissions desk – try a Saturday dance at the community hall in West Mabou or a Thursday evening dance in Glencoe Mills. Ceilidhs at the music center itself are held at 11:30am Monday to Friday during summer.

Creignish B&B (☎902-625-5709; www.bb-canada.com/159.html; 2154 Hwy 19; s/d $30/60; ☻Jun-Nov) is a 'recycled school house' that's been turned into a guesthouse and artist's haven. Wildflowers, shells and bones are everywhere and there's even a giant stuffed tuna hanging on the ceiling. 'Improvised' arts and crafts classes are offered and owner Sandra can point you to the best-hidden secrets of Cape Breton Island. Rooms are large and comfortable, and the B&B is only a 10-minute drive from the causeway.

Mabou

Although it looks unlikely at first glance, micro Mabou is the not-so-underground hot spot of Cape Breton's Celtic music scene. Among lush hills and quiet inlets you can hike away your days and dance away your nights – and don't forget to scorch your tonsils with single malt whiskey at the distillery down the road.

◉ Sights & Activities

Mabou is more a place to experience than to see specific sights. Take any turn off Hwy 19 and see where it takes you.

★ Glenora Inn & Distillery   DISTILLERY
(📞902-258-2662, 800-839-0491; www.glenoradistillery.com; Hwy 19; guided tours incl tasting $7; ⏰tours hourly 9am-5pm Jun-Oct) Take a tour and taste the rocket fuel at the only distillery making single malt whiskey in Canada. Then, stop for an excellent meal at the gourmet pub (there are daily lunchtime and dinner ceilidhs) or even for the night. Cave-like rooms ($125 to $150 per night) are perfect for sleeping it off if you've been drinking the local beverage; the chalets ($175 to $240) are a better choice if you want brighter surroundings. It's 9km north of Mabou.

Cape Mabou Highlands   HIKING
Within the Cape Mabou Highlands, an extensive network of hiking trails extends between Mabou and Inverness toward the coast west of Hwy 19. The trails are sometimes closed when the fire danger is high; otherwise, hikes ranging from 4km to 12km start from three different trailheads. An excellent trail guide ($5) is available at the grocery store across the road from the Mull Café & Deli when the trails are open. Maps are also posted at the trailheads.

🛏 Sleeping & Eating

Clayton Farm B&B   B&B $$
(📞902-945-2719; 11247 Hwy 19; s/d $75/100; ⏰May-Nov; @🛜) This 1835 farmhouse sits on a working red-angus ranch and is run by hardworking Isaac Smith. Paraphernalia of old Cape Breton life and of Isaac's family are casually scattered throughout the common areas and comfortable guest rooms. It's rustically perfect.

Duncreigan Country Inn   INN $$
(📞902-945-2207, 800-840-2207; www.duncreigan.ca; Hwy 19; r incl breakfast $135-195; 🛜) Nestled in oak trees on the banks of the river, this inn has private, spacious rooms, some with terraces and water views. Bikes are available to guests and there's a licensed dining room that serves breakfast to guests or dinner by reservation (mains $10 to $23).

★ Red Shoe Pub   PUB $$
(📞902-945-2996; www.redshoepub.com; 11533 Hwy 19; mains $9-22; ⏰11:30am-11pm Mon-Wed, to 2am Thu-Sat, noon-11pm Sun) Straddling the spine of the Ceilidh Trail, this pub is the beating heart of Mabou. Gather round a local fiddle player (often from the Rankin family) while enjoying a pint and a superb meal. The desserts, including the gingerbread with rum-butterscotch sauce and fruit compote, are divine. Don't be afraid to stay on after dinner to get to know some locals and maybe a few travelers, too. Check the website for details of performances.

Inverness

Row upon row of company housing betrays the history of coal mining in Inverness, the first town of any size on the coast. Its history and people are captured evocatively by writer Alistair MacLeod. His books are for sale at the **Bear Paw** (📞902-258-2528; Hwy 19), next to the Royal Bank.

Beginning near the fishing harbor, there are kilometers of sandy **beach** with comfortable water temperatures in late summer. A **boardwalk** runs 1km along the beach.

In the old train station just back from the beach, the **Inverness Miners' Museum** (📞902-258-3822; 62 Lower Railway St; admission by donation; ⏰9am-5pm Mon-Fri, noon-5pm Sat & Sun) presents local history. **Inverness County Centre for the Arts** (📞902-258-2533; www.invernessarts.ca; 16080 Hwy 19; ⏰10am-5pm) is a beautiful establishment with several galleries and an upmarket gift shop featuring work by local and regional artists. It's also a music venue with a floor built for dancing, of course.

MacLeods Inn B&B (📞902-253-3360; www.macleods.com; Broad Cove Rd, off Hwy 19; r $75-125; ⏰mid-Jun–mid-Oct; 🛜) is a high-end B&B for a not-so-high-end price about 5km north of Inverness. The house is big and modern, but the decoration is in keeping with Cape Breton heritage.

Cabot Trail & Cape Breton Highlands National Park

One of Canada's most dramatic parks and its lively surrounds are accessible via the famous Cabot Trail. The drive is at its best along the northwestern shore of Cape Breton and then down to Pleasant Bay. Be sure to take advantage of the many stops for scenic views; otherwise, keep your eyes on this very circuitous road. Of course, it's even better if you can explore on foot, hiking through a tapestry of terrain to reach vistas looking out over an endless, icy ocean.

Chéticamp

While Mabou is the center of Celtic music, lively Chéticamp throws in some folky notes and French phrases to get your feet moving to Acadian tunes. The town owes much of its cultural preservation to its geographical isolation; the road didn't make it this far until 1949. Today, it's a gateway to Cape Breton Highlands National Park, and has some top-notch museums and live-music opportunities – there's always something going on. The 1893 Church of St Pierre dominates the town with its silver spire and colorful frescoes, but the rest of this seaside town is modern and drab.

Chéticamp is also known for its crafts, particularly hooked rugs, and as a pioneer of the cooperative movement. Check out the rug displays at Les Trois Pignons and take notice of all those co-ops around town: the Credit Union, co-op grocery store, and more.

Visitors information and internet access are available at Les Trois Pignons.

⊙ Sights & Activities

Les Trois Pignons   MUSEUM
(☑ 902-224-2642; www.lestroispignons.com; 15584 Cabot Trail; admission $5; ⊙ 9am-5pm) This excellent museum explains how rug hooking went from being a home-based activity to an international business. Artifacts, including hooked rugs, illustrate early life and artisanship in Chéticamp. Almost everything here – from bottles to rugs – was collected by one eccentric local resident.

Centre de la Mi-Carême   MUSEUM
(☑ 902-224-1016; www.micareme.ca; 12615 Cabot Trail; admission $5; ⊙ 9am-5pm) Mi-Carême, celebrated in the middle of Lent, is Chéticamp's answer to Mardi Gras. Locals wear masks and disguises and visit houses, trying to get people to guess who they are. This museum covers the history of the celebration and displays traditional masks.

Whale Cruisers   BOAT TOUR
(☑ 902-224-3376, 800-813-3376; www.whalecruisers.com; Government Wharf; adult/child $38/17) Several operators sell tours from the Government Wharf, across and down from the church. Captain Cal is the most experienced and offers three-hour expeditions up to four times daily. It's wise to reserve your trip a day in advance in midsummer.

🛏 Sleeping & Eating

Accommodations are tight throughout July and August. It's advisable to call ahead or arrive early in the afternoon.

THE ACADIANS

When the French first settled the area around the Minas Basin, they called the region Arcadia, a Greek and Roman term for 'pastoral paradise.' This became Acadia and by the 18th century, the Acadians felt more connection with the land here than with the distant Loire Valley they'd come from.

To the English, however, they would always be French, with whom rivalry and suspicion was constant. Considering it an affront to their Catholic faith, the Acadians refused to take an oath of allegiance to the English king after the Treaty of Utrecht granted Nova Scotia to the British. When hard-line lieutenant governor Charles Lawrence was appointed in 1754, he became fed up with the Acadians and ordered their deportation. The English burned many villages and forced some 14,000 Acadians onto ships.

Many Acadians headed for Louisiana and New Orleans; others went to various Maritime points, New England, Martinique in the Caribbean, Santo Domingo in the Dominican Republic, or back to Europe. Not once were they greeted warmly with open arms. Some hid out and remained in Acadia. In later years many of the deported people returned but found their lands occupied. In Nova Scotia, Acadians resettled the Chéticamp area on Cape Breton Island and the French Shore north of Yarmouth. New Brunswick has a large French population stretching up the east coast past the Acadian Peninsula at Caraquet.

Maison Fiset House B&B $$
(☑ 902-224-1794, 855-292-1794; www.maisonfiset-house.com; 15050 Cabot Trail; r $169-219; ☎) A little luxury in Chéticamp is found in this grand old 1895 home, once owned by the town's first doctor. If you're in a suite, lounge in your Jacuzzi tub and enjoy the ocean views. Most importantly, experience the full-fledged Acadian hospitality from your host Lyne.

Chéticamp Outfitters Inn B&B B&B $$
(☑ 902-224-2776; www.cheticampns.com/cheticampoutfitters; 13938 Cabot Trail; r $65-120, chalet with kitchen $135; ⊘ Apr-Nov; ☎) Just 2km south of town, this place offers a range of well-priced choices in Acadian style. Views stretch from the sea to the mountain, wildflowers burst from every corner of the garden, and you might even see a passing moose. Very full breakfasts are served in the panoramic dining area by energetic hosts.

Acadian Crafts & Cuisine ACADIAN $$
(☑ 902-224-2170; 15067 Main St; mains $10-15; ⊘ 9am-9pm) This Acadian-only restaurant serves home-style dishes, such as Laurette's meat pie (an Acadian-style pork pie) or get a sample plate to try a bit of everything. Ruddy-cheeked serving ladies wear traditional Acadian bonnets and treat everyone like kin.

☆ Entertainment

Doryman's Beverage Room LIVE MUSIC
(☑ 902-224-9909; 15528 Cabot Trail) This drinking establishment hosts 'sessions' (cover $8), with a fiddler and piano players from Mabou each Saturday (2pm to 6pm), and an acoustic Acadian group at 8pm Sunday, Tuesday, Wednesday and Friday.

Cape Breton Highlands National Park

One-third of the Cabot Trail runs through this extensive **park** (www.pc.gc.ca/capebreton; adult/child/vehicle & passengers $7.80/3.90/19.60) of woodland, tundra, bog and startling sea views. Established in 1936 and encompassing 20% of Cape Breton's landmass, it's the fancy feather in Nova Scotia's island cap.

There are two park entrances: one at Chéticamp and one at Ingonish. Purchase an entry permit at either park entrance. A one-day pass is good until noon the next day. Wheelchair-accessible trails are indicated on the free park map available at either entrance.

🏃 Activities

Hiking

Two trails on the west coast of the park have spectacular ocean views. **Fishing Cove Trail** gently descends 330m over 8km to the mouth of rugged Fishing Cove River. You can opt for a steeper and shorter hike of 2.8km from a second trailhead about 5km north of the first. Double the distances if you plan to return the same day. Otherwise, you must preregister for one of eight backcountry sites ($9.80) at the Chéticamp Information Centre (p91). Reviews of trails in and near the park are available at www.cabottrail.com.

Most other trails are shorter and close to the road, many leading to ridge tops for impressive views of the coast. The best of these is **Skyline Trail**, a 7km loop that puts you on the edge of a headland cliff right above the water. The trailhead is about 5.5km north of Corney Brook Campground.

Just south of Neil's Harbour, on the eastern coast of the park, the **Coastal Trail** runs 11km round-trip and covers more gentle coastline.

Cycling

Don't make this your inaugural trip: the riding is tough, there are no shoulders in many sections and you must be comfortable sharing the incredible scenery with RVs. Alternatively, you can mountain bike on four inland trails in the park. Only **Branch Pond Lookoff Trail** offers ocean views.

Sea Spray Outdoor Adventures (☑ 902-383-2732; www.cabot-trail-outdoors.com; 1141 White Point Rd; bicycle rental per day/week $45/160; ⊘ 9am-5pm Jun-Oct) in Smelt Brook near Dingwall rents bikes and will do emergency repairs on the road. It also offers help planning trips and leads organized cycling, kayaking and hiking tours.

🛏 Sleeping

Towns around the park offer a variety of accommodations. Cape Breton Highlands National Park has six drive-in **campgrounds** (campsites/RV sites from $17.60/29.40) with discounts after three days. Most sites are first-come, first-served, but wheelchair-accessible sites, group campsites and backcountry sites can be reserved for $9.80. In the smaller campgrounds, further from the park entrances, just pick a site and self-register. To camp at any of the three larger ones near the park entrances, register at the closest information center.

The 162-site **Chéticamp Campground** is behind the information center. There are no 'radio free' areas, so peace and quiet is not guaranteed.

Corney Brook (20 sites), 10km further north, is a particularly stunning campground high over the ocean. There's a small playground, but it would be a nerve-racking place to camp with small kids. **MacIntosh Brook** (10 sites) is an open field 3km east of Pleasant Bay. It has wheelchair-accessible sites. **Big Intervale** (10 sites) is near a river 11km west of Cape North.

Near the eastern park entrance, you have a choice of the 256-site **Broad Cove Campground** at Ingonish and the 90-site **Ingonish Campground**, near Keltic Lodge at Ingonish Beach. Both have wheelchair-accessible sites. These large campgrounds near the beach are popular with local families in midsummer.

From late October to early May, you can camp at the Chéticamp and Ingonish Campgrounds for $22, including firewood. In truly inclement weather, tenters can take refuge in cooking shelters with woodstoves.

❶ Information

Chéticamp Information Centre (☎902-224-2306; www.parkscanada.gc.ca; 16646 Cabot Trail; ⊗8:30am-7pm) Has displays and a relief map of the park, plus a bookstore. Ask the staff for advice on hiking or camping.

Ingonish Information Centre (☎902-285-2535; 37677 Cabot Trail; ⊗8am-8pm May-Oct) On the eastern edge of the park, it's much smaller than the center at Chéticamp and has no bookstore.

Pleasant Bay

A perfect base for exploring the park, Pleasant Bay is a carved-out bit of civilization hemmed in on all sides by wilderness. It's an active fishing harbor known for its whale-watching tours and Tibetan monastery. If you are in the area on Canada Day (July 1), try to be in the stands for the annual monks versus townspeople baseball game. There are lots of fish-and-chip and burger places around town, but no really special places to eat.

◉ Sights & Activities

Gampo Abbey   MONASTERY
(☎902-224-2752; www.gampoabbey.org; ⊗tours 1:30-3:30pm Mon-Fri Jun-Sep) This abbey, 8km north of Pleasant Bay past the village of Red River, is a monastery for followers of Tibetan Buddhism. Ane Pema Chödrön is the founding director of the abbey and a noted Buddhist author, but you aren't likely to see her here as she is often on the road. You can visit the grounds any time during the day, but you get a more authentic experience with a tour – a friendly monk escorts you.

Whale Interpretive Centre   MUSEUM
(☎902-224-1411; www.whalecentre.ca; 104 Harbour Rd; adult/child $5/4; ⊗9am-5pm Jun-Oct) Stop here before taking a whale-watching tour from the adjacent wharf. Park entrance permits are for sale, and internet access is available at the C@P site downstairs.

Pollett's Cove   HIKING
The popular, challenging 20km-return hiking trail to Pollett's Cove begins at the end of the road to Gampo Abbey. There are great views along the way and perfect spots to camp when you arrive at the abandoned fishing community. This is not a Parks Canada trail, so it can be rough underfoot.

Captain Mark's Whale &
Seal Cruise   BOAT TOUR
(☎902-224-1316, 888-754-5112; www.whaleandsealcruise.com; adult $35-44, child $15-22; ⊗May-Sep) Depending on the season, two to five daily tours can be taken in the lower-priced 'Cruiser' motorboat or closer to the action in a Zodiac. Captain Mark promises not only guaranteed whales, but also time to see seabirds and seals, as well as Gampo Abbey. There's a discount of up to 10% if you reserve a spot on the earliest (9:30am) or latest (5pm) tour. Tours leave from the wharf next to the Whale Interpretive Centre.

🛏 Sleeping

Cabot Trail Backpackers   HOSTEL $
(☎902-224-1976; www.cabottrail.com/hostel; 23349 Cabot Trail; dm/r $28/68; @🛜) Bright and basic, this very friendly 18-bed hostel has a common kitchen and barbecue area. The office for Cabot Trail Whale Watching is here.

Bay St Lawrence

Bay St Lawrence is a picturesque little fishing village at the very north edge of Cape Breton Island.

Captain Cox (☑888-346-5556, 902-383-2981; Bay St Lawrence Wharf; adult/child $45/25) has been taking people to see whales aboard the 35ft *Northern Gannet* since 1986. He does trips at 10:30am, 1:30pm and 4:30pm in July and August. Call for spring and fall schedules.

Jumping Mouse Campground (☑902-383-2914; www.ecocamping.ca; 3360 Bay St Lawrence Rd; campsites/cabins $25/40; ⊙Jun-Sep) is an ecofriendly campground with 10 oceanfront sites (no cars allowed). Reservations are accepted for multinight stays and for a beautifully built four-bunk cabin. There are hot showers, a cooking shelter, frequent whale sightings and the whole place is nearly bug-free.

To enjoy Aspy Bay and its spectacular beach just for an afternoon, stop at nearby **Cabot's Landing Provincial Park** (www.parks.gov.ns.ca).

Meat Cove

The northernmost road in Nova Scotia finishes at the steep, emerald coast of Meat Cove, 13km northwest of Bay St Lawrence (the last 7km of the road is gravel). As well as watching for frolicking whales in unbelievably clear water, keep an eye on the earth for orchids – some rare species here aren't found anywhere else in Nova Scotia.

� Activities

Cape St Lawrence Lighthouse HIKING
From Meat Cove, a 16km hiking trail continues west to Cape St Lawrence lighthouse and Lowland Cove. Spend an hour gazing over the ocean and you're guaranteed to see pods of pilot whales. They frolic here all spring, summer, and into the fall. Carry a compass and refrain from exploring side paths; locals have gotten lost in this area.

Grassy Point HIKING
For a shorter hike, you can't beat the views over the coast from Grassy Point. The small foot trail (about 40 minutes return) starts just past the campground. Sit for a while at the point to look for whales and nesting bald eagles.

🛏 Sleeping

At the time of research, the old Meat Cove Lodge across from the Welcome Center had been torn down and the owner had plans to build a new structure. Check online or ask around starting from the 2014 summer season.

Meat Cove Campground CAMPGROUND $
(☑902-383-2379, 902-383-2658; www.meatcove-campground.com; 2475 Meat Cove Rd; campsites $25-30, cabins $60; ⊙Jun-Nov) Meat Cove Campground is spectacular, perched on a grassy bluff high above the ocean out in the middle of nowhere. Four cabins with no electricity or plumbing share the magnificent view; bring your own bedding. Be prepared for high winds.

Hine's Ocean View Lodge HOSTEL $
(☑902-383-2512; www.hinesoceanviewlodge.ca; r $60; ☎⚡) This isolated spot, high up its own road (signposted off Meat Cove Road), has plain almost-dormitory style rooms and a shared kitchen. Cash only.

ⓘ Information

Meat Cove Welcome Center (☑902-383-2284; 2296 Meat Cove Rd; ⊙8am-8:30pm Jul-Sep) Stop by the Meat Cove Welcome Center to get excellent information on hiking trails, check email and grab a bite to eat (from sandwiches to lobster suppers). Leave your car here if there's no room at the trailhead.

Ingonish

At the eastern entrance to Cape Breton Highlands National Park are Ingonish and Ingonish Beach, small towns lost in the background of motels and cottages. This is a long-standing popular destination, but there are few real attractions. There are several hiking trails and an information center nearby in the national park.

◉ Sights & Activities

Ingonish Beach BEACH
This long, wide strip of sand is tucked in a bay surrounded by green hills.

Highlands Links Golf Course GOLF
(☑800-441-1118, 902-285-2600; www.highlandslinksgolf.com; per round $91) Reputed to be one of the best golf courses in the world.

🛏 Sleeping & Eating

Driftwood Lodge   INN $
(📞 902-285-2558; www.driftwoodlodge.ca; 36125 Cabot Trail; r $55, ste with kitchen $85-100; ☉ May-Nov; 🕸) Located 8km north of the Ingonish park entrance, this funky cabin-meets-hotel establishment is a steal. The owner works at the park and is a mine of info about hiking and activities. There's a fine-sand beach just below the lodge.

Keltic Lodge   HOTEL $$$
(📞 902-285-2880, 800-565-0444; www.signature-resorts.com; Ingonish Beach; r $155-280, cottages $315-395; ☉ May-Oct; 🕸🏊🍴) The finest digs in the area are scattered within this theatrical Tudor-style resort erected in 1940. It shares Middle Head Peninsula with the famous **golf course** and the **Ingonish Campground**. The lodge is worth visiting even if you're not a guest for its setting and the **hiking trail** to the tip of the peninsula just beyond the resort.

You must have a valid entry permit to the national park, as the lodge, the golf course and the hiking trail are all within park boundaries.

★ **Main Street Restaurant & Bakery**   CANADIAN $$
(📞 902-285-2225; 37764 Cabot Trail, Ingonish Beach; lunch around $10, dinner $10-24; ☉ 7am-9pm Tue-Sat) By far the best breakfast stop (from $6) near the park and also a great stop for lunch and dinner. Sandwiches and French toast are made with thick fresh bread and the seafood plates are immense.

The specialty is the lobster angel-hair pasta with crab and mussels in a brandy cream sauce, but the lobster dinners get our vote for best value of its kind on the island.

White Point to Neil's Harbour

On your way south to Ingonish, leave the Cabot Trail to follow the rugged, windswept White Point Rd via Smelt Brook to the fishing villages of **White Point** and **Neil's Harbour**. These are gritty, hard-working towns, but there is some nice architecture, colorful homes, and illuminated, slightly disorienting views of Cape North to Meat Cove when the sun hits them at the end of the day. These are villages where there are as many fishing boats as houses – the area feels distinctly off the beaten tourist track.

Stay the night at homey **Two Tittle** (📞 866-231-4087, 902-383-2817; www.twotittle.com; 2119 White Point Rd, White Point; r $60-100; 🕸), which smells like supper and whose grandparent-like proprietors are in most evenings watching *Wheel of Fortune*. Don't miss the short but gorgeous walk out back to the Two Tittle Islands the B&B is named for and look out for whales and eagles.

The perfect stop for lunch or dinner is **Chowder House** (chowder from $6, suppers from $14; ☉ 11am-8:30pm), out beyond the lighthouse at Neil's Harbour. It's famous for its chowder, but also serves great-value suppers of snow crab, lobster, mussels and more. There are plenty of dining locals, who like to chat with folks from far away while they splatter themselves with seafood juice.

Around St Ann's Bay

Settle into the artsy calm of winding roads, serene lakes, eagles soaring overhead and a never-ending collection of artists' workshops that dot the Cabot Trail like Easter eggs. Although you could skip the drive around St Ann's Bay and take a $5.50 ferry to Englishtown, you'd be missing a unique leg of the trail. If you explore deeper, you'll discover walking trails to waterfalls, and scenic vistas, Mi'kmaw culture and a decidedly interesting mishmash of characters.

👁 Sights & Activities

Don't leave the area without stopping in at an **artist's workshop** or two; you'll find pottery, leather and pewter workers, a crazy wonderful hat shop and more. The artists are easy to find – just keep an eye out for signs along the main road.

Gaelic College of Celtic Arts & Crafts   CULTURAL BUILDING
(📞 902-295-3411; www.gaeliccollege.edu; 51779 Cabot Trail; 5-day course incl lodging $705-805; ☉ 9am-5pm Jun-Oct) At the end of St Ann's Bay, the college teaches Scottish Gaelic, bagpipe playing, Highland dancing, weaving and more. The college's **Great Hall of the Clans Museum** (admission $3) traces Celtic history from ancient times to the Highland clearances.

🛏 Sleeping & Eating

The Maven Gypsy B&B & Cottages   B&B $$
(📞 902-929-2246; www.themavengypsy.com; 41682 Cabot Trail, Wreck Cove; r $92-117; ☉ Jun-Nov; 🕸🍴) At this adorable butter-yellow cottage three minutes' walk to the beach,

enjoy friendly hosts and fresh baked goods for breakfast.

Chanterelle Country Inn & Cottages INN $$
(☑ 902-929-2263, 866-277-0577; www.chanterelle-inn.com; 48678 Cabot Trail, North River; r $145-225, restaurant mains $20-28, 4-course set menu veg/nonveg $38/45; ☺ May-Nov; 🐾) ❧ Unparalleled as an environmentally friendly place to stay, the house and cabins are on 60 hectares overlooking rolling pastures and bucolic bliss. Meals (breakfast and dinner) are served on the screened-in porch. If you're not staying, you can reserve for dinner at the highly reputed restaurant.

Clucking Hen Deli & Bakery CAFE $
(☑ 902-929-2501; 45073 Cabot Trail; mains $5-15; ☺ 7am-7pm May-Oct) A sign reads 'no fowl moods in here.' Listen to the local 'hens' cluck away while you eat a delicious meal of homemade breads, soup and salad.

Bras d'Or Lake & Around

The highlands meet the lowlands along the shores of this inland saltwater sea, where eagles nest and puffins play. At 1099 sq km, it's the biggest lake in Nova Scotia and all but cleaves Cape Breton Island in two.

Baddeck

An old resort town in a pastoral setting, Baddeck is on the north shore of Bras d'Or Lake, halfway between Sydney and the Canso Causeway. It's the most popular place to stay for those who intend to do the Cabot Trail as a one-day scenic drive.

⊙ Sights & Activities

★ **Alexander Graham Bell National Historic Site** MUSEUM
(☑ 902-295-2069; www.parkscanada.gc.ca; 559 Chebucto St; adult/child $7.80/3.90; ☺ 9am-6pm) The inventor of the telephone is buried near his summer home, Beinn Bhreagh, which is visible across the bay from Baddeck. The excellent museum of the Alexander Graham Bell National Historic Site, at the eastern edge of town, covers all aspects of his inventions and innovations.

Although nothing looks spectacular at first glance, it's the story of the man that will hook you. See medical and electrical devices, telegraphs, telephones, kites and seaplanes and then learn about how they all work.

Bras d'Or Lakes & Watershed Interpretive Centre MUSEUM
(☑ 902-295-1675; www.brasdor-conservation.com; 532 Chebucto St; admission by donation; ☺ 11am-7pm Jun-Oct) This center explores the unique ecology of the enormous saltwater lake.

Amoeba SAILING
(www.amoebasailingtours.com; 2hr tours $25; ☺ Jun-Oct) Classic schooner sailing tours on the Bras d'Or Lake bring you past Alexander Graham Bell's grand Beinn Bhreagh mansion and under soaring bald eagles.

🛏 Sleeping & Eating

Broadwater Inn & Cottages INN $$
(☑ 902-295-1101, 877-818-3474; www.broadwater.baddeck.com; 975 Bay Rd; r $95-150, ste $225, cottages $105-225; ☺ May-Nov; 🐾🐕) In a tranquil spot 1.5km east of Baddeck, this c 1830 home once belonged to JAD McCurdy, who worked with Alexander Graham Bell on early aircraft designs. The rooms in the inn are full of character, have bay views and are decorated with subtle prints and lots of flair. Modern self-contained cottages are set in the woods and are great for families.

Only the B&B rooms include breakfast.

Mother Gaelic's B&B $$
(☑ 902-295-2885, 888-770-3970; www.mother-gaelics.com; 26 Water St; d $105, with shared bath $60-80; ☺ May-Oct) Named for the owner's great-grandmother, who was a bootlegger patronized by Alexander Graham Bell, this sweet cottage opposite the waterfront has the feel of an uncluttered summer home.

Lynwood Inn INN $$
(☑ 902-295-1995; www.lynwoodinn.com; 441 Shore Rd; r $100-230; 🐾) Rooms in this enor-

---

DON'T MISS

HIGHLAND VILLAGE MUSEUM

Explore Scottish heritage through the **Highland Village Museum** (☑ 902-725-2272; http://highlandvillage.novascotia.ca; 4119 Hwy 223 Iona; adult/child $9/4; ☺ 9:30am-5:30pm), a living history museum perched on a hilltop overlooking the Bras d'Or Lake. Costumed Scots demonstrate day-to-day activities of early settlers' lives and there are Celtic-inspired workshops from spring through fall – check the website for scheduling.

mous inn go far beyond the hotel standard, with Victorian wooden beds, muted color schemes and airy, spacious living spaces. There's a family-style restaurant downstairs that serves breakfast, lunch and dinner; breakfast is not included in room rates.

Highwheeler Cafe & Deli CAFE $
(486 Chebucto St; sandwiches $9; ⊘ 6am-8pm) This place bakes great bread and goodies (some gluten-free), and makes big tasty sandwiches (including vegetarian), quesadillas, soups and more. Finish off on the sunny deck licking an ice-cream cone. Box lunches for hikers are also available.

Baddeck Lobster Suppers SEAFOOD $$$
(☑ 902-925-3307; 17 Ross St; dinners $33; ⊘ 4-9pm Jun-Oct) In the former legion hall, this high production, arguably high-priced institution gets live lobsters in the pot then to you lickety-split. Meals come with just about everything and, although not spectacularly prepared, could fuel you for days.

☆ Entertainment

Baddeck Gathering Ceilidhs LIVE MUSIC
(☑ 902-295-2794; www.baddeckgathering.com; St Michael's Parish Hall, 8 Old Margaree Rd; adult/child $10/5; ⊘ 7:30pm Jul & Aug) Nightly fiddling and dancing. The parish hall is just opposite the VIC right in the middle of town.

❶ Information

Visit Baddeck (www.visitbaddeck.com) Has maps, and info on tour operators, golf courses and more.
Visitors Information Centre (VIC; ☑ 902-295-1911; 454 Chebucto St; ⊘9am-7pm Jun-Sep)

Wagmatcook & Around

Stop in the Mi'kmaw community of Wagmatcook just west of Baddeck to visit the **Wagmatcook Culture & Heritage Centre** (☑ 902-295-2492, 902-295-2999; www.wagmatcook.com; Hwy 105; ⊘ 9am-8pm May-Oct, call for hours Nov-Apr) This somewhat empty cultural attraction offers an entryway into Mi'kmaw culture and history.

★ **Bear on the Lake Guesthouse** (☑ 866-718-5253; www.bearonthelake.com; 10705 Hwy 105; dm/r $32/78; ⊜), between Wagmatcook and the next town of Whycocomagh, is a fun place overlooking the lake. Everything is set up for backpacker bliss, from the drive-share board to the big sunny deck and inviting communal areas. This place is so

popular that a whole other building of two dorm rooms and a kitchen was being built in a beautiful forest when we passed; there are also rooms with private sitting areas on the top level of the house. Owner Carmen is the perfect social soldier.

Also on Hwy 105, 12km southwest of Baddeck, is **Herring Choker Deli** (☑ 902-295-2275; 1958 Hwy 105; sandwiches $4.85; ⊘9am-5pm). Arguably the region's best pit stop, the deli serves gourmet sandwiches, soups and salads. Or drive a little farther to the **Dancing Goat** (6289 Cabot Trail, Northeast Margaree; sandwiches $8; ⊘8am-5pm Sat-Thu, to 8pm Fri), which is out of the way (it's 32 km from the Margaree Forks turnoff from Hwy 105), but worth the drive. Everything is homemade, most ingredients are local and hearty breakfasts are as good as you'll get on Cape Breton. Big sandwiches and salads can be eaten in or taken away for hiking. A second, more convenient location is planned in Inverness.

North Sydney

North Sydney is a small, friendly industrial town with few sites, though there are some excellent-value places to stay and eat.

Reserve accommodations if you're coming in on a late ferry or going out on an early one. Most North Sydney motels and B&Bs are open year-round, and it's understood that guests will arrive and leave at all hours. Most places to stay are along Queen St about 2km west of the ferry terminal.

🛏 Sleeping & Eating

Heritage Home B&B B&B $
(☑ 866-601-4515, 902-794-4815; www.bbcanada.com/3242.html; 110 Queen St; r $60-100; ⊜⊛) This exceptionally well decorated and maintained Victorian home is an extremely elegant place to stay for the price. Breakfasts are home cooked and most rooms have private bathrooms.

A Boat to Sea B&B $$
(☑ 902-794-8326, 855-580-9540; www.aboattosea.com; 61 Queen St; r $95-105; ⊜⊛) Right on the waterfront and surrounded by beautiful gardens (look for bald eagles), this grand home is decorated with stained glass and a quirky antiques collection. Relax on the waterfront patio and enjoy hearty breakfasts. There are only three rooms, so book ahead in high season.

★**Lobster Pound & Moore**   SEAFOOD **$$**
(✆902-794-2992; 161 Queen St; mains $15-35; ⏱lunch & dinner Tue-Sun) With the standard lobster here weighing in at almost a kilo (2lb), show up hungry because portions are massive. But big quantity doesn't affect the freshness, high quality and all around deliciousness of the food. Try Korean grilled steaks, seafood stew, or the ravioli stuffed with fresh lobster and topped with even more. Decor is chic bistro meets seafood shack.

★**Black Spoon**   MODERN CANADIAN **$$**
(✆902-241-3300; 320 Commercial St; mains $10-17; ⏱11am-8pm Mon-Thu, to 9pm Fri & Sat) At this hip black and beige restaurant, dine on local faves with a delectable twist, like breaded haddock with mango salsa, or the colorful grilled vegetable salad with goat cheese. There's also espresso drinks, cocktails and a reasonable wine list.

❶ Getting There & Away

Marine Atlantic ferry (✆800-341-7981; www.marine-atlantic.ca) services Newfoundland.
Maritime Bus runs regular services to Halifax (one-way $68.50).

Bay Luxury Shuttle (✆855-673-8083; www.capebretonshuttle.ca) runs from Glace Bay to Halifax (one-way $65) via North Sydney, Sydney and Hwy 105; you can get it to stop or pick up along the way.

Sydney

POP 31,597

The second-biggest city in Nova Scotia and the only real city on Cape Breton Island, Sydney is the embattled core of the island's collapsed industrial belt. The now-closed steel mill and coal mines were the region's largest employers and now the city feels a bit empty, but there are some lovely older houses, especially in the North End residential areas where most of the B&Bs are found. Overall, the city is well serviced and you get more bang for your buck staying here as a base to explore Louisbourg and the Cabot Trail than you would in more scenic areas.

⦿ Sights

Downtown, Charlotte St is lined with stores and restaurants and there's a pleasant boardwalk along Esplanade.

The North End historic district has a gritty charm. There are eight buildings older than 1802 in a two-block radius in North End. Three are open to the public.

St Patrick's Church Museum   HISTORIC BUILDING
(✆902-562-8237; 87 Esplanade; admission $2; ⏱9am-5pm) St Patrick's Church Museum is the oldest Catholic church on Cape Breton Island.

Cossit House   HISTORIC BUILDING
(✆902-539-7973; http://cossithouse.novascotia.ca; 75 Charlotte St; adult/concession $2/1; ⏱9am-5pm Mon-Sat, 1-5pm Sun Jun-Oct) The 1787 Cossit House is the oldest house in Sydney.

Jost Heritage House   HISTORIC BUILDING
(✆902-539-0366; 54 Charlotte St; admission $3; ⏱9am-5pm Mon-Sat, 1-5:30pm Sun) Just down the road from Cossit House, Jost Heritage House features a collection of model ships and an assortment of medicines used by an early-20th-century apothecary.

Cape Breton Centre for Heritage & Science   MUSEUM
(✆902-539-1572; 225 George St; admission $2; ⏱9am-5pm Mon-Sat) In the lyceum, this center explores the social and natural history of Cape Breton Island.

⦿ Tours

Ghosts & Legends of Historic Sydney   WALKING TOUR
(✆902-539-1572; www.oldsydney.com; tours per person $12; ⏱7pm Tue & Wed Jul & Aug) This recommended walking tour leaves from St Patrick's Church Museum, does the loop of historic buildings and finishes with tea and scones at the lyceum.

🛏 Sleeping & Eating

Most establishments in Sydney are open year-round.

★**Colby House**   B&B **$$**
(✆902-539-4095; www.colbyhousebb.com; 10 Park St; r $100-120; 🛜) It's worth staying in Sydney for the affordable luxe of this exceptional B&B. The owner used to travel around Canada for work and she decided to offer everything she wished she'd had while on the road. The result is a mix of heritage and modern design, the softest sheets you can imagine, guest bathrobes, plenty of delicious-smelling soaps, chocolates next to the bed and so many other comfort-giving details we can hardly begin to list them.

Gathering House B&B

B&B $$

(📞 866-539-7172, 902-539-7172; www.gatheringhouse.com; 148 Crescent St; r $75-150; 🛜 📶) This welcoming, ramshackle Victorian home is close to the heart of town. Staying here makes you feel like you're part of a big, lively family.

Flavors

MODERN CANADIAN $$

(📞 902-562-6611; 6 Pitt St; lunch/dinner mains around $10/20; ⊙8:30am-8:30pm Mon-Sat; 🍴) What the setting lacks in feng shui – it has small tables and a strange street-side patio setup – the restaurant makes up for in delicious food prepared from locally sourced ingredients. Start with mains like maple-seared salmon or roast pork loin with wild-blueberry sauce, then finish with a homemade ice-cream sandwich with coconut cookies rolled in toffee bits. Vegan and gluten-free options are also available.

Allegro Grill

MODERN CANADIAN $$

(📞 902-562-1623; 222 Charlotte St; mains $9-25; ⊙11am-3pm Mon-Fri, 5-9pm Tue-Fri, 11am-10pm Sat) Seafood and meat lovers should go here. This simple-looking spot serves not-so-simple specialties, including their famous, handmade turkey andouille sausages.

🍷 Drinking & Entertainment

A lot of touring bands make the trek to Sydney. Fiddlers and other traditional musicians from the west coast of the island perform here or at the Savoy in Glace Bay. Gigs are about $12.

Governors Pub & Eatery

PUB

(www.governorseatery.com; 233 Esplanade; mains $9-22; ⊙11am-11pm) Easily the most popular place in Sydney, stop in to mingle with the after-work crowd for drinks, dine on gourmet pub grub made with local ingredients, and stay on for live-music events like Wednesday night Irish jam sessions. Check the website for what's on.

ℹ️ Information

Visitors Information Centre (VIC; 20 Keltic Dr; ⊙8:30am-6pm) Off Kings Rd, just south of town.

ℹ️ Getting There & Away

The Sydney airport is none too busy. Air Canada flies between Sydney and Halifax, while Westjet has direct Toronto flights. **Air St-Pierre** (📞 877-277-7765, 902-562-3140; www.airsaintpierre.com) flies to St-Pierre ($250 one-way, two hours) on Thursdays and Sundays from early July to early September.

Bay Luxury Shuttle (p96) has shuttle services to Halifax.

Glace Bay

Glace Bay, 6km northeast of Sydney, would be just another fading coal town were it not for its exceptional **Cape Breton Miners' Museum** (📞 902-849-4522; www.minersmuseum.com; 42 Birkley St; tour & mine visit adult/child $12/10, restaurant mains $8-14; ⊙museum 10am-6pm, restaurant 11am-8pm); it's off South St less than 2km east from the town center. The highlight of this museum is the adventure under the seafloor to visit closed-down mines with a retired miner as a guide (it's your lucky day if you get Abbie). The museum's **restaurant** is highly recommended and offers seafood, sandwiches and burgers; there's a daily lunch buffet from noon to 2pm.

The town's grand 1920 **Savoy Theatre** (📞 902-842-1577; www.savoytheatre.com; 116 Commercial St) is the region's premier entertainment venue.

Louisbourg

Louisbourg, 37km southeast of Sydney, is famous for its historic fortress. The town itself has plenty of soul, with its working fishing docks, old-timers and a friendly vibe.

⊙ Sights & Activities

Starting from the trailhead at the lighthouse at the end of Havenside Rd, a rugged 6km **trail** follows the coast over bogs, barrens and pre-Cambrian polished granite. Bring your camera to capture the views back toward the fortress at the national historic site.

Louisbourg National Historic Site

HISTORIC SITE

(📞 902-733-2280; 259 Park Service Rd; adult/child $17.60/8.80; ⊙9am-5:30pm) Budget a full day to explore this extraordinary historic site that faithfully re-creates Fortress Louisbourg as it was in 1744, right down to the people – costumed thespians take their characters and run with them. Built to protect French interests in the region, it was also a base for cod fishing and an administrative capital. Louisbourg was worked on continually from 1719 to about 1745. The British took it in a 46-day siege in 1745 but it would change hands twice more. In 1760, after British troops under the command of General James Wolfe took Québec City, the walls of Louisbourg were destroyed and the city was burned to the ground.

In 1961, with the closing of many Cape Breton Island coal mines, the federal government funded the largest historical reconstruction in Canadian history as a way to generate employment, resulting in 50 buildings open to visitors. Workers in period dress take on the lives of typical fort inhabitants.

Free guided tours around the site are offered throughout the day. Travelers with mobility problems can ask for a pass to drive their car up to the site; there are ramps available to access most buildings. Be prepared for lots of walking, and bring a sweater and raincoat even if it's sunny when you start out. There's also an ever-changing array of tours and activities on offer, from nighttime candlelit walks to period dinner theater; check the website for what's on each season.

Though the scale of the reconstruction is massive, three-quarters of Louisbourg is still in ruins. The 2.5km **Ruins Walk** guides you through the untouched terrain and out to the Atlantic coast. A short **interpretive walk** opposite the visitors center discusses the relationship between the French and the Mi'kmaq and offers some great views of the whole site.

Three restaurants in the site serve food typical of the time. **Hotel de la Marine** and the adjacent **L'Épée Royale** (grilled cod with soup $14, 3-course meal $20) are where sea captains and prosperous merchants would dine on fine china with silver cutlery. Servers in period costume also dish out grub at **Grandchamps House** (meals $9-15), a favorite of sailors and soldiers. Wash down beans and sausage with hot buttered rum ($4). Otherwise buy a 1kg ration ($4) of soldiers' bread at the Destouches Bakery. There's also a small coffee shop between the restaurants serving hot drinks and a few snacks.

🛏 Sleeping & Eating

Stacey House B&B   B&B $
(☎902-733-2317; www.bbcanada.com/thestaceyhouse; 7438 Main St; r $60-90; ⊗Jun-Oct; 🗢) Interesting knickknacks, such as antique teddy bears, dolls and model ships, are harmoniously placed throughout this pretty house.

★**Cranberry Cove Inn**   INN $$
(☎800-929-0222, 902-733-2171; www.cranberrycoveinn.com; 12 Wolfe St; r $105-160; ⊗May-Nov; 🗢) From the dark pink facade to the period-perfect interior of mauves, dusty blues and antique lace, you'll be transported back in time through rose-colored glasses at this stunning B&B. Each room is different and several have Jacuzzis and fireplaces.

Spinning Wheel B&B   B&B $$
(☎902-733-3332, 866-272-3222; www.spinningwheelbedandbreakfast.com; 5 Riverdale St; d with shared bathroom $65-75, d with private bathroom $90; ⊗May-Nov; 🗢) Try this place if everything else in town is full, which it will be during high season. It's not a looker, but the cleanliness, friendly hosts and made-to-order breakfasts more than make up for it.

Grubstake   CANADIAN $$
(☎902-733-2308; 7499 Main St; lunch mains $8-17, dinner mains $16-32; ⊗lunch & dinner) This informal restaurant is the best place to eat in town. The menu features burger platters at lunch and pastas and fresh seafood for dinner.

★**Beggar's Banquet**   SEAFOOD $$$
(☎888-374-8439; Point of View Suites, 15 Commercial St Extension; meals $38; ⊗6-8pm Jul-Sep) Finally, here's a chance for you to get into period costume and gorge on a feast of local seafood in a replicated 18th-century tavern. There's a choice of four delicious and copious mains including crab and lobster. It's located at the Point of View Suites.

☆ Entertainment

Louisbourg Playhouse   THEATER
(☎902-733-2996; 11 Lower Warren St; tickets from $15; ⊗8pm-late Jun-Aug) A cast of young, local musicians entertain all summer long in this 17th-century-style theater.

❶ Information

Tourist Information Office (☎902-733-2720; 7535 Main St; ⊗9am-7pm) Right in the center of town.

EASTERN SHORE

If you want to escape into the fog, away from summer tourist crowds, this is the place to do it. Running from Cape Canso at the extreme eastern tip of the mainland to the outskirts of Dartmouth, the Eastern Shore has no large towns and the main road is almost as convoluted as the rugged shoreline it follows. If you want to experience wilderness and are willing to hike or kayak, this is your heaven.

Guysborough

Guysborough was settled by United Empire Loyalists after the American Revolution. Over the years it became another particularly scenic yet economically challenged Eastern Shore village until Glynn Williams and his brand Authentic Seacoasts came to town. With an estimated $8 million investment, the town is now home to a charming waterfront golf course, a craft brewery, a fair-trade coffee company, a bakery-cafe, Debarres Manor inn and the Rare Bird Pub; a huge distillery was planned for construction when we passed. Not only has Guysborough become an activity-filled holiday hamlet, but the community has jobs they may have never had otherwise. Meanwhile, the old-time charm and natural beauty of the place has remained wonderfully intact.

◎ Sights & Activities

The 26km **Guysborough Trail**, part of the Trans Canada Trail (TCT), is great for biking and hiking and the sheltered coves beg to be kayaked

Old Court House Museum   MUSEUM
(✐ 902-533-4008; 106 Church St; ⊙ 9am-5pm Mon-Fri, 10am-4pm Sat & Sun) **FREE** The Old Court House Museum displays artifacts related to early farming and housekeeping. It also offers tourist information and guides to hiking trails.

⊨ Sleeping & Eating

Boylston Provincial Park   CAMPGROUND $
(✐ 902-533-3326; www.parks.gov.ns.ca; off Hwy 16; campsites $18) The 36 shaded sites are never all taken. From the picnic area on the highway below the campground, a footbridge leads to a small island on the coast about 12km north of Guysborough.

★ Desbarres Manor   INN $$$
(✐ 902-533-2099; www.desbarresmanor.com; 90 Church St; r from $199; ☎) This tastefully renovated 1830 grand mansion with massive, opulent rooms is reason enough to come to Guysborough. With extraordinary service, fine dining and a range of activities on of-

fer including canoeing, walking and golfing, it's one of the most luxurious properties in Nova Scotia.

Rare Bird Pub   PUB $$
(✐ 902-533-2128; www.rarebirdpub.com; 80 Main St; mains $9-15; ⊙ 11am-2am) The Bird is a quintessential stop for a swig of local ale, a pot of mussels, rocking live east coast music on weekends and fiddlers on the wharf below on Wednesdays. Check the website for schedules.

Canso

Mainland North America's oldest seaport is a cluster of boxy fishermen's houses on a treeless bank of Chedabucto Bay. Long dependent on the fishery, Canso has been decimated by emigration and unemployment since the northern cod stocks collapsed around 1990.

◎ Sights & Activities

The cape surrounding the village has some very off-the-beaten-track opportunities for hiking, kayaking, birdwatching and surfing.

Grassy Island National Historic Site   HISTORIC SITE
(✐ 902-366-3136; 1465 Union St; admission $3; ⊙ 10am-6pm Jun-Sep) An interpretive center on the waterfront tells the story of Grassy Island National Historic Site, which lies just offshore and can be visited by boat until 4pm. In 1720 the British built a small fort to offset the French who had their headquarters in Louisbourg, but it was totally destroyed in 1744. Among the ruins today, there's a self-guided **hiking trail** with eight interpretive stops explaining the history of the area. The boat to Grassy Island departs from the center upon demand, weather permitting.

Whitman House Museum   MUSEUM
(✐ 902-366-2170; 1297 Union St; ⊙ 9am-5pm Jun-Sep) **FREE** The **tourist office** is at the 1885 Whitman House Museum, which holds reminders of the town's history and offers a good view from the widow's walk on the roof.

Chapel Gully Trail   HIKING
This is a 10km boardwalk and hiking trail along an estuary and out to the coast. It begins near the lighthouse on the hill behind

SABLE ISLAND

This ever-shifting, 44km-long spit of sand lies some 300km southeast of Halifax and has caused more than 350 documented shipwrecks. But what makes Sable Island most famous is that it's home to one of the world's only truly wild horse populations.

The first 60 ancestors of today's Sable Island horses were shipped to the island in 1760 when Acadians were being deported from Nova Scotia by the British. The Acadians were forced to abandon their livestock and it appears that Boston merchant ship owner Thomas Hancock helped himself to their horses then put them to pasture on Sable Island to keep it low profile. The horses that survived became wild.

Today the island works as a research center; scientists come every year, mostly to study the birds, seals and horses. Since 2003, natural gas fields run by Exxon have been working only 10km from the island but, so far, there has been little environmental conflict.

It's complicated and expensive but not impossible to visit Sable Island as a layperson – in fact, about 50 to 100 adventurous souls make it there each year. Contact **Sable Island Station** (☑ 902-453-9350; gforbes@ca.inter.net), in conjunction with Environment Canada, for information about where to get necessary permissions and independently arrange transport.

the hospital at the eastern end of Canso. A large map is posted at the trailhead.

🎏 Festivals & Events

★ **Stan Rogers Folk Festival** MUSIC
(www.stanfest.com; ☉1st weekend Jul) Most people who come to Canso come for the Stan Rogers Folk Festival, the biggest festival in Nova Scotia. It quadruples the town's population, with six stages showcasing folk, blues and traditional musicians from around the world. Accommodations are pretty much impossible to get unless you reserve a year ahead. Locals set up 1000 campsites for the festival; check the website for details and try to get a campsite away from the festival site if sleep is a priority.

🛏 Sleeping

Last Port Motel MOTEL $$
(☑ 902-366-2400; www.lastportmotel.ca; 10 Hwy 16; r $80-100) The only place to stay is the basic Last Port Motel just out of town.

Sherbrooke

The pleasant little town of Sherbrooke, 123km west of Canso and 63km south of Antigonish, is overshadowed by its historic site, which is about the same size.

The local tourist office is at **Sherbrooke Village** (☑902-522-2400; http://sherbrookevillage.novascotia.ca; Hwy 7; adult/child $10.75/4.75; ☉9:30am-5:30pm Jun-Oct), which re-creates everyday life from 125 years ago through buildings, demonstrations and costumed workers. There are 25 buildings to visit in this living museum that effectively helps its visitors step back in time.

On a quiet farm, **Days Ago B&B** (☑866-522-2811, 902-522-2811; www.bbcanada.com/daysago; 15 Cameron Rd; r $70-80, chalet $80-90; 🐾) will lull you with its slower pace. There's a sunporch for sitting on, or you can take out a kayak. Rooms in the house have a shared bathroom, while the loft-style chalet has its own bathroom.

You'll find coffee and good food at godsend **Village Coffee Grind** (sandwiches around $9; ☉8am-6pm Tue-Sat, 10am-2pm Sun) on the town's minuscule main drag.

Taylor Head Provincial Park

A little-known scenic highlight of Nova Scotia, this spectacular **park** (☑902-772-2218; www.parks.gov.ns.ca; 20140 Hwy 7) encompasses a peninsula jutting 6.5km into the Atlantic. On one side is a long, very fine, sandy beach fronting a protected bay. Some 17km of hiking trails cut through the spruce and fir forests. The **Headland Trail** is the longest at 8km round-trip and follows the rugged coastline to scenic views at Taylor Head. The shorter **Bob Bluff Trail** is a 3km round-trip hike to a bluff with good views. In spring you'll see colorful wildflowers, and this is a great birdwatching venue. Pack the picnic cooler and plan on spending a full day hiking, lounging and, if you can brave the cool water, swimming.

Tangier

About 10km southwest of Taylor Head Provincial Park, Tangier is one of the best settings for kayaking in the Maritimes. Highly recommended **Coastal Adventures Sea Kayaking** (☑902-772-2774; www.coastaladventures.com; off Hwy 7; ☉Jun-Sep) offers introductions to sea-kayaking (half-/full-day $75/115), rentals (single/double kayaks $45/65) and guided trips. The establishment also has a cozy, excellent-value B&B, **Paddlers Retreat** (s $50, d $60-85; ☉mid-Jun–mid-Oct; ☎☀).

Murphy's Camping on the Ocean (☑902-772-2700; www.murphyscampingontheocean.ca; 291 Murphy's Rd; campsites/RV sites $27/39, trailer rental $70-90; ☉mid-May–mid-Oct; ☎☀) gets you out of your tent and into the water to collect mussels; you eat your labors at a beach barbecue to the music of yarns told by Brian the owner. There are RV sites, RV rental, secluded tent sites and a very rudimentary room above the dock that can sleep four people. Boat rental is $75 per hour and there's also drop-off and pickup services for camping on the islands.

Don't miss a snack stop at **J Willy Krauch & Sons Ltd** (☑902-772-2188; 35 Old Mooseland Rd, off Hwy 7; ☉10am-5pm Mon-Fri, 9am-5pm Sat & Sun), famed for making the tastiest smoked fish in the province. Choose from a variety of salmon, eel, mackerel and more – don't forget to bring some crackers.

Charlotte Lake to Jedore

The tiny **Fisherman's Life Museum** (☑902-889-2053; http://fishermanslife.novascotia.ca; 58 Navy Pool Loop; adult/child $4/2.75; ☉10am-5pm Jun-Oct), 45km toward Halifax from Tangier, should really be renamed. The man of the house used to row 16km to get to his fishing grounds, leaving his wife and 13 daughters at home. The museum really captures women's domestic life of the early 20th century. Costumed local guides offer tea and hospitality.

Some 6km down the highway towards Halifax, **Memory Lane Heritage Village** (5435 Clam Harbour Rd, Lake Charlotte; adult/child $6/4; ☉11am-4pm Jun-Oct) re-creates the 1940s via antique cars, a farmstead with animals (great for kids), mid-century-style meals and displays of then new fangled (but now old) washing machines, appliances and more.

New Brunswick

Includes ➡

Best Places to Eat

➡ Rossmount Inn Restaurant (p118)

➡ North Head Bakery (p124)

➡ East Coast Bistro (p128)

Best Places to Stay

➡ Carriage House Inn (p107)

➡ Algonquin Resort (p118)

➡ Inn at Whale Cove (p123)

➡ Mahogany Manor (p127)

Why Go?

In the early 20th century, New Brunswick was a Very Big Deal. Millionaire businesspeople, Major League Baseball players and US presidents journeyed here to fish salmon from its silver rivers and camp at rustic lodges in its deep primeval forests. But over the decades, New Brunswick slipped back into relative obscurity. Today, some joke that it's the 'drive-through province,' as vacationers tend to hot-foot it to its better-known neighbors Prince Edward Island (PEI) and Nova Scotia.

But the unspoiled wilderness is still here. There are rivers for fly-fishing, coastal islands for kayaking, snowy mountains for skiing and quaint Acadian villages for exploring. So do yourself a favor, and don't just drive through. Prince Edward Island will still be there when you're done, we promise.

When to Go
Fredericton

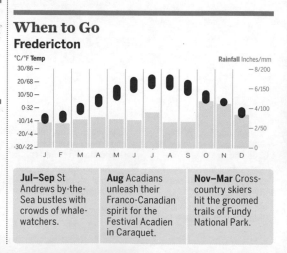

Jul–Sep St Andrews by-the-Sea bustles with crowds of whale-watchers.

Aug Acadians unleash their Franco-Canadian spirit for the Festival Acadien in Caraquet.

Nov–Mar Cross-country skiers hit the groomed trails of Fundy National Park.

New Brunswick Highlights

① Feel the power of the highest tides in the world at **Cape Enrage** (p132).

② Discover the history of picturesque **St Andrews by-the-Sea** (p115).

③ Dip your canoe paddle in the **Chiputneticook Lakes** (p114).

④ Breathe in the fresh sea air and unwind on peaceful, isolated **Grand Manan Island** (p122).

⑤ Stretch out on the sandy beach or splash in the lagoon at **Kouchibouguac National Park** (p138).

⑥ Live history at **King's Landing Historical Settlement** (p110) and **Acadian Historic Village** (p141).

⑦ Taste the delicacies at weekly farmers markets in **Fredericton** (p108) and **Moncton** (p135).

History

What is now New Brunswick was originally the land of the Mi'kmaq and, in the western and southern areas, the Maliseet Aboriginals. Many places still bear their aboriginal names, although the Aboriginal people (who today number around 17,000) are now concentrated on small pockets of land.

Following in the wake of explorer Samuel de Champlain, French colonists arrived in the 1600s. The Acadians, as they came to be known, farmed the area around the Bay of Fundy. In 1755 they were expelled by the English, many returning to settle along the Bay of Chaleur. In the years following, the outbreak of the American Revolution brought an influx of British Loyalists from Boston and New York seeking refuge in the wilds of New Brunswick. These refugees settled the valleys of the Saint John and St Croix Rivers, established the city of Saint John and bolstered the garrison town at Fredericton.

Through the 1800s, lumbering and shipbuilding boomed, and by the start of the 20th century, other industries, including fishing, had developed. That era of prosperity ended with the Great Depression. Today, pulp and paper, oil refining and potato farming are the major industries.

Land & Climate

The province encompasses a varied geography of moist, rocky coastal areas, temperate inland river valleys and a heavily forested and mountainous interior. There are four distinct seasons. Summers are generally mild with occasional hot days. The Fundy shore is prone to fog, particularly in the spring and early summer. The primary tourist season lasts from late June to early September. Many tourist facilities (beaches, organized tours and some accommodations in resort areas) shut down for the remainder of the year.

Language

New Brunswick is Canada's only officially bilingual province, although only about one-third of the population speaks both French and English (compared to 17% nationwide). Around 34% of the population is of French ancestry, concentrated around Edmundston, the Acadian Peninsula, along the east coast and Moncton. You will rarely have a problem being understood in English or French.

ℹ Getting There & Around

There are tourist information centers at all border crossings and in most towns. These are open from mid-May to mid-October only.

AIR

Air Canada has several daily flights from Halifax, Montréal and Toronto into Moncton, Saint John and Fredericton. Moncton has service from Toronto on WestJet; and a daily direct flight from Newark on United. WestJet also flies into Saint John from Toronto.

BOAT

The Bay Ferries' **Princess of Acadia** (📞888-249-7245, 506-649-7777; www.bayferries.com; adult/child 0-5yr/child 6-13yr/senior $43/5/28/33, car/bicycle $86/10) sails between Saint John and Digby, Nova Scotia, year-round. The three-hour crossing can save a lot of driving.

Arrive early or call ahead for vehicle reservations, as the ferry is very busy in July and August. Even with a reservation, arrive an hour before departure. Walk-ons and cyclists should be OK any time. There's a restaurant and a bar.

Fundy Isles ferries also serve the islands. Book ahead where possible and/or arrive early.

BUS

Maritime (📞1-800-575-1807; www.maritime-bus.com) services the major transportation routes in New Brunswick, with service to Nova Scotia, PEI and into Québec as far as Rivière-du-Loup, where buses connect with **Orléans Express** (📞888-999-3977; www.orleansexpress.com) services to points west.

REGIONAL DRIVING DISTANCES

Edmundston to Saint John: 375km

Fredericton to Miramichi: 180km

St Andrews by-the-Sea to Moncton: 254km

CAR & MOTORCYCLE

For drivers, the main access points into New Brunswick are Edmundston, Maine, Houlton, Nova Scotia or PEI. If you're going to PEI, there's no charge to use the Confederation Bridge eastbound from Cape Jourmain – you pay on the way back. Traffic is generally light, although crossing the Maine border usually means a delay at customs.

TRAIN

VIA Rail (☑ 888-842-7245; www.viarail.ca) operates passenger services between Montréal and Halifax ($219, 15½ hours, daily except Tuesday), with stops in Campbellton, Miramichi and Moncton.

FREDERICTON

POP 50,600

This sleepy provincial capital does quaint very well. The St John River curves lazily through Fredericton, past the stately government buildings on the waterfront and the university on the hill. Its neatly mowed, tree-lined banks are dotted with fountains, walking paths and playing fields. On warm weekends, 'The Green,' as it's known, looks like something out of a watercolor painting – families strolling, kids kicking soccer balls, couples picnicking.

On a flat, broad curve in the riverbank, the small downtown commercial district is a neat grid of redbrick storefronts. Surrounding it are quiet residential streets lined with tall, graceful elms shading beautifully maintained Georgian and Victorian houses and abundant flower beds. A canopy of trees spreads over the downtown, pierced here and there by church spires.

◉ Sights

The two-block strip along Queen St between York and Regent Sts is known as the Historic Garrison District. In 1875, Fredericton became the capital of the newly formed province of New Brunswick, and the garrison housed British soldiers for much of the late 18th and early 19th centuries. It's now a lively multi-use area with impressive stone architecture.

Old Government House　　HISTORIC BUILDING
(www.gnb.ca/lg/ogh; 51 Woodstock Rd; ⊘10am-4pm Mon-Sat, noon-4pm Sun) **FREE** This magnificent sandstone palace was erected for the British governor in 1826. The representative of the queen moved out in 1893 after the province refused to continue paying his expenses, and during most of the 20th century the complex was a Royal Canadian Mounted Police (RCMP) headquarters. It now evocatively captures a moment in time with tours led by staff in period costume. New Brunswick's current lieutenant governor (Graydon Nicholas, a member of the Maliseet Nation and the first aboriginal lawyer in Atlantic Canada) lives on the 3rd floor.

★**Beaverbrook Art Gallery**　　MUSEUM
(www.beaverbrookartgallery.org; 703 Queen St; adult/child $10/5, pay as you wish Thu after 5pm; ⊘10am-5pm Mon-Wed, Fri & Sat, to 9pm Thu, noon-5pm Sun) This relatively small but excellent gallery was one of Lord Beaverbrook's gifts to the town. The exceptional collection includes works by international heavyweights and is well worth an hour or so. Among others you will see Constable, Dali, Gainsborough and Turner, Canadian artists Tom Thompson, Emily Carr and Cornelius Kreighoff as well as changing contemporary exhibits of Atlantic art.

Officers' Square　　HISTORIC SITE
(www.downtownfredericton.ca; btwn Carleton & Regent Sts; ⊘ceremonies 11am & 4pm daily & 7pm Tue & Thu Jul & Aug) Once the military parade ground, the Garrison District's Officers' Square now hosts a full-uniform changing of the guard ceremony in summertime. Also in summer the Calithumpians Outdoor Summer Theatre performs daily at 12:15pm weekdays and 2pm weekends. The free historical skits are laced with humor. Summer evenings bring jazz, Celtic and rock concerts – see the website for schedules.

York Sunbury Historical Museum　　MUSEUM
(☑506-455-6041; www.yorksunburymuseum.com; Officers' Sq; adult/student $5/2; ⊘10am-5pm Apr-Nov, by appointment Dec-Mar) Housed in the 19th-century officers' quarters on the west side of Officers' Sq, this museum's collection preserves the city's past. Displays feature military pieces used by local regiments and by British and German armies from the Boer War and both world wars, furniture from a Loyalist sitting room and a Victorian bedroom, and aboriginal and Acadian artifacts. Don't miss the Coleman Frog, a 42lb creature of Fredericton legend. Real or plaster? Decide for yourself.

Soldiers' Barracks　　HISTORIC BUILDING
(cnr Queen & Carleton Sts; ⊘10am-5pm Tue-Sun) **FREE** See how the common soldier lived in

Fredericton

Fredericton

the 1820s (lousy food, too much drink) at this grim stone barracks in the Garrison District. The adjacent 1828 **Guard House** was also unpleasant (plank beds, thin straw mattresses), but the conditions for those held in cells were truly nasty. Threaten your kids! The lower section of the barracks is now used as artisan studios.

Old Loyalist Burial Ground   CEMETERY
(Brunswick St; ⊗8am-9pm) This Loyalist cemetery, dating back to 1784, is an atmospheric, thought-provoking history lesson of its own, revealing large families and kids dying tragically young. The Loyalists arrived from the 13 colonies after the American Revolution of 1776.

Christ Church Cathedral
CHURCH

(www.christchurchcathedral.com; 168 Church St) Built in 1853, this cathedral is a fine early example of 19th-century Gothic Revival style and has exquisite stained glass. It was modeled after St Mary's in Snettisham, Norfolk.

🏃 Activities

Small Craft Aquatic Centre
BOATING

(off Woodstock Rd; boat hire per hour $10; ☺ May-Sep) This small center, on the St John River beside Old Government House, rents out canoes, kayaks and rowboats. On offer are weekly passes, guided canoe and kayak tours, one-hour to three-day river ecology trips, and instruction in either canoeing or kayaking.

Lighthouse on the Green
HIKING, BIKING

(cnr Regent St & St Anne Point Dr; ☺ 9am-6pm) There are 70km of recreational trails around town and along the river that either begin or intersect at this riverfront lighthouse, which doubles as an info center and small museum. Pick up a map inside. In summer, enjoy weekend concerts and Wednesday night yoga on the lighthouse deck.

👉 Tours

Heritage Walking Tours
WALKING TOUR

(☺ 10am, 2:30pm & 5pm daily Jul & Aug, 4pm Jun & Sep-Nov) FREE Enthusiastic young people wearing historic costumes lead good, free hour-long tours of the river, the government district or the Historic Garrison District, departing from City Hall.

Haunted Hikes
WALKING TOUR

(www.calithumpians.com; 796a Queen St; adult/child $14/9; ☺ 9:15pm Mon-Sat Jul & Aug) Actors masquerading as ghoulish thespians run entertaining Fredericton ghost tours.

✨ Festivals & Events

Notable Acts Summer Theatre Festival
THEATER

(www.nbacts.com; ☺ end Jul) Showcases new and noted playwrights with street and theater presentations.

Harvest Jazz & Blues Festival
MUSIC

(www.harvestjazzandblues.com; ☺ Sep) This weeklong event transforms the downtown area into the 'New Orleans of the North.' Jazz, blues and Dixieland performers arrive from across North America.

Silver Wave Film Festival
FILM

(www.swfilmfest.com; ☺ early Nov) Three days of New Brunswick, Canadian and international films and lectures organized by the NB Filmmakers' Cooperative.

🛏 Sleeping

There are a number of budget and midrange motels on the Fredericton Bypass and its parallel Prospect St (southwest of town).

Fredericton International Hostel
HOSTEL $

(☎ 506-450-4417; fredericton@hihostels.ca; 621 Churchill Row; dm members/nonmembers $30/35; ☺ office 8am-noon & 6-10pm; ☺ @) This dark, rambling residence hall is part university student housing, part travelers' lodging. The big, slightly creepy basement has a laundry and pool tables.

Town and Country Motel
MOTEL $

(☎ 506-454-4223; 967 Woodstock Rd; s & d $90, tw $100; ✸) In a quiet riverside setting, you'll find sparkling clean and bright modern rooms with kitchenettes and big picture windows framing a gorgeous view of the river. It's on the walking/cycling path 3km west from the city center.

★ Carriage House Inn
B&B $$

(☎ 506-452-9924, 800-267-6068; www.carriage-house-inn.net; 230 University Ave; r incl breakfast $105-139; ☺✸🛜) In a shady Victorian neighborhood near the Green, this beautifully restored 1875 Queen Anne was built for a lumber baron and former Fredericton mayor. The grand common room has polished hardwood floors, antiques, comfy sofas, fireplaces and a grand piano. Upstairs, the guest rooms have high ceilings, four-posters, period wallpapers and vintage artwork. There is a deep veranda for lounging.

Brennan's B&B
B&B $$

(☎ 506-455-7346; www.bbcanada.com/3892.html; 146 Waterloo Row; r incl breakfast $95-135; ☺✸@) Built for a wealthy merchant family in 1885, this turreted white riverfront mansion is now a handsome four-room B&B. The better rooms have hardwood floors and water views.

Crowne Plaza Lord Beaverbrook
HOTEL $$$

(☎ 506-455-3371; www.cpfredericton.com; 659 Queen St; r $120-270; ✸🛜✸) Always bustling with weddings, conventions and business travelers, this 1948 downtown hotel is another one of Lord Beaverbrook's legacies to the city. The lobby has a touch of vintage glamour, and the 168 rooms are modern and comfortable. Check out the beaver mosaics on the facade.

✖ Eating

For a small city, Fredericton offers a wide, cosmopolitan cross section of restaurants, most in the walkable downtown. Fredericton has also embraced coffee culture in several appealing venues.

WW Boyce Farmers Market   MARKET $
(www.boycefarmersmarket.com; 665 George St; ◉6am-1pm Sat) This Fredericton institution is great for picking up fresh fruit, vegetables, meat, cheese, handicrafts, dessert and flowers. Many of the 150 or so stalls recall the city's European heritage, with everything from German-style sausages to French duck pâtés to British marmalade. There is also a restaurant where Frederictonians queue to chat and people-watch.

Second Cup   CAFE $
(www.secondcup.com; Kings Place Mall, 440 King St; snacks $3-7; ◉6:30am-9pm Mon-Sat, 9am-10pm Sun; 🛜) Warm lighting, world music and the aroma of fresh-roasted coffee beans draw a loyal clientele of office workers, passers-by and aspiring novelists toiling away on their laptops.

Caribbean Flavas   CARIBBEAN $$
(www.caribbeanflavas.ca; 123 York St; mains $16-25; ◉11:30am-2:30pm Tue-Fri & 4:30-8:30pm Tue-Sat) A bright nook dishing up the tastes and colors of the Caribbean. Great for a casual, flavorful meal. BYOB.

Chez Riz   INDIAN $$
(📞506-454-9996; 366 Queen St; mains $16-23; ◉11:30am-2:30pm Mon-Fri, 5-9pm Mon-Sat) Delicious Indian and Pakistani cuisine in a darkly stylish, romantically lit cave of a place.

Schnitzel Parlour   GERMAN $$
(📞506-450-2520; www.facklemanschocolate-heaven.com; 3136 Woodstock Rd; mains $19-24; ◉5:30-10pm Tue-Sat) Specializing in hearty, old-fashioned German fare, this cozy countryside restaurant has richly spiced goulash (the secret ingredient is chocolate), wild-boar stew and six kinds of schnitzel on homemade *spätzle* (soft egg noodles). BYOB. The on-site **Chocolaterie Fackleman** (open from noon) sells truffles and traditional central European tortes. The

restaurant is about 8km west of town on Woodstock Rd.

Blue Door   FUSION $$$
(📞506-455-2583; www.thebluedoor.ca; 100 Regent St; mains $14-28; ◉11:30am-2pm Tue-Fri, 5-9pm Mon-Sat) This local hot spot serves upscale fusion dishes such as Gorgonzola bruschetta, maple-miso cod and chicken curry in a dim, urban-chic dining room. Retro cocktails such as Singapore slings and Harvey Wallbangers are real favorites.

🍷 Drinking & Nightlife

In the evenings, the bars, pubs and rooftop patios of King and Queen Sts come alive.

Lunar Rogue Pub   PUB
(www.lunarrogue.com; 625 King St; ◉10am-late Mon-Sat, 11am-10pm Sun) This jolly locals' joint has a good beer selection and a fine assortment of single malts. The patio is wildly popular during the warmer weather.

Boom! Nightclub   CLUB
(www.boomnightclub.ca; 474 Queen St; cover charge $5-8; ◉8pm-late Wed-Sun) A hip gay bar and dance club welcoming folks of all stripes.

☆ Entertainment

For the scoop on concerts, art gallery openings and other happenings around town, pick up a copy of *here*, a free entertainment weekly available all over town.

Outdoor Summer Concerts   LIVE MUSIC
(www.tourismfredericton.ca) FREE In summer, downtown venues from Officers' Sq to the Lighthouse on the Green feature live local music ranging from highland bagpipes and drums to country and blues. Check the website for schedules.

Playhouse   THEATER
(www.theplayhouse.nb.ca; 686 Queen St) The Playhouse stages concerts, theater, ballet and shows throughout the year.

ℹ Information

Dr Everett Chalmers Hospital (📞506-452-5400; 700 Priestman St) Located 2km south of the city center.

Fredericton Public Library (12 Carleton St; ◉10am-5pm Mon, Tue, Thu & Sat, to 9pm Wed & Fri) Free internet access is first-come, first-served.

Main Post Office (📞506-444-8602; 570 Queen St; ◉8am-5pm Mon-Fri) General

NEW BRUNSWICK ITINERARIES

Four Days

Spend the first day at **King's Landing Historical Settlement** (p110). Land in **Fredericton** on Saturday morning – peruse the stalls at the **WW Boyce Farmers Market** (p108), and nip into the **Beaverbrook Art Gallery** (p105) to see a few old masters and contemporary Canadian art. Follow the **Old River Road** through Gagetown to the port city of **Saint John**, stopping at a few pottery studios on the way. Hit Saint John on a Saturday night – catch some live Maritime music at **O'Leary's pub** (p128) or a play at the **Imperial Theatre** (p128). The next morning, head west along the Fundy coast to catch the ferry to **Grand Manan Island**. Take your pick of whale-watching tours, hiking, cycling or relaxing on the veranda with a book.

One Week

Back on the mainland from Grand Manan, take the scenic route east through **St Martins, Sussex** and **Fundy National Park** (p130). Stop for a dip in the ocean at **Parlee Beach** near Shediac, then head north toward Bouctouche. Get a taste of Acadian culture at **Le Pays de la Sagouine** (p137), then round out the experience with a visit to the modern village of **Caraquet** and a time trip to the early 19th century at **Acadian Historic Village** (p141). Alternatively, head up to the **Miramichi** for a few days of salmon fishing and tubing on the famed river.

Outdoor Adventures

Start with a couple of days camping by the ocean, kayaking along the dunes and exploring the cycling and hiking trails at **Kouchibouguac National Park**. Spend a day or a week hiking the northern end of the **International Appalachian Trail** up over Mt Carleton, around **Grand Manan** or along the **Fundy Trail Parkway** (p132). Take a seakayaking expedition in **Passamaquoddy Bay** (p119), then spend a week canoe-tripping through the **Chiputneticook Lakes**. Do a week-long cycling trip up the **St John River Valley** or day trips around **Grand Manan, Fredericton** and **Sussex.** Leave a couple of days for whale-watching and a boat excursion to **Machias Seal Island** to see the puffins.

Canoe maps for the Nepisiquit, Restigouche, Southwest Miramichi, St Croix and Tobique Rivers are available from **Service New Brunswick** (www.snb.ca; $7 each). It also distributes a guide to the **New Brunswick Trail** ($13) and a snowmobile trail map (free).

delivery mail addressed to Fredericton, NB E3B 4Y1, is held here.

Visitors Center (☑888-888-4768, 506-460-2129; www.tourismfredericton.ca; City Hall, 397 Queen St; ◷9am-8pm) Free city parking passes provided here.

ⓘ Getting There & Away

AIR

Fredericton International Airport (YFC; www.yfcmobile.ca) is on Hwy 102, 14km southeast of town.

BUS

The **Maritime Bus Terminal** (☑1-800-575-1807; www.maritimebus.com; 150 Woodside Lane) is a few kilometers southwest of downtown. Some useful destinations:
Moncton ($44, 2¼ hours, two daily)
Charlottetown, PEI ($69, 5½ hours, two daily)

Bangor, Maine ($58, 7½ hours, one daily)
Saint John ($31, 1½ hours, two daily)

CAR & MOTORCYCLE

Cars with out-of-province license plates are eligible for a free three-day parking pass for downtown Fredericton May to October, available at the visitors center at City Hall. In-province visitors can get a one-day pass.

Avis, Budget, Hertz and National car-rental agencies all have desks at the airport.

ⓘ Getting Around

A taxi to the airport costs $18 to $22.

Bicycle rentals are available at **Radical Edge** (☑506-459-3478; www.radicaledge.ca; 386 Queen St; rental per day $25).

The city has a decent bus system, **Fredericton Transit** (☑506-460-2200); tickets cost $2 and include free transfers. Service runs Monday through Saturday from 6:15am to 11pm. Most city bus routes begin at King's Place Mall, on King St between York and Carleton.

UPPER ST JOHN RIVER VALLEY

The St John River rises in the US state of Maine, then winds along the western border of the province past forests and beautiful lush farmland. It then drifts through Fredericton between tree-lined banks and flows around flat islands between rolling hills before emptying into the Bay of Fundy 700km later. The broad river is the province's dominant feature and for centuries has been its major thoroughfare. The valley's soft, eye-pleasing landscape makes for scenic touring by car, or by bicycle on the Trans Canada Trail (TCT), which follows the river for most of its length.

Two automobile routes carve through the valley: the quicker Trans-Canada Hwy (Hwy 2), mostly on the west side of the river, and the more scenic old Hwy 105 on the east side, which meanders through many villages. Branching off from the valley are Hwy 17 (at St-Léonard) and Rte 385 (at Perth-Andover), which cut northeast through the Appalachian highlands and lead to rugged Mt Carleton Provincial Park.

King's Landing Historical Settlement

One of the province's best sites is this worthwhile recreation of an early-19th-century **Loyal-ist village** (☑506-363-4999; www.kingslanding.nb.ca; adult/child/family $16/11/38; ⊘10am-5pm Jun-Oct), 36km west of Fredericton. A community of 100 costumed staff create a living museum by role-playing in 11 houses, a school, church, store and sawmill typical of those used a century ago, providing a glimpse and taste of pioneer life in the Maritimes. Demonstrations and events are staged throughout the day and horse-drawn carts shunt visitors around. The prosperous Loyalist life reflected here can be tellingly compared to that at the Acadian Historic Village in Caraquet. The **King's Head Inn**, a mid-1800s pub, serves traditional food and beverages, with a nice authentic touch – candlelight. The children's programs make King's Landing ideal for families, and spe-

cial events occur regularly. It's not hard to while away a good half-day or more here.

About 10km south, busy, resortlike **Mactaquac Provincial Park** (day use per vehicle $7) has swimming, fishing, hiking, picnic sites, camping, boat rentals and a huge **campground** (☑506-363-4747; 1256 Hwy 105; campsites/RV sites $24/28; ⊘Jun-Oct).

Hartland

This tiny country hamlet has the granddaddy of New Brunswick's many wooden covered bridges. The photogenic 390m-long **Hartland covered bridge** over the St John River was erected in 1897 and is a national historic site. The picnic tables overlooking the river and the bridge at the tourist information center are five-star lunch spots (fixings at the grocery store across the road). Otherwise, the village has a rather forlorn atmosphere.

Rebecca Farm B&B (☑506-375-1699; 656 Rockland Rd; d incl breakfast $100-130; ⊖❋☎), about 4km from the town center, is a scrupulously maintained 19th-century farmhouse that sits in the midst of gorgeously hilly potato fields.

Florenceville & Around

The tidy and green riverside village of Florenceville is ground zero of the global french-fry industry. It's home to the McCain Foods frozen-foods empire, which is sustained by the thousands of hectares of potato farms that surround it in every direction. Started by the McCain brothers in 1957 and still owned by the family, the company produces one-third of the world's french-fry supply at its Florenceville factory and 54 like it worldwide. That adds up to one million pounds of chips churned out every hour and $5.8 billion in annual net sales.

Worth a stop is the **Potato World Museum** (www.potatoworld.ca; Rte 110; tours adult/child $5/4, experiential tours $10/8; ⊘9am-6pm Mon-Fri, to 5pm Sat & Sun). It's a cheesy name, but the museum is a tasteful, top-class interactive exposition of the history of the humble potato in these parts and its continuing centrality to the provincial economy. In this area, school kids are still given two weeks off in the autumn to help bring in the harvest. The museums' new experiential tour lets you get your hands

SCENIC DRIVE: LOWER ST JOHN RIVER VALLEY

The main Hwy (Rte 7) between the capital and the port city of Saint John barrels south through a vast expanse of trees, trees and more trees. A far more scenic route (albeit about twice as long) follows the gentle, meandering St John River through rolling farmland and a couple of historic villages down to the Fundy coast.

Start on the north side of the river in Fredericton, and follow Rte 105 south through Maugerville to Jemseg. At Exit 339, pick up Rte 715 South which will take you to the **Gagetown ferry landing** (⊙24hr year-round) **FREE**. This is the first of a system of eight free cable ferries that crisscross the majestic St John River en route to the city of Saint John. You will never have to wait more than a few minutes for the crossing, which generally takes five to 10 minutes.

When you reach the opposite bank, head north a couple of miles to visit the pretty 18th-century village of **Gagetown** – well worth a look-see. Front St is lined with craft studios and shops and a couple of inviting cafes. Stop into the excellent **Queen's County Museum** (69 Front St; adult/child $3/free; ⊙10am-5pm) housed in Sir Leonard Tilley's childhood home, built in 1736. The top-notch staff will show you through the exhibits spanning pre-Colonial aboriginal history in the area, 18th-century settler life, and up to WWII. **Gagetown Cider Company** (☑506-488-2147; 127 Fox Rd; ⊙1-6pm) offers tours by appointment.

Explore scenic Gagetown Creek by boat. **Village Boatique** (☑877-488-1992; 50 Front St) has canoe/kayak rentals for $10/15 per hour, $50/75 per day. Homey **Step-Aside Inn** (☑506-488-1808; stepamau@nbnet.nb.ca; 58 Front St; s/d incl breakfast $80/95; ⊙May-Dec; ⊜✿☎) has four bright rooms with views of the river. To eat, grab a smoked-meat sandwich and a beer at the **Old Boot Pub** (48 Front St; ⊙11am-10pm) on the riverfront.

From Gagetown, head south on Rte 102, known locally as 'the Old River Road,' denoting its status as the major thoroughfare up the valley in the kinder, simpler era between the decline of the river steamboats and the construction of the modern, divided highway. The grand old farmhouses and weathered hay barns dotted at intervals along the valley belong to that earlier age. The hilly 42km piece of road between Gagetown and the **Evandale ferry landing** (⊙24hr year-round) **FREE** is especially picturesque, with glorious panoramic views of fields full of wildflowers, white farmhouses and clots of green and gold islands set in the intensely blue water of the river.

A hundred years ago, tiny Evandale was a bustling little place, where a dance band would entertain riverboat passengers stopping off for the night at the **Evandale Resort** (☑506-468-2222; ferry landing; r $139-199), now restored to its Victorian grandeur. It has six rooms and a fine-dining restaurant. On the other side of the water, Rte 124 takes you the short distance to the **Belleisle ferry** (⊙24hr year-round) **FREE**. The ferry deposits you on the rural Kingston Peninsula, where you can cross the peninsula to catch the **Gondola Point Ferry** (signposted off Hwy 1 at Exit 141) **FREE** and head directly into Saint John.

dirty – literally – by planting potato seeds and cutting your own french fries. If all the spud talk leaves you peckish, slip into a potato barrel chair at the on-site **Harvest Cafe** (lunch $5-7; ⊙11am-4pm Mon-Fri). The museum is 2km off Hwy 2 at Exit 152 toward Centreville on Rte 110.

Just outside Florenceville is the **Tannaghtyn B&B** (☑866-399-6966, 506-392-6966; www.tannaghtyn.ca; 4169 Rte 103, off Rte 110, Connell; r incl breakfast $95-140; ✿☎), set high on a ridge with a spectacular view of the St John River and the green and gold patchwork of farms on the opposite side. Both stylish and cozy, the house is furnished with dramatic Canadian art, comfy sofas and beds made up with linens dried in the fresh country air. Plus, there's a hot tub under the stars. Besides the Harvest Cafe, Florenceville has a half-dozen middle-of-the-road restaurants serving three meals a day.

Maritime (☑1-800-575-1807; www.maritimebus.com; 8738 Main St) buses stop at the Irving gas station in Florenceville.

Mt Carleton Provincial Park & the Tobique Valley

From his workshop on the forested banks of the Tobique River at the foot of Mt Carleton, Nictau canoe-maker Bill Miller rhapsodizes that 'If you telephone heaven, it's a local call.' He may be right.

The 17,427-hectare **provincial park** offers visitors a wilderness of mountains, valleys, rivers and wildlife including moose, deer, bear and, potentially, the 'extinct' (but apparently regularly seen) eastern cougar. The main feature of the park is a series of rounded glaciated peaks and ridges, including Mt Carleton, which at 820m is the Maritimes' highest. This range is an extension of the Appalachian Mountains, which begin in the US state of Georgia and end in Québec. Mt Carleton is little known and relatively unvisited, even in midsummer. It could be the province's best-kept secret.

The park is open from mid-May to October; entry is free. Hunting and logging are prohibited in the park, and all roads are gravel-surfaced. The nearest town is **Riley Brook**, 30km away, so bring all food and a full tank of gas.

🏃 Activities

Canoeing

The Mt Carleton area boasts superb wilderness canoeing. In the park itself, the Nictau and Nepisiguit chains of lakes offer easy day-tripping through a landscape of tree-clad mountains. For experienced canoeists, the shallow and swift Little Tobique River rises at Big Nictau Lake, winding in tight curls through dense woods until it joins the Tobique itself at Nictau. The more remote Nepisiguit River flows out of the Nepisiguit Lakes through the wilderness until it empties into the Bay of Chaleur at Bathurst, over 100km away.

The lower reaches of the Tobique, from Nictau, through minute Riley Brook and down to Plaster Rock is a straight, easy paddle through forest and meadow that gives way to farmland as the valley broadens, with a couple of waterfront campgrounds along the way. The easy 10km between Nictau and the Bear's Lair landing in Riley Brook makes for a relaxing afternoon paddle.

Don McAskill at **Bear's Lair** (☑506-356-8351; www.bearslairhunting.com; 3349 Rte 385, Riley Brook; boats per day $40) has boats and can provide expert knowledge on canoeing in these parts. He also offers a shuttle service between your put-in and take-out point (eg boat delivery to Mt Carleton Provincial Park and transport of your vehicle down to Riley Brook is $45). In the park, **Guildo Martel** (☑506-235-2499) rents canoes and kayaks for the day on the edge of Big Nictau Lake at Armstrong Campground.

Fiddles on the Tobique (☑506-356-2409; ⊗late Jun) is a weekend festival held annually in Nictau and Riley Brook. It is a magical idea: a round of community-hall suppers, jam sessions and concerts culminating in a Sunday afternoon floating concert down the Tobique River from Nictau to Riley Brook. Upward of 800 canoes and kayaks join the flotilla each year – some stocked with musicians, some just with paddlers – and 8000 spectators line the river banks to watch. By some accounts, the event has been damaged by its own popularity, devolving into a boisterous booze cruise. Others call it a grand party and good fun.

On land, **Bill Miller** (☑506-356-2409; www.millercanoes.com; 4160 Rte 385, Nictau) welcomes visitors to his cluttered canoe-making workshop in Nictau (population roughly 12), where he and his father and grandfather before him have handcrafted wooden canoes since 1922. Also worth a stop is the **Tobique Salmon Barrier** (⊗9am-5pm) FREE, signposted from the road at Nictau, located at the confluence of the Little Tobique and Campbell Rivers. There is a spectacular view from the Department of Fisheries office situated on a bluff overlooking the water. From here, officers keep a 24-hour watch on the Atlantic salmon, which are trucked up by road from below the Mactaquac Dam at Fredericton and held here until spawning time, in order to protect their dwindling numbers from poachers.

Hiking

The best way to explore Mt Carleton is on foot. The park has a 62km network of trails: most of them are loops winding to the handful of rocky knobs that are the peaks. The International Appalachian Trail (IAT) passes through here.

The easiest peak to climb is Mt Bailey; a 7.5km loop trail to the 564m hillock begins near the day-use area. Most hikers can walk this route in three hours. The highest peak is reached via the Mt Carleton Trail, a 10km route that skirts over the 820m knob, where there's a fire tower. Plan on three to four hours for the trek and pack your parka; the wind above the tree line can be brutal.

The most challenging hike is the Sagamook Trail, a 6km loop to a 777m peak with superlative vistas of Nictau Lake and the highlands area to the north of it; allow three hours for this trek. The Mountain Head Trail connects the Mt Carleton and Sagamook Trails, making a long transit of the range possible.

All hikers intending to follow any long trails must register at the visitors center or park headquarters before hitting the trail. Outside the camping season (mid-May to mid-September), you should call ahead to make sure the main gate will be open, as the Mt Carleton trailhead is 13.5km from the park entrance. Otherwise park your car at the entrance and walk in – the Mt Bailey trailhead is only 2.5km from the gate.

🛏 Sleeping & Eating

There is lodging, a general store, gas station and restaurant in Riley Brook. The park has four public-use **campgrounds** (☑506-235-0793; www.friendsofmountcarleton.ca). In addition to Armstrong Brook, there are the semiwilderness campgrounds of Franquelin and Williams Brook, with outhouses and fire pits (bring your own water), and the ultraremote Headwaters campground on the slopes of Mt Carleton.

The town of Plaster Rock, situated 54km downriver toward the Trans-Canada Hwy (Rte 385), also has several serviceable motels and a couple of casual restaurants.

Bear's Lair INN **$**
(☑506-356-8351; www.bearslairhunting.com; 3349 Rte 385, Riley Brook; r from $60; ⊜) If any place in the province captures the essence of life in the north woods, this is it. A cozy log hunting lodge set on the banks of the Tobique River, it is busiest during fall hunting season – the high-ceilinged main lodge is adorned with numerous taxidermied specimens – but is also a relaxing base for outdoor enthusiasts year-round. The guest rooms are spick and span and the lodge's friendly owners offer meals, canoe/kayak rentals and guided hunting trips.

Armstrong Brook Campground CAMPGROUND **$**
(☑506-235-0793; campsites/RV sites $10/18; ⊙May-Oct) The park's largest campground has 89 sites nestled among the pines on the north side of Nictau Lake, 3km from the entrance. It has toilets, showers and a kitchen shelter, but no sites with hookups. RV drivers often have their noisy generators running, so tenters should check out the eight tent-only sites along Armstrong Brook on the north side of the campground.

ℹ Information

At the entrance to the park is a **visitors center** (☑506-235 0793; www.friendsofmount-carleton.ca; off Rte 385; ⊙8am-8pm May-Oct) for maps and information.

WORLD CLASS (POND) HOCKEY

As anyone who has been in the country for more than five minutes knows, Canadians love their hockey. For many, this affection (obsession?) is wrapped up in happy childhood memories of bright winter afternoons chasing a puck up and down a frozen pond or backyard rink.

Every February, the small forest town of Plaster Rock (population 1200), 84km from Mt Carleton, hosts the **World Pond Hockey Tournament** (www.worldpondhockey. com; Rte 109, Plaster Rock) FREE. Twenty rinks are plowed on Roulston Lake, which is ringed by tall evergreens, hot-chocolate stands and straw-bale seating for the 8000-odd spectators drawn to the four-day event. The tournament is wildly popular, with 120 amateur four-person teams traveling in from places as far flung as England, Egypt and the Cayman Islands. Anyone can register to play, but they will have to defeat the Boston Danglers, who have scrambled over squads such as the Skateful Dead, the Raggedy Ass River Boys and the Boiled Owls to put a lock on the championship trophy several years running.

If you want to play, register early. If you want to watch, pack your long johns and a toque (wool hat) and book your accommodations early. If the motels are full, the organizers keep a list of local folks willing to billet out-of-towners in their homes for the weekend.

CHIPUTNETICOOK LAKES

Tucked away on New Brunswick's southwest border with the USA state of Maine is a little-known but spectacular chain of wilderness lakes. Stretching for 180km along the international border, the forest-ringed Chiputneticook Lakes offer canoeing enthusiasts the chance to slip away into the wild for a few weeks. The nonprofit **St Croix International Waterway Commission** (www.stcroix.org; 5 Rte 1, St Stephen) maintains a network of backcountry campsites on the islands and lakeshores along the chain and publishes a detailed map of the waterway ($10). It includes the St Croix River, a popular three- to four-day paddling route beginning south of the lakes. Canoe rentals are available in Saint John and Fredericton. Note: the lakes are not patrolled by the park service, and paddlers should be experienced and well equipped.

There are a couple of fishing lodges on Palfrey Lake accessible via Rte 630. Day-trippers can use the scenic lakeshore campsites at **Spednik Lake Provincial Park** (free; maintained by volunteers), where there is a hiking trail through the woods, primitive toilets and fire rings. Bring your own water. Take Rte 3 north from St Stephen, then bear left on Rte 630 to reach the park gate.

There is also an **office** at the park headquarters in St Quentin(☑ 506-235-6040; dnr. Mt.carleton@gnb.ca; 11 Gagnon St).

Grand Falls

With a drop of around 25m and a 1.6km-long gorge with walls as high as 80m, these falls merit a stop in this otherwise un-scenic town. The Grand Falls are best in spring or after heavy rain – in summer, much of the water is diverted for generating hydroelectricity – yet the gorge is appealing any time.

In the middle of town, overlooking the falls, the **Malabeam Reception Centre** (25 Madawaska Rd; ☺ 9am-9pm Jul & Aug, 10am-6pm May, Jun & Sep) **FREE** doubles as a tourist office. Among the displays is a scale model of the gorge showing its extensive trail system.

A 253-step stairway down into the gorge begins at **La Rochelle** (1 Chapel St; tours adult/child $4/2, self-guided tours per family $5; boat trips adult/family $12/28; ☺ May-Oct), across the bridge from the Malabeam Reception Centre and left on Victoria St. Boats maneuver for 45-minute trips up the gorge. These run up to eight times a day but only in midsummer when water levels are low (it's too dangerous when the river is in full flood). Buy the boat ticket at La Rochelle first, as it includes admission to the stairway to the base of the gorge.

There are dramatically situated tent and RV sites at the **Falls and Gorge Campground** (☑ 877-475-7769; 1 Chapel St; campsites/RV sites $18/25). **Côté's** (☑ 877-444-2683; www.cotebb-inn.com; 575 Broadway Blvd West; r incl breakfast $103-175) is a homey, five-room B&B with a patio and hot tub.

Le Grand Saut (www.legrandsautristorante.com; 155 Broadway Blvd; mains $11-22; ☺ 10:30am-10pm), a popular, two-tiered spot with an inviting deck out front, serves up salads, pastas, pizzas and steaks.

① Getting There & Away

Maritime (☑ 1-800-575-1807; www.maritimebus.com; 555 Madawaska Rd) buses stop at the Esso station, just west of downtown.

Hwy 108 (known locally as the Renous Hwy) cuts across the province through Plaster Rock to the east coast, slicing through forest for nearly its entirety. It is tedious, but fast. Watch out for deer and moose.

Edmundston

Although working-class Edmundston, with a large paper mill, a utilitarian town center and a mainly bilingual French citizenry, doesn't bother much with tourism, it's a convenient stopover when heading east from Québec.

Halfway between the Québec border and Edmundston in the small community of St-Jacques is the **New Brunswick Botanical Garden** (www.jardinbotaniquenb.com; off Rte 2; adult/child $14/7; ☺ 9am-8pm). Here, 80,000 plants, accompanied by classical music, will brighten your day. It also has neat temporary exhibitions, such as a butterfly garden.

Edmundston is the eastern terminus of the **Petis Témis Interprovincial Linear Park** (www.petit-temis.com), a 134km cycling/hiking trail between Edmundston and Rivière-du-Loup, Québec. It follows an old railbed along the Madawaska River and the shores of Lake

Témiscouata, passing by several small villages and campgrounds along the way.

Get out of gritty Edmundston and sleep next to the botanical gardens at **Auberge Les Jardins** (☑506-739-5514; www.lesjardinsinn.com; 60 Rue Principale, St-Jacques; r $89-180; 🛋🖃), a gracious inn whose 17 rooms are each decorated with a different Canadian flower or tree theme. There's also a modern motel in back, and a wood-and-stained-glass **dining room** that's considered one of the best restaurants in the province (check out the fabulous wine list). Several motels line the highway and old Hwy 2 (Blvd Acadie).

For eats, head to **Bel Air** (☑506-735-3329; 174 Victoria St, cnr Blvd Hébert; mains $6-15; ⊘24hr). A city landmark since the 1950s, this is a total classic, right down to the seasoned, uniformed servers. The you-name-it menu includes acceptable Italian, Chinese, seafood and basic Canadian fare.

The **Provincial Tourist Office** (Hwy 2; ⊘8am-9pm Jun-Sep) is about 20km north at the Québec border.

Maritime (www.maritimebus.com; 191 Victoria St) buses depart from the downtown terminal.

WESTERN FUNDY SHORE

Almost the entire southern edge of New Brunswick is presided over by the constantly rising and falling, always impressive waters of the Bay of Fundy.

The resort town of St Andrews by-the-Sea, the serene Fundy Isles, fine seaside scenery and rich history make this easily one of the most appealing regions of the province. Whale-watching is a thrilling area activity. Most commonly seen are the fin, humpback and minke, and less so, the increasingly rare right whale. Porpoises and dolphins are plentiful. And let's not overlook the seafood – it's bountiful and delicious.

St Stephen

Right on the US border across the river from Calais, Maine, St Stephen is a busy entry point with small-town charm and one tasty attraction. It is home to Ganong, a family-run chocolate business, operating since 1873, whose products are known around eastern Canada. The five-cent chocolate nut bar was invented by the Ganong brothers in 1910, and they can also be credited with developing the heart-shaped box of chocolates seen everywhere on Valentine's Day.

The old Ganong chocolate factory on the town's main street is now the **Chocolate Museum** (www.chocolatemuseum.ca; 73 Milltown Blvd; adult/student/family $10/8.50/30; ⊘9:30am-6:30pm Mon-Sat, 11am-3pm Sun), with tasteful (and tasty) interactive displays of everything from antique chocolate boxes to manufacturing equipment. The adjacent **shop** sells boxes of Ganong hand-dipped chocolates and is free to visit. Try the iconic chicken bone (chocolate-filled cinnamon sticks) or the old-fashioned Pal-O-Mine candy bar.

The museum also offers a **guided heritage walking tour** (adult/child/family $13/10/40; ⊘Jun-Aug) of St Stephen. Once a year, during **Chocolate Fest** (www.chocolate-fest.ca; ⊘1st week Aug), the town celebrates all things chocolate with a parade, tours of the factory with unlimited sampling of the goods, and games for the kids.

There are five very comfortable rooms complemented by a quiet garden at **Blair House** (☑888-972-5247, 506-466-2233; www.blairhouseinn.nb.ca; 38 Prince William St; s/d incl breakfast from $90/110; 🖃🖧🖿), a fabulous Victorian home. You can walk the main street easily from here. There are also a few run-down motels on the outskirts of town if you are desperate.

Home cooking is served up at **Carman's Diner** (☑506-466-3528; 164 King St; mains $4-16; ⊘7am-10pm), a 1960s throwback with counter stools and jukeboxes at the tables.

The **tourist office** (cnr Milltown Blvd & King St; ⊘8am-9pm Jun-Sep) is in the old train station.

❶ Getting There & Away

Across the border in Calais, Maine, **West's Coastal Connection** (☑800-596-2823) buses connect to Bangor. They usually leave from Carmen's Hometown Pizzeria on Main St, but call ahead to confirm. In Bangor, buses use the Greyhound terminal and connect to Bangor airport.

St Andrews by-the-Sea

St Andrews is a genteel summer resort town. Blessed with a fine climate and picturesque beauty, it also has a colorful history. Founded by Loyalists in 1783, it's one of the oldest towns in the province. It's busy with holidaymakers and summer residents in July and August, but the rest of the year there are more seagulls than people.

The town sits on a peninsula pointing southward into the Bay of Fundy. Its main drag, Water St, is lined with restaurants and souvenir and craft shops.

St Andrews by-the-Sea

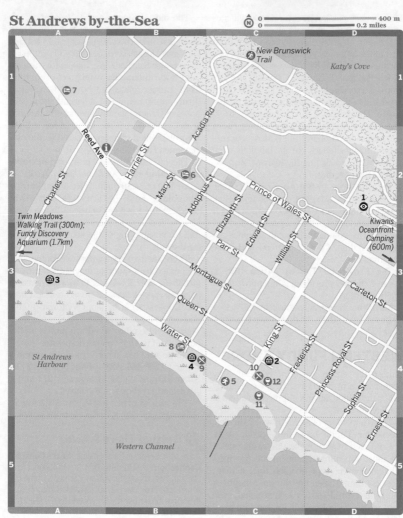

⊙ Sights

Fundy Discovery Aquarium AQUARIUM
(www.huntsmanmarine.com/aquarium; 1 Lower
Campus Rd; adult/child $12/9; ⊘10am-5pm)
This aquatic center focuses on the local
marine ecology; a 20,000-sq-ft aquarium
has most specimens that are found in Bay
of Fundy waters, including seals (feedings
at 11am and 4pm), lobsters and sturgeon.
Kids (and parents) love the touch pool re-
served just for slippery skates.

Minister's Island ISLAND
(www.ministersisland.ca; adult/child $15/10;
⊘May-Oct) This picturesque tidal island was
once used as a summer retreat by William
Cornelius Van Horne, builder of the Canadian Pacific Railway and one of Canada's
wealthiest men. **Covenhoven**, his splendid
50-room Edwardian cottage, is now open
to visitors – check out the tower-like stone
bathhouse, the tidal swimming pool and the
château-like barn.

The island can be visited at low tide, when
you can drive (or walk, or bike) on the hard-
packed sea floor. A few hours later it's 3m

St Andrews by-the-Sea

under water, so you need to be careful! During high tide, a ferry departs from Bar Rd. To get to Minister's Island from downtown St Andrews, follow Rte 127 northeast for about 1km and then turn right on Bar Rd.

Kingsbrae Garden　　　　　　GARDEN
(www.kingsbraegarden.com; 220 King St; adult/student/family $16/12/38, tours per person $3; ⊙9am-6pm May-Oct) Extensive, multihued Kingsbrae Garden is considered one of the best horticultural displays in Canada. Check out the wollemi pine, one of the world's oldest and rarest trees.

Sunbury Shores Arts & Nature Centre　　　　　　GALLERY
(www.sunburyshores.org; 139 Water St; ⊙9am-4:30pm Mon-Fri, noon-4pm Sat & Sun) FREE This nonprofit educational and cultural center offers courses in painting, weaving, pottery and other crafts for a day, weekend or week, as well as natural science seminars. Various changing exhibits run through summer.

St Andrews Blockhouse　　HISTORIC BUILDING
(Joe's Point Rd; ⊙9am-8pm Jun-Aug, to 5pm early Sep) FREE The restored wooden Blockhouse Historic Site is the only one left of several that were built here for protection in the War of 1812. If the tide is out, there's a path that extends from the blockhouse out across the tidal flats.

Sheriff Andrew House　　HISTORIC BUILDING
(cnr King & Queen Sts; admission by donation; ⊙9:30am-4:30pm Mon-Sat, 1-4:30pm Sun Jul-Sep) This 1820 neoclassical house has been restored to look like a middle-class home in the 1800s, and it's attended by lively and informative costumed guides.

Atlantic Salmon Interpretive Centre　　MUSEUM, AQUARIUM
(www.salarstream.ca; Chamcook Lake No 1 Rd, off Rte 127; adult/student/child $6/4/3; ⊙9am-5pm) This handsome lodge has an in-stream aquarium, guided tours and displays devoted to the life and trials of the endangered wild Atlantic salmon, once so plentiful in provincial rivers and bays.

🏃 Activities

Eastern Outdoors　　BIKING, KAYAKING
(☎506-529-4662; www.easternoutdoors.com; 165 Water St; mountain bikes per hr/day $20/35, kayaks per day $55; ⊙May-Oct) This St Andrews–based outfitter offers a variety of trips, including two-hour sunset paddles ($49) and multiday camping expeditions (from $145 per day).

Twin Meadows Walking Trail　　WALKING
The 800m Twin Meadows Walking Trail, a boardwalk and footpath through fields and woodlands, begins opposite 165 Joe's Point Rd beyond the blockhouse.

👉 Tours

Several companies offering boat trips and whale-watching cruises have offices by the wharf at the foot of King St. They're open from mid-June to early September. The cruises (around $60) take in the lovely coast. Seabirds are commonplace and seeing whales is the norm. The ideal waters for watching these beasts are further out in the bay, however, so if you're heading for the Fundy Isles, do your trip there.

Jolly Breeze　　BOAT TOUR
(☎506-529-8116; www.jollybreeze.com; adult/child $55/39; ⊙tours 9am, 12:45pm, 4:30pm Jun-Oct) This antique-style tall ship sails around Passamaquoddy Bay looking for seals and whales.

Quoddy Link Marine　　BOAT TOUR
(☎506-529-2600; adult/child $58/36; ⊙Jul-Oct) Serious whale-watchers should hop aboard this catamaran, staffed by trained marine biologists. There are one to three tours daily.

🛏 Sleeping

Kiwanis Oceanfront Camping　CAMPGROUND $
(📞877-393-7070; www.kiwanisoceanfrontcamping.com; 550 Water St; campsites/RV sites $31/38; ☺Apr-Oct) Situated at the far eastern end of town on Indian Point, this is mainly a gravel parking area for trailers, although there are some grassy spots.

Picket Fence Motel　MOTEL $
(📞506-529-8985; www.picketfencenb.com; 102 Reed Ave; r $90-105; ❉🛜) Modern, neat-as-a-pin motel rooms within walking distance of the main drag. Ultrafriendly management to boot.

★Rossmount Inn　INN $$
(📞506-529-3351; www.rossmountinn.com; 4599 Rte 127; r incl breakfast $125-138; ☺Apr-Dec; 🛜) Flags flap in the breeze in front of this stately yellow summer cottage, perched atop a manicured slope overlooking Passamaquoddy Bay. Inside, the 18 rooms have a stylish mix of antiques and modern decor, with hand-carved wooden furniture and snowy white linens. Many people consider the hotel restaurant to be the town's best. Rossmount Inn is about 3km north of downtown St Andrews on Rte 127.

★Algonquin Resort　HOTEL $$$
(📞855-529-8693, 506-529-8823; www.algonquinresort.com; 184 Adolphus St; r $189-389; ❉🛜🏊) The doyenne of New Brunswick hotels, this Tudor-style 'Castle-by-the-Sea' has sat on a hill overlooking town since 1889. With its elegant veranda, gardens, rooftop terrace, golf course, tennis courts and indoor pool with waterslides, it's worth a look even if you're not spending the night. A revamped spa is due to open in early 2014.

Treadwell Inn　B&B $$$
(📞888-529-1011, 506-529-1011; www.treadwellinn.com; 129 Water St; r incl breakfast $150-250; ☺❉🛜) Big, handsome rooms in an 1820 ship chandler's house, some with private decks and ocean views.

🍽 Eating

In keeping with its genteel atmosphere, St Andrews has embraced the custom of afternoon cream tea. For lunch and dinner, there are a range of nice options, mostly clustered around Water St.

Sweet Harvest Market　CAFE $
(182 Water St; mains $5-11; ☺8am-5pm Mon-Sat, 9am-3pm Sun) Cheerful counter staff create wholesome soups, salads, sandwiches and sweets that are way beyond average standard, and chowder that is truly outstanding. The coffee's good, too.

Clam Digger　SEAFOOD $
(4468 Hwy 127, Chamcook; mains $6-15; ☺11:30am-3pm & 5-9pm Apr-Sep) Cars park three-deep outside this teeny red-and-white seafood shack that's a summertime tradition in these parts. Order your clam platter or juicy, dripping cheeseburger, and claim one of the red-painted picnic tables. Don't forget an ice cream cone! It's in Chamcook, about 9 km north of St Andrews.

★Rossmount Inn Restaurant　MODERN CANADIAN $$
(📞506-529-3351; www.rossmountinn.com; 4599 Rte 127; mains $18-30; ☺5-9:30pm) The Swiss chef-owner makes wonderful use of local bounty in this warm, art-filled dining room. The ever-changing menu might include foraged goose-tongue greens and wild mushrooms, periwinkles (a small shellfish) or New Brunswick lobster. They each play a part in complex, exquisite dishes – say, lobster with nasturtium flower dumplings and vanilla bisque, or foie gras with cocoa nibs and bee balm–poached peach. Reservations are crucial. The restaurant is 3km north of town.

Garden Cafe　CAFE $$
(www.kingsbraegarden.com; 220 King St; $9-17, cream teas $13, plus admission to Kingsbrae Garden; ☺10am-5pm May-Oct) At Kingsbrae Garden, the terrace cafe serves high tea and sandwiches and salads for lunch with a glass of wine or local ale.

Gables　SEAFOOD $$
(📞506-529-3440; 143 Water St; mains $10-20; ☺11am-10pm) Seafood and views of the ocean through a row of tall windows dominate this comfortable place. To enter, head down the alley onto a gardenlike patio on the water's edge.

🍷 Drinking & Nightlife

Afternoon cocktails at the Algonquin Resort are a must. In the evenings, several downtown pubs serve up beer, music and camaraderie.

Shiretown Pub
PUB

(www.kennedyinn.ca; 218 Water St; ⊙11am-2am)
On the ground floor of the delightfully
creaky Kennedy Inn, this old-school English pub draws a mixed-age crowd of par-
tiers. Early afternoons mean sipping New
Brunswick–brewed Picaroons bitter on the
porch, while late nights bring live music
and raucous karaoke.

Red Herring Pub
PUB

(211 Water St; ⊙noon-2am) A fun, slightly divey downtown bar with pool tables, live
music and frosty Canadian beers.

ⓘ Information

The main **tourist office** (www.townofstandrews.
ca; 46 Reed Ave; ⊙8am-8pm May-Sep; 🕾) has
free walking-tour brochures that include a map
and brief description of some of the most note-
worthy places. It also has free internet access.

ⓘ Getting There & Around

HMS Transportation (www.hmstrans.com; 260
Water St) rents cars for $60 to $80 per day with
200 free kilometers; you must arrange your own
collision insurance coverage.

New River Provincial Park

Just off Hwy 1, about 35km west of Saint
John on the way to St Stephen, this large
park has one of the best beaches along the
Fundy shore, a wide stretch of sand bor-
dered on one side by the rugged coastline of
Barnaby Head. During camping season the
park charges a $7 fee per vehicle for day use,
which includes parking at the beach and
Barnaby Head trailhead.

You can spend an enjoyable few hours
hiking Barnaby Head along a 6km network
of nature trails. The **Chittick's Beach Trail**
leads through coastal forest and past four
coves, where you can check the catch in a
herring weir or examine tidal pools for marine life. Extending from this loop is the
2.5km **Barnaby Head Trail**, which hugs
the shoreline most of the way and rises
to the edge of a cliff 15m above the Bay of
Fundy.

The park's **campground** (📞506-755-4042;
newriver@gnb.ca; 78 New River Beach Rd; camp-
sites/RV sites $22/24.50; ⊙May-Sep) is across
the road from the beach and features 100 secluded sites, both rustic and with hookups,
in a wooded setting. Drawbacks are the
gravel emplacements and traffic noise.

FUNDY ISLES

The thinly populated, unspoiled Fundy Isles
are ideal for a tranquil, nature-based escape.
With grand scenery, colorful fishing wharves
tucked into coves, supreme whale-watching,
uncluttered walking trails and steaming
dishes of seafood, the islands will make
your everyday stresses fade away and your
blood pressure ease. The three main islands
each have a distinct personality and offer a
memorable, gradually absorbed peace. Out
of the summer season, all are nearly devoid
of visitors and most services are shut.

Deer Island

Deer Island, the closest of the three main
Fundy Isles, is a modest fishing settlement
with a lived-in look. The 16km-by-5km
island has been inhabited since 1770, and
1000 people live here year-round. It's well
forested, and deer are still plentiful. Lobster
is the main catch and there are half a dozen
wharves around the island.

Deer Island can be easily explored on a
day trip. Narrow, winding roads run south
down each side toward Campobello Island
and the ferry (drive defensively).

⊙ Sights & Activities

At **Lamberts Cove** is a huge lobster pound
used to hold live lobster (it could well be
the world's largest). Another massive pound
squirms at **Northern Harbor**.

At the other end of the island is the
16-hectare **Deer Island Point Park** where
Old Sow, the world's second-largest natural
tidal whirlpool, is seen offshore a few hours
before high tide. Whales pass occasionally.

At the end of Cranberry Head Rd is a deserted **beach**. Most land on the island is privately owned, so there are no hiking trails.

ⓖ Tours

Whales usually arrive in mid-June and stay
until October. Ask at any motel or restaurant
about whale-watching tours.

Seascape Kayak Tours
KAYAKING

(📞866-747-1884, 506-747-1884; www.seascape-
kayaktours.com; 40 NW Harbour Branch Rd,
Richardson; half-/full-day trips $85/150) Offers
guided paddling excursions around Deer
Island and Passamaquoddy Bay. Multiday
island-jumping camping trips are also
available.

Fundy Isles

Sleeping & Eating

Deer Island Point Park
CAMPGROUND $

(📞 506-747-2423; www.deerislandpointpark.com; 195 Deer Island Point Rd; campsites $25-30; ⊙ Jun-Sep) Set up your tent on the high bluff and spend an evening watching the Old Sow whirlpool. The campground is directly above the Campobello ferry landing.

Sunset Beach Cottage & Suites
INN $$

(📞 506-747-2972; www.cottageandsuites.com; 21 Cedar Grove Rd, Fairhaven; r $80, cottage per week $840; ⊙ May-Oct; ❄) On a secluded cove, this two-story unit has five tidy, basic suites with carpet and unstylish plaid bedding. Upper floors have better views. The private barbecues and the pool and hot tub overlooking the bay are major draws. The furnished cottage (sleeps four maximum) is nice for families.

45th Parallel Motel & Restaurant
SEAFOOD $

(📞 506-747-2222; www.45thparallel.ca; 941 Hwy 772, Fairhaven; mains $6-25; ⊙ 7:30am-9pm) The specialty is seafood at this small, rustic country classic with a homey feel and great food. Ask to see Herman, the monster lobster. The creaky-but-clean motel rooms (from $62) are a fine bargain, too.

ℹ Information

There's a summertime **tourist information kiosk** (www.deerisland.nb.ca; ⊙ 10am-3pm Thu-Tue) at the ferry landing.

ℹ Getting There & Away

A free government-run ferry (25 minutes) runs to Deer Island from Letete, which is 14.5km south of St George on Hwy 172 via Back Bay. The ferries run year-round every half-hour from 6am to 7pm, and hourly from 7pm to 10pm. Get in line early on a busy day.

The private **East Coast Ferries** (www.east-coastferries.nb.ca; car & driver $16, additional passenger $3; ⊙ 9am-6pm end Jun–mid-Sep) links Deer Island Point to Eastport, Maine, an attractive seaside town. It leaves for Eastport every hour on the hour.

Campobello Island

The atmosphere on Campobello is remarkably different from that of Deer Island. It's a gentler and more prosperous island, with straight roads and better facilities. The wealthy have long been enjoying Campobello as a summer retreat. Due to its accessibility and proximity to New England, it feels as much a part of the USA as of Canada, and most of the tourists here are Americans.

Like many moneyed families, the Roosevelts bought property in this peaceful coastal area at the end of the 1800s, and it is for this that the island is best known. The southern half of Campobello is almost all park, and a golf course occupies still more.

Come to the island prepared. There's a single grocery store, two ATMs, a liquor store and a pharmacy, but no gas station – the 1200 residents of the 16km-long Campobello must cross the bridge to Lubec, Maine, to fill their tanks. They generally use the same bridge to go elsewhere in New Brunswick, as the Deer Island ferry only operates in the summer.

◉ Sights & Activities

★ Roosevelt Campobello International Park   PARK

(www.fdr.net; Hwy 774; ☺ sunrise-sunset year-round, cottage tours Jun-Sep) The southern-most green area of Campobello Island is this 1200-hectare park. Its biggest visitor attraction is the **Roosevelt Cottage**, the 34-room lodge where Franklin D Roosevelt grew up (between 1905 and 1921) and visited periodically throughout his time as US president (1933–45). The tomato-red Arts and Crafts–style structure is furnished with original Roosevelt furniture and artifacts. Adjacent **Hubbard House**, built in 1898, is also open to visitors. The grounds are open all the time, and you can peek through the windows when the doors are closed.

The park is just 2.5km from the Lubec bridge, and from the Roosevelt mansion's front porch you can look directly across to Eastport, Maine. You'd hardly know you were in Canada.

Unlike the manicured museum area, most of the international park has been left in its natural state to preserve the flora and fauna that Roosevelt appreciated so much. A couple of gravel roads meander through it, leading to beaches and 7.5km of nature trails. It's a surprisingly wild, little-visited part of Campobello Island. Deer, moose and coyote call it home, and seals can sometimes be seen offshore on the ledges near Lower Duck Pond, 6km from the visitors center. Look for eagles, ospreys and loons.

Herring Cove Provincial Park   PARK

Along the northern boundary of Roosevelt Campobello International Park is Herring Cove Provincial Park. This park has 10km of walking trails as well as a campground and a picnic area on an arching 1.5km beach. It makes a fine, picturesque place for lunch.

Wilson's Beach   VILLAGE

Ten kilometers north of Roosevelt Park, Wilson's Beach has a large pier with fish for sale, and a sardine-processing plant with an adjacent store. There are various services and shops here in the island's biggest community.

East Quoddy Head Lighthouse   LIGHTHOUSE

Four kilometers north of Wilson's Beach is East Quoddy Head Lighthouse. Whales browse offshore and many people sit along the rocky shoreline with binoculars enjoying the sea breezes.

☞ Tours

Island Cruises   CRUISE

(☎ 506-752-1107,   888-249-4400;   www.bayof-fundywhales.com; 62 Harbour Head Rd, Wilson's Beach; adult/child $52/42; ☺ Jul-Oct) Offers 2½-hour whale-watching cruises.

🛏 Sleeping & Eating

There are very few restaurants on Campo-bello, and the pickings across the bridge in Lubec, Maine, aren't much better. For self-catering, there's a Valufoods supermarket in Welshpool.

Herring Cove Provincial Park   CAMPGROUND $

(☎ 506-752-7010; www.tourismnewbrunswick.ca; 136 Herring Cove Rd; campsites/RV sites $22/24; ☺ Jun-Sep) This 76-site park on the east side of the island, 3km from the Deer Island ferry, has some nice secluded sites in a forest setting, plus there's a sandy beach and ample hiking.

Pollock Cove Cottages   COTTAGES $$

(☎ 506-752-2300; senewman@nbnet.nb.ca; 2455 Rte 774, Wilson's Beach; cottages $75-175; @) Simple, clean one- and two-bedroom cottages with million-dollar views.

Owen House B&B   B&B $$

(☎ 506-752-2977; www.owenhouse.ca; 11 Welsh-pool St, Welshpool; d incl breakfast with/without bathroom from $122/114) A classic seaside vacation home of yesteryear, complete with antique spool beds made up with quilts, cozy reading nooks and lots of windows on the ocean.

Family Fisheries Restaurant   SEAFOOD $$

(Hwy 774, Wilson's Beach; mains $9-23; ☺ 8am-7:30pm, later in summer) Part of a fresh fish market, this ultracasual seafood shack specializes in fish-and-chips, lip-smacking chowders, and lobster rolls.

❶ Information

For further information see www.visitcampo-bello.com. There's also a **visitors center** (Hwy 774; ☺ 10am-5pm) at Roosevelt Campobello International Park.

❶ Getting There & Away

East Coast Ferries (www.eastcoastferries. nb.ca; car & driver $16, additional passenger $3; ☺ 9am-7pm) connects Deer Island to Welshpool on Campobello Island (25 minutes, half-hourly).

NEW BRUNSWICK CAMPOBELLO ISLAND

Grand Manan Island

Cue the Maritime fiddle music. As the ferry from the mainland rounds the northern tip of Grand Manan Island (population 2700), Swallowtail Lighthouse looms into view, poised atop a rocky, moss-covered cliff. Brightly painted fishing boats bob in the harbor. Up from the ferry dock, the tidy village of North Head spreads out along the shore: a scattering of clapboard houses and shops surrounded by well-tended flower gardens and tall, leafy trees.

Grand Manan is a peaceful, unspoiled place. There are no fast-food restaurants, no trendy coffeehouses or nightclubs, no traffic lights and no traffic. Just a ruggedly beautiful coastline of high cliffs and sandy coves interspersed with spruce forest and fields of long grass. Along the eastern shore and joined by a meandering coastal road sit a string of pretty and prosperous fishing villages. There is plenty of fresh sea air and that rare and precious commodity in the modern world: silence, broken only by the rhythmic ocean surf. Some people make it a day trip, but lingering is recommended.

The ferry disembarks at the village of North Head at the north end of the island. The main road, Rte 776, runs 28.5km down the length of the island along the eastern shore. It connects all of Grand Manan's settlements en route to the lighthouse, which is perched atop a bluff at South Head. You can drive from end to end in about 45 minutes. The western side of Grand Manan is uninhabited and more or less impenetrable: a sheer rock wall rising out the sea, backed by dense forest and bog, broken only at Dark Harbour where a steep road drops down to the water's edge. A hiking trail provides access to this wilderness.

◎ Sights

Swallowtail Lighthouse   LIGHTHOUSE

Whitewashed Swallowtail Lighthouse (1860) is the island's signature vista, cleaving to a rocky promontory about 1km north of the ferry wharf. Access is via steep stairs and a slightly swaying suspension bridge. Since the light was automated in 1986, the site has been left to the elements. Nevertheless, the grassy bluff is a stupendous setting for a picnic. It has a wraparound view of the horizon and seals raiding the heart-shape fishing weirs (an ancient type of fishing trap made from wood posts) below.

All of the approximately 30 weirs dotting the waters around Grand Manan are named, some dating back to the 19th century. They bear labels such as 'Ruin,' 'Winner,' 'Outside Chance' and 'Spite,' evoking the heartbreak of relying on an indifferent sea for a living. A tear made by a marauding seal in a net can free an entire catch of herring in a single night.

Grand Manan Historical Museum   MUSEUM

(www.grandmananmuseum.ca; 1141 Rte 776, Grand Harbour; adult/student & senior $5/3; ⊘9am-5:30pm Mon-Sat) This museum makes a good destination on a foggy day. Its diverse collection of local artifacts provides a quick primer on island history. Here you can see a display on shipwreck lore and the original kerosene lamp from nearby Gannet Rock lighthouse (1904). There is also a room stuffed with 200-plus taxidermied birds (including the now-extinct passenger pigeon). The museum hosts a number of evening lectures and community classes and activities.

Seal Cove   HISTORIC SITE

Seal Cove is the island's prettiest village. Much of its charm comes from the fishing boats, wharves and herring-smoking sheds clustered around the tidal creek mouth. For a century, smoked herring was king on Grand Manan. A thousand men and women worked splitting, stringing and drying fish in 300 smokehouses up and down the island. The last smokehouse shut down in 1996. Although herrings are still big business around here, they're now processed at a modern cannery. Today, the sheds house an informal **Sardine Museum** (admission by donation; ⊘11am-4pm Tue-Sat). On display are the world's largest sardine can (alleged) and an authentically smelly exhibit on the smoking process.

🏃 Activities

Sea Watch Tours   BIRDWATCHING

(☑506-662-8552, 877-662-8552; www.seawatchtours.com; Seal Cove fisherman's wharf; adult/child $86/48; ⊘Mon-Sat Jul & Aug) Make the pilgrimage out to isolated Machias Seal Island to see the Atlantic puffins waddle and play on their home turf. Access is limited to 15 visitors a day, so reserve well in advance. Getting onto the island can be tricky, as the waves are high and the rocks slippery. Wear sturdy shoes.

Whales-n-Sails Adventures BOAT TOUR
(✆506-662-1999, 888-994-4044; www.whales-n-sails.com; North Head fisherman's wharf; adult/child $66/46; ☉Jul-Sep) A marine biologist narrates these exhilarating whale-watching tours aboard the sailboat *Elsie Menota*. You'll often see puffins, razorbills, murre and other seabirds.

Hiking Trails HIKING
Seventy kilometers of hiking trails crisscross and circle the island. Grab the comprehensive guide, *Heritage Trails and Footpaths on Grand Manan* ($5), available at most island shops. Stay well away from the cliff edges; unstable, undercut ground can give way beneath your feet.

For an easy hike, try the 1.6km shoreline path from Long Pond to Red Point (about a one-hour round-trip; suitable for children). In Whale Cove, the Hole-in-the-Wall is an often photographed natural arch jutting into the sea. It's a short hike from the parking area.

Adventure High KAYAKING, CYCLING
(✆506-662-3563; www.adventurehigh.com; 83 Rte 776, North Head; day tours $45-110, bicycles per half-day/day/week $16/22/130; ☉May-Oct) This outfitter offers tours of the Grand Manan coastline ranging from two-hour sunset paddles to multiday Bay of Fundy adventures.

🛏 Sleeping

Anchorage Provincial Park CAMPGROUND $
(✆506-662-7022; Rte 776 btwn Grand Harbour & Seal Cove; campsites/RV sites $24/26; ☉May-Sep) Family-friendly camping in a large field surrounded by tall evergreens, located 16km from the ferry. There's a kitchen shelter for rainy days, a playground, laundry and a long pebbly beach. Get down by the trees to block the wind. Anchorage adjoins some marshes, which comprise a migratory bird sanctuary, and there are several short hiking trails.

Hole-in-the-Wall Campground CAMPGROUND $
(✆506-662-3152, 866-662-4489; www.grandmanancamping.com; 42 Old Airport Rd, North Head; campsites/cabins $27/40; ☉May-Oct) These spectacular cliff-top campsites are secluded among the rocks and trees, with fire pits, picnic tables and breathtaking views. Choose an inland site if you sleepwalk or suffer from vertigo. Showers and laundry facilities are available, as well as a couple of spotless, simple cabins, furnished with bunk beds and a microwave.

Shorecrest Lodge INN $$
(✆506-662-3216; www.shorecrestlodge.com; 100 Rte 776, Seal Cove; r $90-135; 🌐) Near the ferry landing, this big, comfy farmhouse has 10 sunny rooms with quilts and antique furniture. A rec room has a TV and a toy train set for the kids. The Austrian owners cook up fresh seafood dinners (mains $18 to $28) and takeout lunches; nonguests can call ahead to order.

★Inn at Whale Cove INN $$
(✆506 662-3181; www.whalecovecottages.ca; Whistle Rd, North Head; s/d incl breakfast $135/145;

NEW BRUNSWICK GRAND MANAN ISLAND

WHOSE ROCK IS IT ANYWAY?

Though Canada and the US share nearly 9000km of border, they manage to play nicely most of the time. So nicely, in fact, that today the sole remaining land dispute between the two countries is over an uninhabited 8-hectare chunk of rock called Machias Seal Island, and a neighboring (and even smaller) island so undistinguished it's referred to only as 'North Rock.'

Foggy, barren and treeless, Machias Seal Island is best known as a nesting site for Atlantic puffins. North Rock is best known for...being a rock. Yet the two tiny islands are part of a dispute that dates back to the 1783 Treaty of Paris, which attempted to draw a border between the newly formed USA and what was then called 'British North America.' Machias Seal Island, approximately equidistant between Maine and New Brunswick's Grand Manan Island, was not directly addressed in the treaty (imagine that!), and has remained part of a 'gray zone' ever since. Canada operates a lighthouse on the island and attempts to maintain it as a bird sanctuary, while some American puffin-boat tour operators challenge Canadian sovereignty. One, the late Captain Barna Nelson of Jonesport, Maine, would parade around the island once a year, waving an American flag. Canada and the US have had the opportunity to resolve the border dispute in international courts, but have declined.

⊙May-Oct) 'Serving rusticators since 1910,' including writer Willa Cather, who wrote several of her novels here in the 1920s and '30s. The main lodge (built in 1816) and half a dozen vine-covered and shingled cottages retain the charm of that earlier era. They are fitted with polished pine floors and stone fireplaces, antiques, chintz curtains and well-stocked bookshelves. Some have kitchens.

Compass Rose   B&B $$
(⏿506-662-8570, off-season 613-471-1772; www. compassroseinn.com; 65 Rte 776, North Head; r incl breakfast $105-149) Cheerful, comfortable guest rooms with a seashore motif and harbor views. Within walking distance of the ferry dock, it has one of the island's most atmospheric restaurants (mains $12-$18) attached.

✗ Eating

The island's scant options are nearly non-existent in the off-season (October to early June). That said, there is some fine eating on Grand Manan. Reservations are essential for dinner due to limited table space island-wide.

★ North Head Bakery   BAKERY $
(www.northheadbakery.ca; 199 Rte 776, North Head; baked goods $1-5; ⊙6:30am-5:30pm Tue-Sat May-Oct) Scrumptious Danish pastries, fruit pies and artisanal breads made with organic flour make this cheerful red-and-white bakery the first stop for many folks just off the ferry. Sit at the lunch counter with a coffee and sandwich and watch the parade.

Sailors Landing   CANADIAN $
(⏿506-662-9620; 1 Ferry Wharf Rd, North Head; mains $5-10; ⊙6am-10pm Mon-Fri, to 11pm Sat, 7am-9pm Sun) In a hangarlike corrugated metal building by the ferry dock, this updated restaurant offers a 'featured menu' daily, plus fresh, locally caught seafood and homemade desserts.

★ Inn at Whale Cove   MODERN CANADIAN $$$
(⏿506-662-3181; www.whalecovecottages.ca; Whistle Rd, North Head; mains $22-28; ⊙5-9pm) Absolutely wonderful food in a relaxed country setting on the cove. The menu changes daily, but includes mouth-watering upscale meals such as Provençal-style rack of lamb, scallop ravioli and a to-die-for hazelnut crème caramel for dessert. Come early and have a cocktail by the fire in the cozy, old-fashioned parlor.

🛍 Shopping

Roland's Sea Vegetables   MARKET
(www.rolandsdulse.com; 174 Hill Rd; ⊙9am-6pm) Grand Manan is one of the few remaining producers of dulse, a type of seaweed that is used as a snack food or seasoning in Atlantic Canada and around the world. Dark Harbour, on the west side of the island, is said to produce the world's best. Dulse gatherers wade among the rocks at low tide to pick the seaweed, then lay it out on beds of rocks to dry just as they've been doing for hundreds of years. Buy some at this little roadside market, which sells various types of edible local seaweeds from nori to sea lettuce to Irish moss. Sandy, Roland's son, recommends sprinkling powdered dulse on fried eggs or baked fish.

ℹ Information

Tourist Information Office (www.grand-manannb.com; 130 Rte 776, North Head; ⊙8am-4pm Mon-Fri, 9am-noon Sat)

ℹ Getting There & Around

The only way to get on and off the island from Blacks Harbour on the mainland to North Head on Grand Manan is by the **government ferry** (⏿506-662-3724; www.coastaltransport.ca; adult/child/car/bicycle $12/6/33/4; 🎟 ticket office at North Head ferry terminal). The crossing takes 1½ hours, and there are seven departures daily in summer. Service is first-come, first-served at Blacks Harbour; plan on arriving at least 45 minutes before departure. In July and August especially there can be long queues for vehicles to board, but cyclists and pedestrians can walk on at any time. No ticket is required for the trip over; book and pay for your return trip in North Head the day before you plan to leave for the mainland. Watch for harbor porpoises and whales en route.

The ferry dock is within walking distance of several hotels, restaurants, shops and tour operators. To explore the whole of the island, bring your own car, as there is no rental company on Grand Manan.

Adventure High (p123) rents bicycles.

SAINT JOHN

POP 70,500

Saint John is the economic engine room of the province, a gritty port city with a dynamism that's missing from the demure capital. The setting is spectacular – a ring of rocky bluffs, sheer cliffs, coves and peninsulas surrounding a deep natural harbor where the mighty Saint John and Kennebecasis Rivers empty into the Bay of Fundy. It can take a bit of imagination to appreciate this natural beauty, obscured as it is by the smokestacks of a pulp mill, oil refinery and garden-variety urban blight. The city is surrounded by an ugly scurf of industrial detritus and a tangle of concrete overpasses. But those who push their way through all this to the historic core are rewarded with beautifully preserved red-brick and sandstone 19th-century architecture and glimpses of the sea down steep, narrow side streets.

Originally a French colony, the city was incorporated by British Loyalists in 1785 to become Canada's first legal city. Thousands of Irish immigrants arrived during the potato famine of the mid-1800s and helped build the city into a prosperous industrial town, important particularly for its wooden shipbuilding. Today, a large percentage of the population works in heavy industry, including pulp mills, refineries and the Moosehead Brewery.

Downtown (known as Uptown) Saint John sits on a square, hilly peninsula between the mouth of the St John River and Courtenay Bay. Kings Sq marks the nucleus of town, and its pathways duplicate the pattern of the Union Jack.

West over the Harbour Bridge (50¢ toll) is Saint John West. Many of the street names in this section of the city are identical to those of Saint John proper, and to avoid confusion, they end in a west designation, such as Charlotte St W. Saint John West has the ferries to Digby, Nova Scotia.

◎ Sights

New Brunswick Museum MUSEUM
(www.nbm-mnb.ca; 1 Market Sq; adult/student/family $8/4.50/17; ☺9am-5pm Mon-Wed & Fri, to 9pm Thu, 10am-5pm Sat, noon-5pm Sun) This is a quality museum with a varied collection. There's a captivating section on marine wildlife with an outstanding section on whales, including a life-size specimen. There are also hands-on exhibits, models of old sailing ships and an original copy of *The Night Before Christmas* written in author Clement Clarke Moore's own hand, which was sent to his godfather Jonathan Odell's family in New Brunswick.

Reversing Rapids RIVER
The Bay of Fundy tides and their effects are a predominant regional characteristic. The rapids here on the St John River are part of that and are one of the best-known sites in the province. However, 'reversing rapids' is a bit of a misnomer. When the high Bay of Fundy tides rise, the current in the river reverses, causing the water to flow upstream. When the tides go down, the water flows in the normal way. Generally, it looks like rapids. **Reversing Rapids Visitors Centre** (200 Bridge Rd; ☺8am-7pm May-Oct), next to the bridge over the river, can supply a 'Reversing Rapids Tide Table' brochure that explains where in the cycle you are.

Loyalist House HISTORIC BUILDING
(120 Union St; adult/child/family $5.50/2.50/7.50; ☺10am-5pm May-Sep) Dating from 1810, the Georgian-style Loyalist House is one of the city's oldest unchanged buildings. It's now a museum, depicting the Loyalist period, and contains some fine carpentry.

Loyalist Burial Ground CEMETERY
This solemn cemetery, with fading tombstones from as early as 1784, is just off Kings Sq, in a park-style setting in the center of town.

Carleton Martello Tower HISTORIC BUILDING
(454 Whipple St; adult/child $3.90/1.90; ☺10am-5:30pm Jun-Sep) Built during the War of 1812, this round stone fort features a restored barracks and other historical displays, but the real reason to go is the panoramic view over Saint John and the Bay of Fundy from the hilltop locale.

Saint John Jewish Historical Museum MUSEUM
(91 Leinster St; admission by donation; ☺10am-4pm Mon-Fri, 1-4pm Sun) This modest museum traces the history of Saint John's once-thriving Jewish community, whose members included Louis B Mayer of Metro-Goldwyn-Mayer Hollywood fame.

🏃 Activities

Reversing Falls Jet Boat Rides BOAT TOUR
(☎506-634-8987; www.jetboatrides.com; Fallsview Ave; adult/child $39/29; ☺Jun-Oct) Offers two types of boat trips. One is a leisurely one-hour sightseeing tour to the Reversing Rapids and around the harbor. The other is a 20-minute 'thrill ride' through the white water at the rapids. Count on getting soaked.

NEW BRUNSWICK SAINT JOHN

Saint John

Saint John

⊙ Sights

Irving Nature Park HIKING
(⊙8am-dusk May-Oct) For those who have
vehicles and an appreciation for nature,
Irving Nature Park is a must for its rugged, unspoiled coastal topography. It's
also a remarkable place for birdwatching,
with hundreds of species regularly spotted.
Seals may be seen on the rocks offshore.
Seven trails of varying lengths lead around
beaches, cliffs, woods, mudflats, marsh and
rocks. Good footwear is strongly recommended.

It's well worth the 5km drive southwest
from downtown to get here. Take Hwy 1
west from town and turn south at Exit 107,
Bleury St. Then take a right on Sand Cove
Rd and continue for 2km to the entrance.

Harbour Passage WALKING
Beginning on a boardwalk at **Market Sq**
(behind the Hilton Hotel), Harbour Passage is a red-paved walk- and cycle-trail
that leads around the harbor, up Bennett
St and down Douglas Ave to the Reversing Falls bridge and lookout. Informative

plaques line the route and it's about a one-hour walk one-way.

Gibson Creek Canoeing CANOEING
(506-672-8964; www.gibsoncreek.ca; tours per day from $65) This company offers guided canoe trips through the numerous intertidal marshes and peaceful rivers close to the city.

Tours

As a popular stop for cruise-ship travelers, Saint John has a surprisingly large range of tour options. Whale-watching, unfortunately, is not an attraction in Saint John, save for the very occasional, very wayward minke.

Saint John Transit Commission BUS TOUR
(506-658-2855; www.saintjohntransit.com; adult/child $22/6; Jun-Sep) Runs two-hour bus tours around the city. Departures and tickets from Reversing Rapids Visitors Centre, Barbour's General Store at Market Sq, and Rockwood Park Campground. Two tours daily.

Words, Walks & Workshops WALKING TOUR
(506-672-8601; walks free-$5; 7pm Tue Jun-Sep) For nearly 30 years David Goss, travel and outdoor columnist, has led themed walks throughout the city and natural environments. The walks have so much flair that locals as well as visitors frequent the fun. Departure locations and hours vary; check with the visitors center.

Roy's Tour DRIVING TOUR
(www.roystours.webs.com; tours per group per hr $50) Knowledgeable local Roy Flowers narrates personalized five- to six-hour taxi tours of the city and surrounds.

Sleeping

Saint John motels sit primarily along Manawagonish Rd, 7km west of uptown. There are also a couple of upscale chain hotels uptown.

Rockwood Park CAMPGROUND $
(506-652-4050; www.rockwoodparkcampground.com; Lake Dr S; campsites/RV sites $25/35; May-Sep;) A couple of kilometers north of the downtown area is huge Rockwood Park, with small lakes, a woodland crisscrossed by walking paths, and a campground in a small open field. Bus 6 to Mt Pleasant from Kings Sq goes within a few blocks Monday to Saturday.

University of New Brunswick Summer Residences RESIDENCE HALL $
(506-648-5755; www.unbsj.ca; off Sandy Point Rd near Rockwood Park; s/d/ste $35/48/72;) From May to August, the University of New Brunswick's Saint John campus offers simple rooms and rather spartan kitchenette suites in two residence halls. The university is 6km north of the city center (take bus 15 from Kings Sq).

★ **Mahogany Manor** B&B $$
(800-796-7755, 506-636-8000; www.sjnow.com/mm; 220 Germain St; d incl breakfast $105-115;) On the loveliest street in Saint John, this gay-friendly, antique-filled Victorian is a wonderful place to temporarily call home. Five rooms are a comfy mix of antiques and plush, modern bedding. The upbeat owners know more about the city than you'll be able to absorb – even which meal to order at which restaurant!

Homeport B&B $$
(506-672-7255, 888-678-7678; www.homeport.nb.ca; 60 Douglas Ave; r incl breakfast $109-175;) Perched above once-grand Douglas Ave, this imposing Italianate-style B&B was once two separate mansions belonging to shipbuilder brothers. It has a boutique-hotel vibe, with a stately parlor, a full bar and 10 sunny guest rooms. Try to snag one with a clawfoot tub. It's about 1km west of the uptown peninsula.

Chipman Hill Suites APARTMENTS $$
(506-693-1171; www.chipmanhill.com; 9 Chipman Hill; ste $79-299;) Chipman has taken historic properties around downtown, renovated them into mini-apartments with kitchens while retaining all the character, and rents them out by the day, week or month. Size and features determine price, but all are a steal.

Eating

★ **Old City Market** MARKET $
(www.sjcitymarket.ca; 47 Charlotte St; lunches $5-10; 7:30am-6pm Mon-Fri, to 5pm Sat) Wedged between North and South Market Sts, this sense-stunning food hall has been home to wheeling and dealing since 1876. The interior of the impressive brick building is packed with produce stalls, bakeries, fishmongers and butcher shops, as well as numerous counters selling a range of delectable prepared meals. Locals head to the lunch counter at Slocum and Ferris.

Look out for bags of dulse, a dried Atlantic seaweed that's eaten like potato chips in these parts.

Java Moose
CAFE $

(www.javamoose.com; 84 Prince William St; snacks $2-5; ⊗8am-6pm; 🛜) Get your caffeine fix at this home-grown coffeehouse with a groovy North Woods vibe.

Infusion
CAFE $

(www.infusiontearoom.ca; Old City Market; snacks $3-6; ⊗7am-7pm; 🛜) In the Old City Market, this warmly lit urban-chic cafe offers dozens of rare and exceptional teas, along with sandwiches and other light fare.

★East Coast Bistro
INTERNATIONAL $$

(☑506-696-3278; www.eastcoastbistro.com; 60 Prince William St; mains $18-25; ⊗11am-4pm Mon, to 9pm Tue-Thu, to 10pm Fri & Sat) Sustainable, local cuisine (they even make their own bread) is the real deal here. East Coast Bistro is one of the standout restaurants in Saint John, offering top-notch cuisine at digestible prices. Pan-fried New Brunswick goat cheese, molasses-glazed Atlantic salmon, and brown-butter apple crumble are just a few of the luscious dishes whipped up in this casual space.

Bourbon Quarter & Magnolia Cafe
CAJUN $$

(☑506-214-3618; Prince William St; mains $10-35; ⊗8am-11pm Mon-Fri, 9am-midnight Sat, to 8pm Sun) Cajun food in Canada? Hip, young Saint Johners don't seem to find anything odd about the idea, flocking to eat fried oysters and muffuletta sandwiches at this recently opened pair of adjacent New Orleans–style restaurants. Bourbon Quarter is more formal, Magnolia a casual lunch spot. Both have live music.

Splash Thai Cuisine
THAI $$

(www.splashthaicuisine.com; 419 Rothesay Ave; mains $18-23; ⊗4-10pm Tue-Sun) Killer Thai specialties that bring back the locals over and over again. Go for the usual suspects or more inventive twists on the old, like mango chicken curry. Soothing low lights and minimalist decor lend the space an upscale, relaxing vibe.

Taco Pica
MEXICAN, GUATEMALAN $$

(www.tacopica.ca; 96 Germain St; mains $10-17; ⊗10am-10pm Mon-Sat) A fusion of authentic Guatemalan and Mexican fare is served in this colorful cantina. An economical introduction to the cuisine is Taco Pica's *pepian –* a simple but spicy beef stew that is as good as you'll find in any Guatemalan household.

Billy's Seafood Company
SEAFOOD $$$

(www.billysseafood.com; 49 Charlotte St; mains $16-32; ⊗11am-10pm Mon-Sat, 4-10pm Sun) Since we are on the east coast after all...this popular casual restaurant at the top of the City Market does seafood with flair.

Thandi
INDIAN $$$

(☑506-648-2377; www.singhdining.com; 33 Canterbury St; mains $17-38; ⊗11am-10pm Mon-Fri, 4pm-midnight Sat, to 10pm Sun) Thandi gets an A+ for atmosphere, with exposed brick, heavy timbers and warm lighting, a stylish backlit bar downstairs, and cozy fireplaces upstairs. The food is good, too – try Indian classics such as lamb korma or shrimp vindaloo, or fusion specialties such as tandoori strip loin or snapper with mango salsa.

🍷 Drinking & Entertainment

There isn't much of a nightclub scene here, but pub culture and live music thrive in a handful of atmospheric waterfront bars in the uptown core. For weekly goings on, pick up the free *here* entertainment paper, available around town.

Big Tide Brewing Company
BREWERY

(www.bigtidebrew.com; 47 Princess St; ⊗11am-midnight Mon-Sat, 3-9pm Sun) This subterranean brewpub is a cozy spot for a pint (try the Confederation Cream Ale or the Whistlepig Stout), a plate of beer-steamed mussels or a friendly game of trivia.

Happinez Wine Bar
BAR

(www.happinezwinebar.com; 42 Princess St; ⊗4pm-midnight Wed & Thu, to 1am Fri, 5pm-1am Sat) For a quiet tipple in a sleek urban environment, duck into this intimate little wine bar.

O'Leary's
PUB

(www.olearyspub.com; 46 Princess St; ⊗11:30am-11pm Mon & Tue, to 2am Wed-Fri, 3pm-2am Sat) Shoot the breeze with local barflies at this pleasantly divey downtown institution.

Imperial Theatre
THEATER

(☑506-674-4100; www.imperialtheatre.nb.ca; 24 Kings Sq S) Now restored to its original 1913 splendor, this is the city's premier venue for performances ranging from classical music to live theater.

ℹ Information

Main Post Office (41 Church Ave W, Saint John West) Send general delivery mail here (Postal Station B, E2M 4X6).

Saint John Library (1 Market Sq; ⊘9am-5pm Mon & Sat, 10am-5pm Tue & Wed, to 9pm Thu & Fri) Free internet access.

Saint John Regional Hospital (☑506-648-6000; 400 University Ave; ⊘24hr) Northwest of the town center.

Visitor & Convention Bureau (☑506-658-2990, 888-364-4444; www.tourismsaintjohn.com; Market Sq; ⊘9:30am-8pm) Knowledge-able, friendly staff. Ask for the self-guided walking-tour pamphlets.

ℹ Getting There & Away

AIR
The airport is 5km east of town on Loch Lomond Rd toward St Martins. Air Canada runs daily flights to Toronto, Montréal and Halifax.

BOAT
There's a daily ferry service between Saint John and Digby, Nova Scotia ($43, three hours).

BUS
The **bus station** (300 Union St; ⊘7:30am-9pm Mon-Fri, 8am-9pm Sat & Sun) is a five-minute walk from town. Routes include Fredericton ($29, 1½ hours) and Moncton ($33, two hours). There's a daily direct bus to Bangor, Maine ($55, 3½ hours), but you'll need to buy your ticket in person.

ℹ Getting Around

TO/FROM THE AIRPORT
City bus 22 links the airport and Kings Sq. A taxi costs around $35.

ℹ MOOSE ON THE LOOSE

Every year, there are around 300 collisions involving moose on the roads in New Brunswick. These accidents are almost always fatal for the animal and about five people a year die this way. Eighty-five percent of moose-vehicle collisions happen between May and October, and most occur at night. Slow down when driving after dusk and scan the verges for animals, using your high beams when there is no oncoming traffic. High-risk zones are posted.

BUS
Saint John Transit (☑506-658-4700) charges $2.50. The most important route is the east–west bus service, which is either bus 1 or 2 eastbound to McAllister Dr and bus 3 or 4 westbound to Saint John West near the ferry terminal. It stops at Kings Sq in the city center. Another frequent service is bus 15 or 16 to the university.

CAR & MOTORCYCLE
Discount Car Rentals (☑506-633-4440; www.discountcar.com; 255 Rothesay Ave) is opposite the Park Plaza Motel. Avis, Budget, Hertz and National all have car-rental desks at the airport.

Parking meters in Saint John require $1 an hour from 8am to 6pm weekdays only. You can park free at meters on weekends, holidays and in the evening. Park free any time on back streets such as Leinster and Princess Sts, east of Kings Sq. The **city parking lot** (11 Sydney St) is free on weekends.

EASTERN FUNDY SHORE

Much of the rugged, unspoiled Eastern Fundy Shore from Saint John to Hopewell Cape remains essentially untouched. Indeed, hikers, cyclists, kayakers and all nature-lovers will be enchanted by this marvelous coast, edged by dramatic cliffs and tides. It's not possible to drive directly along the coastline from St Martins to Fundy National Park; a detour inland by Sussex is necessary, unless you're prepared to hike.

St Martins

A 40km drive east of Saint John, St Martins is a winsome seaside hamlet surrounded by steep cliffs and flower-studded pastureland. Once a sleepy wooden shipbuilding center, it now draws hikers, bikers and scenic-drive takers to the 11km **Fundy Trail Parkway** (www.fundytrailparkway.com), which winds along a jaw-dropping stretch of coastline. In town, check out the impressive red sandstone sea caves of Mac's Beach, accessible by foot when the tide is low. The village's twin covered bridges are a popular photo op, so bring your camera.

River Bay Adventures (☑506-663-9530; www.riverbayadventures.com; tours from $50, kayaks half-/full day $33/52) runs two- to three-hour guided sea-kayaking trips to the caves and islands along the coast.

St Martin's Country Inn (☑800-566-5257, 506-833-4534; www.stmartinscountryinn.ca;

WORTH A TRIP

SCENIC DRIVE: KENNEBECASIS RIVER VALLEY

On a Saturday in summer, do what loads of Saint Johners do and take the Gondola Point Ferry (p111) to the bucolic Kingston Peninsula, then follow Rte 845 east to the **Kingston Farmers Market** (Rte 845, Kingston; ⊘8am-1pm Sat). Sample the fresh fruits and vegetables and various ethnic foods on offer or stop for lunch at the restored 1810 **Carter House Tea Room** (874 Rte 845; cakes & teas $4-8; ⊘9:30am-4:30pm Tue-Sat), which is, of course, haunted – by a ghost who likes to tidy up and rearrange the books.

Leave the city folk behind, continuing on Rte 845 into the bustling community of Hampton, where you pick up Rte 121, which follows the north side of the Kennebecasis River through farm country and the villages of Norton and Apohaqui into **Sussex** (population 4200).

Sussex is a working farming community nestled in a green valley dotted with dairy farms. The old-fashioned main street could be a movie set for a heartwarming 1950s coming-of-age story (but please, enough with the outdoor murals!). The well-preserved railway station houses the tourist information center, a small museum devoted to the area's military regiment, and Sully's Ice Cream Parlour.

If you stick around until evening, keep up the 1950s time trip with a double-bill at the **Sussex Drive-In** (☑506-432-9114; www.sussexdrivein.com; Rte 2; adult/child $10/6; ⊘dusk Fri-Sun May-Sep). You can pitch your tent at the attached **Town & Country Campark** (☑506-432-9114; www.sussexdrivein.com; campsites/RV sites $24/31). You can also bed down at **Jonah Place B&B** (☑866-448-8800, 506-433-6978; www.jonahplace.com; 977 Main St; r incl breakfast from $99; ⊜@⊚). The classy and cozy **Broadway Cafe** (☑506-433-5414; 73 Broad St; mains lunch $8, dinner $17-35; ⊘10am-3pm Mon & Tue, to 9pm Wed-Sat) is the place to eat in town.

Gasthof Old Bavarian (☑506-433-4735; www.oldbavarian.ca; 1130 Knightville Rd; mains $10-24; ⊘noon-10pm Fri-Sun) is the place for a truly memorable meal in the countryside. On a country road in a quiet valley settled by German and Dutch farmers, this place could have been transported – beer steins and all – from the Black Forest. The decor is Bavarian hunting lodge, with low timbered ceilings, heavy wooden furniture and cheerful blue-and-white-checked tablecloths. The plates of schnitzel and sausages made on the family farm are plain beautiful: they're decorated with purple cabbage, fresh-picked greens and creamy white dumplings, with hearty flavors to match. Despite being more or less in the middle of nowhere, this place is always packed for dinner, so reservations are recommended. It's cash only.

Hang a left out of Gasthof's back onto the Knightville Rd, then left again onto Country View Rd at Anagance Ridge, then right onto Rte 890 into Petitcodiac. This stretch of road affords breathtaking vistas of rolling green countryside that'll make you want to sell up, move here and raise chickens. If you can work up an appetite, stroll through the greenhouses and have a healthy organic lunch or tea and cake at **Cornhill Nursery & Cedar Cafe** (www.cornhillnursery.com; 2700 Rte 890; mains $8-12; ⊘8am-4pm May-Oct). From Petitcodiac you can rejoin Hwy 1, heading east to Moncton or west back to Fundy Park and Saint John. The views of the valley from Hwy 1 between Hampton and Sussex are also lovely.

303 Main St; r $110-165; ⊜❉⊚), the towering mansion overlooking the bay, is the most deluxe place in town and also offers delectable meals (mains $19 to $24) in its delightful, caught-in-time dining room.

Right on Mac's Beach, the resort-style **Seaside Restaurant** (81 Mac's Beach; mains $8-18; ⊘11am-7pm) serves fish and chips, scallops, chowder and more. Now you know you are on holiday.

Fundy National Park

This **national park** (www.pc.gc.ca/fundy; daily permits adult/child/family $7.80/3.90/19.60) is one of the country's most popular. Highlights are the world's highest tides, the irregularly eroded sandstone cliffs and the wide beach at low tide that makes exploring the shore for small marine life and debris such a treat. The park features an extensive network of impressive hiking trails.

🏃 Activities

Cycling

Mountain biking is permitted on six trails: Goose River, Marven Lake, Black Hole, East Branch, Bennett Brook (partially open) and Maple Grove. Surprisingly, at last report there were no bicycle rentals in Fundy National Park or in nearby Alma. Contact the visitors centers to find current information on this.

Hiking

Fundy features 120km of walking trails, where it's possible to enjoy anything from a short stroll to a three-day trek. Several trails require hikers to ford rivers, so be prepared.

The most popular backpacking route is the **Fundy Circuit**, a three-day trek of 45km through the heart of the park. Hikers generally spend their first night at Marven Lake and their second at Bruin Lake, returning via the Upper Salmon River. First, stop at the visitors center to reserve your wilderness campsites ($10 per night; call ahead for reservations).

Another overnight trek is the **Goose River Trail**. It joins the Fundy Circuit, and is accessible by road from St Martins. This undeveloped three-day trek is one of the most difficult in the province. While you can cycle to Goose River, the trail beyond can only be done on foot.

Enjoyable day hikes in Fundy National Park include the **Coppermine Trail**, a 4.4km loop which goes to an old mine site; and the **Third Vault Falls Trail**, a challenging one-way hike of 3.7km to the park's tallest falls. In summer, rangers lead a variety of family-friendly educational programs, including night hikes.

Skiing

In the winter, 25km of park trails are groomed for fantastic cross-country skiing, with additional snowshoeing tracks through the forest.

Swimming

The ocean is pretty bracing here; luckily, there's a heated saltwater **swimming pool** (adult/child $3/1.50; ⊘11am-6:30pm Jul & Aug) not far from the park's southern entrance.

🛏 Sleeping

The park has three campgrounds and 13 wilderness sites. **Camping reservations** (☑877-737-3783; www.pccamping.ca) must be made at least three days in advance. The park entry fee is extra and is paid upon arrival.

With bathhouses and showers, **Chignecto North** (campsites/RV sites $26/36) is a good pick for families. The 131-site **Headquarters Campground** (campsites/RV sites $26/37) is near the visitors center. It's the only area open for winter camping. Along the coast, 8km southwest of the visitors center, is **Point Wolfe Campground** (campsites $26) and its 181 sites with sea breezes and cooler temperatures. To reserve a backcountry site ($10), call either of the visitors centers.

Fundy Highlands Inn & Chalets CABINS, MOTEL $$
(☑506-887-2930, 888-883-8639; www.fundyhighlandchalets.com; 8714 Hwy 114; r $95-105, cabins from $115; ⊘May-Oct) Simple but charming little cabins, all with decks, kitchenettes and superlative views, and a small, well-kept motel.

ℹ Information

Headquarters Visitors Centre (☑506-887-6000; ⊘10am-6pm) At the park's south entrance

Wolfe Lake Information Centre (☑506-432-6026; Hwy 114; ⊘10am-6pm Jul & Aug) At the park's north entrance.

THE TIDES OF FUNDY

The tides of the Bay of Fundy are the highest in the world. A Mi'kmaq legend explains the tide as the effect of a whale's thrashing tail sending the water forever sloshing back and forth. A more prosaic explanation is in the length, depth and gradual funnel shape of the bay itself.

The contrasts between the high and ebb tide are most pronounced at the eastern end of the bay and around the Minas Basin, with tides of 10m to 15m twice daily 12½ hours apart. The highest tide ever recorded anywhere was 16.6m, the height of a four-story building, at Burncoat Head near Noel, Nova Scotia.

NEW BRUNSWICK FUNDY NATIONAL PARK

DON'T MISS

SCENIC DRIVE: FUNDY TRAIL PARKWAY

This magnificent **parkway** (www.fundytrailparkway.com; adult/child/family $5.50/3.50/13; ⊙6am-8pm May-Oct) traverses a rugged section of what has been called the only remaining coastal wilderness between Florida and Newfoundland. The 11km-long parkway to Big Salmon River put an end to the unspoiled wilderness part. There is now a lovely stretch of pavement with numerous viewpoints, picnic areas and parking lots. Eventually, it will extend to Fundy National Park. Nova Scotia is visible across the bay. There is also a separate 16km-long very steep and hilly hiking/biking trail.

On Saturdays, Sundays and holidays, a free hourly **shuttle bus** operates from noon to 6pm, ferrying hikers up and down the trail between the parkway entrance and Big Salmon River. In the off-season, the main gate is closed, but you can park at the entrance and hike or pedal in.

At Big Salmon River a suspension bridge leads to a vast wilderness hiking area beyond the end of the road. Hikers can make it from Big Salmon River to Goose River in Fundy National Park in three to five days. At last report, no permits or permissions were required to do so. But beyond Big Salmon River, be prepared for wilderness, rocky scree and even a rope ladder or two.

You can spend the night here, too, at **Hearst Lodge** (r incl breakfast & dinner per person $109; ⊙Jun-Sep), a cabin-on-steroids built by newspaper magnate J Randolph Hearst.

Alma

The tiny village of Alma is a supply center for the park. It has accommodations, restaurants, a small gas station, grocery store, liquor outlet and laundry. Most facilities close in winter, when it becomes a ghost town. Down on the beach is a statue of Molly Kool, the first female sea captain on the continent.

Fresh Air Adventure (☏800-545-0020, 506-887-2249; www.freshairadventure.com; 16 Fundy View Dr; tours from $55; ⊙Jun-Sep) offers myriad kayaking tours, from two-hour trips to multiday excursions, in and around Fundy.

For accommodations, **Parkland Village Inn** (☏506-887-2313; www.parklandvillageinn.com; 8601 Hwy 114; r incl breakfast $95-160) is a busy 60-year-old inn with comfy, renovated rooms, some with killer Bay of Fundy views. At the inn, **Tides Restaurant** (8601 Hwy 114; mains $12-22; ⊙noon-8pm) is a beachy, fine-dining place that does top-rate seafood and excellent ribs. The casual takeout patio has fish-and-chips and cold beer.

Cape Enrage & Mary's Point

From Alma, old Rte 915 yields two sensational, yet relatively isolated, promontories high over the bay.

See the 150-year-old lighthouse at the windblown, suitably named **Cape Enrage** (www.capenrage.ca; off Rte 905; adult/child $5/3; ⊙9am-8pm). The cape was restored and is still expertly run by local high-school students and volunteer mentors from the area. On-site guides offer **climbing** ($85 for two hours) and **rappelling** ($90 for two hours) off the steep rock faces. Or you can simply wander the beach looking for fossils (low tide only!).

When all that activity gets you hungry, head to the **Cape House Restaurant** (mains $13-28; ⊙11:30am-11pm). Here in the original lighthouse-keeper's house you can enjoy the dramatic view while dining on pan-seared local scallops, foraged fiddlehead ferns and lobster tacos.

At Mary's Point, 22km east, is the **Shepody Bay Shorebird Reserve** (Mary's Point Rd, off Hwy 915) FREE. From mid-July to mid-August hundreds of thousands of shorebirds, primarily sandpipers, gather here. Nature trails and boardwalks lead through the dikes and marsh. The interpretive center is open from late June to early September, but you can use the 6.5km of trails any time.

Hopewell Rocks

At Hopewell Cape, where the Petitcodiac River empties into Shepody Bay, are the **Hopewell Rocks** (www.thehopewellrocks.ca; off Hwy 114; adult/child/family $9/6.75/24, shuttle per person $2; ⊙8am-8pm; ♿). The 'rocks' are bizarre sandstone erosion formations known as 'flowerpots,' rising several stories from the ocean floor. Some look like arches, others like massive stone mushrooms, still others like enormous ice-cream cones. Crowds come from all over the world to marvel at their Dr Seussian look, making the rocks New Brunswick's top attraction (and certainly one of its most crowded). You can only walk amid the rocks at low tide – check the tide tables at any tourist office or area hotel. At high tide, the rock towers are still visible from the trails that wind through the woods above.

The park features a large interpretive center with educational displays, two cafes, picnic areas and several kilometers of well-trafficked trails. In high season, the massive parking lot is choked with cars and the staircases down to the beaches suffer human traffic jams.

Another way to visit the rocks is by kayak. **Baymount Outdoor Adventures** (☑877-601-2660; www.baymountadventures.com; tours adult/child $62/52; ☉Jun-Sep) offers two-hour paddling tours.

There are several motels in the Hopewell Rocks vicinity, including the family-run **Hopewell Rocks Motel** (☑506-734-2975; www.hopewellrocksmotel.com; 4135 Hwy 114; r incl breakfast $110; ☎☒), with 39 tidy rooms, a heated pool and an adjacent lobster restaurant. Prices are halved in the low season.

SOUTHEASTERN NEW BRUNSWICK

The southeastern corner of New Brunswick province is a flat coastal plain sliced by tidal rivers and salt marshes. Moncton, known as 'Hub City,' is a major crossroads with two well-known attractions where nature appears to defy gravity. Southeast, toward Nova Scotia, are significant historical and bird-life attractions.

Moncton

POP 64,100

Once a major wooden shipbuilding port, Moncton is now the fastest-growing city in the Maritimes, with an economy built on transportation and call centers drawn here by the bilingual workforce. It's a pleasant, suburban city, with a small redbrick

downtown along the muddy banks of the Petitcodiac River. There are some decent restaurants, bars and a bustling Acadian farmers market. Apart from that, there is little to detain the visitor.

◉ Sights

Magnetic Hill AMUSEMENT PARK
(www.magnetichill.com; cnr Mountain Rd & Hwy 2; admission per car $5; ☉8am-8pm May-Sep) At Magnetic Hill, one of Canada's best-known (though not best-loved) attractions, gravity appears to work in reverse. Start at the bottom of the hill in a car and you'll drift upward. You figure it out. After hours and out of season, it's free. It's a goofy novelty, worth the head-scratching laugh, but all the money-generating, spin-off hoopla now surrounding the hill is a bit much. Family-oriented attractions include a zoo, faux village hawking ice cream and souvenirs, and a water park. Magnetic Hill is about 10km northwest of downtown off Mountain Rd.

Tidal Bore Park PARK
(Main St; ☉24hr) The tourist literature talks up the twice-daily return of the waters of the tidal Petitcodiac River. In theory, the tide comes in as one solid wave, unfurled like a carpet across the muddy riverbed in one dramatic gesture; the height of this oncoming rush can allegedly vary from just a few centimeters to about 1m. In reality, it usually just looks like a big mud seep, and is, well...boring.

Casino New Brunswick CASINO
(www.casinonb.ca; 21 Casino Dr; ☉10am-3am) The province's first full-service casino, this 24,000-sq-foot gambling palace brings a touch of Vegas to Moncton. It packs in crowds with its 500 slot machines, poker room, numerous bars and buffets, and an entertainment venue boasting big-name performers such as the Beach Boys and Bill Cosby. The casino is about 9km northwest of the town center off Mountain Rd.

☞ Tours

Roads to Sea BUS TOUR
(☑506-850-7623; www.roadstosea.com; ☉May-Oct) Roads to Sea offers 3½-hour bus tours ($85) to Hopewell Rocks (p132), an eight-hour guided trip that takes in the Rocks, Fundy National Park, Cape Enrage and a few covered bridges and lighthouses ($160),

Moncton

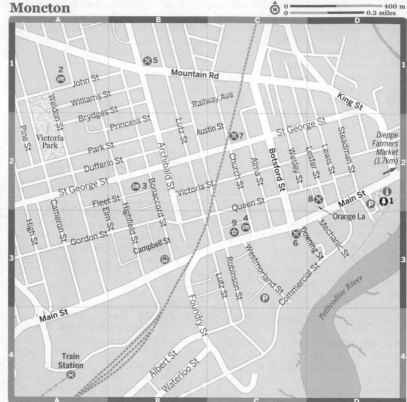

Moncton

◎ Sights
1 Tidal Bore Park.....................................D2

🛏 Sleeping
2 Auberge au Bois Dormant Inn................A1
3 C'mon Inn...B2
4 L'Hotel St James..................................C3

⊗ Eating
5 Cafe Archibald....................................B1
6 Café Cognito.......................................C3
7 Calactus..C2
8 Pump House..D2

✪ Entertainment
9 Capitol Theatre...................................C3

---

as well as a two-hour tour of the Moncton sights ($45).

🛏 Sleeping

Reservations are a good idea as the city is a major conference destination and often gets packed solid. Most of the chain hotels are clustered around Magnetic Hill.

C'mon Inn HOSTEL $

(☎506-854-8155, 506-530-0905; www.moncton-hostel.ca; 47 Fleet St; dm/r $35/70; 🛜) Moncton's only hostel is housed in a rambling Victorian two blocks from the bus station. The five-bunk dorm rooms and private singles and doubles with shared bathroom are nothing fancy, but they are clean and comfortable. There is a kitchen for guest use and lots of space for lounging on the verandas.

Auberge au Bois Dormant Inn B&B $$

(☑506-855-6767, 866-856-6767; www.auberge-auboisdormant.com; 67 John St; s $85-120, d $95-130; 😊 ❄ @ 🛜) A gracious Victorian renovated with crisp modern flair. This gay-friendly establishment is on a quiet, tree-lined residential street and puts on a three-course breakfast spread. Some rooms have private balconies.

L'Hotel St James BOUTIQUE HOTEL $$$

(☑888-782-1414; www.stjamesgatecanada.com; 14 Church St; r $159-289; 🛜) On the 2nd floor of a 19th-century brick shop building, this downtown boutique hotel has 10 stylish urban-chic guest rooms that wouldn't look a bit out of place in Montréal or New York. Swank design touches include mod tile walls, crisp white linens, huge flatscreen TVs and iPod docks. There's a popular pub and restaurant downstairs.

✖ Eating

Cafe Archibald FRENCH, CANADIAN $

(221 Mountain Rd; mains $8-12; ⊙7am-11pm) At this stylish bistro, crepes are the house specialty, whipped up in the open stainless-steel kitchen and served at redwood and zebra-print banquettes or on the inviting screened-in porch. Alternatively, feast on the wild mushroom and basil pizza with a leafy salad.

Café Cognito CAFE $

(700 Main St; snacks $3-8; ⊙7:30am-5:30pm Mon-Fri, 9am-4pm Sat) Get your morning joe at downtown's Café Cognito, a tiny European-style cafe with exposed brick walls and a handful of bistro tables.

Calactus VEGETARIAN $

(☑506-388-4833; www.calactus.ca; 125 Church St; mains $10-13; ⊙11am-10pm; 🖉) Shangri-la for vegetarians! Enjoy the freedom to order anything off the globally inspired menu, which contains everything from felafel plates, to tofu cheese pizza, to fried Indian *pakoras*. The natural wood, warm earth colors and burbling fountain create a soothing atmosphere.

Pump House BREWERY $$

(www.pumphousebrewery.ca; 5 Orange Lane; mains $8-15; ⊙11:30am-late) The Pump is where the locals unwind and you can get a good burger, steak-based meal or wood-fired pizza. Of the brews made on the premises, the Muddy River stout is tasty – or try the beer sample tray.

Little Louis' MODERN CANADIAN $$$

(☑506-855-2022; www.littlelouis.ca; 245 Collishaw St; mains $24-34; ⊙5-10pm) The odd location of this nouvelle-cuisine bistro – upstairs in a faceless industrial strip mall – only adds to its speakeasy vibe. The atmosphere is cozy, with low lights, white tablecloths and jazzy live music. Local foodies rave about dishes such as foie gras with apple-wine jelly, or crispy steelhead trout with shitake and saffron-vanilla butter. Whatever you do, always start with raw local oysters on the half shell with fresh horseradish. The wine list racks up awards on a regular basis.

🍷 Drinking & Entertainment

Moncton has a lively little rock and indie music scene, with several bars and clubs clustered around central Main St. The free *Here* magazine has the rundown on the city's vibrant (read: raucous) nightlife.

Capitol Theatre THEATER

(www.capitol.nb.ca; 811 Main St) You can sip a glass of wine during the interval at the grand Capitol Theatre, a 1922 vaudeville house that has been restored to its original glory. It is the venue for concerts and live theater throughout the year.

🔒 Shopping

Dieppe Farmers Market MARKET

(www.marchedieppemarket.com; cnr Acadie Ave & Gauvin Rd, Dieppe; ⊙7am-1:30pm Sat) A great place to get a taste of New Brunswick's vibrant Acadian culture is this weekly market. Stalls overflow with locally made cheeses, cottage wines and homemade preserves as well as Acadian dishes such as *tourtière* (a meat pie), *fricot à la poule* (home-style chicken stew) and rabbit pie. You can nibble sweet pastries such as *plogues* and *guaffres* while browsing the craft stalls. To get there from downtown, head 2km east on Main St, which becomes Champlain, to Acadie Ave. Look for the yellow roof.

ⓘ Information

Moncton Hospital (☑506-857-5111; 135 MacBeath Ave) Emergency room.

Moncton Public Library (644 Main St; ⊙9am-8:30pm Tue-Thu, to 5pm Fri & Sat; 🛜) Free internet access.

St George St After Hours Medical Clinic (☑506-856-6122; 404 St George Blvd; ⊙5:30-8pm Mon-Fri, noon-3pm Sat, Sun & holidays) No appointment is required to see a doctor here. Adjacent to Jean Coutu Pharmacy.

Visitors Information Center (www.gomoncton.com; Bore Park, Main St E; ⊘8:30am-6:30pm)

ℹ Getting There & Away

AIR

Greater Moncton International Airport (YQM; www.gmia.ca) is about 6km east of Champlain Place Shopping Centre via Champlain St. Air Canada runs daily flights to Toronto and Montréal.

BUS

Maritime (☑1-800-575-1807; www.maritimebus.com; 92 Lester St) runs to Fredericton ($34, two hours), Saint John ($34, two hours), Charlottetown, PEI ($34, three hours) and Halifax ($49, four hours).

CAR & MOTORCYCLE

If you need wheels, Avis, Budget, Hertz and National all have car-rental desks at the airport, or try **Discount Car Rentals** (☑506-857-2323; www.discountcar.com; 1543 Mountain Rd).

Parking can be a hassle in Moncton: the parking meters ($1 per hour) and 'no parking' signs extend far from downtown. The municipal parking lot at Moncton Market on Westmorland St charges $1/$8 per hour/day and is free on Saturday, Sunday and evenings after 6pm. Highfield Sq Mall on Main St provides free parking for its clients.

TRAIN

With **VIA Rail** (www.viarail.ca; 1240 Main St), the Ocean line goes through northern New Brunswick, including Miramichi and Campbellton, and into Québec, on its way to Montréal (from $135). The train to Halifax (from $39) departs six days a week.

ℹ Getting Around

The airport is served by bus 20 from Champlain Pl nine times a day on weekdays. A taxi to the center of town costs about $15.

Codiac Transit (www.codiactranspo.ca) is the local bus system, with 40 wi-fi-equipped buses going all over town.

Sackville

Sackville is a small university town that's in the right place for a pit stop – for birds and people. The **Sackville Waterfowl Park**, across the road from the university off East Main St, is on a major bird migration route. Boardwalks with interpretive signs rise over portions of it. The **Wildlife Service** (17 Waterfowl Lane, off E Main St; ⊘8am-4pm Mon-Fri) has

information and a wetlands display at one of the entrances. Enthusiasts should also see the **Tantramar Wetlands Centre** (www.wet-ed.com; 223 Main St; ⊘8am-4pm Mon-Fri) **FREE**, with its walking trail and educational office, behind the high school.

Mel's Tea Room (17 Bridge St; mains $4-10; ⊘7:30am-8pm) has been operating in the center of town since 1919, now with the charm of a 1950s diner – with a jukebox and prices to match.

Fort Beauséjour National Historic Site

Right by the Nova Scotia border, this **national historic site** (www.pc.gc.ca/fort-beausejour; adult/child/family $3.90/1.90/9.50; ⊘interpretive center 9am-5pm Jun-Oct), 1.5km west of the visitors center, preserves the remains of a French fort built in 1751 to hold the British back. It didn't work. Later it was used as a stronghold during the American Revolution and the War of 1812. Only earthworks and stone foundations remain, but the view is excellent, vividly illustrating why these crossroads of the Maritimes were fortified by two empires.

To find out more, visit the **New Brunswick Visitors Centre** (☑506-364-4090; 158 Aulac Rd; ⊘9am-9pm), off Hwy 2 in Aulac, at the junction of roads leading to all three Maritime provinces.

NORTHUMBERLAND SHORE

New Brunswick's Northumberland Shore stretches from the Confederation Bridge to Kouchibouguac National Park and is dotted with fishing villages and summer cottages. Shediac, on all lobster-lovers' itineraries, is a popular resort town in a strip of summer seaside and beach playgrounds. A good part of the population along this coast is French-speaking, and Bouctouche is an Acadian stronghold. Further north, Kouchibouguac National Park protects a large swath of scenic coastal ecosystems.

Cape Jourimain

Near the bridge to PEI, the **Cape Jourimain Nature Centre** (www.capejourimain.ca; Rte 16; ⊘8am-7pm May-Oct) **FREE** sits in a

675-hectare national wildlife area that protects this undeveloped shoreline and its migratory birds. Seventeen kilometers of trails wind through salt marshes, dunes, woods and beach. A four-story lookout provides views of the surroundings and Confederation Bridge.

There's a **visitors center** (Hwy 16; ⊗8am-9pm May-Sep) by the bridge.

Shediac

Shediac, a self-proclaimed lobster capital, is a busy summer beach town and home of the annual July lobster fest. The many white lights sprinkled around town all summer lend a festive air. Don't fail to have your picture taken with the 'World's Largest Lobster' sculpture – you can't miss it!

It seems on any hot weekend that half the province is flaked out on the sand at **Parlee Beach**, turning the color of cooked lobster. South at Cap Pelé are vast stretches of more sandy shorelines. Terrific **Aboiteau Beach** comprises over 5km of unsupervised sand, while others have all amenities and lifeguards.

Shediac Bay Cruises (⊡888-894-2002, 506-532-2175; www.lobstertales.ca; Pointe-du-Chene wharf; adult/child $68/46) takes passengers out on the water, pulls up lobster traps, then shows you how to cook and eat 'em.

Shediac is ringed with shantytown-like RV campgrounds whose only appeal is their proximity to Parlee Beach. More upscale lodgings are found at **Maison Tait** (⊡506-532-4233; www.maisontaithouse.com; 293 Main St; r incl breakfast from $189; 🛜), a luxurious 1911 mansion with nine sun-drenched rooms, and **Auberge Gabriele Inn** (⊡877-982-7222, 506-532-8007; www.aubergegabrieleinn.com; 296 Main St; r $110-165; 🅿🅰), with simple, country-chic rooms above a popular restaurant.

Tops for dining out are **Paturel's Shore House** (⊡506-532-4774; Rte 133; mains $18-27; ⊗4-10pm) for fresh seafood, or the restaurant at Maison Tait for fine dining and romantic ambience. Grab fresh seafood and strawberry daiquiris at always-packed **Captain Dan's** (www.captaindans.ca; mains $11-28) at the busy Pointe-du-Chene wharf. After dinner, catch a flick at the wonderfully retro **Neptune Drive-In** (www.neptunedrivein.ca; 691 Main St; ⊗Jun-Sep).

MR BIG

Kenneth Colin (KC) Irving was born in Bouctouche in 1899. From a modest beginning selling cars, he built up a business Goliath spanning oil refining, shipyards, mass media, transportation, pulp and paper, gas stations, convenience stores and more. The name is everywhere. At least 8% of the province's workforce is employed by an Irving endeavor. KC died in 1992, leaving his three sons to carry on the vast Irving Group empire.

Bouctouche

This small, surprisingly busy waterside town is an Acadian cultural focal point with several unique attractions. The **visitors information center** (Hwy 134; ⊗9am-5pm Jun-Sep) at the town's south entrance features a boardwalk out over the salt marsh.

⊙ Sights

Le Pays de la Sagouine HISTORIC PARK
(www.sagouine.com; 57 Acadie St; adult/child/family $20/12/45; ⊗10am-5:30pm Jul & Aug) Sitting on a small island in the Bouctouche River, this reconstructed Acadian village has daily programs in English and French. There are interactive cooking and craft demos, historical house tours and live music, as well as several cafes in which to sample old-fashioned Acadian cuisine. In July and August there's a supper theater at 7pm Monday to Saturday ($66).

Irving Eco Centre PARK
(www.irvingecocentre.com; 1932 Hwy 475; ⊗interpretive center 10am-6pm May-Oct) On the coast 9km northeast of Bouctouche, this nature center protects and makes accessible 'La Dune de Bouctouche,' a beautiful, long sandspit jutting into the strait. The interpretive center has displays on the flora and fauna, but the highlight is the **boardwalk** that snakes above the sea grass along the dunes for 2km. The peninsula itself is 12km long, taking four to six hours to hike over the loose sand and back. There are several naturalist-led tours daily. There's a 12km hiking/cycling trail through mixed forest to Bouctouche town, which begins at the Eco Centre parking lot.

KC Irving, founder of the Irving empire, was from Bouctouche, and there's a large bronze statue of him in the town park.

Olivier Soapery   MUSEUM
(www.oliviersoaps.com; 831 Rte 505, Ste-Anne-de-Kent) This old-fashioned soap factory advertises its 'museum' on what seems like every highway in New Brunswick. It's really more of a store, with tons of luscious-smelling hand-molded soaps, but it does have regular talks on the soap-making process and a few interesting historical displays.

🛏 Sleeping & Eating

Chez les Maury   CAMPGROUND $
(☑ 506-743-5347; www.fermemaury.com; 2021 Rte 475; campsites $25; ☺ May-Oct) On the grounds of a family-run vineyard, this small, basic campground has toilets, showers and a tiny private beach across the way.

Le Vieux Presbytère   INN $$
(☑ 506-743-5568; www.vieuxpresbytere.nb.ca; 157 Chemin du Couvent; d incl breakfast $119-165; 🛜) This former priest's residence was once a popular religious retreat for Acadians from across the province. The best rooms, with high molded ceilings and simple, sunny decor, are in the older part of the building.

Restaurant La Sagouine   ACADIAN $
(43 Blvd Irving; mains $8-18; ☺ 6am-10pm) Fried clams or a traditional Acadian dinner are on offer here. Be sure to get a seat on the outdoor patio.

Kouchibouguac National Park

Beaches, lagoons and offshore sand dunes extend for 25km here, inviting strolling, birdwatching and clam-digging. The **park** (www.pc.gc.ca; adult/child $7.80/3.90; ☺ 8am-dusk) encompasses hectares of forest and salt marshes, crisscrossed or skirted by bike paths, hiking trails and groomed cross-country ski tracks. Kouchibouguac (*koosh*-e-boo-gwack), a Mi'kmaq word meaning 'river of long tides,' also has moose, deer and black bear.

🏃 Activities

Cycling & Kayaking
Kouchibouguac has 60km of bikeways – crushed gravel paths that wind through the park's backcountry. **Ryan's Rental Centre** (☑ 506-876-3733; bicycles per hour/day $6/28, canoes/kayaks per day $30/50), near the South Kouchibouguac campground, rents out bicycles, canoes and kayaks. From Ryan's you can cycle a 23km loop and never be on the park road. The calm, shallow water between the shore and the dunes, which run for 25km north and south, makes for a serene morning paddle.

Hiking
The park has 10 trails, mostly short and flat. The excellent **Bog Trail** (1.9km) is a boardwalk beyond the observation tower, and only the first few hundred meters are crushed gravel. The **Cedars Trail** (1.3km) is less used. The **Osprey Trail** (5.1km) is a loop trail through the forest. **Kelly's Beach Boardwalk** (600m one-way) floats above the grass-covered dunes. When you reach the beach, turn right and hike 6km to the end of the dune. Take drinking water.

Swimming
The lagoon area is shallow, warm and safe for children, while adults will find the deep water on the ocean side invigorating.

🛏 Sleeping & Eating

Kouchibouguac has two drive-in campgrounds and three primitive camping areas totaling 359 sites. The camping season is from mid-May to mid-October, and the park is very busy throughout July and August, especially on weekends. **Camping reservations** (☑ 877-737-3783; www.pccamping.ca) are taken for 60% of the sites. Otherwise, get on the lengthy 'roll call' waiting list – it can take two or three days to get a site. The park entry fee is extra.

South Kouchibouguac (campsites $28) is the largest campground. It's 13km inside the park near the beaches in a large open field ringed by trees, with sites for tents and RVs, showers and a kitchen shelter.

On the north side of Kouchibouguac River, **Cote-a-Fabien** (campsites $19) is the best choice for those seeking a bit of peace and privacy. There is water and vault toilets, but no showers. Some sites are on the shore, others nestled among the trees, with a dozen walk-in sites (100m; wheelbarrows are provided for luggage) for those who want a car-free environment. The Osprey hiking trail starts from here. No reservations accepted.

The three primitive campgrounds cost $10 per person per night; they have only vault toilets. **Sipu** and **Petit-Large** have water pumps. **Pointe-a-Maxime** is the most difficult to get to (access by water only), but this does not translate into remote seclusion. There is a constant stream of passing motorized boat traffic from the fishing wharf nearby.

There are a couple of snack bars and a restaurant in the park, but you should stock up on groceries in nearby St-Louis-de-Kent.

❶ Information

Visitors Center (www.pc.gc.ca/kouchibouguac; 186 Hwy 117; ◷8am-8pm)

❶ Getting There & Away

It is difficult to get to and around the park without a car or bicycle. The distance from the park gate to the campgrounds and beaches is at least 10km. The nearest bus stop is in Rexton, 16km south of the park, where **Maritime** (☑1-800-575-1807; www.maritimebus.com; 126 Main St) buses stop at the Circle K gas station. There is one bus a day heading south to Moncton ($16), and one a day heading north to Miramichi ($23).

MIRAMICHI RIVER VALLEY AREA

In New Brunswick, the word Miramichi refers to both the city and the river, but it connotes even more: an intangible, captivating mystique. The spell the region casts emanates partially from the Acadian and Irish mix of folklore, legends, superstitions and tales of ghosts. It also seeps from the dense forests and wilderness of the area and from the character of the residents, who wrestle a livelihood from these natural resources. The fabled river adds its serpentine cross-country course, crystal tributaries and world-renowned salmon fishing. The region produces some wonderful rootsy music and inspires artists, including noted writer David Adams Richards, whose work skillfully mines the temper of the region.

Miramichi

The working-class river city of Miramichi is an amalgam of the towns of Chatham, Newcastle, Douglastown, Loggieville, Nelson and several others along a 12km stretch of the Miramichi River near its mouth. Miramichi, with its Irish background, is an English-speaking enclave in the middle of a predominantly French-speaking region.

Though surrounded by two paper mills and sawmills, central Newcastle is pleasant enough. In the central square is a statue to Lord Beaverbrook (1879–1964), one of the most powerful press barons in British history and a major benefactor of his home province. His ashes lie under the statue presented as a memorial to him by the town. Beaverbrook's boyhood home, the 1879 **Beaverbrook House** (www.beaverbrookhouse.com; 518 King George Hwy; ◷9am-5pm Mon-Fri, 10am-5pm Sat, 1-5pm Sun Jun-Aug) **FREE**, is now a museum.

Miramichi is a mill town, not a tourist center, but traditional folk-music enthusiasts might want to pay a visit for the **Irish Festival** (www.canadasirishfest.com; ◷mid-Jul) and the **Miramichi Folksong Festival** (www.miramichifolksongfestival.com; ◷early Aug), the oldest of its kind in North America.

🛏 Sleeping & Eating

Enclosure Campground CAMPGROUND $
(☑506-622-0680; 8 Enclosure Rd, Derby Junction; campsites/RV sites $31/36; ◷May-Oct) Southwest of Newcastle off Hwy 8, this former provincial park includes a nice wooded area with spacious quasi-wilderness sites for tenters.

Governor's Mansion B&B $$
(☑506-622-3036, 877-647-2642; www.governorsmansion.ca; 62 St Patrick's St, Miramichi; r incl breakfast from $80) On the south side of the river overlooking Beaubears Island is the creaky-but-elegant Victorian Governor's Mansion (1860), onetime home of the first Irish lieutenant governor of the province. Rooms are a tad frilly but provide a cozy place to rest your head.

Cunard CHINESE $$
(www.cunardrestaurant.com; 32 Cunard St, Chatham; mains $11-23; ◷noon-10pm) Surprisingly decent Canadianized Chinese food, such as chicken chow mein and honey-garlic spareribs, in a classic, lacquer-and-dragon-print dining room.

❶ Information

Tourist Information Center (www.discovermiramichi.com; 199 King St; ◷10am-5pm Jun-Sep) The tourist information center is downtown at Ritchie's Wharf, a down-at-heel riverfront boardwalk park.

❶ Getting There & Away

Maritime (📞1-800-575-1807; www.maritime-bus.com; 201 Edward St) buses depart from the Best Value Inn. Daily buses leave for Fredericton ($54, 2½ hours), Saint John ($49, five hours) and Campbellton ($44, three hours).

The **VIA Rail station** (www.viarail.ca; 251 Station St at George St) is in Newcastle. Trains from Montréal and Halifax stop here.

Miramichi River Valley

The Miramichi is actually a complex web of rivers and tributaries draining much of central New Brunswick. The main branch, the 217km-long Southwest Miramichi River, flows from near Hartland through forest to Miramichi where it meets the other main fork, the Northwest Miramichi. For over a hundred years, the entire system has inspired reverent awe for its tranquil beauty and incredible Atlantic salmon fly-fishing. Famous business tycoons, international politicians, sports and entertainment stars and Prince Charles have all wet lines here. Even Marilyn Monroe is said to have dipped her toes in the water. The legendary fishery has had some ups and downs with overfishing, poaching and unknown causes (perhaps global warming) affecting stocks, but they now seem back at sustainable levels.

◉ Sights

Atlantic Salmon Museum   MUSEUM
(www.atlanticsalmonmuseum.com; 263 Main St, Doaktown; adult/child $5/3; ⊙9am-5pm Apr-Oct) Learn about historic Doaktown's storied fishing history and check out the salmon and trout aquarium.

Metepenagiag Heritage Park   HISTORIC SITE
(📞506-836-6118; www.metpark.ca; 2156 Micmac Rd, Red Bank; adult/child $8/6; ⊙10am-5pm) On the Esk River, the Metepenagiag Heritage Park has interpretive tours of Mi'kmaq culture and history on a 3000-year-old archaeological site.

🏃 Activities

Sport fishing remains the main activity, but is tightly controlled for conservation. Licenses are required and all anglers must employ a registered guide. A three-day license for nonresidents is $60. All fish under 35cm or over 63cm must be released. Salmon fishing on the Miramichi is primarily hook and release, to preserve the precious and endangered species. (Most of the salmon served up in the province is, in fact, salmon farmed in the Bay of Fundy.)

WW Doak & Sons (www.doak.com; 331 Main St, Doaktown) is one of Canada's best fly-fishing shops. It sells a huge number of flies annually, some made on the premises. A wander around will get an angler pumped.

Despite the presence of the king of freshwaters, there are other pastimes to enjoy. The **Miramichi Trail**, a walking and cycling path along an abandoned rail line, is now partially complete, with 75km of the projected 200km usable.

At McNamee, the pedestrian Priceville Suspension Bridge spans the river. It's a popular put-in spot for canoeists and kayakers spending half a day paddling downriver to Doaktown. Several outfitters in Doaktown and Blackville offer equipment rentals, shuttle services and guided trips for leisurely canoe, kayak or even tubing trips along the river. Try **Gaston Adventure Tours** (bgaston@nbnet.nb.ca; canoe tours $60-180), with personalized fishing trips and falls tours run by Bev Gaston of the Atlantic Salmon Museum.

🛏 Sleeping & Eating

Beautiful rustic lodges and camps abound, many replicating the halcyon days of the 1930s and '40s. Check out www.miramichirivertourism.com for links to more accommodations and fishing outfitters. Restaurants are few and far between – plan to pack in your own supplies.

O'Donnell's Cottages &
Expeditions   MOTEL, COTTAGES **$$**
(📞800-563-8724, 506-365-7636; www.odonnellscottages.com; 439 Storeytown Rd, Doaktown; cottages from $129) Cozy log cabins on the riverbank. Offers a variety of outdoor activities.

❶ Information

Tourist Office (www.doaktown.com; 263 Main St; ⊙10am-5pm) The tourist office is in the Salmon Museum in Doaktown, the center of most valley activity.

NORTHEASTERN NEW BRUNSWICK

The North Shore, as it is known to New Brunswickers, is the heartland of Acadian culture in the province. The region was settled 250 years ago by French farmers and fishers, starting from scratch again after the upheaval of the Expulsion, frequently intermarrying with the original Mi'kmaq inhabitants. The coastal road north from Miramichi, around the Acadian Peninsula and along Chaleurs Bay to Campbellton passes through small fishing settlements and peaceful ocean vistas. At Sugarloaf Provincial Park, the Appalachian Mountain Range comes down to the edge of the sea. Behind it, stretching hundreds of kilometers into the interior of the province, is a vast, trackless wilderness of rivers and dense forest, rarely explored.

Tracadie-Sheila

Unmasking a little-known but gripping story, the **Historical Museum of Tracadie** (Rue du Couvent; adult/child $3/free; ⊙9am-5pm Mon-Fri, noon-5pm Sat & Sun) focuses on the leprosy colony based here from 1868 to as late as 1965. The nearby cemetery has the graves of 60 victims of Hansen's Disease (leprosy).

Caraquet

The oldest of the Acadian villages, Caraquet was founded in 1757 by refugees from forcibly abandoned homesteads further south. It's now the quiet, working-class center of the peninsula's French community. Caraquet's colorful, bustling fishing port, off Blvd St-Pierre Est, has an assortment of moored vessels splashing at the dock. East and West Blvd St-Pierre are divided at Rue le Portage.

The tourist office and all of the local tour operators are found at the **Carrefour de la Mer** complex, with its Day Adventure Centre, restaurant and views down on the waterfront near the fishing harbor.

⊙ Sights

Acadian Historic Village HISTORIC PARK
(www.villagehistoriqueacadien.com; 14311 Hwy 11; adult/student/family $17.50/15.50/42; ⊙10am-6pm Jun-Sep) Acadian Historic Village, 15km west of Caraquet, is a major historical reconstruction set up like a village of old. Thirty-three original buildings relocated to the site and animators in period costumes reflect life from 1780 to 1880. A good three to four hours is required. To eat there are old-fashioned sit-down Acadian meals at La Table des Ancêtres, the 1910 historical menu at the Château Albert dining room, and several snack bars. The village has a program for kids ($35), which provides them with a costume and seven hours of supervised historical activities.

✯✯ Festivals & Events

The largest annual Acadian cultural festival, **Festival Acadien** (www.festivalacadien.ca), is held here the first two weeks of August. It draws 100,000 visitors; over 200 performers including singers, musicians, actors, dancers from Acadia and other French regions (some from overseas) entertain. Especially picturesque is the annual blessing of the fleet, when a flotilla of fishing vessels cruises the harbor with ribbons and flags streaming from their rigging. The culminating Tintamarre Parade is a real blowout.

⨳ Sleeping & Eating

Maison Touristique Dugas INN, CAMPGROUND $
(☎506-727-3195; www.maisontouristiquedugas. ca; 683 Blvd St-Pierre W; campsites/r/ste from $20/85/119, cabins $99) A few miles west of Caraquet, five generations of the friendly Dugas family have run this rambling, something-for-everyone property. The homey,

NEW BRUNSWICK TRACADIE-SHEILA

WORTH A TRIP

SCENIC DRIVE: THE ACADIAN PENINSULA

Take a run out to the very northeastern tip of the province – a chain of low, flat islands pointing across the Gulf of St Lawrence to Labrador. Rte 113 cuts across salt marsh and scrub arriving first in Shippagan, home of the province's largest fishing fleet, where crab is king. Visit the sea creatures at the **Aquarium & Marine Centre** (www.aquariumnb. ca; 100 Aquarium St; adult/child $8.50/5.50; ⊙10am-6pm Jul-Sep). Kids will love the touch tanks full of sea creatures, and the seals (fed at 11am and 4pm).

Hop the bridge to Lamèque, a tidy fishing village that has hosted the **Lamèque International Baroque Festival** (☎800-320-2276, 506-344-5846; www.festivalbaroque. com; ⊙late Jul) for over 30 years. Note the red, white and blue Acadian flags flying from nearly every porch. Rte 113 continues north to Miscou Island. Stop to walk the boardwalk trail over a cranberry bog before the road dead-ends at the lighthouse.

antique-filled 1926 house has 11 rooms with shared bathrooms. There are five clean, cozy cabins with private bathrooms and cooking facilities in the backyard, a small field for RVs beyond that, and a quiet, tree-shaded campground for tenters.

★**Hotel Paulin** HOTEL $$
(☎866-727-9981, 506-727-9981; www.hotelpaulin. com; 143 Blvd St-Pierre W; r incl breakfast $128, r incl breakfast & 4-course dinner from $195) Scrimp elsewhere and splurge on a night at the exquisite Hotel Paulin. This vintage seaside hotel overlooking the bay was built in 1891 and has been run by the Paulin family since 1907. The rooms are sunny and polished, done up in crisp white linens, lace and antiques. If you are staying elsewhere, make reservations for dinner; the hotel has earned a reputation for fine cuisine. An example: fiddlehead fern soup followed by Acadian chicken fricot with herb dumplings (table d'hôte $45).

Château Albert INN $$$
(☎506-726-2600; www.villagehistoriqueaca-dien.com/chateauanglais.htm; Acadian Historic Village; d incl dinner & theater package $275) For complete immersion in the Acadian Historic Village, spend the night in early-20th-century style – no TV, no phone, but a charming, quiet room restored to its original 1909 splendor (with a modern bath). The original Albert stood on the main street in Caraquet until it was destroyed by fire in 1955. Packages are available that include dinner in the period dining room downstairs and a ride in a Ford Model T.

Le Caraquette CANADIAN $$
(89 Blvd St-Pierre; mains $8-14) Overlooking the harbor, this casual family-run restaurant serves Maritime standards such as fried clams and mayonnaise shrimp salad along with French-Canadian specialties such as poutine and smoked-meat sandwiches.

ℹ️ Information

Tourist Office (www.ville.caraquet.nb.ca; 51 Blvd St-Pierre Est; ◷9am-5pm Jun-Sep)

ℹ️ Getting There & Away

Public transportation around this part of the province is very limited as Maritime buses don't pass this way. Van shuttles connect with the bus or train in Miramichi or Bathurst. Ask for details at the tourist office.

Campbellton

Campbellton is a pleasant but unremarkable mill town on the Québec border. There are really only two reasons to come here: to transit to or from Québec, or to hike, ski and camp at Sugarloaf Provincial Park. The lengthy Restigouche River, which winds through northern New Brunswick and then forms the border with Québec, empties to the sea here. The Bay of Chaleur is on one side and dramatic hills surround the town on the remaining sides.

Dominated by Sugarloaf Mountain, which looks vaguely like one of its other namesakes in Rio, **Sugarloaf Provincial Park** (www.parc-sugarloafpark.ca; 596 Val d'Amours Rd) FREE is off Hwy 11 at Exit 415. From the base, it's just a half-hour walk to the top – well worth the extensive views.

The last naval engagement of the Seven Years' War was fought in the waters off this coast in 1760. The Battle of Restigouche marked the conclusion of the long struggle for Canada by Britain and France. Sugarloaf Provincial Park has 76 **campsites** (☎506-789-2366; www.parcsugarloafpark.ca; 596 Val d'Amours Rd; campsites/RV sites $25/32; ◷May-Sep) in a wooded setting 4km from Campbellton.

You can also crash comfortably at **Campbellton Lighthouse Hostel** (☎506-759-7044; campbellton@hihostels.ca; 1 Ritchie St; dm $27; ◷Jun-Aug; 🛜). This clean hostel is in a converted lighthouse by the Restigouche River, near the Maritime bus stop and Campbellton's 8.5m **salmon sculpture**.

Alternatively, **Maison McKenzie House B&B** (☎506-753-3133; www.bbcanada.com/4384. html; 31 Andrew St; r with shared bathroom incl breakfast $75-100; ◓🛜) is a homey 1910 house handy to downtown. For $60, the folks here will rent you a kayak and drop you off upriver.

The helpful provincial **tourist office** (☎506-789-2367; 56 Salmon Blvd; ◷8am-9pm May-Sep) is next to City Centre Mall.

ℹ️ Getting There & Away

Maritime (☎1-800-575-1807; www.maritimebus. com; 46 Water St) stops at the Pik-Quik convenience store, near Prince William St. The bus departs daily for Fredericton ($82, six hours) and Moncton ($59, six hours). Twice a day (once in the morning and once in the afternoon), an **Orléans Express** (www.orleansexpress.com) bus leaves from the Pik-Quick for Gaspé ($41, six hours) and Québec City ($91, seven hours). The **VIA Rail station** (www.viarail.ca; 99c Roseberry St) is conveniently central.

Prince Edward Island

Best Places to Eat

➡ Lot 30 (p152)

➡ Shipwright's Café (p165)

➡ Inn at Bay Fortune (p156)

➡ Pearl (p164)

➡ Lobster suppers at town halls and churches around the province

Best Places to Stay

➡ Fairholm Inn (p150)

➡ Barachois Inn (p161)

➡ Great George (p150)

➡ Maplehurst Properties (p155)

➡ Willowgreen Farm (p166)

Why Go?

Prince Edward Island (PEI) is as pretty as a storybook, and it just so happens that the island's depiction in a storybook (Lucy Maud Montgomery's *Anne of Green Gables*) is what has made the place famous. And like Anne Shirley, the heroine of that book, the island is a red-head – from tip to tip, sienna-colored soil peeks out from under potato plants, and the shores are lined with rose and golden sand. Meanwhile the Green Gables–esque landscape is a pastoral green patchwork of rolling fields, tidy gabled farmhouses and seaside villages.

Yet despite the pervasive splendor of the province, the first thing most visitors notice, and fall in love with, is PEI's charm and relaxed atmosphere. The 'Gentle Island' really lives up to its nickname, and the least authentic things you'll find here are the orange nylon braids of little girls in tourist spots dressed up as 'Anne.'

When to Go
Charlottetown

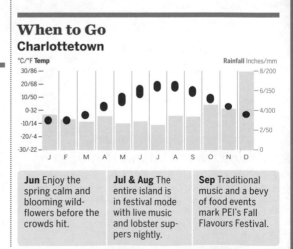

Jun Enjoy the spring calm and blooming wildflowers before the crowds hit.

Jul & Aug The entire island is in festival mode with live music and lobster suppers nightly.

Sep Traditional music and a bevy of food events mark PEI's Fall Flavours Festival.

Prince Edward Island Highlights

1 Be transported into the pages of *Anne of Green Gables* while visiting the Green Gables House in **Cavendish** (p163).

2 Eat your fill of lobster with all the fixings at **New Glasgow** (p161) or **St Ann** (p162).

3 Follow the floating boardwalk across the salt marsh and over the sand dunes onto the empty beach at **Greenwich** (p157).

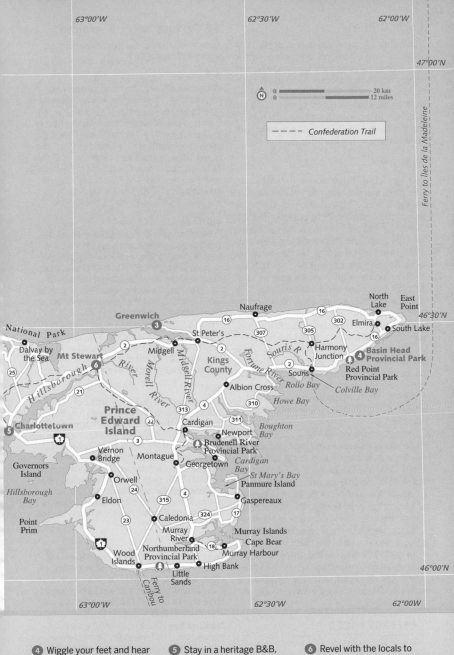

4 Wiggle your feet and hear a squeak at the 'singing sands' of **Basin Head Provincial Park** (p156).

5 Stay in a heritage B&B, wander the scenic waterfront and enjoy the charms of **Charlottetown** (p147).

6 Revel with the locals to rocking live music at homey venues like the **Trailside Cafe** (p157) in Mt Stewart.

Local Culture

The defining feature of island culture is its rural roots – most islanders are just one or two generations removed from the family farm or fishing boat, or are still there working it. There are descendants of the original Mi'kmaq (mig-*maw*) population and small pockets of French Acadians in the eastern and western parts of the province. Most islanders, however, trace their heritage to the British Isles.

History

Its Aboriginal inhabitants, the Mi'kmaq, knew the island as Abegeit – 'Land Cradled on the Waves.' Although Jacques Cartier of France first recorded PEI's existence in 1534, European settlement didn't begin until 1603. Initially small, the French colony grew only after Britain's expulsion of the Acadians from Nova Scotia in the 1750s. In 1758 the British took the island, known then as Île St Jean, and expelled the 3000 Acadians. Britain was officially granted the island in the Treaty of Paris of 1763.

To encourage settlement, the British divided the island into 67 lots and held a lottery to give away the land. Unfortunately, most of the 'Great Giveaway' winners were speculators and did nothing to settle or develop the island. The questionable actions of these absentee landlords hindered population growth and caused incredible unrest among islanders.

One of the major reasons PEI did not become part of Canada in 1867 was because union did not offer a solution to the land problem. In 1873 the Compulsory Land Purchase Act forced the sale of absentee landlords' land and cleared the way for PEI to join Canada later that year. Foreign land ownership, however, is still a sensitive issue in the province. The population has remained stable, at around 140,000, since the 1930s.

In 1997 PEI was linked to New Brunswick and the mainland by the Confederation Bridge – at almost 13km, it's the world's longest artificial bridge over ice-covered waters.

PEI FAST FACTS

➡ Population: 145,000

➡ Area: 5700 sq km

➡ Capital: Charlottetown

➡ Quirky fact: Kilos of potatoes produced per year – 1.3 billion

---

❶ Getting There & Around

There is little public transportation on PEI so most people rent a car.

AIR

Charlottetown's airport is 8km from town and serves all flights entering and leaving the province.

Air Canada has daily flights to Charlottetown from Halifax and Toronto, and from Montréal in the high season (June to September). WestJet offers direct flights to Charlottetown from Toronto and Ottawa. From June to September, Delta Airlines runs one daily direct flight to Charlottetown from New York and Boston, respectively. **Sunwing** (☑ 877-786-9464; www.flysunwing. com) flies from Toronto during the summer.

BICYCLE

Cyclists and pedestrians are banned from the Confederation Bridge and must use the 24-hour, demand-driven shuttle service (bicycle/pedestrian $8.25/4.25). On the PEI side, go to the bridge operations building at Gateway Village in Borden-Carleton; on the New Brunswick side, the pickup is at the Cape Jourimain Nature Centre at exit 51 on Rte 16.

While your easiest option to get around the island is by car, bicycle is also a fine choice. The flat and well-maintained Confederation Trail (p151) runs the length of the island through some beautiful countryside and small towns.

BOAT

Northumberland Ferries (☑ 888-249-7245, 902-566-3838; www.peiferry.com) runs the ferry service that links Wood Islands, in PEI's southeast, to Caribou, Nova Scotia, from May to December. There are up to nine daily sailings in each direction during the summer, and five in the fall and spring (car/pedestrian/motorcycle $67.50/17/40). Note that vehicle fees include all passengers for the 1¼-hour trip. All tickets are round-trip fare even if you're only taking the ferry one way. The ferry operates on a first-come, first-served basis.

BUS

Trius Transit Lines (☑ 902-566-5664; www. triustransit.ca) Runs local services within Charlottetown and Summerside and its County Line Express runs between the two ($9 each way) three times a day via Rte 2. Schedules are available on the website.

Maritime Bus (☑ 800-575-1807; www.maritimebus.com; 7 Mt Edward Rd, Charlottetown) Has services to Charlottetown from Moncton, New Brunswick ($42.87 one-way, three hours) two times a day, with stops at Borden-Carleton and Summerside en route. There are two buses a day to Halifax ($72.35 one-way, 5½ hours), with a transfer in Amherst, Nova Scotia.

REGIONAL DRIVING DISTANCES

North Cape to East Point: 273km

Halifax to Charlottetown: 227km

Charlottetown to Montréal: 1199km

Advanced Shuttle (☑ 877-886-3322; www. advancedshuttle.ca; Nassau St, University Ave, Charlottetown) A convenient service from Charlottetown or Summerside to Halifax or any point along the way (adult one-way $69). The van has a bicycle carrier.

East Connection (☑ 902-393-5132) Departs Charlottetown daily around noon for Souris, arriving at 1pm in time for the 2pm ferry. The shuttle van leaves Souris at 1:30pm, arriving at Charlottetown an hour later.

CAR & MOTORCYCLE

The **Confederation Bridge** (☑ 888-437-6565, 902-437-7300; www.confederationbridge.com; car/motorcycle $43/17; ⊘ 24hr) is the quickest way to get to PEI from New Brunswick and east central Nova Scotia. Unfortunately, the 1.1m-high guardrails rob you of any hoped-for view. The toll is only charged on departure from PEI, and includes all passengers.

If you're planning to travel one way on the bridge and the other way by ferry, it's cheaper to take the ferry to PEI and return via the bridge.

CHARLOTTETOWN

POP 34,562

PEI's capital is just about the perfect size, with a collection of stylish eateries and a lively cultural scene. Couple this with quiet streets for strolling, abundant greenery and a well-preserved historical core, and you have plenty of small-town appeal.

History

Charlottetown is named after the exotic consort of King George III. Her African roots, dating back to Margarita de Castro Y Sousa and the Portuguese royal house, are as legendary as they are controversial. While many believe the city's splendid harbor was the reason Charlottetown became the capital, the reality was less glamorous. In 1765 the surveyor-general decided on Charlottetown because he thought it prudent to bestow the poor side of the island with some privileges. Thanks to the celebrated 1864 conference, however, Charlottetown is etched in Canadian history as the country's birthplace.

⊙ Sights

All of the major sights are within the confines of Old Charlottetown, which makes wandering between them as rewarding as wandering through them.

Province House
National Historic Site   HISTORIC SITE

(☑902-566-7626; http://www.pc.gc.ca/lhn-nhs/pe/provincehouse/index.aspx; 165 Richmond St; admission $3.40; ⊘8:30am-5pm) Charlottetown's centerpiece is the imposing, yet welcoming, neoclassical Province House. The symmetry of design is carried throughout, including two brilliant skylights reaching up through the massive sandstone structure. It was here in 1864, within the Confederation Chamber, that 23 representatives of Britain's North American colonies first discussed the creation of Canada. Along with being the 'birthplace of Canada,' the site is home to Canada's second-oldest active legislature.

Several rooms have been restored, and in July and August actors in period garb wander the halls and regularly come together to perform reenactments of the famous conference. Enjoy the *Great Dream,* a 17-minute film about the monumental 1864 conference.

Founders' Hall   MUSEUM

(☑800-955-1864, 902-368 1864; www.foundershall.ca; 6 Prince St; adult/child $9.50/6.25; ⊘8:30am-8pm) Opened in 2001, this high-tech multimedia exhibit, housed in an old train station, swamps your senses with facts and fun about Canada's history since 1864. It's sure to entertain children and the child in you.

Beaconsfield Historic
House   NOTABLE BUILDING

(☑902-368-6603; 2 Kent St; adult/student/family $5/4/14; ⊘10am-5pm) With its crowning belvedere, intricate gingerbread trim and elegant 19th-century furnishings, Beaconsfield House is the finest Victorian mansion in Charlottetown. Have a wander or sit on the verandah and be stunned by the view.

Government House   NOTABLE BUILDING

(☑902-368-5480; ⊘10am-4pm Mon-Fri Jul & Aug) FREE Within the sprawling gardens of Victoria Park is Government House. This striking colonial mansion, with its grand hall, Palladian window and Doric columns, has been home to PEI's lieutenant governors since 1835. In 2003 the Hon JL Bernard

Charlottetown

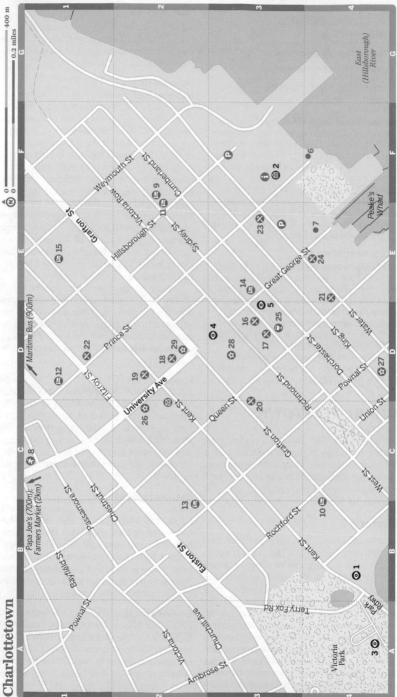

Charlottetown

broke with an almost 170-year-old tradition and opened its doors to the public.

St Dunstan's Basilica　　NOTABLE BUILDING
(☑902-894-3486; 45 Great George St; ⊗9am-5pm) FREE Rising from the ashes of a 1913 fire, the three towering stone spires of this neo-Gothic basilica are now a Charlottetown landmark. The marble floors, Italianate carvings and decoratively embossed ribbed ceiling are surprisingly ornate.

Tours

Self-guided walking tour booklets are available for just a Loonie ($1) at the tourist office.

Confederation Players　　WALKING TOUR
(☑1800-565-0278; 6 Prince St; adult/child $15/8; ⊗daily Jul & Aug) There is no better way to tour Charlottetown. Playing the fathers and ladies of Confederation, actors garbed in 19th-century dress educate and entertain through the town's historic streets. Tours leave from Founders' Hall, and there are three variations on the theme: historic Great George St, Island Settlers and the haunts of local ghosts.

Peake's Wharf Boat Cruises　　BOAT CRUISE
(☑902-566-4458; www.peakeswharfboattours. com; 1 Great George St; 70min cruise $20; ⊗2:30pm, 6:30pm & 8pm Jun-Aug) Observe sea life, hear interesting stories and witness a wonderfully different perspective of Charlottetown from the waters of its harbor. An

excellent seal-watching trip ($28) departs at 2:30pm, returning at 5pm.

Harbour Hippo Hippopotabus　　BUS & BOAT TOUR
(☑902-628-8687; www.harbourhippo.com; 2 Prince St; 1hr tour adult/child $24/16) Want to explore historic Charlottetown but afraid the kids will get bored? Hop on this amphibious bus that takes you to all the sights on land, then floats in the water.

Festivals & Events

Charlottetown Festival　　THEATER
(☑800-565-0278; www.charlottetownfestival.com; ⊗mid-May–mid-Oct) This theatrical festival features free outdoor performances, a children's theater and dance programs.

Festival of Small Halls　　MUSIC
(www.smallhalls.com; ⊗mid-Jun) Island musicians, dancers and storytellers who have 'made it' out of the province return to their homeland to perform in rural community halls around PEI during this 11-day festival.

Old Home Week　　CULTURE
(☑902-629-6623; www.oldhomeweekpei.com; ⊗mid-Aug) Held at the Provincial Exhibition grounds, this event features carnival rides, musical entertainment, games of chance, harness racing and traditional livestock shows.

Fall Flavours
FOOD

(☑866-960-9912; www.fallflavours.ca; ⊙last 3 weeks of Sep) Now one of the island's largest festivals, this massive kitchen party, set on the Charlottetown waterfront, merges great traditional music with incredible seafood. Don't miss the oyster-shucking championships or the chowder challenge.

🛏 Sleeping

Old Charlottetown's charms and proximity to major sights and restaurants makes it the most enviable area to rest your head. During summer, Charlottetown hums with activity, so it's wise to book ahead. In the off-season, accommodations are plentiful and most places reduce their rates. Parking is freely available at, or close to, all accommodations.

Spillett House B&B
B&B $

(☑902-892-5494; www.spilletthouse.pe.ca; 157 Weymouth St; s/d without bathroom incl breakfast $50/60; 🖥) This lovely heritage home is scrupulously clean, with polished hardwood floors and antique furnishings, homemade quilts on the beds and lace curtains on the windows. Kids are welcome and there are storage facilities for bicycles.

Charlottetown Backpackers
B&B $

(☑902-367-5749; www.charlottetownbackpackers. com; 60 Hillsborough St; dm/r incl breakfast $32/80; 🖥) Impossible to miss with its bright red-and-white paint job and happy hostellers milling about on the lawn, this superbly happening backpackers has cozy single-sex or mixed dorms, a good kitchen and a quirky common room with a turntable and a rather epic vinyl collection. Be prepared for spontaneous barbecues and pub outings.

Charlotte's Rose Inn
INN $$

(☑888-237-3699, 902-892-3699; www.charlottes-rose.ca; 11 Grafton St; r incl breakfast $120-195, apt $195; ❀🖥) Miss Marple must be around here somewhere. This decadent Victorian has true English flair with bodacious rose-printed wallpaper, lace canopies, big fluffy beds and grand bathrooms. There's a fire in the parlor for guests to enjoy along with complimentary tea and cakes. A modern loft apartment can accommodate five and has its own private rooftop deck.

Aloha Tourist Home
B&B $$

(☑855-892-5642, 902-892-5642; www.alohaam-igo.com; 234 Sydney St; r incl breakfast $90-150; 🖥) A welcoming choice that's really a heritage B&B complete with antiques and comfy beds, but without the hefty price tag. The serve-yourself breakfasts are gourmet, the location is central and the owner is sweet and helpful. Lower-end rooms have shared bathrooms. There's one family-sized room for $225 and all prices drop considerably outside the high season.

★Fairholm Inn
B&B $$$

(☑888-573-5022, 902-892-5022; www.fairholm. pe.ca; 230 Prince St; ste incl breakfast $129-289; 🖥) This historic inn was built in 1838 and is a superb example of the picturesque movement in British architecture. Take tea while enjoying the morning sun in the beautiful conservatory, wander the gardens or hole up with a book in the library. Luxurious English fabrics, beautiful PEI artwork and grand antiques fill each suite. Light a fire, soak in your tub and sink back into the elegant days of the 19th century.

★Great George
INN $$$

(☑800-361-1118, 902-892-0606; www.thegreat-george.com; 58 Great George St; d incl breakfast $175-219, ste $269-899; ❀🖥) This colorful collage of celebrated buildings along Charlottetown's most famous street has rooms ranging from plush and historic to bold and contemporary – but all are simply stunning. It's both gay- and family-friendly. A babysitting service is available, as is a fitness room.

Fitzroy Hall B&B
B&B $$$

(☑866-627-9766; www.fitzroyhall.com; 45 Fitzroy St; d $99-190, ste $225-300; 🖥) A perfect blend of elegance and comfort, this house is as grand as they come, while the welcome is warm and down to earth. The innkeepers have put some serious thought into how to make their guests comfortable: the answer is found with refined antiques, muted color schemes, and details like hidden alcoves with fridges and hot pots for guests to keep cold drinks or make tea.

🍴 Eating

Thanks largely to the Culinary Institute at Charlottetown's Holland College, which keeps churning out talented chefs, the city has a heaped helping of fine eateries. During summer, Victoria Row's pedestrian mall and the waterfront are hot spots for diners and drinkers. Pubs are also a great place to go for good-value eating.

★ **Leonard's**   CAFE **$**
(University Ave; sandwiches from $5; ☺9am-5pm
Tue-Sat) Find absolute comfort in this little
cafe full of cushioned seating and soothing
country-style muted hues. Treat yourself to
excellent German pastries, salads and creative sandwiches as well as all-day breakfasts made with free-range eggs, a great
cheese selection and cold cuts like Black
Forest ham. Wash it down with farmers
market teas and espresso.

Young Folk & the Kettle Black   CAFE **$**
(98 Water St; light lunches $9; ☺8am-8pm Mon-
Thu, to 10pm Fri & Sat, 11am-6pm Sun) A cozy
bakery and cafe that feels like a mix between a rural farmhouse and an urban art
gallery. Enjoy great coffee, breakfasts and
light lunches.

Splendid Essence   TAIWANESE **$**
(☎902-566-4991; 186 Prince St; mains $6-12;
☺11:30am-3pm & 5-8pm; ✐) Savory Taiwanese
vegetarian dishes are served in this cozy
Victorian, fitted out with warm wood pan-
eling and intimate booths upholstered in
red, green and gold and accented with Chinese art. Recommended are the spicy vegetables and fried rice chased with a steaming
mug of hot almond milk.

Farmers Market   MARKET **$**
(☎902-626-3373; 100 Belvedere Ave; ☺9am-2pm
Sat, also Wed Jul & Aug) Come hungry and
empty-handed. Enjoy some prepared island
foods or peruse the cornucopia of fresh organic fruit and vegetables. The market is
north of the town center off University Ave.

Papa Joe's   CANADIAN **$**
(345 University Ave; mains $10-15; ☺11am-9pm)
This family-style restaurant is superpopular

with locals. Here, all pretensions are
checked at the door as you dine on bacon-
wrapped meatloaf, turkey pot pie or a
steak sandwich. Wednesdays go exotic
with Indian cuisine served all day.

Water Prince Corner Shop   SEAFOOD **$$**
(☎902-368-3212; 141 Water St; meals $10-27;
☺9:30am-8pm) When locals want seafood
they head to this inconspicuous, sea-blue
eatery near the wharf. It is deservedly
famous for its scallop burgers, but it's also
the best place in town for fresh lobster.
You'll probably have to line up for a seat,
otherwise order takeout lobster, which gets
you a significant discount.

Sirinella   ITALIAN **$$**
(☎902-628-2271; 83 Water St; lunch $8-17, din-
ner $15-28; ☺11:30am-2pm & 5-10pm Mon-Fri,
5-10pm Sat) Cross the threshold of this
charming restaurant and you are transported to seaside Italy. It's nothing fancy,
just little round white-clothed tables, some
Mediterranean oil paintings and incredibly
authentic Italian fare.

**Daniel Brennan Brick
House**   MODERN CANADIAN **$$**
(☎902-566-4620; 125 Sydney St; mains $13-32;
☺11am-9pm Mon-Thu, to 10pm Fri & Sat, 4-10pm
Sun) The chic ambience of this heritage
brick building is matched by creative
dishes inspired by island culture and made
with local ingredients. Try the lobster
poutine, seafood bouillabaisse, Thai curry
chicken or just a good PEI beef burger.
Don't leave without enjoying a cocktail or
dessert in the upstairs lounge.

PRINCE EDWARD ISLAND CHARLOTTETOWN

CYCLING THE CONFEDERATION TRAIL

Following the rail-bed of Prince Edward Island's erstwhile railway, the 357km-long Con-
federation Trail is almost entirely flat as it meanders around hills and valleys. There are
some sections of the trail that are completely canopied by lush foliage, and in late June
and the early weeks of July the trail is lined with bright, flowering lupines. There's per-
haps no better way to enjoy the fall's change of colors than by riding the trail.

The 279km tip-to-tip route from Tignish, near North Cape, to Elmira, near East Point,
is a rewarding workout, passing through idyllic villages, where riders can stop for meals
or rest for the night. Note that the prevailing winds on PEI blow from the west and south-
west, so cycling in this direction is easier. Branches connect the trail to the Confedera-
tion Bridge, Charlottetown, Souris and Montague.

Provincial **tourist offices** (www.gov.pe.ca/visitorsguide) have excellent route maps
and their website offers a plethora of planning and trail information. The bicycle rental
shops in Charlottetown also run superb island-wide tours.

Pilot House
MODERN CANADIAN $$

(☑902-894-4800; 70 Grafton St; mains $19-37; ⊙11am-10pm Mon-Sat) The oversized wood beams and brick columns of the historic Roger's Hardware building provide a bold setting for fine dining or light pub fare. A loyal clientele tucks into lobster-stuffed chicken, vegetarian pizza or seafood torte. Lunch specials start at $10.

★ Lot 30
MODERN CANADIAN $$$

(☑902-629-3030; 151 Kent St; mains $22-55; ⊙from 5pm Tue-Sun) Anyone who's anyone goes to Lot 30, but show up unknown and in jeans and you'll be treated just as well. Tables are in view of each other so you can see the ecstatic expressions of food bliss on the merry diners' faces; dishes from *beurre blanc* to curry are spiced to perfection.

For a treat, try the excellent-value five-course tasting menu ($60) – small servings of a starter, three mains and a dessert sampler. Staff are wine-pairing masters, the eclectic ever-changing menu is made with local seasonal ingredients and the chef is happy to cater to food allergies and special needs. This really is a Charlottetown highlight.

Claddagh Room
SEAFOOD $$$

(☑902-892-6992; 131 Sydney St; mains $19-45; ⊙5-10pm Mon-Sat) Locals herald the Claddagh Room as one of the best seafood restaurant in Charlottetown. Trust 'em! The Irish-inspired Galway Bay Delight features a coating of fresh cream and seasonings over scallops and shrimp that have been sautéed with mushrooms and onions, then flambéed with Irish Mist liqueur.

🍷 Drinking

Charlottetown has an established and burgeoning drinking scene. Historic pubs dot the old part of town. Most bars and pubs have a small cover charge (about $5) on weekends, or when there is live music. People spill into the streets at 2am when things wrap up.

★ Gahan House
PUB

(☑902-626-2337; 126 Sydney St; ⊙11am-10pm or 11pm Sun-Thu, to midnight or 1am Fri & Sat) Within these homey, historic walls the pub owners brew PEI homegrown ales. Sir John A's Honey Wheat Ale is well worth introducing to your insides, as is the medium- to full-bodied Sydney Street Stout. The food here is also great – enjoy with friends old and new.

Marc's Studio
BAR

(☑902-566-4620; 125 Sydney St; ⊙4:30pm-midnight) Climb the stairs for a cocktail or a nightcap. Think plenty of art by the late, local artist Marc Gallant (who restored this building in the 1980s) and cozily grouped sofas set against exposed brick walls. It usually closes around midnight, but will stay open until the crowd thins out.

☆ Entertainment

From early evening to the morning hours, Charlottetown serves up a great mix of theater, music, island culture and fun. Throughout the city and across PEI, various venues host traditional ceilidhs (*kay*-lees). They are sometimes referred to as 'kitchen parties' and usually embrace gleeful Celtic music and dance. If you have the chance to attend one, don't miss it. The Friday edition of the *Guardian* newspaper and the free monthly *Buzz* list times and locations of upcoming ceilidhs, along with other details of the entertainment scene.

City Cinema
CINEMA

(☑902-368-3669; 64 King St) A small independent theater featuring Canadian and foreign-language films.

Confederation Centre of the Arts
THEATER

(☑800-565-0278, 902-566-1267; www.confederationcentre.com; 145 Richmond St) This modern complex's large theater and outdoor amphitheater host concerts, comedic performances and elaborate musicals. *Anne of Green Gables – The Musical* has been entertaining audiences here as part of the Charlottetown Festival since 1964, making it Canada's longest-running musical. You'll enjoy it, and your friends will never have to know.

Mack
THEATER

(www.charlottetownfestival.com/theatres-themack.php; 28 University Ave) An intimate venue where guests sit at round tables. *O Come Ye* is a comedy about PEI shown through summer, while *Late Night at the Mack* (selected dates through summer) gets performers from the Confederation Centre of the Arts at a sort of open-mike show where they can show off their talents.

Olde Dublin Pub
LIVE MUSIC

(☑902-892-6992; 131 Sydney St; admission $8) A traditional Irish pub with a jovial spirit and live entertainment nightly during the summer months. Celtic bands and local notables take to the stage and make for an engaging night out.

Baba's Lounge
LIVE MUSIC

(☑ 902-892-7377; 81 University Ave; admission $8) Located above Cedar's Eatery, this welcoming, intimate venue hosts great local bands playing their own tunes. Occasionally there are poetry readings.

Benevolent Irish Society
LIVE MUSIC

(☑ 902-963-3156; 582 North River Rd; admission $10; ⊙8pm Fri) On the north side of town, this is a great place to catch a ceilidh. Come early, as seating is limited.

ℹ Information

Main Post Office (☑ 902-628-4400; 135 Kent St)

Police, Ambulance & Fire (☑ 911)

Polyclinic Professional Centre (☑ 902-629-8810; 199 Grafton St; ⊙5:30-8pm Mon-Fri, 9:30am-noon Sat) Charlottetown's after-hours, walk-in medical clinic.

Queen Elizabeth Hospital (☑ 902-8894-2111; 60 Riverside Dr; ⊙24hr) Emergency room.

Royal Canadian Mounted Police (☑ 902-368-9300; 450 University Ave) For nonemergencies only.

Visit Charlottetown (www.visitcharlottetown.com) A helpful website with upcoming festival information, city history and visitor information.

Visitors Centre (☑ 888-734-7529, 902-368-4444; www.peiplay.com; 6 Prince St; ⊙9am-10pm Jul & Aug, reduced hours Sep-Jun) Located in Founders' Hall, this visitors center is the island's main tourist office. It has all the answers, a plethora of brochures and maps, and free internet access.

ℹ Getting There & Away

AIR

Charlottetown Airport (YYG; ☑ 902-566-7997; www.flypei.com) is 8km north of the city center at Brackley Point and Sherwood Rds. A taxi to/from town costs $12, plus $3.50 for each additional person.

CAR & MOTORCYCLE

With next to no public transportation available, rental cars are the preferred method for most travelers going to/from Charlottetown. During the summer cars are in short supply, so make sure you book ahead.

Nationwide companies such as Avis, Budget, National and Hertz have offices in town and at the airport. Note that the airport desks are strictly for people with reservations.

BUS

For information, see p146.

ℹ Getting Around

BICYCLE

Riding is a great way to get around this quaint town. **MacQueen's Bicycles** (☑ 902-368-2453; www.macqueens.com; 430 Queen St; per day/week $25/125) rents a variety of quality bikes. Children's models are half price. **Smooth Cycle** (☑ 902-566-5530; www.smoothcycle.com; 330 University Ave; per day/week $26/110) also provides super service. Both of these operators also offer excellent customized island-wide tours of the Confederation Trail.

CAR & MOTORCYCLE

The municipal parking lots near the tourist office and Peak's Wharf charge $6 per day. One Loonie gets you two hours at any of the town's parking meters, which operate between 8am and 6pm on weekdays.

PUBLIC TRANSPORTATION

Trius Transit Lines (www.triustransit.ca) operates the anemic city transit within Charlottetown (one-way fare $2.25). One bus makes various loops through the city, stopping sporadically at the Confederation Centre between 9:20am and 2:40pm.

TAXI

Fares are standardized and priced by zones. Between the waterfront and Hwy 1 there are three zones. Travel within this area is about $11, plus $3 per extra person. **City Taxi** (☑ 902-892-6567; www.citytaxipei.com) and **Yellow Cab PEI** (☑ 902-566-6666; www.yellowcabpei.com) provide good service.

EASTERN PRICE EDWARD ISLAND

You can make your own tracks across Kings County, the eastern third of the province and PEI's most under-touristed region. From stretches of neatly tended homesteads to the sinuous eastern shore with its protected harbors, sweeping beaches and country inns, majestic tree canopies seem to stretch endlessly over the scenic heritage roads. The 338km Points East Coastal Drive winds along the shore, hitting the highlights.

Orwell

Situated 28km east of Charlottetown, via Hwy 1, is **Orwell Corner Historic Village** (☑ 902-651-8510; www.orwellcorner.ca; off

Hwy 1; adult/child $7.50/4.50; ☺9am-4:30pm), a living re-creation of a 19th-century farming community, complete with bonneted school teacher and a blacksmith. Check the website for special events. The **Sir Andrew MacPhail Homestead** (✆902-651-2789; www. macphailhomestead.ca; 271 MacPhail Park Rd; ☺9am-5pm Wed & Sun Jun-Dec), a further 1km down the road, is open for tea on summer afternoons (light lunches around $12).

Point Prim

This skinny bucolic spit of land is covered in wild rose, Queen Anne's lace and wheat fields through summer and has views of red sand shores on either side. At the tip is the province's oldest **lighthouse** (adult/child $7/2; ☺9am-6pm); we think it's one of the prettiest spots on the island. Climb up the steep lighthouse steps to pump the foghorn and for panoramas over the south coast on sunny days.

Many folks come out this way to dig razor, soft shell, bar and quahog clams with **Happy Clammers** (✆866-887-3238; www. experiencepei.ca; adult/child $90/25 minimum 4 people). Once you've filled your buckets, go home to Gilbert and Goldie's house to steam up your catch and to dine on other treats cooked up by this charming local family.

Get even more into the treasures of this coast with **Seaweed Secrets** (✆866-887-3238; www.experiencepei.ca; adult/child $90/25, min/max 4/8 people; ☺Mon, Tue, Thu & Fri), where you can harvest seaweed and learn about which types are edible or have medicinal qualities; it's all led by a local family who have been in the industry for generations, plus a knowledgeable marine botanist.

Eat at **Chowder House** (chowder with a biscuit $8; ☺11am-7pm), a homey cafe near the lighthouse reminiscent of Cape Cod circa 1950; it serves a mean chowder and homemade pie.

Wood Islands

Wood Islands is the jumping-off point for ferries to Nova Scotia. A **visitors information center** (✆902-962-7411; Plough Waves Centre, cnr Hwy 1 & Rte 4; ☺10:30am-9pm) is just along the road from the terminal.

If you'll be waiting a while at the terminal, **Wood Islands Provincial Park** and its 1876 lighthouse are well worth the short walk. Munch a rock crab sandwich or a lobster roll at **Crabby's Seafood** (snacks $4-7; ☺noon-6pm Jun-Sep) near the ferry terminal.

Murray River & Around

From Wood Islands, Rte 4 heads east along the Northumberland Strait, veering inland at High Bank toward the lively and surprisingly artsy fishing settlement of Murray River. The coastal road becomes Rte 18, keeping the sea in view as it rounds Cape Bear, passing the lighthouse before looping back through the village of Murray Harbour and into Murray River. This stretch of flat, empty road offers superbly serene scenery and excellent cycling possibilities. Cyclists can follow the coastal road from Murray River, then loop back on the extension of the Confederation Trail at Wood Islands.

Head towards the coast from Murray River along Rte 348 (Gladstone Rd) to find **Newman Estate Winery** (✆902-962-4223; www.newmanestatewinery.com; 9404 Gladstone Rd, Gladstone; ☺by appointment). This lovely place specializes in blueberry wines, but has recently began making white wine from grapes.

For more wine tasting on a grander scale, cruise over to Little Sands, 9km from the Wood Islands Ferry, where **Rossignol Estate Winery** (✆902-962-4193; Rte 4; ☺10am-5pm Mon-Sat, 1-5pm Sun May-Oct) has free tastings and specializes in fruit wines. The divine blackberry mead has won a string of gold medals and the wild rose liquor made from rose hips is also well worth a try; call ahead for winter hours.

Brehaut's Restaurant (✆902-962-3141; Murray Harbour; dinner under $8; ☺8am-9pm Mon-Sat, 11am-9pm Sun) is the place to stop in the area for a hearty meal. There are cozy booths and nooks filled with happy diners in this big, red wooden house. The seafood chowder gets rave reviews.

Panmure Island

Duck off Hwy 17 and ride the tarmac to the tip of Panmure Island, known for its variety of beaches: white sand and cold water line the ocean side, while pink sands and warmer water run along the St Mary's Bay side. Joined to the main island by a causeway, the island offers sweeping vistas of sand dunes and ocean surf, grazing horses and a gaily painted **lighthouse** (✆902-838-3568; tours $5; ☺9:30am-5pm Jul & Aug, hours vary

Jun & Sep). You can climb the tower for $4. There's an annual **powwow** (☎902-892-5314; www.ncpei.com/powwow-trail.html; ⊙mid-Aug) held each year with drumming, crafts and a sweat tent – it attracts around 5000 visitors, so don't expect any secluded beaches!

Bring a picnic for the supervised beach at **Panmure Island Provincial Park** (☎902-838-0668; Hwy 347; campsites $21; ⊙Jun-Sep). The park campground has every amenity for its 44 sites (most unserviced) tucked under the trees and along the shore. For something more luxurious stay at the grand **Maplehurst Properties** (☎902-838-3959; www.maplehurstproperties.com; Rte 347; d $145-190, cottage $1500 per week; ⊙May-Nov; ☎). Marsha Leftwich has mustered every glimmer of her native Southern hospitality to create this exceptional B&B that drips with gorgeous chandeliers as well as fresh baked muffins and treats.

Montague & Around

The fact that Montague isn't flat gives it a unique, inland feel. Perched on either side of the Montague River, the busy little town is the service center for Kings County; its streets lead from the breezy, heritage marina area to modern shopping malls, supermarkets and fast-food outlets.

In the old train station on the riverbank there's an **Island Welcome Center** (☎902-838-0670; cnr Rtes 3 & 4; ⊙8am-7pm Jul & Aug, 9am-4:30pm May, Jun, Sep & Oct). Here, you can hop on the Confederation Trail, which follows the former rail line; rent bikes at **Pines Bicycle Rentals** (☎902-838-3650; 31 Riverside Dr; bike rental half-/full day $20/30; ⊙8am-8pm).

On the other side of the river, the statuesque former post office and customs house (1888) overlooks the marina, and houses the **Garden of the Gulf Museum** (☎902-838-2467; 564 Main St S; adult/child under 12yr $3/free; ⊙9am-5pm Mon-Fri Jun-Sep). Inside are several artifacts illustrating local history.

Just north of town, development meets nature at **Brudenell River Provincial Park** (☎902-652-8966; off Rte 3; campsites $21, RV sites $24-28; ⊙May-Oct), which is a park and resort complex. Options range from kayaking to nature walks and golf on two championship courses. You can also take a one-hour horseback trail ride through the sun-dappled forest and onto the beach with **Brudenell Riding Stables** (☎902-652-2396; www.brudenellriding-stables.com; 1hr ride $35; ⊙Jun-Sep).

🛏 Sleeping & Eating

★**Knox's Dam B&B**   B&B $$
(☎866-245-0037, 902-838-4234; www.bbcanada.com/3963.html; cnr Rtes 353 & 320; r incl breakfast $85-100; ⊙Apr-Nov; ☎) This cheerful, red Victorian country home is constantly serenaded by the babble and flow of Knox dam on the Montague River. Guest rooms are thoughtfully appointed with soft linens, the old-fashioned elegance of a claw-foot tub and

---

WORTH A TRIP

DISTILLERIES

Two distinctly different distilleries operate on PEI, echoing the province's fame for bootlegging during Prohibition. Even today many families distill their own moonshine (which is technically illegal) and this is what is often mixed in punch and cocktails at country weddings and parties.

Prince Edward Distillery (☎902-687-2586; www.princeedwarddistillery.com; Rte 16, Hermanville; ⊙11am-6pm) specializes in potato vodka that, even in its first year of production, has turned international heads (some calling it among the finest of its class). Stop in for tours of the immaculate distillery and to taste the different vodkas (potato, grain and blueberry) as well as the newer products such as bourbon, rum, whiskey, pastis and a very interesting and aromatic gin.

Myriad View Distillery (☎902-687-1281; www.straightshine.com; 1336 Rte 2, Rollo Bay; ⊙11am-6pm Mon-Sat, 1-5pm Sun) produces Canada's first and only legal moonshine. The hardcore Straight Lightning Shine is 75% alcohol and so potent it feels like liquid heat before it evaporates on your tongue. Take our advice and start with a micro-sip! A gulp could knock the wind out of you. The 50% alcohol Straight Shine lets you enjoy the flavor a bit more. Tours and tastings are free and the owner is happy to answer any questions.

It's about a 10-minute drive on Hwy 307 between the two places.

modern amenities such as satellite TV. Rooms overlook the prize-winning flower gardens or the bountiful vegetable patch, there's good trout fishing at the dam and your hosts couldn't be kinder.

Windows on the Water Café MODERN CANADIAN **$$**
(☑902-838-2080; cnr Sackville & Main Sts; mains $9-17; ☺11:30am-9:30pm May-Oct) Enjoy a flavorful array of seafood, chicken and vegetarian dishes on the deck overlooking the water and, sort of, the road. Try the lobster quiche and leave room for a freshly baked dessert.

Georgetown

The many heritage buildings in Georgetown are testament to the town's importance as a shipbuilding center in the Victorian era. Today it's a sleepy village cum tourist spot thanks to its great places to eat and waterfront setting. It's also the site of **Tranquility Cove Adventures** (☑902-969-7184; www.tranquilitycoveadventures.com; Fisherman's Wharf, 1 Kent St; half-/full day tours $55/98) that leads excellent fishing and clamming trips as well as kundalini yoga on a deserted island. Check the website for details on other exciting packages.

🛏 Sleeping & Eating

★**Georgetown Inn & Dining Room** INN **$$**
(☑877-641-2414, 902-652-2511; www.peigeorgetownhistoricinn.com; 62 Richmond St; r incl breakfast $105-155; 🛜) Right in the center of Georgetown, this place is as equally well known for its PEI-themed rooms (including a Green Gables room) as for its fine casual island-fare dining.

Clamdigger's Beach House & Restaurant SEAFOOD **$$**
(☑902-652-2466; 7 West St; mains $12-37; ☺11am-9pm) Some claim this place serves PEI's best chowder, but no matter what your opinion, you can't help but ooh and aah about the water view from the deck or through the dining room's giant windows.

Cardigan Lobster Suppers LOBSTER SUPPER **$$**
(☑902-583-2020; www.peicardiganlobstersuppers.com; Rte 311; adult/child $39/26; ☺5-9pm Jun-Oct) In tiny Cardigan, enjoy a five-course lobster supper in a heritage building on Cardigan Harbor.

DON'T MISS

BASIN HEAD PROVINCIAL PARK

While this park (off Rte 16) is home to the **Basin Head Fisheries Museum** (☑902-357-7233; adult/student $4.50/2; ☺9am-6pm Jun-Sep), its star attraction is the sweeping sand of golden **Basin Head Beach**. Many islanders rank this as their favorite beach and we have to agree. The sand is also famous for its singing – well, squeaking – when you walk on it. Unfortunately, the sand only performs when dry, so if it's been raining, it's no show. Five minutes of joyous 'musical' footsteps south from the museum and you have secluded bliss – enjoy!

Souris

Wrapped around the waters of Colville Bay is the bustling fishing community of Souris (*sur*-rey). It owes its name to the French Acadians and the gluttonous mice who repeatedly ravaged their crops. It's now known more for its joyous annual music festival than for the hungry field rodents of old. The **PEI Bluegrass & Old Time Music Festival** (☑902-569-3153; www.bluegrasspei.com/rollobay; Rte 2; ☺early Jul) draws acts from as far away as Nashville. Come for just a day, or camp out for all three.

This is a working town that's a friendly jumping-off point for cycling the coastal road (Rte 16) and the Confederation Trail, which comes into town. Souris is also the launching point for ferries to the Îles de la Madeleine in Québec.

🛏 Sleeping & Eating

Inn at Bay Fortune INN **$$**
(☑902-687-3745; www.innatbayfortune.com; 758 Rte 310; r from $135, ste $225-335; ✳🛜) Find some of PEI's most upscale rooms at this waterside inn about 12km south of Souris, as well as one of the island's best restaurants (meals from $60). Chef Domenic Serio has created a menu that captures the essence of PEI flavors; highlights include tartar of PEI scallops with strawberry and balsamic salsa or crispy beef short ribs with roasted organic shiitake mushrooms. Rooms are modern with country flair; the most fun rooms, tiny units in a tower with nearly 360-degree

views, are the least expensive. The price goes up with size, culminating in private cottages.

21 Breakwater   CANADIAN **$$**
(21 Breakwater St; mains $10-20; ⊙11:30am-8pm Mon-Sat) Souris' most elegant option is in a bright, historic mansion overlooking the industrial waterfront. The menu focuses on the usual suspects such as burgers, pasta with scallops, steamed mussels or chowder, but the preparation is top notch as is the service.

East Point to Naufrage

Built the same year Canada was unified, the **East Point Lighthouse** (☑902-357-2106; adult/ child $4/2; ⊙10am-6pm Jun-Aug) still stands guard over the northeastern shore of PEI. After being blamed for the 1882 wreck of the British *Phoenix,* the lighthouse was moved closer to shore. The eroding shoreline is now chasing it back. There's a gift shop and a little cafe next to the lighthouse that serves good-value lobster rolls ($9.50), hearty chowder and nice sandwiches.

The wooded coast and lilting accents of the north shore make for an interesting change of pace. Giant white windmills march across the landscape. **North Lake** and Naufrage harbors are intriguing places to stop and, if you feel so inclined, join a charter boat in search of a monster 450kg tuna.

The **railway museum** (☑902-357-7234; Rte 16A; adult/student/family $3/2/10; ⊙10am-6pm Jun-Sep) in Elmira includes a quirky miniature train ride (adult/student/family $8/5/16) that winds through the surrounding forest. The station marks the eastern end of the Confederation Trail.

Treat yourself to one of the most luxurious stays on the island at **Johnson Shore Inn** (☑902-687-1340; www.johnsonshoreinn.com; 9984 Northside Rd, Hermanville; r $175-350; ⊙May-Feb; ☎), run by the same effervescent couple who own Prince Edward Distillery (p155). Besides being impeccably run, the inn is blessed with a stunning setting on a red bluff that looks over endless sea.

St Peter's to Mt Stewart

The area between these two villages is a hot-bed for cycling. The section of the Confederation Trail closest to St Peter's flirts with the shoreline and rewards riders with an eyeful of the coast. In Mt Stewart three riverside

sections of the Confederation Trail converge, giving riders and hikers plenty of attractive options within a relatively compact area. Both the Confederation Trail and a **provincial tourist office** (☑902-961-3540; Rte 2; ⊙8am-7pm Jul & Aug, 9am-4:30pm Jun, Sep & Oct) are found next to the bridge in St Peter's.

🛏 Sleeping & Eating

Inn at St Peters Village   INN **$$$**
(☑800-818-0925, 902-961-2135; www.innatstpeters. com; 1168 Greenwich Rd; d $125-265; ☎) Even with its large, comfortable rooms and stunning water views, the main reason to come to this inn is to dine on some of PEI's finest fare at the sunset-facing restaurant (lunch mains from $17, dinner mains from $22). Rooms are simply and elegantly decorated with antique furniture, but even if you don't stay here we highly recommend stopping in for a meal (even you, sweaty bikers).

⭐ **Trailside Cafe & Inn**   CAFE **$$**
(☑902-628-7833; www.trailside.ca; 109 Main St, Mt Stewart; mains $12-17) It's a cafe, it's a music venue, it's a cozy and affordable inn (rooms $89). In all ways this place exudes the best of PEI. Grab a pot of mussels or a taster plate of local cheeses and a beer and let the live local music tingle your spine. Check the website for showtimes and ticket sales.

> **WORTH A TRIP**
>
> ## GREENWICH
>
> Massive, dramatic and ever-shifting sand dunes epitomize the amazing area west of Greenwich. These rare parabolic giants are fronted by an awesome, often empty beach – a visit here is a must. Preserved by Parks Canada in 1998, this 6km section of shore is now part of Prince Edward Island National Park.
>
> Avant-garde meets barn at the **Greenwich Interpretation Centre** (☑902-961-2514; Hwy 13; ⊙9:30am-7pm Jul & Aug, to 4:30pm May, Jun, Sep & Oct), where an innovative audiovisual presentation details the ecology of the dune system and the archaeological history of the site. The highlight though is getting out into the tree-eating dunes. Four walking trails traverse the park; the **Greenwich Dunes Trail** (4.5km return, 1½ hours) is especially scenic.

If you can't make a nighttime show, try and make it to the Hillsborough River Gospel Brunch, on every Sunday May through September for $20 including brunch.

CENTRAL PRICE EDWARD ISLAND

Central PEI contains a bit of all that's best about the island – verdant fields, quaint villages and forests undulating north to the dramatic sand-dune-backed beaches of Prince Edward Island National Park. Anne of Green Gables, the engaging heroine of Lucy Maud Montgomery's 1908 novel, has spawned a huge global industry focused on the formerly bucolic hamlet of Cavendish. However, this being PEI, even its most savagely developed patch of tourist traps and commercial detritus is almost quaint – freshly painted and flower bedecked.

For those entering central PEI via the Confederation Bridge, it's worth stopping at the **Gateway Village Visitors Information Centre** (☑ 902-437-8570; Hwy 1; ⊙ 8:30am-8pm), just off the bridge on the PEI side, for its free maps, brochures, restrooms and an excellent introductory exhibit called *Our Island Home* (open May to November). Staff can point you to the Confederation Trail, which starts nearby.

Victoria

The shaded, tree-laden lanes of this lovely little fishing village – a place to wander and experience more than 'see' – scream out character and charm. The entire village still fits neatly in the four blocks laid out when the town was formed in 1819. Colorful clapboard and shingled houses are home to more than one visitor who was so enthralled by the place they decided to stay. There's a profusion of art, cafes and eateries, as well as an excellent summer theater festival.

◉ Sights & Activities

Lighthouse Museum   MUSEUM
(admission by donation; ⊙ 9am-5:30pm Jun-Aug) This museum has an interesting exhibit on local history. If it's closed, get the key from the shop across the road.

By the Sea Kayaking   KAYAKING
(☑ 877-879-2572, 902-658-2572; www.bytheseakayaking.ca; kayak rentals per hr/day $25/50) Paddle round the bay on your own or on a

guided tour, then take a dip off the beach at **Victoria Harbour Provincial Park** (FREE), where there are change rooms available. The outfit also operates popular 'I Dig Therefore I Clam' clamming expeditions ($7) and offers bike rentals (per hour/day $15/30).

🛏 Sleeping & Eating

Orient Hotel B&B   B&B $$
(☑ 800-565-6743, 902-658-2503; www.theorienthotel.com; 34 Main St; r incl breakfast $85-105, ste $125-160; ☎) A delightful Victorian confection of buttercup yellow, red and blue, this historic seaside inn is a perfect jewel.

★ Landmark Café   CAFE $$
(☑ 902-658-2286; 12 Main St; mains $12-25; ⊙ 11:30am-10pm May-Sep) People come from miles around for the wonderful imaginative food at this family-run cafe. Prepared with wholesome ingredients, every colorful menu item from lasagnas and homemade soups to Cajun stir-fries and feta-stuffed vine leaves is a winner. Enjoy the photos on the wall of the family's annual exotic trips and their equally multicultural music selection, softly pumping through the cafe.

☆ Entertainment

Victoria Playhouse   THEATER
(☑ 902-658-2025, 800-925-2025; www.victoriaplayhouse.com; 20 Howard St; tickets $30; ⊙ 8pm Jun-Sep) The ornate red velvet and gold theater at Victoria Playhouse presents a series of plays over the summer, with concerts from some of the region's finest musicians on Monday nights.

Prince Edward Island National Park

Heaving dunes and red sandstone bluffs provide startling backdrops for some of the island's finest stretches of sand; welcome to **Prince Edward Island National Park** (☑ 902-672-6350; www.pc.gc.ca/pei; day pass adult/child $7.80/3.90). This dramatic coast, and the narrow sections of wetland and forests behind it, is home to diverse plants, animals and birdlife, including the red fox and endangered piping plover.

The park is open year-round, but most services only operate between late June and the end of August. Entrance fees are charged between mid-June and mid-September, and admit you to all park sites, except the House of Green Gables (p163). If you're planning to stay longer than five days, look into a seasonal pass. The park maintains an information desk at the Cavendish Visitor Centre (p164).

The following sights and sleeping and eating options are organized from east to west covering the park-run facilities and private operations inside and out of the park.

◉ Sights & Activities

Beaches lined with marram grasses and wild rose span almost the entire length of the park's 42km coastline. In most Canadians' minds, the park is almost synonymous with these strips of sand. **Dalvay Beach** sits to the east, and has some short hiking trails through the woods. The landscape flattens and the sand sprawls outward at **Stanhope Beach**. Here, a boardwalk leads from the campground to the shore. Backed by dunes, and slightly west, is the expansive and popular **Brackley Beach**. On the western side of the park, the sheer size of **Cavendish Beach** makes it the granddaddy of them all. During summer this beach sees copious numbers of visitors beneath its hefty dunes. If crowds aren't your thing, there are always the pristine sections of sand to the east. Lifeguards are on duty at Cavendish, Brackley and Stanhope Beaches in midsummer. A beautiful bike lane runs all the way along this coast.

🛏 Sleeping

Parks Canada operates three highly sought-after **campgrounds** (☏800-414-6765; campsites/RV sites $28/36; ☉ Jun-Aug), which are spread along the park's length. They all have kitchen shelters and showers. For an additional fee of $11, you can reserve a campsite online at www.reservation.parkscanada.gc.ca (or it's $13.50 by phone). You can request a campground, but not a specific site; you must accept whatever is available when you arrive. While 80% of sites can be booked in advance, the remaining sites are first-come, first-served, so it's wise to arrive early.

Stanhope Campground, on Gulfshore East Pkwy, is nestled nicely in the woods behind the beach of the same name. There is a well-stocked store on-site.

Robinsons Island Campground, also on Gulfshore East Pkwy, is open from late June. The most isolated of the three sites, it's set at the end of Brackley Point. It's not too much fun if the wind gets up.

The proximity of **Cavendish Campground**, off Rte 6, to the sights makes it the most popular. It has exposed oceanfront sites and ones within the shelter and shade of the trees. Don't be lured by the view – it's nice, but sleep is better.

Dalvay by the Sea

Standing proudly near the east end of the park, and overlooking the beach named after it, is Dalvay, a historic mansion. Built in 1895 this majestic building is now owned by Parks Canada and operated as an **inn** (☏888-366-2955, 902-672-2048; www.dalvaybythesea.com; Gulfshore East Pkwy; r incl breakfast $174-344, cottages $404-444; ❄🛜☒). It's easily the most luxurious and stunning accommodations on the north shore. Each plush room's view and antique furnishings are refreshingly unique. The majestic **dining room** (dinner $18-36; h breakfast, lunch and dinner Jul-Aug) prepares remarkable dishes ranging from hazelnut- and sage-crusted rack of lamb to fresh island lobster. It is open to nonguests, and both lunch and afternoon tea (from 2pm to 4pm) are reasonably priced. The inn also rents bicycles ($9/26 per hour/day).

Brackley Beach

Brackley Beach isn't so much a town as a rural area with a few scattered amenities and the main beach access to the central eastern beaches of Prince Edward Island National Park. It's a short enough drive from Charlottetown (21km) so that even if you're not staying overnight, it's fun to catch a movie at **Brackley Beach Drive-In** (☏902-672-3333; www.drivein.ca; 3164 Rte 15; adult/child $9/6; ☉May-Sep). Check the website for what's showing.

Shaw's Hotel & Cottages (☏902-672-2022; www.shawshotel.ca; Rte 15, 99 Apple Tree Rd; d $85-260, cottages $155-500; ❄🛜), open since 1860, is Canada's oldest family-operated inn. The hotel occupies 30 hectares of the family farm, with a private lane leading to Brackley Beach, a 600m walk away. Rooms in the inn have old-fashioned simplicity. One- to four-bedroom cottages, ranging from rustic to modern, are scattered around the property. A children's program runs in July and August, with hay rides, games, trips to the beach and a supervised supper hour. The **dining room** (☏902-672-2022; mains $22-33; ☉8-10am & 5:45-9:30pm) is open to outside guests;

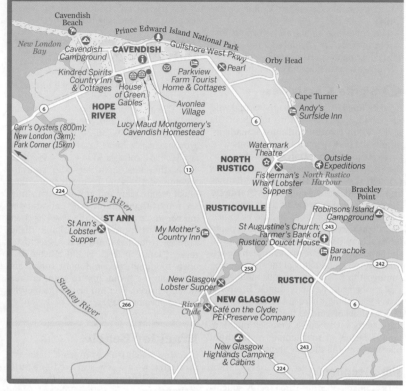

Cavendish
Beach

New London
Bay

Cavendish
Campground

CAVENDISH

Prince Edward Island National Park

Gulfshore West Pkwy

Orby Head

Kindred Spirits
Country Inn
& Cottages

House
of Green
Gables

Parkview
Farm Tourist
Home & Cottages

Pearl

**HOPE
RIVER**

Avonlea
Village

Cape Turner

Andy's
Surfside Inn

Carr's Oysters (800m);
New London (3km);
Park Corner (15km)

Lucy Maud Montgomery's
Cavendish Homestead

6

13

Watermark
Theatre

**NORTH
RUSTICO**

Fisherman's
Wharf Lobster
Suppers

Outside
Expeditions

North Rustico
Harbour

Brackley
Point

224

Hope River

ST ANN

RUSTICOVILLE

Robinsons Island
Campground

St Ann's
Lobster
Supper

My Mother's
Country Inn

St Augustine's Church;
Farmer's Bank of
Rustico; Doucet House

243

Barachois
Inn

242

258

RUSTICO

Stanley River

266

New Glasgow
Lobster Supper

River
Clyde

NEW GLASGOW

Café on the Clyde;
PEI Preserve Company

6

New Glasgow
Highlands Camping
& Cabins

243

224

reservations are recommended for the popular Sunday evening buffet ($40; held in July and August).

For near-the-beach budget digs you won't find better than the clean and superfriendly **Brackley Beach Hostel** (☑902-672-1900; www.brackleybeachhostel.com; 37 Britain Shore Rd; dm/q $27/59; ☏) housed in a big barn about 2km from the shoreline. There are several eight-bed dorm rooms and a few quads as well as plenty of showers and an equipped kitchen.

While over-the-top springs to mind, **Dunes Café & Gallery** (☑902-672-2586; Rte 15; dinner mains $16-25; ☉11:30am-10pm) is a nice change of pace. Honestly, where else on the island can you enjoy Vietnamese rice-noodle salad in the shade of a giant Buddha? Come in for a coffee, a meal or just to roam the eclectic mix of Asian and island art in the sprawling glass gallery and garden.

Rustico

The seafront Acadian settlement at Rustico dates back to 1700, and several fine historic buildings speak of this tiny village's former importance. Most prominent is **St Augustine's Church** (1830), the oldest Catholic church on PEI. The old cemetery is on one side of the church, the solid red-stone **Farmer's Bank of Rustico** is on the other. The bank operated here from 1864 to 1894; it was a forerunner of the credit-union movement in Canada. Beside the bank is **Doucet House**, an old Acadian dwelling that was relocated here. A **museum** (☑902-963-2194; adult/student $4/2; ☉9:30am-5:30pm Mon-Sat, 1-5pm Sun) describing the settlement of the community and the establishment of the bank is now housed in the two secular buildings.

PRINCE EDWARD ISLAND RUSTICO

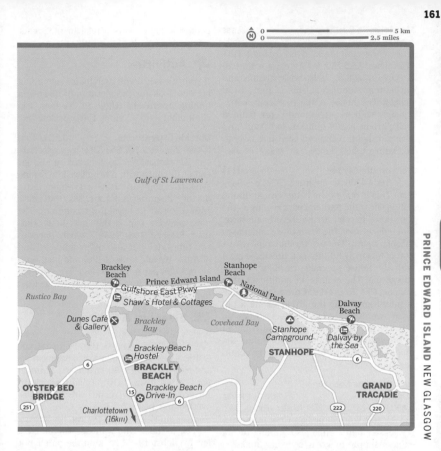

In a prime location just across the street from the towering old church, **Barachois Inn** (☑800-963-2194, 902-963-2906; www.barachoisinn.com; 2193 Church Rd; d incl breakfast $140-275; ✳️🛜) is one of the finest B&Bs on PEI. The grand Acadian-style mansion is decorated not only with the standard sublime selection of antiques, but also with very eclectic paintings, which makes walking around the many common areas like touring an art museum. Bathrooms are nearly equal in size to the enormous rooms, and hidden in the basement of the newer annex (built to copy the older building to perfection) is an exercise room, sauna and conference area.

New Glasgow

New Glasgow is a quiet town that spreads elegantly across the shores of the River Clyde. This is the favorite lobster supper getaway for folks from Charlottetown, although it's becoming equally respected for its luscious preserves.

🛏 Sleeping & Eating

New Glasgow Highlands Camping & Cabins CAMPGROUND $
(☑902-964-3232; www.campcabinpei.com; Rte 224; campsites/RV sites $32/38, cabins $60; ☺Apr-Nov; 🛜🏊) The 20-odd sites here are properly spaced in the forest, each with its own fire pit. For rainy days there are simple cooking facilities in the lodge. Add a laundry, a small store, a heated swimming pool and a mystifying absence of bugs, and you're laughing. There are also bright cabins, each with two bunks, a double bed, a sofa and a picnic table, but no linen or pillows; bathrooms are shared. Be sure to book ahead and don't even think about making late-night noise – peace is the word.

My Mother's Country Inn B&B $$

(☎800-278-2071, 902-964-2508; www.mymoth-erscountryinn.com; Rte 13; d incl breakfast $110-225, cottages $125-250; ☞) An oasis within 20 hectares of rolling hills, brisk streams and enchanting woodlands, this is pure, rural delight. The house is the essence of country style with sea-green and ochre painted walls, bright pastel quilts, wood floors and plenty of light. A big red barn just begs to be photographed beside a storybook brook.

Café on the Clyde CAFE $$

(☎902-964-4300; dinner mains $13-20; ☺9am-8pm) This is one of the better casual dining options near the national park as long as the tour buses haven't arrived before you have. Sun reflects in off the River Clyde and makes this place glow. The vegetarian wraps with a hint of feta truly hit the spot; finish the meal with the house specialty, raspberry cream cheese pie. The cafe is an addition to the famous **PEI Preserve Company** (☺9am-8pm Jun-Sep). While the preserves are a tad pricey, we think they're worth every penny; if you're not going to buy, at least come in to browse the free samples. Don't pass the orange ginger curd or the raspberry champagne preserves.

New Glasgow Lobster Supper LOBSTER SUPPER $$

(☎902-964-2870; Rte 258; lobster dinners $32; ☺4-8:30pm) You can make a right mess with the lobster here, while also gorging on an endless supply of great chowder, mussels, salads, breads and homemade desserts.

St Ann

St Ann is so small you hardly even know you've arrived. Yet on a summer evening, follow the traffic and wafts of lobster steam to **St Ann's Lobster Supper** (☎902-621-0635; Rte 224; lobster dinners $32; ☺4:30-8:30pm), which rivals New Glasgow as PE Islanders' favorite lobster supper.

North Rustico

Within a few minutes of arrival, it is pretty obvious that this is not simply a tourist town. Rickety, boxy fishermen's houses painted in navies, brick reds and beiges, line a deep harbor that is simply packed with fishing vessels. A walk east from the pier along the boardwalk, and out to North Rustico Harbour, is a great way to take in the sights, sounds and smells of this little village.

Activities

If your idea of ocean activity is reeling in a big one, look for the plethora of **deep-sea fishing operators** (three to 3½ hour trip adult/child $45/35) along Harbourview Dr.

Outside Expeditions CYCLING, KAYAKING

(☎800-207-3899, 902-963-3366; www.getoutside.com; 374 Harbourview Dr) Situated at the far end of the harbor in a bright-yellow fishing shed, this company runs a 1½-hour introductory 'Beginner Bay' tour ($39) that starts with a lesson in kayaking techniques. The most popular trip is the three-hour 'Harbour Passage' tour ($59), which operates two times daily. It also offers guided 'Land of Anne' bicycle tours ($120) and bike rentals ($20/35 per half-/full day). Trips are operated in the off-season, whenever at least four people want to go.

Sleeping & Eating

Andy's Surfside Inn INN $

(☎902-963-2405; andyssurfsideinn@gmail.com; Gulfshore West Pkwy; d with shared bathroom incl light breakfast $50-75; ☞) Inside the national park, 2.7km toward Orby Head from North Rustico, is this very rustic, rambling house overlooking beautiful Doyle's Cove. It has been an inn since the 1930s, and the kitchen is open to those who want to bring home a few live lobsters. Sit back on the porch, put your feet up and thank your lucky stars.

Fisherman's Wharf Lobster Suppers LOBSTER SUPPER $$$

(☎902-963-2669; 7230 Main St; lobster dinners $32; ☺noon-9pm) During the dinner rush in July and August this huge place has lines of people out the door. It's a fun, casual, holiday-style restaurant offering excellent value – that is if you don't wreck your shirt! Come hungry, as there are copious servings of chowder, tasty local mussels, rolls and a variety of desserts to go with your pound of messy crustacean. If things go your way, you may get a table with an ocean view.

Entertainment

Watermark Theatre THEATER

(☎902-963-3963; www.watermarktheatre.com; North Rustico Village; tickets $28-39) Opened in 2008 in honor of the 100th anniversary of the publication of *Anne of Green Gables*, this theater presents plays from the life and times of Lucy Maud Montgomery. Performances are in a renovated 19th-century church that Montgomery herself attended. Seats sell out fast, so book in advance!

Cavendish

Anyone familiar with *Anne of Green Gables* might have lofty ideas of finding Cavendish as a quaint village bedecked in flowers and country charm; guess again. While the Anne and Lucy Maud Montgomery sites are right out of the imagination-inspiring book pages, Cavendish itself is a mishmash of manufactured attractions with no particular town center. The junction of Rte 6 and Hwy 13 is the tourist center and the area's commercial hub. When you see the service station, wax museum, church, cemetery and assorted restaurants, you know you're there. This is the most-visited community on PEI outside of Charlottetown and, although an eyesore in this scenic region, it is a kiddie wonderland. To get out of the world of fabricated and fictional free-for-all, head to beautiful **Cavendish Beach**; it gets crowded during summer months, but with perfect sand and a warm(ish) ocean in front, you won't really care.

If you haven't read the 1908 novel, this is the place to do it – not just to enjoy it, but to try and understand all the hype. The story revolves around Anne Shirley, a spirited 11-year-old orphan with red pigtails and a creative wit, who was mistakenly sent from Nova Scotia to PEI. The aging Cuthberts (who were brother and sister) were expecting a strapping boy to help them with farm chores. In the end, Anne's strength of character wins over everyone in her path.

◉ Sights

House of Green Gables　　　HISTORIC SITE
(☑902-672-7874; Rte 6; adult/child $6.30/3.15; ◷10am-5pm Mon-Sat) Cavendish is the home town of Lucy Maud Montgomery (1874–1942), author of *Anne of Green Gables*. Here she is simply known as Lucy Maud or LM. Owned by her grandfather's cousins, the now-famous House of Green Gables and its Victorian surrounds inspired the setting for her fictional tale.

In 1937 the house became part of the national park and it's now administered as a national heritage site, celebrating Lucy Maud and Anne with exhibits and audio-visual displays.

ⓘ IN LUCY MAUD'S FOOTSTEPS

To really get a feel for the *Anne of Green Gables* scenery get out and walk the green, gentle creek-crossed woods that Lucy Maud herself knew like the back of her hand. The best way is to start at the Lucy Maud Montgomery's Cavendish Homestead where you can buy a combo ticket that includes the House of Green Gables for $8.50. Then walk the 1.1km return trail to the House of Green Gables through the 'Haunted Wood.' In this way you arrive to a magical view from below the house rather than via a big parking lot and modern entrance. Once you're at the House of Green Gables you can enjoy the site plus many other surrounding trails including 'Lover's Lane,' before hoofing it back to the homestead.

Lucy Maud Montgomery's Cavendish Homestead　　HISTORIC SITE
(☑902-963-2231; Rte 6; adult/child $4/2; ◷9am-6pm) This is considered hallowed ground to Anne fans worldwide. Raised by her grandparents, Lucy Maud lived in this house from 1876 to 1911 and it is here that she wrote *Anne of Green Gables*. You'll find the old foundation of the house, many interpretive panels about Lucy Maud, a small on-site museum and a bookshop.

Avonlea Village　　　AMUSEMENT PARK
(☑902-963-3050; www.avonlea.ca; Rte 6; adult/family $19/70; ◷10am-5pm) Delve deeper into Anne fantasy at this theme park where costumed actors portray characters from the book and perform dramatic moments and scenes from Green Gable chapters. Beyond the theatrical exploits, the park offers you cow-milking demonstrations, a ride in a horse-drawn wagon and other period farm activities. Check the website for the day's schedule.

🛏 Sleeping & Eating

While accommodations are numerous, remember that this is the busiest and most expensive area you can stay. There are bargains and more bucolic settings east, toward North Rustico.

Parkview Farm Tourist Home & Cottages B&B **$**

(📞 800-237-9890, 902-963-2027; www.peionline.com/al/parkview; 8214 Rte 6; r with shared bathroom incl light breakfast $65-70, 2-bedroom cottages $165-265; 🐾🐕) This fine choice is set on a working dairy farm, 2km east of Cavendish. Ocean views, bathrooms and the prerequisite flowered wallpaper and frills abound in this comfortable and roomy tourist home. Each of the seven cottages, which are available May to mid-October (the B&B is open year-round), contains a kitchen and a barbecue, as well as a balcony to catch those dramatic comings and goings of the sun.

Kindred Spirits Country Inn & Cottages INN **$$**

(📞 800-461-1755, 902-963-2434; www.kindredspirits.ca; Rte 6; d $85-320, cottages $105-500; ❄️🐕🐾) A huge, immaculate complex, this place has something for everyone from a storybook-quality inn-style B&B to deluxe suites. Rooms are every Anne fan's dream, with dotty floral prints, glossy wood floors and fluffy, comfy beds. Downstairs the lounge has a fireplace that will make you wish it would snow and couches perfect for snuggling up with a mug of cocoa.

Carr's Oysters SEAFOOD **$$**

(📞 902-886-3355; Stanley Bridge Wharf, Rte 6; mains $14-32; ⊙10am-7pm) Dine on oysters straight from Malpeque Bay or lobster, mussels and seafood you've never even heard of like quahogs from this place's saltwater tanks. There are also plenty of fish on offer from salmon to trout. The setting over the bay is sociable and bright and there's also an on-site market selling fresh and smoked sea critters.

⭐ **Pearl** MODERN CANADIAN **$$$**

(📞 902-963-2111; 7792 Cavendish Rd; mains $22-32, brunch $8-12; ⊙from 4:30pm daily, 10am-2pm Sun) This shingled house just outside Cavendish is surrounded by flowers and is an absolutely lovely place to eat. There are plenty of unusual and seasonally changing options like ice-wine-infused chicken liver pâté on a Gouda brioche for starters and locally inspired mains such as delicious butter-poached scallops.

ℹ️ Information

Cavendish Visitor Centre (📞 902-963-7830; cnr Rte 6 & Hwy 13; ⊙9am-9pm)

New London & Park Corner

New London and Park Corner both have strong ties to Lucy Maud Montgomery, and are thus caught up in the everything-Anne pandemonium. The most charming place to stop for a bite to eat and a cup of tea is the **Blue Winds Tea Room** (📞 902-886-2860; 10746 Rte 6, New London; meals $10-14; ⊙11am-6pm Mon-Thu, to 8pm Fri-Sun) about 500m southwest of Lucy Maud Montgomery's birthplace and surrounded by English gardens. Of course like everything else in this region, they've got to be 'Anne,' so order a raspberry cordial or some New Moon Pudding – both recipes have been taken from Lucy Maud's journals.

⊙ Sights & Activities

Lucy Maud Montgomery Birthplace MUSEUM

(📞 902-886-2099; cnr Rtes 6 & 20; admission $4; ⊙9am-5pm) This house is now a museum that contains some of Lucy Maud's personal belongings, including her wedding dress.

Anne of Green Gables Museum MUSEUM

(📞 902-886-2884; 4542 Rte 20; adult/child $5/1; ⊙9am-6pm May-Oct) Surrounded by a luscious 44-hectare property, this is the charming home Lucy Maud liked to call Silver Bush. It was always dear to her and she chose the parlor for her 1911 wedding. Silver Bush hosts the Anne of Green Gables Museum. It contains such items as her writing desk and autographed first-edition books.

Lucy Maud Montgomery Heritage Museum MUSEUM

(📞 902-886-2807; 4605 Rte 20; admission $4; ⊙9:30am-6pm) The building that houses this museum is believed to be the home of Lucy Maud's grandfather and there's a lot of Anne paraphernalia. Take a guided tour; there's a guarantee that if you're not absolutely fascinated, you don't pay the admission.

Annie's Table COOKERY

(📞 902-314-9666; www.annies-table.com; 4295 Graham's Rd, New London; 2hr course $50) Learn the secrets of local lavender, discover how to make PEI spuds spectacular, wrangle seafood into deliciousness or get acquainted with Acadian food at a cookery course in this remodeled antique church. On staff are several chefs and a sommelier to make sure the food is as beautiful as the setting.

MALPEQUE

So where is this place where all the oysters come from, you might ask. The tiny hamlet of Malpeque takes you off the beaten path, past shadeless, rolling farmland to a tiny bay simply jam-packed with fishing boats and their colorfully painted storage barns. Don't miss lunch at **Malpeque Oyster Barn** (Malpeque Wharf; 6 oysters $14; ⊙ 11am-9pm Mon-Sat, noon-9pm Sun), one of PEI's more authentically ambient cafes, in the top of a fisherman's barn and overlooking the bay and its oyster-filled action. Downstairs is a seafoodmonger where you can pick up fresh local sea critters to take away.

To get even closer to the crustaceans, hop in a sea kayak or on a stand up paddle board with **Malpeque Bay Kayak Tour Ltd** (☑ 866-582-3383; www.peikayak.ca; 3hr kayak tour $55).

Kensington & Around

Kensington is a busy market town about halfway between Cavendish and Summerside. It's a good place to replenish supplies and the closest service center for those attending the **Indian River Festival** (www.indianriverfestival.com) when some of Canada's finest musicians (from Celtic to choral) play in the wonderfully acoustic St Mary's Church, from June through September.

Home Place Inn & Restaurant (☑ 866-522-9900, 902-836-5686; www.thehomeplace.ca; 21 Victoria St E; d incl breakfast $89-109, ste $149; ⊙ May-Oct; 🛜) exudes country elegance at its finest. In the morning you may be awakened with scents of freshly baking cinnamon rolls and there's a licensed pub and restaurant on the premises.

In nearby Margate, **Shipwright's Café** (☑ 902-836-3403; cnr Rtes 6 & 233; dinner mains $25-35; ⊙ 11:30am-3:30pm Mon-Fri, from 5pm daily) is housed in an 1880s farmhouse overlooking rolling fields and flower gardens. It earns rave reviews for its seafood dishes and vegetarian fare concocted from organic herbs and vegetables from the gardens. Try the 'Salute to Our Greenhouse' salad, a paella endowed with the island's best seafood and creations with PEI beef.

WESTERN PRINCE EDWARD ISLAND

Malpeque and Bedeque Bays converge to almost separate the western third of PEI from the rest of the province. This region sits entirely within the larger Prince County, and it combines the sparse pastoral scenery of Kings County's interior with some of Queens County's rugged coastal beauty.

The cultural history here stands out more than elsewhere on the island. On Lennox Island a proud Mi'kmaq community is working to foster knowledge of its past, while French Acadians are doing the same in the south, along Egmont and Bedeque Bays.

Summerside

While it lacks the elegance and cosmopolitan vibe of Charlottetown, Summerside is a simpler, seaside-oriented place with everything you need in one small, tidy package. Recessed deep within Bedeque Bay and PEI's second-largest 'city,' this tiny seaside village possesses a modern waterfront and quiet streets lined with leafy trees and grand old homes. The two largest economic booms in the province's history, shipbuilding and fox breeding, shaped the city's development in the 19th and early 20th centuries. Like Charlottetown, its outskirts are plagued by unsightly development – you'll find most of Summerside's interesting bits along, or near to, Water St, which runs parallel to the waterfront.

⊙ Sights & Activities

The Confederation Trail makes its journey right through town and passes behind the library on Water St.

Spinnaker's Landing   BOARDWALK

This redeveloped waterfront is the highlight of Summerside. A continually expanding boardwalk allows you to wander and enjoy the harbor and its scenic surrounds. There are some very nice eateries, a stage for live music in the summer and numerous shops. A mock lighthouse provides adults with a nice lookout and some local information, while a large model ship is a dream

PRINCE EDWARD ISLAND KENSINGTON & AROUND

Summerside

playground for kids. Backing all of this is the modern **Eptek Exhibition Centre** (📞902-888-8373; 130 Harbour Dr; admission by donation; ⏱10am-4pm), which features local and traveling art exhibitions.

🛏 Sleeping & Eating

★**Willowgreen Farm**   B&B $$
(📞888-436-4420, 902-436-4420; www.willow-greenfarm.com; 117 Bishop Dr; d incl breakfast $60-118; 🛜) With the Confederation Trail at its back door, and the College of Piping & Celtic Performing Arts out its front door, this rambling farmhouse is an incredibly great-value place to stay; you feel like you're in the coun-

try, but actually you're in central Summerside. Rooms are bright, and the bold country interior is a refreshing change from busy period decors. Read beside the woodstove or check out some of the more interesting farm animals.

Summerside Bed & Breakfast   B&B $$
(📞902-620-4993;www.summersideinnbandb.com; 98 Summer St; r $115; ❋🛜) Poetically located on the corner of Summer and Winter Sts; the room you should obviously angle for is the bright and spacious Spring Room. This fine heritage building has been home to two Canadian premiers and boasts plenty of sitting areas and charm. Your friendly hosts prepare delicious hot breakfasts.

Five Eleven West   CANADIAN $$
(Credit Union Place, 511 Notre Dame St; mains $10-19; ⏱11:30am-2pm Mon-Fri, 5-8pm daily) Summerside's most modern eatery is tucked into a very unlikely corner of the town's multipurpose sports complex. Once you find it (to the left of the snack bar) be prepared to be impressed. Everything from the massive portion of beer-battered fish and chips to Madras chicken over rice, steamed mussels and prime rib is beautifully prepared, and the ambience is chic.

☆ Entertainment

Harbourfront Theatre THEATER
(☑800-708-6505, 902-888-2500; www.harbour-fronttheatre.com; 124 Harbour Dr) This modern theater is in the same complex as the Eptek Exhibition Centre and is the venue for a changing series of plays, comedy and more. It also hosts the **Summer on the Waterfront Festival** (☉ Jul- mid-Sep), which showcases local and well-known Canadian musical acts.

Feast Dinner Theatres THEATER
(☑902-888-2200, 888-748-1010; 618 Water St E; dinner & show $40; ☉6:30pm Mon-Sat Jun-Dec) Most locals start to giggle when they speak of their last time at Feast Dinner Theatres. You will find it below Brothers Two Restaurant and it is the longest-running theater restaurant in Atlantic Canada. Music, script and improvisation combine with audience participation to make for a truly memorable evening. And that's not all: the food's not too shabby, either.

College of Piping & Celtic Performing Arts MUSIC
(☑902-436-5377; 619 Water St E; ceilidhs adult/student $12/7; ☉9am-9pm, ceilidhs 7pm) In celebration of Celtic dance and music, this school provides visitors with free 20-minute miniconcerts from Monday to Friday at 11:30am, 1:30pm and 3:30pm – expect bagpipes, singing and dancing. Inspired? Then get yourself out to the 'Highland Storm,' a Celtic music and dance extravaganza with a cast of 30 of the island's best performers. The show is on three days a week through summer.

❶ Information

Provincial Tourist Office (☑902-888-8364; Harbourfront Theatre, 124 Harbour Dr; ☉9am-7pm Jul & Aug, reduced hours May, Jun, Sep & Oct) Pick up a copy of the useful walking-tour pamphlet, which details the town's finer 19th-century buildings.

❶ Getting There & Away

Maritime Bus (p146) stops at the **Irving gas station** (☑902-436-2420; 96 Water St) in the center of town and has services to Charlottetown ($14.25, one hour), Moncton ($29.50, two hours) and Halifax ($53.25, 3½ hours). On request, bus shuttles pick up at the Esso station on Hwy 1A at the end of Water St E.

Région Évangéline

The strongest French Acadian ancestry on the island is found here, between Miscouche and Mont Carmel. Some 6000 residents still speak French as their first language, although you'll have trouble discerning this region from others in the province. There is one notable exception: the red, white, blue and yellow star of the Acadian flag hangs proudly from many homes. It was in Miscouche, on August 15, 1884, that the Acadian flag was unfurled for the very first time. The yellow star represents the patron saint of the Acadians, the Virgin Mary.

A favorite stop on this stretch is the **Bottle Houses** (☑902-854-2987; Rte 11, Cape Egmont; adult/child $5/2; ☉9am-8pm), the artful and monumental recycling project of Edouard Arsenault. Over 25,000 bottles of all shapes and sizes (that Edouard collected from the community) are stacked in white cement to create a handful of buildings with light-filled mosaic walls.

The very worthwhile **Acadian Museum** (☑902-432-2880; 23 Maine Dr E; admission $5; ☉9:30am-7pm), in Miscouche, uses 18th-century Acadian artifacts, texts, visuals and music to enlighten visitors about the tragic and compelling history of the Acadians on PEI since 1720. The introspective video introduces a fascinating theory that the brutal treatment of the Acadians by the British may have backhandedly helped preserve a vestige of Acadian culture on Prince Edward Island.

Tyne Valley

This area, famous for its Malpeque oysters, is one of the most scenic in the province. The village, with its cluster of ornate houses, gentle river and art studios, is definitely worth a visit.

Green Park Provincial Park, 6km north of the village, hosts the **Green Park Shipbuilding Museum & Historic Yeo House** (☑902-831-7947; Rte 12; adult $5; ☉9am-5pm). The museum and restored Victorian home, along with a re-created shipyard and partially constructed 200-tonne brigantine, combine to tell the story of the booming shipbuilding industry in the 19th century.

The park has 58 **campsites** (☑902-831-7912; off Rte 12; campsites $23-25, with hookups $30, cabins with shared bathroom $45; ☉Jun-Sep) spread within a mixed forest. The dozen cabins just beyond the campground are a steal.

Not surprisingly, the specialty at **Landing Oyster House & Pub** (☑902-831-3138; 1327 Port Hill Station Rd; mains $8-13; ☺11am-9pm Mon & Tue, to 11pm Wed, to midnight Thu-Sat, 8am-8pm Sun) is deep-fried oysters – definitely indulge. Live bands (cover $4 to $8) play here on Friday night, and also on Saturday during July and August.

Lennox Island

Set in the mouth of Malpeque Bay, sheltered behind Hog Island, is Lennox Island and its 250 Mi'kmaq people. The island is connected by a causeway, making it accessible from the town of East Bideford off Rte 12.

The **Lennox Island Aboriginal Ecotourism Complex** (☑866-831-2702; 2 Eagle Feather Trail; adult/student $4/3; ☺10am-6pm Mon-Sat Jun-Sep) opened its doors in June 2004. Inside there are small, changing exhibits and information about the two excellent **interpretive trails** around the island. These trails consist of two loops, forming a total of 13km, with the shorter one (3km) being accessible to people in wheelchairs – if you're lucky and someone's around, a local will guide you for a small fee. Also ask at the center if anything else is on offer, as it seems to change frequently.

Tignish

Tignish is a quiet town tucked up near the North Cape; it sees only a fraction of PEI's visitors. The towering **Church of St Simon & St Jude** (1859) was the first brick church built on the island. Have a peek inside – its ceiling has been restored to its gorgeous but humble beginnings, and the organ (1882) is of gargantuan proportions.

The Confederation Trail begins (or ends!) two blocks south of the church on School St. The **Tignish Cultural Centre** (☑902-882-1999; 305 School St; ☺8am-4pm Mon-Fri) FREE, near the church, has a good exhibition of old maps and photos and tourist information.

North Cape

The drive toward North Cape seems stereotypically bucolic, until the moment your eyes rise above the quaint farmhouses to see the heavens being churned by dozens of sleek behemoth-sized white blades.

The narrow, windblown North Cape is not only home to the **Atlantic Wind Test**, but also to the longest **natural rock reef** on the continent. At low tide, it's possible to walk out 800m, exploring tide pools and searching for seals. The expanded **interpretive center** (☑902-882-2991; admission $6; ☺9:30am-8pm), at the northern end of Rte 12, provides high-tech displays dedicated to wind energy, and informative displays on the history of the area. The aquarium is always a hit with kids. The **Black Marsh Nature Trail** (2.7km) leaves the interpretive center and takes you to the west side of the cape – at sunset these crimson cliffs simply glow against the deep-blue waters.

Above the interpretive center, the atmospheric **Wind & Reef Restaurant & Lounge** (☑902-882-3535; mains $9-29; ☺lunch & dinner) attracts visitors and locals out for a treat. The menu and view are equally vast and pleasing.

West Coast

In Miminegash, stop into the **Seaweed Cafe** (meals $5-12) that serves a special seaweed pie, although nothing about this fluffy, creamy creation reeks of the beach.

Inland at O'Leary is the **Canadian Potato Museum** (☑902-859-2039; 1 Dewar Lane; admission $8; ☺9am-5pm Mon-Sat, 1-5pm Sun May-Oct). It's a bit like a giant school science fair project with hallways of information panels and pictures on the walls.

Between Miminegash and West Point, Rte 14 hugs the shore and provides stunning vistas. It's perhaps the finest drive on the island. Off Hwy 14, the striking black-and-white-striped **West Point Lighthouse** (☑800-764-6854, 902-859-3605; www.westpointlighthouse.com; ☺8am-9:30pm) dates from 1875. There's a small **museum** (admission $4; ☺9am-9pm), where you can climb the tower for a breathtaking view. Part of the former lighthouse keepers' quarters have been converted into a nine-room **inn** (www.westpointlighthouse.com; d $170; ☺Jun-Sep; ❄�); the Tower Room is actually in the old lighthouse tower. The **restaurant** (meals $8-18; ☺8am-8pm) is locally famous for its clam chowder.

Cedar Dunes Provincial Park (☑902-859-8785; campsites $23-25, RV sites $26-27) has tent space in an open grassy field adjacent to West Point Lighthouse. Its red-sand beach is an island gem.

Newfoundland & Labrador

Best Places to Eat

➡ Chinched (p179)

➡ Bonavista Social Club
(p191)

➡ Lighthouse Picnics (p185)

Best Places to Stay

➡ Tuckamore Lodge (p207)

➡ Artisan Inn (p189)

➡ Skerwink Hostel (p189)

➡ The Cliffhouse (p188)

Why Go?

Canada's easternmost province floats in a world of its own. Blue icebergs drift by. Puffins flap along the coast. Whales spout close to shore. The island even ticks in its own offbeat time zone (a half-hour ahead of the mainland) and speaks its own dialect (the *Dictionary of Newfoundland English* provides translation, me old cock).

Outside of the good-time capital St John's, it's mostly wee fishing villages that freckle the coast, some so isolated they're reached only by boat. They offer plenty of hiking and kayaking escapes where it will just be you, the local family who's putting you up for the night and the lonely howl of the wind.

If you're looking to get off the beaten path – to see Viking vestiges, eat meals of cod tongue and partridgeberry pie, and share fish tales over shots of rum – set a course for this remote hunk of rock.

When to Go

St John's

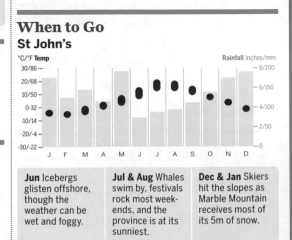

Jun Icebergs glisten offshore, though the weather can be wet and foggy.

Jul & Aug Whales swim by, festivals rock most weekends, and the province is at its sunniest.

Dec & Jan Skiers hit the slopes as Marble Mountain receives most of its 5m of snow.

Newfoundland & Labrador Highlights

① See live music, a ghost tour and history in North America's oldest city, **St John's** (p172).

② Watch whales and puffins at **Witless Bay Ecological Reserve** (p184).

③ Explore a 1000-year-old Viking pad at the sublime

L'Anse aux Meadows National Historic Site (p205).

④ Hike the mountains and kayak the lakes at **Gros Morne National Park** (p200).

⑤ Try out the modern outport life in **Fogo** (p198).

⑥ Hike, ogle icebergs and sip

Moose Joose in **Twillingate** (p196).

⑦ Get your French fix with wine, chocolate éclairs and baguettes in **St-Pierre** (p192).

⑧ Learn Basque whaling history then walk past ancient whale bones at **Red Bay** (p218).

History

The Paleoindians walked into Labrador 9000 years ago. They hunted seals, fished for salmon and tried to stay warm. The Vikings, led by Leif Eriksson, washed ashore further south at L'Anse aux Meadows in Newfoundland in AD 1000 and established North America's first European settlement.

John Cabot (Italian-born Giovanni Caboto) sailed around the shores of Newfoundland next. It was 1497, and he was employed by England's Henry VII. Cabot's stories of cod stocks so prolific that one could nearly walk on water spread quickly throughout Europe. Soon the French, Portuguese, Spanish and Basques were also fishing here.

The 1713 Treaty of Utrecht ceded all of Newfoundland to England. The land remained a British colony for most of the next two centuries, with life revolving around the booming fishing industry. Newfoundland's Aboriginal people, the Beothuk, did not fare well after settlement began. Diseases and land conflicts contributed to their demise by 1829.

Ever true to its independent spirit, Newfoundland was the last province to join Canada, doing so in 1949. While Labrador was always part of the package, it wasn't until 2001 that it became part of the provincial name.

Language

Two hundred years ago, coastal fishing families from Ireland and England made up almost the entire population. Since then, as a result of living in isolated outposts, their language has evolved into almost 60 different dialects. Strong, lilting inflections, unique slang and colorful idioms pepper the language, sometimes confounding even residents.

The authoritative source is the *Dictionary of Newfoundland English* (www.heritage.nf.ca/dictionary).

> ⓘ **PLANNING YOUR TRIP**
>
> ➡ Book ahead for rental cars and accommodations. If arriving during mid-July to early August, secure a car by April or May and don't wait much longer to book a room. **Newfoundland & Labrador Tourism** (www. newfoundlandlabrador.com) has listings.
>
> ➡ Driving distances are lengthy so have realistic expectations of what you can cover. For instance, it's 708km between St John's and Gros Morne National Park. The **Road Distance Database** (www.stats.gov.nl.ca/DataTools/RoadDB/Distance) is a good reference.
>
> ➡ Know your seasons for puffins (May to August), icebergs (June to early July) and whales (July to August). Icebergs, in particular, can be tricky to predict. Check **Iceberg Finder** (www.icebergfinder.com) to get the drift.

Land & Climate

It isn't called the Rock for nothing. Glaciers tore through, leaving behind a rugged landscape of boulders, lakes and bogs. The interior remains barren, while the island's cities and towns congregate at its edges near the sea.

NEWFOUNDLAND & LABRADOR

NEWFOUNDLAND ITINERARIES

Five Days

Start in **St John's** by visiting Signal Hill (p172) and **Cape Spear** (p183). Both are historic sites, but they also offer walking trails and views where you just may see an iceberg, whale, or both. At night sample St John's eateries, funky shops and music-filled pubs.

After a couple of days of 'big city' life, move on through the Avalon Peninsula. Cruise to see whales and puffins at **Witless Bay Ecological Reserve** (p184), plan a picnic in **Ferryland** (p185) or visit the birds at **Cape St Mary's** (p188).

Spend the last day or two soaking up the historic eastern communities of **Trinity** (p188) and **Bonavista** (p190) and the cliff-side hikes inbetween.

10 Days

Do the five-day itinerary and then go west, possibly via a quick flight to Deer Lake (p200), and view the mighty fjords of **Gros Morne National Park** (p200) and take in the monumental Viking history at **L'Anse aux Meadows** (p205). With a few extra days you could sail across the Strait of Belle Isle and slow waaay down among the wee towns and bold granite cliffs of the **Labrador Straits** (p215).

> ### REGIONAL DRIVING DISTANCES
> ....
> **St John's to Port aux Basques:** 905km
>
> **St John's to Gros Morne:** 708km
>
> **Gros Morne to St Anthony:** 372km

Labrador is more sparse than Newfoundland, puddled and tundralike, with mountains thrown in for good measure.

In July and August daytime highs average 20°C. These are also the driest months; it rains or snows about 15 out of every 30 days. Wintertime temperatures hover at 0°C. Fog and wind plague the coast much of the year (which makes for a lot of canceled flights).

Parks & Wildlife

Whales, moose and puffins are Newfoundland's wildlife stars, and most visitors see them all. Whale-watching tours depart from all around the province and will take you close to the sea mammals (usually humpback and minke). Puffins flap around Witless Bay and Elliston. Moose nibble shrubs near roadsides throughout the province, so keep an eye out while driving. Some visitors also glimpse caribou near the Avalon Wilderness Reserve, which is special because usually these beasts can only be seen in the High Arctic. Caribou herds also roam in Labrador, though their numbers have been declining sharply in recent years.

ℹ Getting There & Around

AIR

St John's International Airport (YYT; www.stjohnsairport.com) is the region's main hub, though Deer Lake Airport (p200) is an excellent option for visitors focusing on the Northern Peninsula. Airlines flying in include **Air Canada** (www.aircanada.com), **Provincial** (www.provincialairlines.ca), **Porter** (www.flyporter.com) and **United** (www.united.com).

BOAT

Marine Atlantic (☑ 800-341-7981; www.marine-atlantic.ca) runs two car/passenger ferries between North Sydney, Nova Scotia and Newfoundland. There's a daily, six-hour crossing to Port aux Basques (western Newfoundland) year-round, and a thrice-weekly, 14-hour crossing to Argentia (on the Avalon Peninsula) in summer. Reservations are recommended, especially to Argentia.

Provincial Ferry Service (www.gov.nl.ca/ferryservices) runs the smaller boats that travel within the province to various islands and coastal towns. Each service has its own phone number with up-to-the-minute information; it's wise to call before embarking.

BUS

DRL (☑ 709-263-2171; www.drl-lr.com) sends one bus daily each way between St John's and Port aux Basques (13½ hours), making 25 stops en route. Other than DRL, public transportation consists of small, regional shuttle vans that connect with one or more major towns. Although not extensive, the system works pretty well and will get most people where they want to go.

CAR

The Trans-Canada Hwy (Hwy 1) is the main cross-island roadway. Driving is often slow-going on heavily contorted, single-lane roads. Watch out for moose, especially at dusk.

ST JOHN'S

POP 106,200

Encamped on the steep slopes of a harbor, with jelly-bean-colored row houses popping up from hilly streets, St John's is often described as looking like a mini San Francisco. And like its American counterpart, it's home to artists, musicians, inflated real estate prices and young, iPhone-using denizens. Yet the vibe of Newfoundland's largest city and capital remains refreshingly small-town. At some point, locals will be sure to let you know St John's is North America's oldest city.

Highlights include the view from Signal Hill, live music and a pint (or shot of rum) in George St's pubs. Many visitors take advantage of the city's beyond-the-norm eating and lodging options by making St John's their base camp for explorations elsewhere on the Avalon Peninsula. Cape Spear, Witless Bay Ecological Reserve and Ferryland are among the easy day trips.

History

St John's excellent natural harbor, leading out to what were once seething seas of cod, prompted the first European settlement here in 1528. During the late 1600s and much of the 1700s, St John's was razed and taken over several times as the French, English and Dutch fought for it tooth and nail. Britain won the ultimate victory on Signal Hill in 1762.

The harbor steadfastly maintained its position as the world trade center for salted cod well into the 20th century. By mid-century, warehouses lined Water St, and the merchants who owned them made a fortune. Come the early 1960s, St John's had more millionaires per capita than any other city in North America.

Today the city's wharves still act as service stations to fishing vessels from around the world and the occasional cruise ship, though the cod industry suffered mightily after a 1992 fishing moratorium. The offshore oil industry now drives the economy.

◎ Sights

Most sights are downtown or within a few kilometers, though be prepared for some serious uphill walking.

Signal Hill National Historic Site HISTORIC SITE
(☑709-772-5367; www.pc.gc.ca/signalhill) The city's most famous landmark offers a glorious view, though there's much more to see. The tiny castle atop the hill is **Cabot Tower** (◎8:30am-5pm Apr-Nov) FREE, built in 1900 to honor both John Cabot's 1497 arrival Queen Victoria's Diamond Jubilee. In midsummer, soldiers dressed as the 19th-century Royal Newfoundland Company perform a **tattoo** (www.rnchs.ca/tattoo; admission $5; ◎11am & 3pm Wed-Thu, Sat & Sun Jul & Aug) and fire cannons.

An **interpretive center** (adult/child $3.90/1.90; ◎10am-6pm May-Oct) features displays on the site's history. The last North American battle of the Seven Years' War took place here in 1762, and Britain's victory ended France's renewed aspirations for control of eastern North America. The tattoo takes place next to the center at O'Flaherty Field.

You can see cannons and the remains of the late-18th-century British battery at **Queen's Battery & Barracks** further up the hill. Inside Cabot Tower, educational displays relay how Italian inventor Guglielmo Marconi received the first wireless transatlantic message from Cornwall, England at the site in 1901. An amateur radio society operates a station in the tower in July and August.

Signal Hill also offers guided tours around the grounds, Thursday lunches where you eat like an 18th-century soldier (complete with rum pairings) and sunset concerts. Check the website's 'Activities' section for details and costs.

An awesome way to return to downtown is along the **North Head Trail** (1.7km) which connects Cabot Tower with the harborfront Battery neighborhood. The walk departs from the tower's parking lot and traces the cliffs, imparting tremendous sea views and sometimes whale spouts. The trailhead isn't marked; look for it right before you enter the lot. It's the path leading furthest to the right. Because much of the trail runs along the bluff's sheer edge, this walk is not something to attempt in icy, foggy or dark conditions. Free maps are available at Cabot Tower.

The site sits 1.5km from downtown, up Signal Hill Rd.

Rooms MUSEUM
(☑709-757-8000; www.therooms.ca; 9 Bonaventure Ave; adult/child $7.50/4, 6-9pm Wed free; ◎10am-5pm Mon, Tue & Thu-Sat, to 9pm Wed, noon-5pm Sun; ☎) Not many museums offer the chance to see a giant squid, hear avantgarde sound sculptures and peruse ancient weaponry all under one roof. But that's the Rooms, the province's all-in-one historical museum, art gallery and archives. Frankly, the building is much more impressive to look at than look in, since its frequently changing exhibits are sparse.

The views from this massive stone-and-glass complex, which lords over the city from a breath-sapping hilltop, are eye-poppers; try the 4th-floor cafe for the best vistas.

Johnson Geo Centre MUSEUM
(☑709-737-7880; www.geocentre.ca; 175 Signal Hill Rd; adult/child $12/6; ◎9:30am-5pm) Nowhere in the world can geo-history, going back to the birth of the earth, be accessed so easily as in Newfoundland, and the Geo Centre does a grand job of making snoreworthy geological information perk up with appeal via its underground, interactive displays.

The center also has a *Titanic* exhibit about how human error and omission, not just an iceberg, caused the tragedy. For instance, the ship's owners didn't supply her with enough lifeboats so as not to 'clutter the deck,' and the crew ignored myriad ice warnings. What any of this has to do with geology remains unclear, but who cares? It's fascinating.

Trails with interpretive panels wind around outside. The Geo Centre is up Signal Hill Rd, about 1km beyond downtown.

NEWFOUNDLAND & LABRADOR ST JOHN'S

NEWFOUNDLAND FAST FACTS

➡ Population: 484,700

➡ Area: 111,390 sq km

➡ Capital: St John's

➡ Quirky fact: Newfoundland has 82 places called Long Pond, 42 called White Point and one called Jerry's Nose

St John's

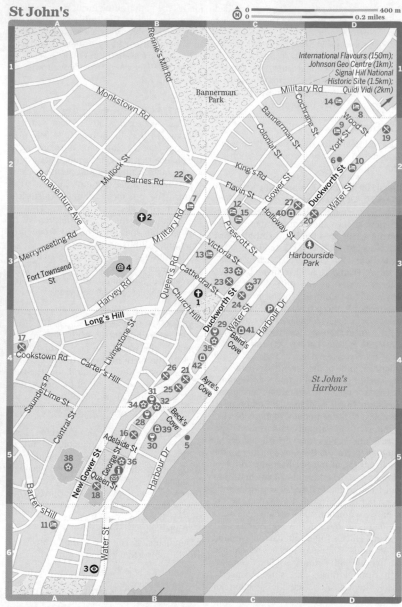

International Flavours (150m);
Johnson Geo Centre (1km);
Signal Hill National
Historic Site (1.5km);
Quidi Vidi (2km)

St John's
Harbour

Basilica of St John the Baptist   CHURCH
(☎709-754-2170; www.thebasilica.ca; 200 Military Rd; ☺9:30am-5pm) Built in 1855, the soaring twin spires of the basilica pierce the sky and are visible all the way from Signal Hill. Its design marks the revival of classical architecture in North America. Inside, 65 stained-glass windows illuminate the remarkable polychromatic Italianate ceiling and its gold-leaf highlights.

The honor of being named a 'basilica' was bestowed on the church by Pope Pius XII on

St John's

its centennial anniversary. Free half-hour tours are offered from 10am Monday to Saturday in July and August, according to demand. The convent behind the church holds the 'Veiled Virgin,' a one-of-a-kind marble statue that spiritual types come to view. Ring the buzzer for entry. to the convent.

Anglican Cathedral of St John the Baptist   CHURCH
(☎709-726-5677; www.stjohnsanglicancathedral.org; 16 Church Hill; ⊙9:30am-4pm) Serving Canada's oldest parish (1699), this is one of the finest examples of ecclesiastical Gothic architecture in North America. Although originally built in the 1830s, all but its exterior walls were reduced to ashes by the Great Fire of 1892. It was rebuilt in 1905. The Gothic ribbed ceiling, graceful stone arches and long, thin, stained-glass windows are timeless marvels.

A 12th-century gargoyle (a gift from the Diocese of Bristol) stands guard over the south transept. Students offer tours (in July and August), organists play concerts (1:15pm Wednesdays year-round) and church ladies serve tea and crumpets.

Quidi Vidi   HISTORIC SITE
Over Signal Hill, away from town, is the tiny picturesque village of Quidi Vidi. Check out the 18th-century battery and the lakeside regatta museum, but make your first stop **Quidi Vidi Brewery** (☎709-738-4040; www.quidividibrewery.ca; 35 Barrows Rd; tours $15; ⊙10am-4pm), which cooks up Newfoundland's most popular microbrews. Located in an old fish-processing plant on the small wharf, it's a scenic place to slake one's thirst.

The fee includes tastings and a bottle to sip while touring. Be sure to try the Iceberg brand, made with water from the big hunks.

Nearby you'll find North America's oldest cottage, the 1750s-era **Mallard Cottage** (www.mallardcottage.ca; 2 Barrows Rd). At press time it was being converted into a restaurant serving Newfoundland comfort foods.

The 1762 **Quidi Vidi Battery**, atop the hill end of Cuckhold's Cove Rd, was built by the French after they took St John's. The British quickly claimed it, and it remained in military service into the 1800s.

Inland from the village, **Quidi Vidi Lake** is the site of the city-stopping St John's

NEWFOUNDLAND & LABRADOR ST JOHN'S

TEA TOMB

All around the Anglican Cathedral of St John the Baptist you'll see signs for 'tea in the crypt.' Sound spooky? It is a bit when you first arrive at the church's basement, what with all the women in flowery dresses and sensible shoes flurrying to and fro. But give it a chance, and **high tea** ($9; 2:30-4pm Mon-Fri Jul & Aug) here becomes more than home-baked cookies and mini-scones. It's a chance to chat with the older generation about jam recipes, tips for summer holidays and the way things used to be (actually, you'll be listening and eating, and they'll do all the talking). The crypt, by the way, has never been used for burials.

Regatta. The **Royal St John's Regatta Museum** (709-576-8921; cnr Lakeview Ave & Clancy Dr, off Forest Rd; by appointment) **FREE** is on the 2nd floor of the boathouse. A popular walking trail leads around the lake.

Quidi Vidi is about 2km from the northeast edge of downtown. Take Plymouth Rd, go left on Quidi Vidi Rd, then right on Forest Rd (which becomes Quidi Vidi Village Rd). For the brewery, bear right onto Barrows Rd. For the battery, veer off on Cuckold's Cove Rd. For the regatta museum, take a left off Forest Rd onto Lakeview Ave. You can also walk from Signal Hill via the Cuckold's Cove Trail, which takes about 30 minutes.

Newman Wine Vaults HISTORIC SITE
(709-739-7870; www.seethesites.ca; 436 Water St; admission by donation; by appointment) Dating from the 1780s, these dark, cool wine vaults are where the Newman company aged its port until 1996 (when EU regulations forced the process back to Portugal). Guides used to give tours, but at press time they were on hold. The vaults often host music, literary and foodie events.

CA Pippy Park PARK
(www.pippypark.com) The feature-filled, 1343-hectare CA Pippy Park coats downtown's northwestern edge. Recreational facilities include walking trails, picnic areas, playgrounds, a golf course and a campground. **Memorial University**, the province's only university, is here too. The university's **botanical garden** (709-737-8590; www.mun.ca/botgarden; adult/child $7/3; 10am-5pm May-Aug, reduced hours Sep-Apr) is at Oxen Pond, at the park's western edge off Mt Scio Rd.

Cultivated areas and a nature reserve fill the botanical landscape. Together, these and the park's **Long Pond** marsh give visitors an excellent introduction to Newfoundland's flora, habitats (including boreal forest and bogs) and animals (look for birds at Long Pond and the occasional moose). Take the 3km **Long Pond Walk** for the full effect.

The **Fluvarium** (709-754-3474; www.fluvarium.ca; 5 Nagle's Pl; adult/child/family $7/4/20; 9am-5pm Mon-Fri, from 10am Sat & Sun Jul & Aug, reduced hours Sep-Jun), a glass-sided cross-section of a 'living' river, is located across the street from the campground. Viewers can peer through large windows to observe the undisturbed goings-on beneath the surface of Nagle's Hill Brook. Numerous brown trout and the occasional eel can be seen. If there has been substantial rain or high winds, all visible life is completely lost in the murkiness.

To get here from downtown, take Bonaventure Ave north to Allandale Rd and follow the signs; it's about 2km.

🏃 Activities

Golf and cross-country skiing enthusiasts can partake in CA Pippy Park.

Excellent walking trails zigzag across the area. The **Grand Concourse** (www.grandconcourse.ca) is an ambitious 160km-long trail network throughout St John's and environs. Many hikes are in the CA Pippy Park and Quidi Vidi Lake areas. Definitely make time for the sea-hugging North Head Trail on Signal Hill. The concourse website has route details for all walks.

The epic **East Coast Trail** (www.eastcoasttrail.ca) stretches 265km from Cape St Francis south to Cappahayden; a further 275km is to be developed. It's part easy coastal walking, part tough wilderness trail. The website has details on free weekly guided hikes; you can also volunteer to do trail cleanup. An excellent stretch runs along the coast from Cape Spear.

☞ Tours

Boat

For most tours, you need to head south of town to Witless Bay.

Iceberg Quest BOAT TOUR
(709-722-1888; www.icebergquest.ca; Pier 6; 2hr tour adult/child $60/28) Departs from St John's harbor and makes a run down to Cape Spear in search of icebergs in June, whales in July and August.

O'Brien's　　　　　　　　　BOAT TOUR
(☎709-753-4850, 877-639-4253; www.obriens-boattours.com; 126 Duckworth St; 2hr tour adult/child $55/25) See whales, puffins and icebergs at Witless Bay. Boats launch from Bay Bulls 31km south, but O'Brien's has a shuttle service (round-trip $25) that picks up from hotels throughout St John's. Buy tickets at O'Brien's shop.

Outfitters　　　　　　　　　KAYAKING
(☎709-579-4453, 800-966-9658; www.theoutfit-ters.nf.ca; 220 Water St; half-/full-day tour $69/169) Popular kayak tours at Bay Bulls, with shuttle service (round-trip $25) from Outfitters' store downtown.

Bus

Jellybean Tours　　　　　　　BUS TOUR
(☎709-754-4789; www.jellybean-tours.com; 8 Gower St) This group, based out of the HI St John's hostel, arranges city tours ($49, four hours) and Cape Spear/Witless Bay tours ($99, six hours) daily, if enough people sign up for it.

Legend Tours　　　　　　　　BUS TOUR
(☎709-753-1497; www.legendtours.ca; 3hr tour $49-59) This award-winning operator covers St John's, Cape Spear and the northeast Avalon Peninsula. The commentary is richly woven with humor and historical tidbits. Call to reserve; they'll pick you up at your hotel or B&B.

Walking

The visitors center has brochures for self-guided walking tours in town. Also check the East Coast Trail website (www.eastcoast-trail.ca) for free guided hikes in the area.

★**St John's Haunted Hike**　　　WALKING TOUR
(www.hauntedhike.com; tours $10; ◷9:30pm Sun-Thu Jun-Sep) The black-caped Reverend Thomas Wyckham Jarvis Esq leads these super-popular explorations of the city's dark corners. He'll spook you with tales of headless captains, murderers and other ghosts. Departure is from the Anglican Cathedral's

west entrance. On midsummer Fridays and Saturdays, the spine-tingling action moves to Signal Hill for a seated, indoor show of ghost stories (8pm, tickets $15).

✸ Festivals & Events

Festival 500　　　　　　　　MUSIC
(www.festival500.com; ◷early Jul) Choirs and beatboxers from around the globe let their voices soar in cool venues citywide. It takes place every other year; upcoming fests are in 2015 and 2017.

Sound Symposium　　　PERFORMING ARTS
(www.soundsymposium.com; ◷early Jul) Held every other year, it's a big, avant-garde week of concerts, workshops, dance, theater and film experiments; next symposiums are in 2014 and 2016.

George Street Festival　　　　MUSIC
(www.georgestreetlive.ca; ◷late Jul/early Aug) The mighty George St becomes one big nightclub for a fabulous week of daytime and nighttime musical performances.

Royal St John's Regatta　　　SPORTS
(www.stjohnsregatta.org; ◷1st Wed Aug) The streets are empty, the stores are closed and everyone migrates to the shores of Quidi Vidi Lake. This rowing regatta officially began in 1825 and is now the oldest continuously held sporting event in North America.

Newfoundland & Labrador Folk Festival　　　　　　　　　　MUSIC
(www.nlfolk.com; ◷early Aug) This three-day event celebrates traditional Newfoundland music, dancing and storytelling. It's held the weekend after the regatta.

Downtown Busker Festival　　CARNIVAL
(www.downtownstjohns.com; ◷early Aug) Jugglers, magicians, acrobats, comedians and more take their performances to the streets for a long weekend.

NEWFOUNDLAND & LABRADOR ST JOHN'S

ST JOHN'S FOR CHILDREN

St John's will keep the wee ones entertained, rain or shine. CA Pippy Park is a kids' haven, with a huge playground, lots of trails and, of course, the Fluvarium. The ever-hungry ducks at the pond in **Bowring Park** (www.bowringpark.com; Waterford Bridge Rd) love company, as do the sea creatures at the Ocean Sciences Centre (p183).

Just knowing a cannon will blast at the end of the tattoo should keep kids riveted at Signal Hill (p172). The various boat tours are also a great bet, but inquire if there are icebergs and whales in the area first. While geology may not initially spark their interest, the fact that the Johnson Geo Centre (p173) is underground may do the trick. Older kids will enjoy the ghostly tales of the St John's Haunted Hike..

🛏 Sleeping

Scores of B&Bs offer a place to rest your head in the heart of St John's; they're usually better value than the hotels and motels. They fill fast, so book ahead. Many have a two-night minimum stay requirement. The ones listed here all serve a hot breakfast. The city's 17% tax is not included in prices listed here. Parking is available at or near all accommodations.

HI St John's   HOSTEL $
(☎709-754-4789; www.hihostels.ca; 8 Gower St; dm $28-33, r $75-89; ☻@☎) It's everything a good hostel should be: well located near the action, spic 'n' span facilities, not too big (16 beds in all), and helpful. A whiteboard lists everything of interest happening in town each day. The hostel also books reasonably priced tours.

Chef's Inn   B&B $$
(☎709-753-3180, 877-753-3180; www.thechefs-inn.ca; 29 Gower St; r $140-170; ☻✳☎) TV chef Todd Perrin owns this snug B&B, and his parents run it. The four rooms are done up in modern, minimalist decor, and each has an en suite bathroom. As you might expect, breakfast is a hearty feed with house-cured bacon and herbs from the garden.

Balmoral House   B&B $$
(☎877-428-1055, 709-754-5721; www.balmoral-house.com; 38 Queen's Rd; r $129-209; ☻✳@) While the Balmoral is a typical B&B in many ways (cherub statues, long wooden antique tables), its owners live off-site and breakfast is self-serve, so it's more relaxed and private than many B&Bs. The beds are bestowed with super-comfy mattresses.

Abba Inn   B&B $$
(☎800-563-3959, 709-754-0058; www.abbainn.com; 36 Queen's Rd; r $139-189; ☻✳@☎) The Abba shares the same building as the Balmoral, and it even shares reservations (ie if one is full, it'll hook you up with the other). Both B&Bs have similar amenities and ambience. If Abba is full, the owner also has nearby Gower House, which is comparable.

Gower House   B&B $$
(☎709-754-0058; www.newfoundland-hotels.com; 180 Gower St; r $129-139; ✳☎) Gower House is more like a boarding house than frilly B&B. Rooms are small, but with restful bedding, a flatscreen TV and amenity-laden en suite bathroom. A university student lives on-site and manages operations (he also cooks the egg-filled breakfast). Gower has the same owner as Abba Inn, but with an even better location.

Narrows B&B   B&B $$
(☎866-739-4850, 709-739-4850; www.thenarrowsbb.com; 146 Gower St; r $130-175; ☻☎) Warm colors mix with elegant trims and large wooden beds in the rooms of this welcoming B&B. There are modern amenities throughout and a gorgeous sitting room and balcony where guests can mingle and swap whale stories.

At Wit's Inn   B&B $$
(☎877-739-7420, 709-739-7420; www.atwitsinn.ca; 3 Gower St; r $129-149; ☻✳@☎) Polished floorboards, plasterwork ceilings, ornate fireplaces, bright-colored walls and beds you'll have trouble leaving make this B&B memorable. The living and dining rooms are as swank as they are comfy.

Foggy Rock B&B   B&B $$
(☎709-697-0077; www.foggyrock.ca; 50 Prescott St; r from $99; ☻☎) Foggy Rock ranks between a B&B and hostel. The four rooms share a couple of bathrooms, and breakfast is do-it-yourself continental. It's not the best value for money in town, but when everything is else is booked up, you'll be glad it's there.

Courtyard St John's   HOTEL $$
(☎709-722-6636; www.marriott.com/yytcy; 131 Duckworth St; r $159-199; ✳@☎) It's the Marriott chain's typical property, with comfy beds. Some rooms have harbor views (about $10 extra).

Leaside Manor   B&B $$
(☎877-807-7245, 709-722-0387; www.leaside-manor.com; 39 Topsail Rd; r $139-249; ☻✳@☎) The higher-end rooms in this old merchant's home have a canopied bed, fireplace and Jacuzzi, which explains why the *Globe and Mail* designated Leaside as one of Canada's 'most romantic destinations.' It's about a half-hour walk from downtown; if you want to be closer, inquire about the downtown apartments.

Delta Hotel   HOTEL $$$
(☎709-739-6404; www.deltahotels.com; 120 New Gower St; r $189-269; ✳@☎⊠) The Delta is the main, amenity-laden business hotel in town; it's located next to the convention center. Parking costs $12.

✗ Eating

Japanese, Indian, Latin and even vegetarian restaurants pop up along Water and Duckworth Sts, providing a variety of food you won't find elsewhere in the province. You'll need reservations several days in advance for high-end and foodie hot spots.

Rocket Bakery   BAKERY $

(www.rocketfood.ca; 272 Water St; mains $5-9; ⊘7:30am-10pm Mon-Sat, 8am-6pm Sun; 🐀) Cheery Rocket is the perfect spot for a cuppa joe, groovy sandwich or sweet treat. Try the hummus on multigrain bread, or maybe a croissant with lemon curd. The fish cakes also win raves. Order at the counter, then take your goodies to the tables in the bright-hued adjoining room.

International Flavours   PAKISTANI $

(☑709-738-4636; 4 Quidi Vidi Rd; mains $8-12; ⊘noon-7pm Tue-Sat; 🖋) Pakistani owner Talat ladles out a whopping spicy plateful of dahl or curry with basmati rice for her daily set meal (one with meat, the other without). She's just beyond downtown, a few minutes' walk up Signal Hill Rd.

Ches's   FAST FOOD $

(☑709-726-2373; www.chessfishandchips.ca; 9 Freshwater Rd; mains $8-15; ⊘11am-2am Sun-Thu, to 3am Fri & Sat) Ches's and its fish and chips are an institution in Newfoundland. No frills, just cod that will melt in your mouth.

Hava Java   CAFE $

(258 Water St; baked goods $3-7; ⊘7:30am-6pm Sun-Wed, to 9pm Thu-Sat; 🐀) The atmosphere at this place is refreshingly antifranchise and pro-tattoo; it just focuses on making the best coffee in town.

Fixed Coffee & Baking   CAFE $

(www.fixedcoffee.com; 183 Duckworth St; baked goods $3-8; ⊘7am-6pm Mon-Fri, from 9am Sat & Sun; 🐀) Fixed pours the city's best hot chocolate and mighty fine coffee and chai, plus it's cheaper than elsewhere. House-made bagels and breads add to the divine aroma.

Sun Sushi   JAPANESE $

(☑709-726-8688; 186 Duckworth St; sushi rolls $4.50-7.50; ⊘noon-10pm Mon-Sat) This un-adorned spot tops the townsfolks' list for reasonably priced sushi. The spicy tuna wins raves.

Hungry Heart   CAFE $$

(☑709-738-6164; www.hungryheartcafe.ca; 142 Military Rd; mains $7-15; ⊘10am-2pm Mon-Sat)

Eat in this warm-toned cafe and you're helping abused women and others in need to train in food service and get back on their feet. Try the curry mango chicken or pulled-pork sandwiches. Saturday brunch brings out the cheese scones with peameal bacon and cherry bread pudding. Lots of baked goodies, too.

Sprout   VEGETARIAN $$

(☑709-579-5485; www.thesproutrestaurant.com; 364 Duckworth St; mains $10-15; ⊘11:30am-9pm Mon-Fri, from 10am Sat; 🖋) It's almost unheard of in Newfoundland: full-on vegetarian food. So savor your marinated tofu burger, walnut-pesto-melt sandwich and brown rice poutine (fries served under miso gravy) before leaving town.

Classic Cafe   CAFE $$

(☑709-726-4444; 73 Duckworth St; mains $14-22; ⊘8am-2:30pm Sun-Tue, to 9pm Wed-Sat) Yes, many tourists eat here, but it's still a swell place to soak up harbor views and fork into Newfie standards like toutons, fish 'n' brewis, seafood chowder and fish-cakes, plus omelettes and sandwiches.

India Gate   INDIAN $$

(☑709-753-6006; www.indiagatenl.com; 286 Duckworth St; mains $12-17; ⊘11:30am-2pm Mon-Fri, 5-10pm daily; 🖋) This is the local Indian favorite, with loads of vegetarian options. Fill up at the weekday all-you-can-eat lunch special for $15.

★Chinched   MODERN CANADIAN $$$

(☑709-722-3100; www.chinchedbistro.com; 7 Queen St; mains $30-35; ⊘6-9:30pm Tue-Sat) 🖋 Chinched is St John's first real foodie res-taurant, the kind that offers mega-quality dishes but without the white-tablecloth pretense. So belly up in the warm, dark-wood room for octopus tacos or Newfoundland wild mushroom risotto. The meaty menu changes regularly. The young chefs' creativity extends to the singular desserts (say, wild nettle ice cream) and spirits (partridgeberry vodka) made in-house.

If you don't want to commit to a full meal, the bar menu lets you sample dishes for $6 to $7.

★Reluctant Chef   MODERN CANADIAN $$$

(☑709-754-6011; www.facebook.com/TheReluc-tantChefRestaurant; 281 Duckworth St; set menu $60; ⊘noon-3:30pm Wed-Fri, 5pm-midnight Mon-Sat) 🖋 Perhaps it should be renamed the 'passionate chef,' given the lovingly pre-

SCRUNCHEONS, TOUTONS & FLIPPER PIE: A GASTRONOMIC GUIDE

Get ready for a whole new culinary vocabulary when you enter Newfoundland. Lesson number one: having a 'scoff' is local parlance for eating a big meal.

Two of Newfoundland's favorite dishes are fish 'n' brewis and Jiggs dinner. Fish 'n' brewis is a blend of salted fish, onions, scruncheons (aka fried pork fat) and a near-boiled bread. Jiggs dinner is a right feast comprising a roast (turkey or possibly moose) along with boiled potatoes, carrots, cabbage, salted beef and pea-and-bread pudding. A touton is fried dough that you dip in gooey molasses.

Cod tongues are the tender, fleshy bits between the lower jaws served battered and fried, while cod cheeks are just that: cheeks from the fish. Fishcakes are a blend of cod, potato and onion mashed together and fried – delicious. Seal flipper pie, on the other hand, is for the brave; the strong flavor of seal meat is definitely an acquired taste.

To finish off your meal, try figgy duff, a thick fig pudding boiled in a cloth bag.

pared, eight-course (give or take) menu that hits the toasty tables here. The dishes always vary; check the Facebook page to see what's cooking. Then plan on a three-hour flavorgasm with 30 other chowhounds under a sparkly chandelier.

Bacalao MODERN CANADIAN $$$
(☎709-579-6565; www.bacalaocuisine.ca; 65 Lemarchant Rd; mains $26-36; ☺noon-2:30pm Tue-Fri, from 11am Sat & Sun, 6-10pm Tue-Sun) 🍴 Cozy Bacalao sources local, sustainable ingredients for its 'nouvelle Newfoundland cuisine.' Dishes include salt cod *du jour* and caribou in partridgeberry sauce, washed down by local beer and wines. Located 1.5km west of downtown; take Water St south to Waldegrave St, then Barters Hill Rd.

Bistro Sofia CAFE $$$
(☎709-738-2060; www.bistrosofia.net; 320 Water St; mains $26-36; ☺9am-11pm; 🛜) Bistro Sofia cooks up high-quality food and serves it casually in a bright, classy coffee shop ambience. Order at the counter, plop down at a roomy table, and wait for your lunch (grilled sandwiches plumped to perfection) or dinner (braised lamb shank or salmon and squash risotto) while sipping coffee or wine.

🍷 Drinking & Nightlife

George St is the city's famous party lane. Water and Duckworth Sts also have plenty of drinkeries, but the scene is slightly more sedate. Bars stay open until 2am (3am on weekends). Expect many places to charge a small cover (about $5) on weekends or when there's live music. Don't forget to try the local Screech rum.

★**Duke of Duckworth** PUB
(www.dukeofduckworth.com; McMurdo's Lane, 325 Duckworth St; ☺noon-late; 🛜) 'The Duke,' as it's known, is an unpretentious English-style pub that represents all that's great about Newfoundland and Newfoundlanders. Stop in on a Friday night and you'll see a mix of blue-collar, white-collar, young and old, perhaps even band members from Great Big Sea plunked down on the well-worn, red-velour bar stools.

The kitchen cooks the ultimate in chicken pot pie, fish and chips and other comfort foods, and 14 beers (including the local Quidi Vidi) flow through the taps. The popular *Republic of Doyle* CBC TV series films here, which explains all the people taking photos of the sign by the door.

Trapper John's Museum & Pub PUB
(www.trapperjohns.com; 2 George St; ☺noon-2am Mon-Wed, to 3am Thu-Sun) It's not the most refined pub in town, but it sure is the most fun place to become an Honorary Newfoundlander, which happens after you kiss Stubby the Puffin (a variation on the usual codfish). The animal traps enshrined throughout grant the 'museum' status.

Gypsy Tea Room BAR
(www.gypsytearoom.ca; 315 Water St; ☺from 11:30am) It holds a well-regarded Mediterranean restaurant and chic lounge, but the courtyard is where you want to be, sipping wine, cocktails and other refreshing beverages under the stars.

Celtic Hearth PUB
(www.theceltichearth.com; 298 Water St; ☺24hr) Get your Guinness and pub grub 24/7.

Velvet CLUB
(twitter.com/Velvetniteclub; 208 Water St; ☺11pm-3am Fri & Sat) This is the premier gay dance bar in Newfoundland. Straights are equally welcome to soak up the fun energy. Located above Rose & Thistle; the entrance is via Mc-Murdo's Lane.

☆ Entertainment

The Scope (www.thescope.ca) has the daily lowdown. Perhaps because this is such an intimate city, word-of-mouth and flyers slapped on light poles are also major vehicles for entertainment information. Venues are close together – have a wander and enjoy.

Live Music

Cover charges range from $5 to $10. **Mighty Pop** (www.mightypop.ca) lists cool upcoming shows.

Ship Pub LIVE MUSIC
(☎709-753-3870; 265 Duckworth St; ☺noon-late) Attitudes and ages are checked at the door of this little pub, tucked down Solomon's Lane. You'll hear everything from jazz to indie, and even the odd poetry reading. Wednesday is folk music night.

Shamrock City LIVE MUSIC
(www.shamrockcity.ca; 340 Water St; ☺noon-late) Bands, most playing Irish and Newfoundland-style music, take the stage nightly at this all-ages pub.

Rose & Thistle LIVE MUSIC
(☎709-579-6662; 208 Water St; ☺9am-late) Pub where well-known local folk musicians strum.

Fat Cat BLUES
(www.fatcatbluesbar.com; George St; ☺8pm-late Tue-Sun) Blues radiates from the cozy Fat Cat nightly during the summer months.

Rock House LIVE MUSIC
(☎709-579-6832; 8 George St) When indie bands visit town, they plug in here.

Theater

Resource Centre for the Arts PERFORMING ARTS
(☎709-753-4531; www.rca.nf.ca; 3 Victoria St) Sponsors indie theater, dance and film by Newfoundland artists, all of which plays downtown in the former longshoremen's union hall (aka LSPU Hall).

Shakespeare by the Sea Festival THEATER
(www.shakespearebytheseafestival.com; tickets $20; ☺early Jul–mid-Aug) Live outdoor productions are presented at Signal Hill, local parks and other venues. Buy all tickets on-site; cash only. Some performances are free.

Sports

St John's IceCaps HOCKEY
(www.stjohnsicecaps.com; 50 New Gower St; ☺Oct-May) The popular IceCaps, part of the American Hockey League, slap the puck at Mile One Centre.

🔒 Shopping

You'll find traditional music, berry jams and local art in the nooks and crannies of Water and Duckworth Sts.

Fred's MUSIC
(☎709-753-9191; www.fredsrecords.com; 198 Duckworth St; ☺9:30am-9pm Mon-Fri, to 6pm Sat, noon-5pm Sun) The town's premier music shop features local music such as Hey Rosetta, Buddy Wasisname, Ron Hynes, The Navigators and Great Big Sea.

Living Planet SOUVENIRS
(☎709-739-6810; www.livingplanet.ca; 181 Water St; ☺10am-5pm Mon-Sat, noon-5pm Sun) For quirky

NEWFOUNDLAND & LABRADOR ST JOHN'S

GETTING SCREECHED IN

Within a few days of your arrival in St John's, you'll undoubtedly be asked by everyone if you've been 'screeched in,' or in traditional Newfoundland slang, 'Is you a screecher?' It's not as painful as it sounds, and is, in fact, locals' playful way to welcome visitors to the province.

Screeching derives from the 1940s when new arrivals were given their rites of passage, and from pranks played on sealers heading to the ice for the first time. Today the ceremony takes place in local pubs, where you'll gulp a shot of rum (there's actually a local brand called Screech), recite an unpronounceable verse in the local lingo, kiss a stuffed codfish and then receive a certificate declaring you an 'Honorary Newfoundlander.' Sure it's touristy, but it's also good fun. The more the merrier, so try to get screeched in with a crowd.

tourist T-shirts and buttons even locals are proud to wear.

Downhome
SOUVENIRS

(☎709-722-2070; 303 Water St; ⊗10am-5:30pm Mon-Sat, noon-5pm Sun) It's touristy, but it does have a fine selection of local goods such as jams, woolen wear, moose cookbooks and the coveted *How to Play the Musical Spoons* CD.

Outfitters
OUTDOOR EQUIPMENT

(☎709-579-4453; www.theoutfitters.nf.ca; 220 Water St; ⊗10am-6pm Mon-Wed & Sat, to 9pm Thu & Fri, noon-5pm Sun) A camping and gear shop where you can get the local outdoorsy lowdown (check the bulletin board).

ⓘ Information

INTERNET ACCESS

Almost all coffee shops and bars have free wi-fi, including Fixed, Hava Java and Duke of Duckworth.

MEDIA & INTERNET RESOURCES

City of St John's (www.stjohns.ca) The 'Visiting Our City' category has descriptions of attractions, accommodations, eateries and events.

Downhome (www.downhomelife.com) A folksy, *Reader's Digest*–style monthly for the region.

Scope (www.thescope.ca) Free alternative newspaper covering local arts and politics.

St John's Telegram (www.thetelegram.com) The city's daily newspaper.

MEDICAL SERVICES

Health Sciences Complex (☎709-777-6300; 300 Prince Phillip Dr) A 24-hour emergency room.

Water St Pharmacy (☎709-579-5554; 335 Water St; ⊗Mon-Sat)

MONEY

Banks stack up near the Water St and Ayre's Cove intersection.

CIBC (215 Water St)

Scotia Bank (245 Water St)

POST

Central Post Office (☎709-758-1003; 354 Water St)

TOURIST INFORMATION

Visitors Centre (☎709-576-8106; www.stjohns.ca; 348 Water St; ⊗9am-4:30pm) Excellent resource with free provincial and city roadmaps, and staff to answer questions and help with bookings.

ⓘ Getting There & Away

AIR

Air Canada (www.aircanada.com), **WestJet** (www.westjet.com), **Provincial Airlines** (www.

provincialairlines.ca) and **Porter Airlines** (www.flyporter.com) are the main carriers. United Airlines schedules the only direct flight from the US. Air Canada offers a daily direct flight to and from London.

BUS

DRL (☎709-263-2171; www.drl-lr.com) sends one bus daily each way between St John's and Port aux Basques ($123, cash only, 13½ hours) via the 905km-long Hwy 1, making 25 stops en route. It leaves at 7:30am from Memorial University's Student Centre, in CA Pippy Park.

CAR & MOTORCYCLE

Avis, Budget, Enterprise, Hertz, National and Thrifty have offices at the airport. **Practicar** (☎709-753-2277; www.practicar.ca; 909 Topsail Rd) is a 20-minute drive from the airport but often has lower rates.

SHARE TAXI

These large vans typically seat 15 and allow you to jump on or off at any point along their routes. You must call in advance to reserve. They pick up and drop off at your hotel. Cash only.

Foote's Taxi (☎800-866-1181, 709-832-0491) Travels daily down the Burin Peninsula as far as Fortune ($45, 4½ hours).

Newhook's Transportation (☎709-682-4877, in Placentia 709-227-2552) Travels down the southwestern Avalon Peninsula to Placentia, in sync with the Argentia ferry schedule ($30, two hours).

Shirran's Taxi (☎709-468-7741) Plies the Bonavista Peninsula daily, making stops at Trinity ($50, 3½ hours) and Bonavista ($40, four hours), among others.

ⓘ Getting Around

TO/FROM THE AIRPORT

St John's International Airport is 6km north of the city on Portugal Cove Rd (Rte 40). A government-set flat rate of $25 (plus $3 for each extra passenger) is charged by taxis to go from the airport to downtown hotels and B&Bs; **Citywide Taxi** (☎709-722-7777) provides the official service. However, when you make the trip in reverse – ie from town to the airport – taxis run on meters and should cost a few bucks less.

CAR & MOTORCYCLE

The city's one-way streets and unique intersections can be confounding. Thankfully, citizens are incredibly patient. The parking meters that line Water and Duckworth Sts cost $1.25 per hour. **Sonco Parking Garage** (cnr Baird's Cove & Harbour Dr; ⊗6:30am-11pm) charges $1.50 for 30 minutes or $11 per day.

ⓘ THE RENTAL CAR CRUNCH

Be warned: rental car fleets are small (thanks to the island's remoteness and short tourist season), which means loads of visitors vie for limited vehicles in midsummer. Costs can rack up to $100 per day (including taxes and mileage fees). Reserve well in advance – April or May is recommended if you're traveling during the mid-July to early August peak – and confirm the booking before you arrive.

PUBLIC TRANSPORTATION

The **Metrobus** (www.metrobus.com) system covers most of the city (fare $2.25). Maps and schedules are online and in the visitors center. Bus 3 is useful; it circles town via Military Rd and Water St before heading to the university. The new 'trolley line' (it's actually a bus) loops around the main tourist sights, including Signal Hill. It costs $5/20 per person/family per day.

TAXI

Except for the trip from the airport, all taxis operate on meters. A trip within town should cost around $8. **Jiffy Cabs** (☑709-722-2222; www.jiffycabs.com) provides dependable service.

AROUND ST JOHN'S

North of St John's

Right out of *20,000 Leagues Under the Sea*, the **Ocean Sciences Centre** (☑709-737-3708; www.mun.ca/osc; ☺10am-5pm Jun-Aug) **FREE** is operated by Memorial University and examines the salmon life cycle, seal navigation, ocean currents and life in cold oceanic regions. The outdoor visitors area consists of local sealife in touch tanks. It's about 8km north of St John's, just before Logy Bay. From the city, take Logy Bay Rd (Rte 30), then follow Marine Dr to Marine Lab Rd and take it to the end.

Secluded and rocky, **Middle Cove** and **Outer Cove** are just a bit further north on Rte 30 – they're perfect for a beach picnic.

North at the head of **Torbay Bight** is the enjoyably short **Father Troy Path**, which hugs the shoreline. The view from **Cape St Francis** is worth the bumpy gravel road from Pouch Cove. There's an old battery and you may just be lucky and see a whale or two.

West of St John's

West of town on Topsail Rd (Rte 60), just past Paradise, is **Topsail Beach** with picnic tables, a walking trail and panoramic views of Conception Bay and its islands.

Bell Island (www.tourismbellisland.com) is the largest of Conception Bay's little landmasses, and it makes an interesting day trip. It's a 14km drive northwest from St John's to Portugal Cove to the ferry (☑709-895-6931) and then a 20-minute crossing (per passenger/car $2.50/7, hourly 6am to 10:30pm). Bell Island has the distinction of being the only place on the continent to have been nailed by German forces in WWII. Its pier and 80,000 tonnes of iron ore were torpedoed by U-boats in 1942. At low tide, you can still see the aftermath. The island sports a pleasant mélange of beaches, coastal vistas, lighthouses and trails. Miners here used to work in shafts under the sea at the world's largest submarine iron mine. The **Iron Ore Mine & Museum** (☑709-488-2880; adult/child $12/5; ☺11am-6pm Jun-Sep) details the operation and gives visitors the chance to go underground; dress warmly.

South of St John's

Cape Spear

A 15km drive southeast of town leads you to the most easterly point in North America. The coastal scenery is spectacular, and you can spot whales through much of the summer. The area is preserved as the **Cape Spear National Historic Site** (☑709-772-5367; www.pc.gc.ca/capespear; Blackhead Rd; adult/child $3.90/1.90; ☺grounds year-round) and includes an **interpretive center** (☺10am-6pm May-Oct), the refurbished 1835 **lighthouse** (☺10am-6pm Jun-Aug, reduced hours May, Sep & Oct) and the heavy gun batteries and magazines built in 1941 to protect the harbor during WWII. A **trail** leads along the edge of the headland cliffs, past 'the most easterly point' observation deck and up to the lighthouse. You can continue all the way to Maddox Cove and Petty Harbour along the East Coast Trail; even walking it a short way is tremendously worthwhile.

Heed all signs warning visitors off the rocks by the water, as rogue waves have been known to sweep in.

You reach the cape from Water St by crossing the Waterford River south of town and then following Blackhead Rd for 11km.

Goulds & Petty Harbour

In Goulds, at the junction of Rte 10 and the road to Petty Harbour, is **Bidgood's** (www.bidgoods.ca; Bidgood's Plaza; ⊗ 9am-7pm Mon-Sat, 10am-5pm Sun). It's just a normal-looking supermarket, except for the fresh seal flipper (in pies, jars or jerky-like strips) and caribou steak purveyed at the back of the store. For the faint of heart, partridgeberry and bakeapple jams are the other Newfoundland specialties on hand.

Its back lapping up against steep rocky slopes, movie-set-beautiful Petty Harbour is filled with weathered boats, wharves and sheds on precarious stilts. **North Atlantic Ziplines** (www.zipthenorthatlantic.com; 2½hr trips adult/child $115/90) is quite scenic. Depending on when you go, you might see whales or moose. There are five trips per day.

AVALON PENINSULA

The landscape along the coastline's twisting roads is vintage fishing-village Newfoundland. Many visitors make day trips to the peninsula's sights from St John's, which is easily doable, but there's something to be said for burrowing under the quilt at night, with the sea sparkling outside your window, in Cupids or Branch. Four of the province's six seabird ecological reserves are in the region, as are 28 of its 41 national historic sites.

Much of the **East Coast Trail** (www.eastcoasttrail.ca) runs through the area; keep an eye out for free guided hikes. The ferry to Nova Scotia leaves from Argentia.

Southeastern Avalon Peninsula

This area, sometimes called the South Shore, is known for its wildlife, archaeology, boat and kayak tours and unrelenting fog. Scenic Rtes 10 and 90, aka the **Irish Loop** (www.theirishloop.com), lasso the region.

Witless Bay Ecological Reserve

This is a prime area for whale-, iceberg- and bird-watching, and several boat tours will take you to see them from the towns of **Bay Bulls** (31km south of St John's) and around **Bauline East** (15km south of Bay Bulls).

Four islands off Witless Bay and southward are preserved as the **Witless Bay Ecological Reserve** (www.env.gov.nl.ca/parks) and represent one of the top seabird breeding areas in eastern North America. Every summer, more than a million pairs of birds gather here, including puffins, kittiwakes, storm petrels and the penguinlike murres. Tour boats sail to the islands, hugging the shore beneath sheer cliffs and giving you a shrieking earful as well as an eyeful.

The best months for trips are late June and July, when the humpback and minke whales arrive to join the birds' capelin (a type of fish) feeding frenzy. If you really hit the jackpot, in early summer an iceberg might be thrown in too.

☞ Tours

Tours from Bay Bulls (ie the big operators O'Brien's and Gatherall's) visit Gull Island, which has the highest concentration of birds. Tours that depart to the south around Bauline East head to nearby Great Island, home to the largest puffin colony. Bauline East is closer to the reserve, so less time is spent en route, but you see the same types of wildlife on all the tours.

Kayaking is also popular in the area. You don't just see a whale while paddling, you feel its presence.

You can't miss the boat operators – just look for signs off Rte 10. Sometimes the smaller companies cancel tours if there aren't enough passengers; it's best to call ahead to reserve and avoid such surprises. The following are recommended tour companies, all operating from mid-May through mid-September. Most depart several times daily between 9:30am and 5pm.

Colbert's Tours   BOAT TOUR
(☏709-334-2098; Rte 10, Bauline East; 1hr tour adult/5-15yr $30/15) It's a 10-minute ride on a 40ft boat to see the puffins and whales.

Gatherall's   BOAT TOUR
(☏800-419-4253; www.gatheralls.com; Northside Rd, Bay Bulls; 1½hr tour adult/child $56/16) A large, fast catamaran gives you as much time at the reserve as O'Brien's. It's also a good choice for people prone to seasickness.

Molly Bawn Tours BOAT TOUR
(📞 709-334-2621; www.mollybawn.com; Rte 10, Mobile; 1hr tour adult/child $40/35) These tours cruise over the waves on a small, 35ft boat. Mobile is halfway between Bay Bulls and Bauline East.

O'Brien's BOAT TOUR
(📞 709-753-4850, 877-639-4253; www.obriens-boattours.com; 2hr tour adult/child $55/25) O'Brien's, on the south side of Bay Bulls, is the granddaddy of tours and includes story-telling, music and more on its nice, big boat. A more expensive but exhilarating option is the two-hour tour in a high-speed Zo-diac ($85). There's a shuttle service from St John's (round-trip $25).

Outfitters KAYAKING
(📞 709-579-4453, 800-966-9658; www.theoutfit-ters.nf.ca; Bay Bulls; half-/full-day tour $69/169) Popular half-day kayak tours leave at 9am and 2pm; full-day tours depart at 9:30am and travel beyond the inner bay of Bay Bulls to the top of the eco reserve. There is a shut-tle service (round-trip $25) from St John's that leaves from Outfitters at 220 Water St.

Stan Cook Sea Kayak
Adventures KAYAKING
(📞 709-579-6353, 888-747-6353; www.wildnfld. ca; Harbour Rd, Cape Broyle; 2½hr tour from $59) Located further south near Ferryland, this company offers great guided tours for begin-ners and advanced paddlers.

La Manche Provincial Park

Diverse bird life, along with beaver, moose and snowshoe hare, can be seen in this lush park only 53km south of St John's. A high-light is the 1.25km trail to the remains of La Manche, a fishing village that was destroyed in 1966 by a fierce winter storm. Upon ar-rival, you'll see the beautiful newly built suspension bridge dangling over the nar-rows – it's part of the East Coast Trail. The trailhead is situated at the park's fire-exit road, past the main entrance.

There is excellent **camping** (📞 709-685-1823; www.nlcamping.ca; Rte 10; campsites $15-23, per vehicle $5; ☺ May-Sep), with many sites overlooking large La Manche Pond; the lat-ter is good for swimming.

Ferryland

Ferryland, one of North America's earliest settlements, dates to 1621, when Sir George

Calvert established the Colony of Avalon. A few Newfoundland winters later he was scurrying for warmer parts. He settled in Maryland and eventually became the first Lord Baltimore. Other English families ar-rived later and maintained the colony de-spite it being razed by the Dutch in 1673 and by the French in 1696.

The seaside surrounds of the **Colony of Avalon Archaeological Site** (📞 709-432-3200; www.colonyofavalon.ca; Rte 10; adult/child $9.50/7.50; ☺ 10am-6pm Jun-Sep) only add to the rich atmosphere, where you'll see ar-chaeologists unearthing everything from axes to bowls. The **visitors center** (📞 709-432-3207) houses interpretive displays and many of the artifacts that have been recovered.

The village's former courthouse is now the small **Historic Ferryland Museum** (📞 709-432-2711; Rte 10; admission $2; ☺ 10am-4pm Mon-Sat, 1-4pm Sun Jul & Aug). The tow-ering hill behind the museum was where settlers climbed to watch for approach-ing warships, or to escape the Dutch and French incursions. After seeing the view, you'll understand why the settlers named the hill 'the Gaze.'

★**Lighthouse Picnics** (📞 709-363-7456; www.lighthousepicnics.ca; Lighthouse Rd, off Rte 10; per person $25; ☺ 11:30am-4:30pm Wed-Sun Jun-Sep; 🐾) 🍴 has hit upon a winning con-cept: it provides a blanket and organic pic-nic meal (say, a curried chicken sandwich, mixed-green salad and lemonade from a Mason jar) that visitors wolf down while sitting in a field overlooking the ocean. It's at Ferryland's old lighthouse; you have to park and hike 2km to reach it, but ooh is it worth it. Reserve in advance.

Avalon Wilderness Reserve

Dominating the interior of the region is the 1070-sq-km **Avalon Wilderness Reserve** (📞 709-635-4520; www.env.gov.nl.ca/parks; free permit required). Illegal hunting dropped the region's caribou population to around 100 in the 1980s. Thirty years later, a couple of thousand now roam the area. Permits for hiking, canoeing and birdwatching in the reserve are available at La Manche Provin-cial Park.

Even if you don't trek into the wilds, you still might see caribou along Rte 10 between Chance Cove Provincial Park and St Stevens.

Mistaken Point Ecological Reserve

This **ecological reserve** (www.env.gov.nl.ca/parks), which Unesco has short-listed for World Heritage site designation, protects 575-million-year-old multicelled marine fossils – the oldest in the world. The only way to reach it is via a free, ranger-guided, 45-minute hike from the **Edge of Avalon Interpretive Centre** (☑709-438-1100; www.edgeofavalon.ca; Rte 10; ⊗May-Oct) in Portugal Cove South.

You can also drive the bumpy gravel road between here and Cape Race. At the end, a lighthouse rises up beside an artifact-filled, replica 1904 Marconi wireless station. It was the folks here who received the fateful last message from the *Titanic*.

The 'Mistaken Point' name, by the way, comes from the blinding fog that blankets the area and has caused many ships to lose their way over the years.

Along Route 90

The area from St Vincent's to St Mary's provides an excellent chance of seeing whales, particularly humpbacks, which feed close to shore. The best viewing is from **St Vincent's beach.** Halfway between the two villages is **Point La Haye Natural Scenic Attraction,** a dramatic arm of fine pebbles stretching across the mouth of St Mary's Bay – it's perfect for a walk.

Salmonier Nature Park (☑709-229-7189; www.env.gov.nl.ca/snp; Rte 90; ⊗10am-5pm Jun-Aug, to 3pm Sep & Oct) **FREE** rehabilitates injured and orphaned animals for release back into the wild. A 2.5km trail through pine woods takes you past indigenous fauna and natural enclosures with moose, caribou and cavorting river otters. There's an **interpretive center** and touch displays for children. The park is on Rte 90, 12km south of the junction with Hwy 1.

Conception Bay

Fishing villages stretch endlessly along Conception Bay's scenic western shore, a mere 80km from St John's. Highlights include Brigus, in all its Englishy, rock-walled glory combined with North Pole history, and Cupids, a 1610 settlement complete with an archaeological dig to explore.

Brigus

Resting on the water and surrounded by rock bluffs is the heavenly village of **Brigus** (www.brigus.net). Its idyllic stone-walled streams meander slowly past old buildings and colorful gardens before emptying into the serene Harbour Pond. During WWI, American painter Rockwell Kent lived here, before his eccentric behavior got him deported on suspicion of spying for the Germans in 1915. The path toward his old cottage makes a great walk.

Captain Robert Bartlett, the town's most famous son, is renowned as one of the foremost Arctic explorers of the 20th century. He made more than 20 Arctic expeditions, including one in 1909, when he cleared a trail in the ice that enabled US commander Robert Peary to make his celebrated dash to the North Pole. Bartlett's house, **Hawthorne Cottage** (☑709-528-4004; www.pc.gc.ca/hawthornecottage; cnr Irishtown Rd & South St; adult/child $5/4; ⊗10am-6pm daily Jul & Aug, Wed-Sun Jun), is a national historic site and museum.

On the waterfront, below the church, is the **Brigus Tunnel,** which was cut through rock in 1860 so Robert Bartlett could easily access his ship in the deep cove on the other side.

Every perfect village needs a perfect eatery. At **North St Cafe** (☑709-528-1350; 29 North St; light meals $6-9; ⊗11am-6pm May-Oct), quiche, fishcakes, scones and afternoon tea are all on order. Brigus has a couple of B&Bs, but we suggest sleeping down the road in Cupids.

Cupids

Merchant John Guy sailed here in 1610 and staked out England's first colony in Canada. It's now the **Cupids Cove Plantation Provincial Historic Site** (☑709-528-3500; www.seethesites.ca; Seaforest Dr; adult/child $6/3; ⊗9:30am-5pm May-Oct). An active archaeological dig is ongoing, and you can take a tour of it. A stone's throw down the road is the **Cupids Legacy Centre** (www.cupidslegacycentre.ca; Seaforest Dr; adult/child $8.50/4.25; ⊗9:30am-5pm Jun-Oct), stuffed with silver coins, bottle shards and some of the other 150,000 artifacts unearthed on-site so far.

Afterward, head to the town's northern edge and hike the **Burnt Head Trail.** Climb to the rocky headlands, past blueberry thickets and stone walls that once fenced settlers' gardens, and look out over the same sea-buffeted coast that drew Guy.

The trail departs from an old Anglican church that has been converted into the divine **Cupid's Haven B&B and Tea Room** (☑709-528-1555; www.cupidshaven.ca; 169 Burnt Head Loop; r $99-149; ☺☎). Each of the four rooms has a private bathroom, vaulted ceilings and Gothic arched windows that let light stream in.

Harbour Grace & Around

A mixed crowd of historic figures has paraded through Harbour Grace over the past 500 years. Notables include the pirate Peter Easton and aviator Amelia Earhart. Learn about them at the redbrick customs house that is now the small **Conception Bay Museum** (☑709-596-5465; www.hrgrace.ca/museum.html; Water St; adult/child $3/2; ☺10am-6pm Jun-Aug). You can visit the airstrip Amelia launched from in 1932 – **Harbour Grace Airfield** (www.hrgrace.ca/air.html; Earhart Rd) – when she became the first woman to cross the Atlantic solo.

It's hard to miss the large ship beached at the mouth of the harbor. This is the **SS Kyle** (1913), wrecked during a 1967 storm. Locals liked the look of it so much they paid to have it restored instead of removed.

Clinging to cliffs at the northern end of the peninsula are the remote and striking villages of **Bay de Verde** and **Grates Cove**. Hundreds of 500-year-old rock walls line the hills around Grates Cove and have been declared a national historic site. Further offshore, in the distance, is the inaccessible **Baccalieu Island Ecological Reserve**, which is host to three million pairs of Leach's storm petrel, making it the largest such colony in the world.

Trinity Bay

Thicker forests, fewer villages and subdued topography typify the shores of Trinity Bay and give the west coast of the peninsula a much more serene feeling than its eastern shore.

Heart's Content

The **Cable Station Provincial Historic Site** (☑709-583-2160; www.seethesites.ca; Rte 80; adult/child $6/3; ☺9:30am-5:30pm May-Oct) tells the story of the first permanent transatlantic cable that was laid here in 1866. The word 'permanent' is significant, because the first successful cable (connected in 1858 to Bull Arm, on Trinity Bay) failed shortly after Queen Victoria and US President James Buchanan christened the line with their congratulatory messages.

Dildo

Oh, go on – take the obligatory sign photo. For the record, no one knows definitively how the name came about; some say it's from the phallic shape of the bay.

Joking aside, Dildo is a lovely village and its shore is a good spot for whale-watching. The **Dildo Interpretation Centre** (☑709-582-3339; Front Rd; adult/child $2/1; ☺10am-4:30pm Jun-Sep) has a whale skeleton and exhibits on the ongoing Dorset Eskimo archaeological dig on Dildo Island. It's not terribly exciting, but outside are excellent photo opportunities with Captain Dildo and a giant squid. Across the street, **Kountry Kravins 'n' Krafts** (☑709-582-3888; ☺9am-8pm Mon-Sat, 10am-6pm Sun Jun-Sep) sells fruit pies and knickknacks (including many 'Dildo' logoed items – always a fine souvenir for folks back home).

Cape Shore

The ferry, French history and lots of birds fly forth from the Avalon Peninsula's southwesterly leg. Newhook's Transportation (p182) connects the towns of Argentia and Placentia to St John's.

Argentia

Argentia's main purpose is to play host to the **Marine Atlantic ferry** (☑800-341-7981; www.marine-atlantic.ca; adult/child $112/54, per car/motorcycle $225/113), which connects Argentia with North Sydney in Nova Scotia – a 14-hour trip. It operates from mid-June to late September with three crossings per week. The boat leaves North Sydney at 5pm Monday, Wednesday and Friday. It returns from Argentia at 5pm Tuesday, Thursday and Saturday. Cabins (four-berth $172) are available. Vehicle fares do not include drivers.

A provincial **visitors center** (☑709-227-5272; Rte 100) is 3km from the ferry on Rte 100. Its opening hours vary to coincide with ferry sailings.

Placentia

In the early 1800s, **Placentia** (www.placentia-tourism.ca) – then Plaisance – was the French capital of Newfoundland, and the French attacks on the British at St John's were based here. Near town, lording over the shores, is **Castle Hill National Historic Site** (☑709-227-2401; www.pc.gc.ca/castlehill; adult/child $3.90/1.90; ☺10am-6pm Jun-Aug), where remains of French and British fortifications from the 17th and 18th centuries provide panoramic views over the town and the surrounding waters.

The fascinating **graveyard** next to the Anglican church holds the remains of people of every nationality who have settled here since the 1670s. The **O'Reilly House Museum** (☑709-227-5568; 48 Orcan Dr; admission $2; ☺11:30am-7:30pm Jun-Aug), within a century-old Victorian home, gives you more of an inside look at the town and its past luxuries. Wander past the other notable buildings, including the **Roman Catholic church** and the **stone convent**. A boardwalk runs along the stone-skipper's delight of a beach.

Philip's Cafe (170 Jerseyside Hill; mains $3-7; ☺7:30am-3:30pm Tue-Sat; 🖘) is a must pre- or post-ferry ride for yummy baked goods and creative sandwiches such as apple and sharp cheddar on molasses-raisin bread. The chef also owns the five-room **Rosedale Manor B&B** (☑877-999-3613; www.rosedalemanor.ca; 40 Orcan Dr; r $99-129; 🖛🖘). It's a 10-minute drive from the Argentia ferry.

Cape St Mary's Ecological Reserve & Around

At the southwestern tip of the peninsula is **Cape St Mary's Ecological Reserve** (www.env.gov.nl.ca/parks) FREE, one of the most accessible bird colonies on the continent. Birders swoon over it, and it's impressive even for those who aren't bird crazy. Stop at the **Interpretive Centre** (☑709-277-1666; ☺9am-5pm May-Oct) and get directions for the 1km trail to Bird Rock. It's an easy footpath through fields of sheep and blue irises, and then suddenly you're at the cliff's edge facing a massive, near-vertical rock swarmed by squawking birds. There are 70,000 of them, including gannets, kittiwakes, murres and razorbills. The reserve is isolated, so you'll have to travel for lodging.

The **Cliffhouse** (☑709-338-2055; www.thecliffhouse.ca; Rte 100; r $100), in the wee town of Branch 22km away, is strongly recommended. Set high on a hill, you can see the ocean and spouting whales from everywhere: the front yard's Adirondack chairs, the porch, the front picture window and all three guest rooms. It's owned by a local family – Chris is a naturalist at the reserve, wife Priscilla is the town mayor and mum Rita cooks breakfast.

Near the reserve turnoff is **Gannet's Nest Restaurant** (☑709-337-2175; Rte 100; mains $8-15; ☺8am-8pm), frying some of the province's crispiest fish and chips and baking a mean rhubarb pie.

EASTERN NEWFOUNDLAND

Two peninsulas seem to grasp awkwardly out at the sea and comprise the sliver that is Eastern Newfoundland. The beloved, well-touristed Bonavista Peninsula projects northward. Historic fishing villages freckle its shores, and windblown walking trails swipe its coast. **Clarenville** (www.clarenville.net) is the Bonavista Peninsula's access point and service center, though there's not much for sightseers.

To the south juts the massive but less-traveled Burin Peninsula, another region of fishing villages. These towns are struggling to find their way in the post-cod world. The ferry for France – yes, France, complete with wine, éclairs and Brie – departs from Fortune and heads to the nearby French islands of St-Pierre and Miquelon, a regional highlight.

Trinity

POP 250

Let's set the record straight: Trinity is the Bonavista Peninsula's most popular stop, a historic town of crooked seaside lanes, storybook heritage houses and gardens with white picket fences. Trinity Bight is the name given to the 12 communities in the vicinity, including Trinity, Port Rexton and New Bonaventure.

While Trinity is movie-set lovely, some visitors have complained that its perfection is a bit boring. But if you like historic buildings and theater along with your scenery – and you're keen for a whale-watch tour – this is definitely your place. It's a tiny town and easily walkable.

First visited by Portuguese explorer Miguel Corte-Real in 1500 and established as a town in 1580, Trinity is one of the oldest settlements on the continent.

◉ Sights & Activities

Trinity Historic Sites
HISTORIC SITE

(☑709-464-3599; adult/child $15/free; ⊙ 9:30am-5pm Jun-Sep) One admission ticket lets you gorge on seven buildings scattered throughout the village.

The **Trinity Historical Society** (www.trinityhistoricalsociety.com) runs four of the sites. The **Lester Garland House** (West St) was rebuilt to celebrate cultural links between Trinity and Dorset, England – major trading partners in the 17th, 18th and 19th centuries. The **Cooperage** (West St) brings on a real live barrel-maker; the **Green Family Forge** (West St) is an iron-tool-filled blacksmith museum and the **Trinity Museum** (Church Rd) displays more than 2000 pieces, including North America's second-oldest fire wagon.

The provincial government operates the other trio of **sites** (www.seethesites.ca), which include costumed interpreters. The **Lester Garland Premises** (West St) depicts an 1820s general store; the **Interpretation Centre** (West St) provides a comprehensive history of Trinity; and **Hiscock House** (Church Rd) is a restored merchant's home from 1910.

Fort Point
HISTORIC SITE

Further afield is Fort Point (aka Admiral's Point), where you'll find a pretty lighthouse and four cannons, the remains of the British fortification from 1745. There are 10 more British cannons in the water, all compliments of the French in 1762. An interpretive center and trail tells the tale. It's accessible from Dunfield, a few kilometers south on Rte 239.

Skerwink Trail
HIKING

The Skerwink Trail (5km) is a fabulous (though muddy) loop that reveals picture-perfect coastal vistas. The trailhead is near the church in Trinity East, off Rte 230.

☞ Tours

Rugged Beauty Tours
BOAT TOUR

(☑709-464-3856; www.ruggedbeautyboat-tours.net; 3hr tour $70; ⊙10am & 2pm May-Oct) Unique trips with Captain Bruce, who takes you to abandoned outports and makes their history come alive. You might even see an eagle along the way.

Sea of Whales
BOAT TOUR

(☑709-464-2200; www.seaofwhales.com; 1 Ash's Lane; 3hr tour adult/child $80/50) Zodiac boats head out in search of whales three times per day.

Trinity Historical Walking Tours
WALKING TOUR

(☑709-464-3723; www.trinityhistoricalwalking-tours.com; Clinch's Lane; adult/child $10/free; ⊙10am Mon-Sat Jul & Aug) These entertaining and educational tours start behind Hiscock House.

⊨ Sleeping & Eating

There are numerous fine inns and B&Bs. Space gets tight in summer, so book ahead. Several snack shops and grocery stores have popped up and are good places to pick up a sandwich or cheese plate that you can take to the picnic tables near the Lester Garland Premises.

★Skerwink Hostel
HOSTEL $

(☑709-557-2015; www.skerwinkhostel.com; dm $25-29, r $55-59; ⊙May-Oct; 🛜) The homey Skerwink, with two six-bed dorms and two private rooms, is part of Hostelling International. All ages of travelers stay here, and a community vibe pervades as lots of locals drop by to chat and play guitar with the staff. Fresh bread and coffee are included for breakfast, and there are bicycles you can use for free.

The hostel also arranges kayak tours (per person $50 for two hours). It's off Rte 230, about 500m from the Skerwink Trail.

★Artisan Inn & Campbell House B&B
B&B $$

(☑709-464-3377, 877-464-7700; www.trinity-vacations.com; High St; r incl breakfast $125-179; ⊙May-Oct; ⊜🛜) Adjacent to each other and managed by the same group, these places are gorgeous. The three-room inn hovers over the sea on stilts; the flower-surrounded, three-room B&B also provides ocean vistas. The inn's Twine Loft restaurant serves a three-course, prix-fixe meal ($39) of local specialties; check the menu posted out front, which changes daily.

Eriksen Premises
B&B $$

(☑877-464-3698, 709-464-3698; www.trinity-experience.com; West St; r incl breakfast $105-170; ⊙May-Oct; ⊜🛜) This Victorian home offers elegance in accommodations and dining (mains $20 to $30, open lunch and dinner). It also books two nearby B&Bs: Kelly's

Landing (four rooms) and Bishop White Manor (nine rooms).

Trinity Mercantile
CAFE $

(www.trinitymercantile.ca; 24 West St; mains $6-15; ⊙8am-9pm; 🐾) It's a great spot for a cup of coffee, baked goods, sandwiches, chowder, salt cod or cold beer.

☆ Entertainment

Rocky's Place Lounge
LIVE MUSIC

(📳709-464-3400; High St; ⊙from 7pm) Rocky's hosts bands from time to time, but even if the mics are quiet it's a friendly place to hoist a brew.

Rising Tide Theatre
THEATER

(📳709-464-3232; www.risingtidetheatre.com; Water St; tickets $27; ⊙Jun-Sep) Alongside the Lester Garland Premises is the celebrated Rising Tide Theatre, which hosts the 'Seasons in the Bight' theater festival and the **Trinity Pageant** (adult/child $19/free; ⊙2pm Wed & Sat), an entertaining outdoor drama on Trinity's history.

❶ Information

RBC Royal Bank (West St; ⊙10:30am-2pm Mon-Thu, to 5pm Fri) No ATM.

Town of Trinity (www.townoftrinity.com) Tourism info.

❶ Getting There & Around

Trinity is 259km from St John's and is reached via Rte 230 off Hwy 1. **Shirran's Taxi** (📳709-468-7741) makes the trip daily from St John's ($50).

Bonavista

POP 3700

'O buona vista!' (Oh, happy sight!), shouted John Cabot upon spying the New World from his boat on June 24, 1497. Or so the story goes. From all descriptions, this pretty spot is where he first set foot in the Americas. Today Bonavista's shoreline, with its lighthouse, puffins and chasms, continues to rouse visitors.

◉ Sights

Cape Bonavista Lighthouse
LIGHTHOUSE

(📳709-468-7444; www.seethesites.ca; Rte 230; adult/child $6/3; ⊙9:30am-5pm May-Oct) Cape Bonavista Lighthouse is a brilliant red-and-white-striped lighthouse dating from 1843. The interior has been restored to the 1870s and is now a provincial historic site. A **puffin colony** lives just offshore; the birds put on quite a show around sunset.

Dungeon Park
PARK

(Cape Shore Rd, off Rte 230) Nowhere is the power of water more evident than at the Dungeon, a deep chasm 90m in circumference that was created by the collapse of two sea caves, through which thunderous waves now slam the coast.

Ryan Premises National Historic Site
HISTORIC SITE

(📳709-468-1600; www.pc.gc.ca/ryanpremises; Ryans Hill Rd; adult/child $3.90/1.90; ⊙10am-6pm Jun-Sep) Ryan Premises National Historic Site is a restored 19th-century saltfish mercantile complex. The slew of white clapboard buildings honors five centuries of fishing in Newfoundland via multimedia displays and interpretive programs.

Ye Matthew Legacy
HISTORIC SITE

(📳709-468-1493; www.matthewlegacy.com; Roper St; adult/child $7.25/3; ⊙9:30am-4:45pm Jun-Sep) The site has an impressive full-scale replica of the ship on which Cabot sailed into Bonavista.

🛏 Sleeping & Eating

HI Bonavista
HOSTEL $

(📳877-468-7741, 709-468-7741; www.hihostels.ca; 40 Cabot Dr; dm $26-30, r $75-120; @🐾) This tidy white-clapboard hostel offers four private rooms, two shared dorm rooms, free bike use and kitchen and laundry facilities. It's a short walk from the center.

Harbourview B&B
B&B $

(📳709-468-2572; 21 Ryans Hill Rd; r incl breakfast $70; ⊙May-Sep; 🐾) The name doesn't lie: you get a sweet view at this simple, four-room B&B, plus an evening snack (crab legs) with owners Florence and Albert.

White's B&B
B&B $

(📳709-468-7018; www.bbcanada.com/3821.htm; 21 Windlass Dr; r incl breakfast $75-85; 🐾@🐾) Low-key White's has three rooms to choose from, all with either private bathroom or en suite. Enjoy the bike rentals, barbecue use and ocean view.

Neil's Yard
CAFE $

(www.neilsyard.org; 27-29 Church St; mains $5-10; ⊙10am-8pm May-Oct; 🐾) A tea lounge serving buckwheat crepes? Neil's Yard is not your usual Newfoundland cafe. The gregarious

ELLISTON: ROOT CELLARS & PUFFINS

The Root Cellar Capital of the World, aka Elliston, lies 6km south of Bonavista on Rte 238. The teeny town was struggling until it hit upon the idea to market its 135 subterranean veggie storage vaults, and then presto – visitors came a knockin'. Actually, what's most impressive is the **puffin colony** just offshore and swarming with thousands of chubby-cheeked, orange-billed birds from mid-May to mid-August. A quick and easy path over the cliffside brings you quite close to them and also provides whale and iceberg views.

Stop at the **visitors center** (☑709-468-7117; www.townofelliston.ca; Main St) as you enter town, and the kindly folks will give you directions to the site along with a map of the cellars (which you're welcome to peek inside).

Work up an appetite while you're here, because **Nanny's Root Cellar Kitchen** (☑709-468-7998; ☺8am-10pm) in historic Orange Hall cooks a mighty fine lobster, Jiggs dinner and other traditional foods, plus she's licensed.

The **Roots, Rants and Roars Festival** (www.rootsrantsandroars.ca) brings crowds in late September. The province's top chefs serve dishes alfresco along a 5km shoreline hiking route.

From the adjoining hamlet of **Maberly** a gorgeous 17km **coastal hiking trail** winds over the landscape to Little Catalina.

English owner will set you up with a steaming mug of exotic tea, while his wife cooks up the crepes, carrot ginger soup, cheesecake with local berries and other healthy fare. Service can be slow, but there's plenty to look at in the attached craft shop.

Walkham's Gate   CAFE **$**
(☑709-468-7004;   www.walkhamsgatepub.ca; mains $5-9; ☺24hr; 🖥) One side is a coffee shop with whopping pies and hearty soups, the other side a congenial pub tended by music-lover Harvey. Located in the town center, near the courthouse.

★**Bonavista Social Club** MODERN CANADIAN **$$**
(☑709-445-5556;   www.bonavistasocialclub.com; Upper Amherst Cove; mains $12-23; ☺11am-8pm Tue-Sun) 🖉 Incredible breads and pizzas emanate from the wood-fired brick oven. Other highlights include the famed rhubarb lemonade and moose burger with partridgeberry ketchup. The young couple who own the restaurant grow many of their ingredients in the surrounding gardens. The goats roaming the grounds provide milk for cheese, while the chickens lay the eggs. Reserve ahead.

The rustic restaurant, complete with ocean-view terrace, is about 15 minutes from Bonavista via Rte 235 (turn left when you see the sign for Upper Amherst Cove). The chef's dad carved all the beautiful wood decor in his workshop next door.

☆ Entertainment

Garrick Theatre   THEATER
(www.garricktheatre.ca; 18 Church St) The artfully restored Garrick shows mainstream and indie films and hosts live music performances.

ℹ Information

Bonavista Community Health Centre (☑709-468-7881; Hospital Rd)
Scotiabank (☑709-468-1070; 1 Church St)
Town of Bonavista (www.townofbonavista.com) Tourism info.

ℹ Getting There & Around

Bonavista is a scenic 50km drive north of Trinity along Rte 230. **Shirran's** (☑709-468-7741) drives up daily from St John's ($40).

Burin Peninsula

It's not exactly lively on the Burin Peninsula, as the besieged fishing economy is felt. Still, the coastal walks inspire, and the region is a low-key place to spend a day or two before embarking toward the baguettes of France (aka St-Pierre).

Marystown is the peninsula's largest town; it's jammed with big-box retailers but not much else. **Burin** is the area's most attractive town, with a gorgeous elevated boardwalk over the waters of its rocky shoreline. **St Lawrence** is known for fluorite mining and scenic coastal hikes. In **Grand**

Bank, there's an interesting self-guided walk through the historic buildings and along the waterfront. Just south is fossil-rich **Fortune**, the jump-off point for St-Pierre.

◉ Sights & Activities

Provincial Seamen's Museum   MUSEUM
(☑709-832-1484; www.therooms.ca/museum; Marine Dr, Grand Bank; admission $2.50; ☺9:30am-4:45pm May-Oct) The impressive-looking Seamen's Museum depicts both the era of the banking schooner and the changes in the fishery over the years.

Burin Heritage Museums   MUSEUM
(☑709-891-2217; Seaview Dr, Burin; ☺9am-6pm Mon-Fri, 10:30am-6pm Sat & Sun Apr-Sep) **FREE** Displays in two historic homes tell of life's highs and lows in remote outports.

Fortune Head Ecological Reserve   PARK
(www.env.gov.nl.ca/parks; off Rte 220; ☺24hr) The reserve protects fossils dating from the planet's most important period of evolution, when life on earth progressed from simple organisms to complex animals some 550 million years ago. The reserve is about 3km west, by the Fortune Head Lighthouse. Kids will appreciate the **Interpretation Centre** (☑709-832-3569; adult/child $5/3; ☺9am-5pm Jun-Aug) with fossils to touch; it's in town by the St-Pierre ferry dock.

Hiking Trails   HIKING
Ask at the Burin Heritage Museum about locating the **Cook's Lookout** trailhead. It's a 20-minute walk from town to the panoramic view. Off Pollux Cres in St Lawrence, the rugged, breath-draining **Cape Trail** (4km) and **Chamber Cove Trail** (4km) shadow the cliff edges and offer amazing vistas to rocky shores and some famous WWII shipwrecks. Another good (and easier) trail is the **Marine Hike** (7km) that traces Admiral's Beach near Grand Bank. It leaves from Christian's Rd off Rte 220.

🛏 Sleeping & Eating

Options are spread thinly. For those heading to St-Pierre, Grand Bank and Fortune are the best bases. Grand Bank has better lodging but it's further, at 8km from the ferry dock. Fortune has a sweet bakery by its dock. For more choices check the **Heritage Run** (www.theheritagerun.com).

Thorndyke B&B   B&B $$
(☑877-882-0820, 709-832-0820; www.the-thorndyke.ca; 33 Water St, Grand Bank; r $95-120;

☺May-Oct; ☻) This handsome old captain's home overlooks the harbor. Antique wood furnishings fill the four light and airy rooms (each with private bathroom). The hosts will provide dinner with advance notice.

Fortune Harbourview B&B   B&B $$
(☑709-832-7666; www.fortuneharbourview.com; 74 Eldon St, Fortune; r $99; ☎) The five rooms aren't fancy, and they're perched on top of a beauty salon, but they're tidy and best of all, located near the ferry to St-Pierre. It's a serve-yourself, continental-style breakfast.

Sharon's Nook & the Tea Room   CAFE $
(☑709-832-0618; 12 Water St, Grand Bank; mains $7-10; ☺7:30am-9pm Mon-Sat, 11am-7:30pm Sun) This countrified eatery serves up lasagna, chili, sandwiches and heavenly cheesecake.

ℹ Getting There & Around
The Burin Peninsula is accessed via Rte 210 off Hwy 1. The drive from St John's to Grand Bank is 359km and takes just over four hours. **Foote's Taxi** (☑800-866-1181, 709-832-0491) travels from St John's down the peninsula as far as Fortune ($45, 4½ hours).

ST-PIERRE & MIQUELON
POP 6100

Twenty-five kilometers offshore from the Burin Peninsula floats a little piece of France. The islands of St-Pierre and Miquelon aren't just Frenchlike with their berets, baguettes and Bordeaux, they *are* France, governed and financed by the *tricolore*.

Locals kiss their hellos and pay in euros, while sweet smells waft from the myriad pastry shops. French cars – Peugeots, Renaults and Citroëns – crowd the tiny one-way streets. It's an eye-rubbing world away from Newfoundland's nearby fishing communities.

St-Pierre is the more populated and developed island, with most residents of its 5500 living in the town of St-Pierre. Miquelon is larger geographically but has only 600 residents overall.

The fog-mantled archipelago has a 20th-century history as colorful as its canary-yellow, lime and lavender houses. Going further back, Jacques Cartier claimed the islands for France in 1536, after they were discovered by the Portuguese in 1520. At the end of the Seven Years' War in 1763, the islands were turned over to Britain, only to

ST-PIERRE'S BOOZY BACKSTORY

When Prohibition dried out the USA's kegs in the 1920s, Al Capone decided to slake his thirst – and that of the nation – by setting up shop in St-Pierre.

He and his mates transformed the sleepy fishing harbor into a booming port crowded with imported-booze-filled warehouses. Bottles were removed from their crates, placed in smaller carrying sacks and taken secretly to the US coast by rumrunners. The piles of Cutty Sark whiskey crates were so high on the docks that clever locals used the wood both to build and heat houses. At least one house remains today and is known as the 'Cutty Sark cottage'; most bus tours drive by.

The visitors center offers a special **Prohibition tour** (per person $25) that covers sites related to the theme. If nothing else, drop by the Hotel Robert near the tourist information center and check out Al Capone's hat; it hangs in the gift shop.

be given back to France in 1816. And French they've remained ever since.

◉ Sights & Activities

In St-Pierre, the best thing to do is just walk around and soak it up – when you're not eating, that is. Pop into stores and sample goods you'd usually have to cross an ocean for. Or conduct research as to the best chocolate-croissant maker. A couple of **walking trails** leave from the edge of town near the power station.

Île aux Marins　　　HISTORIC SITE
(3hr tour €24; ⊙9am & 1:30pm May-Sep) The magical Île aux Marins is a beautiful abandoned village on an island out in the harbor. A bilingual guide will walk you through colorful homes, a small schoolhouse museum and the grand church (1874). Book tours at the visitors center. You can also go over on the boat (€3) *sans* guide, but be aware most signage is in French.

L'Arche Museum　　　MUSEUM
(☑508-410-435; www.arche-musee-et-archives. net; Rue du 11 Novembre; adult/child €4/2.50; ⊙10am-noon & 1:30-5pm Tue-Sun Jun-Sep) The well-done exhibits cover the islands' history, including Prohibition times. The showstopper is the **guillotine** – the only one to slice in North America. Islanders dropped the 'timbers of justice' just once, in 1889, on a murderer. The museum also offers bilingual **architectural walking tours** (€6.50 or €8.50).

Miquelon & Langlade　　　ISLANDS
The island of Miquelon, 45km away, is less visited and less developed than St-Pierre. The village of **Miquelon**, centered on the church, is at the northern tip of the island. From nearby l'**Étang de Mirande** a walking trail leads to a lookout and waterfall. From the bridge in town, a scenic 25km road leads across the isthmus to the wild and uninhabited island of Langlade. There are some wild horses, and around the rocky coast you'll see seals and birds.

Cemetery　　　CEMETERY
(Ave Commandant Roger Birot) The cemetery, with its above-ground mausoleums, provides an atmospheric wander.

Les Salines　　　NEIGHBORHOOD
(Rue Boursaint & the waterfront) Old-timers hang out around this scenic cluster of multi-hued fishing shacks.

Fronton　　　PELOTE
(Rue Maître Georges Lefèvre & Rue Gloanec) Watch locals play the Basque game of *pelote* (a type of handball) at the outdoor court here.

☞ Tours

Chez Janot　　　BOAT TOUR
(www.chezjanot.fr; adult/child €73/50; ⊙Jun-Sep) It offers full-day, bilingual tours by Zodiac covering both Miquelon and Langlade. Book at the visitors center.

★★ Festivals & Events

From mid-July to the end of August, folk dances are often held in St-Pierre's square.

Bastille Day　　　CULTURAL
(⊙Jul 14) The largest holiday of the year.

Basque Festival　　　CULTURAL
(⊙mid-Aug) A weeklong festival with music, marching and invigorating street fun.

🛏 Sleeping & Eating

There are about a dozen accommodations on St-Pierre; all include continental

NEWFOUNDLAND & LABRADOR ST-PIERRE & MIQUELON

breakfast. Book ahead in summer. Great eateries abound, not surprisingly; make reservations to ensure a table. Several bars and restaurants are on Rue Albert Briand.

Bernard Dodeman B&B   B&B $

(☏508-413-060; www.pensiondodeman.com; 15 Rue Paul Bert; r €55; ☺@☎) The Dodeman's three simple rooms share two bathrooms and a communal TV parlor. It's a 15-minute walk from the ferry, on a hill above town.

Auberge Quatre Temps B&B   B&B $

(☏508-414-301; www.quatretemps.com; s/d €70/78; @☎) Quatre Temps is a 15-minute schlep from the ferry dock, but don't let that deter you. All six rooms have their own bathroom. There's a fine terrace where you can buy drinks and sip alfresco. The owner also runs the Saveurs des Îles restaurant.

Nuits St-Pierre   B&B $$

(☏508-412-720; www.nuits-saint-pierre.com; 10 Rue du Général Leclerc; r €125-150; ☺☎) St-Pierre's most upscale lodging aims for the honeymoon crowd. The five rooms, each with private bathroom and downy, above-the-norm beds, are named after famous French authors. There's free pickup from the airport or ferry. The attached tea salon is open every afternoon from 2pm to 6pm and is a must for a restorative beverage and slice of cake.

★ Guillard Gourmandises   BAKERY $

(23 Rue Boursaint; pastries €1-3; ⊙7am-noon & 2-5:30pm Tue-Sat, to 4:30pm Sun) Holy mother! These cream-plumped chocolate éclairs, macarons and gateaux are the reason you came to France, right?

Saveurs des Îles   FRENCH $$$

(☏508-410-360; www.restaurant-saveursdesiles. com; 6 Rue Maître Georges Lefèvre; mains €16-20; ⊙11:30am-2pm & 6:30-10pm) The candlelit wood bar, gauzy curtains, crooners on the stereo and cocktail list lend a sexy vibe to this restaurant. Staff chalk the daily specials on the board, say, of fresh-plucked fish or snails with garlic cream. A fine wine selection, of course, washes it down.

L'Atelier Gourmand   FRENCH $$$

(☏508-415-300; www.lateliergourmandspm.com; 12 Rue du 11 Novembre; mains €15-26; ⊙noon-2pm & 6-10:30pm; ☎) Crowds of diners tuck into classic, delicious, French fare at this cozy restaurant with a streetfront patio. The heaping bowl of mussels, toasted goat cheese salad and white chocolate crème

brûlée are among the dishes that will haunt your dreams.

ℹ Information

Americans, EU citizens and all visitors except Canadians need a passport for entry. Those staying longer than 30 days also need a visa. Other nationalities should confirm with their French embassy if a visa is needed prior to arrival. Canadians can enter with a driver's license.

Business Hours Most shops and businesses close between noon and 1:30pm. Some stores also close on Saturday afternoons, and most are closed on Sunday.

Customs To merit the duty-free waiver on alcohol, you must stay on the islands at least 48 hours.

Language French, but many people also speak English.

Money Many merchants accept the loonie, though they return change in euros. If you're staying more than an afternoon, it's probably easiest to get euros from the local ATMs.

Telephone Calling the islands is an international call, meaning you must dial 011 in front of the local number. Phone service links in to the French system, so beware of roaming charges on your mobile.

Time Half an hour ahead of Newfoundland Time.

Tourist Information (www.st-pierre-et-mique-lon.com) The visitors center, near the ferry dock, provides a map showing all the banks, restaurants etc. Staff also provides information on the islands' hotels and tours and make bookings for free.

Voltage 220V; Canadian and American appliances need an electrical adapter.

ℹ Getting There & Away

AIR

Air St-Pierre (www.airsaintpierre.com) flies to St John's, Montréal and Halifax. There are two to three flights weekly to each city. Taxis to/from the airport cost around €5.

BOAT

From Fortune on Newfoundland, the **St-Pierre Ferry** (☏709-832-3455; www.saintpierreferry. ca; 14 Bayview St; adult/child return $93/58) makes the hour-long trip to and from the island once daily (twice on Wednesdays) in July and August. It runs less often the rest of the year. Departure times vary, so check the schedule. The boats carry foot passengers only. You can leave your car in the parking lot by the dock (per day $9).

ℹ️ Getting Around

Much can be seen on foot. Roads are steep, so prepare to huff and puff. The visitors center rents bicycles (per half/full day €10/15). Local ferries head to Miquelon and Langlade; check with the visitors center for schedules and costs.

CENTRAL NEWFOUNDLAND

Central Newfoundland elicits fewer wows per square kilometer than the rest of the province, but that's because huge chunks of the region are pure bog land and trees. The islands of Notre Dame Bay – particularly Twillingate, when icebergs glide by – are exceptional exceptions.

Terra Nova National Park

Backed by lakes, bogs and hilly woods, and fronted by the salty waters of Clode and Newman Sounds, **Terra Nova National Park** (📞709-533-2801; www.pc.gc.ca/terranova; adult/child/family per day $5.80/2.90/14.70) is spliced by Hwy 1 running through its interior. It's not nearly as dramatic as the province's other national parks, though it does offer moose, bear, beaver and bald eagles, as well as relaxed hiking, paddling, camping and boat tours.

Make your first stop the **visitors center** (📞709-533-2942; Hwy 1; ⊙10am-6pm Jul & Aug, to 4pm May, Jun & Sep), which has oodles of park information, ranger-guided programs and marine displays with touch tanks and underwater cameras. It's 1km off Hwy 1 at Salton's Day-Use Area, 80km east of Gander.

◉ Sights & Activities

Terra Nova's 14 hiking trails total almost 100km; pick up maps at the visitors center. Highly recommended is the **Malady Head Trail** (5km), which climaxes at the edge of a headland cliff offering stunning views of Southwest Arm and Broad Cove. **Sandy Pond Trail** (3km) is an easy loop around the pond – your best place to spot a beaver. The area is also a favorite for **swimming**, with a beach, change rooms and picnic tables. In winter, the park grooms trails here for cross-country skiing.

The epic **Outport Trail** (48km) provides access to backcountry campgrounds and abandoned settlements along Newman

Sound. The loop in its entirety is rewarding, but be warned: parts are unmarked, not to mention mucky. A compass, a topographical map and ranger advice are prerequisites for this serious route.

Kayak rentals are available at the kiosk by the visitors center. Inquire about the **Sandy Pond-Dunphy's Pond Route** (10km), a great paddle with only one small portage.

About 15km from the park's western gate, the **Burnside Archaeology Centre** (📞709-677-2474; www.digthequarry.com; Main St; adult/child $2/1; ⊙9am-6pm Jul-Oct) catalogs artifacts found at local Beothuk sites; ask about **boat tours** (per adult/child $45/25) to the more far-flung settlements. Also in the region is **Salvage**, a photographer's-dream fishing village with well-marked walking trails. It's near the park's north end on Rte 310, about 26km from Hwy 1.

☞ Tours

Departures are from the visitors center.

Coastal Connections   BOAT TOUR
(📞709-533-2196; www.coastalconnections.ca; 2½hr tours adult/child $65/35; ⊙9:30am & 1pm May-Oct) Climb aboard for a trip through Newman Sound, where you'll pull lobster pots, examine plankton under the microscope and engage in other hands-on activities. It's common to see eagles, less so whales.

🛏️ Sleeping

Camping is the only option within the park itself. Those with aspirations of a bed should head to Eastport; it's near the park's north end on Rte 310, about 16km from Hwy 1. For camping reservations (recommended on summer weekends), call **Parks Canada** (📞877-737-3783; www.pccamping.ca; reservation fee $10.80) or go online.

Backcountry Camping   CAMPGROUND $
(free permit required, campsites $16) There are several backcountry sites around the Outport Trail, Beachy Pond, Dunphy's Island and Dunphy's Pond, reached by paddling, hiking or both. Register at the visitors center.

Newman Sound Campground CAMPGROUND $
(campsites $26-30) This is the park's main (noisier) campground, with 343 sites, a grocery store and laundromat. It's open for winter camping, too.

Malady Head Campground   CAMPGROUND **$**
(campsites $17-22) Located at the park's north-
ern end, Malady Head is smaller, quieter
and more primitive (though it does have
showers).

Gander

POP 11,000

Gander sprawls across the juncture of Hwy
1 and Rte 330, which leads to Notre Dame
Bay. It is a convenient stopping point and
offers a couple of sights for aviation buffs.

There is a **visitors center** (www.gander-
canada.com; ⊘8am-8pm Jun-Sep, 8:30am-5pm
Oct-May) on Hwy 1 at the central entry into
town. For aviation fanatics, the **North Atlantic Aviation Museum** (☑709-256-2923;
www.northatlanticaviationmuseum.com; Hwy 1;
adult/child $6/5; ⊘9am-7pm daily Jul & Aug, to
4pm Mon-Fri Sep-Jun) has exhibits detailing
Newfoundland's air contributions to WWII
and the history of navigation. Just east on
Hwy 1 is the sobering **Silent Witness Monument**, a tribute to 248 US soldiers whose
plane crashed here in December 1985.

Sinbad's Hotel & Suites (☑709-651-2678;
www.steelehotels.com; Bennett Dr; r $95-130) has
clean, basic hotel rooms within the center of
Gander. Big box retailers are everywhere, as
this is the region's main town. If you need to
stock up on anything, do it here.

The **Gander Airport** (YQX; www.gander-
airport.com) gets a fair bit of traffic. **DRL**
(☑709-263-2171; www.drl-lr.com) buses stop at
the airport en route to St John's (four hours)
and Port aux Basques (nine hours).

Twillingate Island & New World Island

POP 2600

This area of Notre Dame Bay gets the most
attention, and deservedly so. Twillingate
(which actually consists of two barely sepa-
rated islands, North and South Twillingate)
sits just north of New World Island. The islands are reached from the mainland via an
amalgamation of short causeways. It's stunningly beautiful, with every turn of the road
revealing new ocean vistas, colorful fishing
wharves or tidy groups of pastel houses
hovering on cliffs and outcrops. An influx
of whales and icebergs every summer only
adds to the appealing mix.

◉ Sights

The sights below are roughly in order of
how you will come across them as you drive
through Twillingate.

★ Prime Berth/Twillingate
Fishing Museum   MUSEUM
(☑709-884-5925; www.primeberth.com; Walter El-
liott Causeway; admission $5, tour $8; ⊘10am-5pm
Jul & Aug) Make this your first stop. Run by an
engaging fisherman, the private museum,
with its imaginative and deceivingly simple
concepts (a cod splitting show!), is brilliant,
and fun for mature scholars and school kids
alike. It's the first place you see as you cross
to Twillingate.

Little Harbour   WATERFRONT
In Little Harbour, en route to the town of
Twillingate, a 5km trail leads past the vestiges of a resettled community and rock arch
to secluded, picturesque **Jone's Cove**.

Auk Island Winery   WINERY
(☑709-884-2707; www.aukislandwinery.com; 29
Durrell St; tastings $3, with tour $5; ⊘9:30am-
6:30pm Jul & Aug, reduced hours Sep-Jun) Visit
the grounds that produce Moose Joose
(blueberry-partridgeberry), Funky Puffin
(blueberry-rhubarb) and other fruity flavors using iceberg water and local berries.
There's also ice cream made from iceberg
water and bicycle rentals (per day $25).

Durrell Museum   MUSEUM
(☑709-884-2780; Museum St, off Durrell St; adult/
child $2/1; ⊘9am-5pm Jun-Sep) Don't neglect
to see scenic Durrell and its museum, dwelling atop Old Maid Hill. The polar bear is a
bonus. Bring your lunch; there are a couple
of picnic tables and a spectacular view.

Twillingate Museum   MUSEUM
(☑709-884-2825; www.tmacs.ca; off Main St;
admission by donation; ⊘9am-5pm May-Sep)
Housed in a former Anglican rectory, the
museum tells the island's history since the
first British settlers arrived in the mid-1700s.
One room delves into the seal hunt and its
controversy. There's a historic **church** next
door.

Long Point Lighthouse   LIGHTHOUSE
(☑709-884-2247; ⊘10am-6pm) **FREE** Long
Point provides dramatic views of the coastal
cliffs. Travel up the winding steps, worn
from lighthouse keepers' footsteps since
1876, and gawk at the 360-degree view. Located at the tip of the north island, it's an

ideal vantage point for spotting icebergs in May and June.

☞ Tours

Fun two-hour tours (per adult/child $44/22) to view icebergs and whales depart daily from mid-May to early September.

Twillingate Adventure Tours BOAT TOUR
(🖉 888-447-8687; www.twillingateadventuretours.com; off Main St) Depart from Twillingate's wharf at 10am, 1pm and 4pm (and sometimes 7pm).

Twillingate Island Boat Tours BOAT TOUR
(🖉 709-884-2242; www.icebergtours.ca; Main St) Depart from the Iceberg Shop (itself worth a peek, with its iceberg pictures and crafts) at 9:30am, 1pm and 4pm.

✯ Festivals & Events

Fish, Fun & Folk Festival MUSIC
(www.fishfunfolkfestival.com; ⊙ late Jul) Traditional music and dance, some of which goes back to the 16th century, merrily take over Twillingate during this weeklong festival.

🛏 Sleeping & Eating

Despite having about 20 lodging options, Twillingate gets very busy in the summer. Book early.

Captain's Legacy B&B B&B $$
(🖉 709-884-5648; www.captainslegacy.com; Hart's Cove; r $95-125; ⊙ May-Oct; ☺ 🗟) A real captain named Peter Troake once owned this historic 'outport mansion,' now a gracious four-room B&B overlooking the harbor.

Paradise B&B B&B $$
(🖉 877-882-1999, 709-884-5683; www.capturegaia.com/paradiseb&b.html; 192 Main St; r $100; ⊙ May-Sep; ☺ 🗟) Set on a bluff overlooking Twillin-

gate's harbor, Paradise offers the best view in town. You can wander down to the beach below, or relax on a lawn chair and soak it all up. Oh, the three rooms are comfy too. Angle for room 1. Cash only.

Anchor Inn Hotel HOTEL $$
(🖉 800-450-3950, 709-884-2777; www.anchorinn-twillingate.com; 3 Path End; r $120-180 ; ⊙ Mar-Dec; 🗟) The waterfront Anchor has rooms with deliciously soft beds. Amenities include the hotel's view-worthy deck and the barbecue grill for do-it-yourself types. There's also an excellent on-site restaurant.

J & J Fish Market SEAFOOD $
(98 Main St; mains $8-16; ⊙ 11am-7pm) It only has six tables, but they're filled with diners shoveling fresh fish, lobster and crab in their gobs.

R&J Restaurant SEAFOOD $
(🖉 709-884-2212; 110 Main St; mains $8-14; ⊙ 8am-11pm) Sink your teeth into fish 'n' brewis, shrimp, scallops or battered fish. Pizzas and burgers are also available.

☆ Entertainment

All Around the Circle Dinner Theatre THEATER
(🖉 709-884-5423; Crow Head; adult/child $32/16; ⊙ 6pm Mon-Sat Jun-Sep) Six of Newfoundland's best will not only cook you a traditional meal, they'll also leave you in stitches with their talented performances. It's just south of the Long Point Lighthouse.

ℹ Information

Town of Twillingate (www.townof twillingate.ca)
Twillingate Tourism (www.visittwillingate.com)

DRIFTING DOWN ICEBERG ALLEY

Each year 10,000 to 40,000 glistening icebergs break off Greenland's glaciers and enter the Baffin and Labrador currents for the three-year trip south to Newfoundland's famed 'Iceberg Alley.' This 480km-long, 98km-wide stretch of sea runs along the province's north and east coasts and is strewn with 'bergs in late spring and early summer. Fogo and Twillingate Islands in Notre Dame Bay and St Anthony on the Northern Peninsula are some of the best places for sightings. Even St John's is graced with a few hundred of the blue-and-white marvels most years (though sometimes the waters remain barren due to climate and current shifts).

To see where the behemoths lurk, check www.icebergfinder.com, the provincial tourism association's website showing where icebergs are floating; you can get weekly email updates on their locations and plan your trip accordingly.

ℹ Getting There & Away

From the mainland, Rte 340's causeways almost imperceptibly connect Chapel Island, tiny Strong's Island, New World Island and Twillingate Island.

Fogo Island & Change Islands

POP 2900

Settled in the 1680s, Fogo is an intriguing and rugged island to poke around. Keep an eye on this place: it has embarked on an ambitious, arts-oriented sustainable tourism plan that's quite progressive for the region. The rare Newfoundland pony roams the Change Islands, which float to the west.

◎ Sights & Activities

On Fogo, the village of **Joe Batt's Arm**, backed by rocky hills, is a flashback to centuries past – though it now has a mod twist thanks to the luxe new Fogo Island Inn. A **farmers market** takes place at the ice rink on Saturday mornings.

Nearby is **Tilting**, perhaps the most engaging village on the island. The Irish roots run deep here and so do the accents. The inland harbor is surrounded by picturesque fishing stages and flakes, held above the incoming tides by weary stilts. There's also the great coastal **Turpin's Trail** (9km) that leaves from Tilting, near the beach at **Sandy Cove**.

On the opposite end of the island is the village of **Fogo** and the indomitable **Brimstone Head**. After you take in the mystical rock's view, do another great hike in town: the **Lion's Den Trail** (5km), which visits a Marconi radio site. Keep an eye out for the small group of caribou that roams the island.

As part of the new development plan, the island is stringing **art studios** along its walking trails, and inviting painters, filmmakers and photographers from around the world for residencies. Ask about the **digital cinema's** current location.

The Change Islands are home to the **New-foundland Pony Sanctuary** (☑709-621-6381; 12 Bowns Rd; admission by donation; ☺by appointment), established to increase numbers of the native, endangered Newfoundland pony. Less than 100 registered beasts of breeding age remain in the province, and this humble stable of 11 ponies is the largest herd. The small creatures are renowned

as hardy workers (especially in winter) with gentle temperaments. Pony rides are available for $5 to $10. Call first to make sure someone is on-site before visiting.

✦ Festivals & Events

Great Fogo Island Punt Race CULTURAL
(www.fogoislandregatta.com; ☺late Jul) Locals row traditionally built wooden boats (called punts) 16km across open sea to the Change Islands and back.

Brimstone Head Folk Festival MUSIC
(www.brimstoneheadfestival.com; ☺mid-Aug) A three-day hootenanny; Irish and Newfoundland music.

🛏 Sleeping & Eating

Peg's B&B B&B $
(☑709-266-2392; www.pegsbb.com; 60 Main St, Fogo; r from $80; ☺May-Oct; ☻🗢) Right in the heart of Fogo village, Peg's four-room place offers up a friendly atmosphere and harbor views.

Foley's Place B&B B&B $
(☑866-658-7244, 709-658-7288; www.foleysplace. ca; 10A Kelley's Island Rd, Tilting; r $85; ☻🗢) The four rooms in this traditional, 100-year-old home are brightly colored, furnished in modern style and have en suite bathrooms.

ROUND OR FLAT?

Despite Columbus' stellar work in 1492 (when he sailed the ocean blue without falling off the earth's edge), and despite modern satellite photos that confirm his findings of a rounded orb, the folks at the Flat Earth Society aren't buying it. A spinning, spherical world hurtling through space would only lead to our planet's inhabitants living a confused and disorientated life, they say.

In 'reality,' the stable and calming flat earth is said to have five striking corners: Lake Mikhayl in Tunguska (Siberia); Easter Island; Lhasa (Tibet); the South Pacific island of Ponape; and Brimstone Head on Fogo Island, right here in Newfoundland. So climb up the craggy spine of Brimstone Head, stare off the abyss to earth's distant edge and judge for yourself if the earth is round or flat. If nothing else, you're guaranteed a stunning view of Iceberg Alley.

Fogo Island Inn
INN $$$

(☑709-658-3444; www.fogoislandinn.ca; Joe Batt's Arm; r incl meals $850-2700) ◢ Opened in 2013, this 29-room, ecofriendly inn is a gorgeous architecturual wonder clasping the edge of the world. Each room has phenomenal views, as does the on-site restaurant (mains $40 to $49, open 7am to 9pm). The chef sources almost everything from island forages. If staff aren't busy, they'll give you a tour of the mod building.

Nicole's Cafe
CAFE $$

(☑709-658-3663; www.nicolescafe.ca; 159 Main Rd, Joe Batt's Arm; mains $16-22; ☺10am-9pm) ◢ Nicole uses ingredients from the island – sustainably caught seafood, root vegetables and wild berries – for her contemporary take on dishes like Jiggs dinner, caribou pâté and the daily vegetarian plate. It's a sunny spot with big wood tables and local artwork and quilts on the walls.

❶ Information

Change Islands (www.changeislands.ca)
Fogo Tourism (www.townoffogoisland.ca)

❶ Getting There & Away

Rte 335 takes you to the town of Farewell, where the ferry sails to the Change Islands (20 minutes) and then onward to Fogo (45 minutes). Five boats leave between 7:45am and 8:30pm. Schedules vary, so check with **Provincial Ferry Services** (☑709-627-3492; www.gov.nl.ca/ferryservices). The round-trip fare to Fogo is $18 for car and driver, and $6 for additional passengers. It's $7 to the Change Islands. Note it is about 25km from Fogo's ferry terminal to Joe Batt's Arm.

Grand Falls-Windsor

POP 13,700

The sprawl of two small pulp-and-paper towns has met and now comprises the community of Grand Falls-Windsor. The Grand Falls portion, south of Hwy 1 and near the Exploits River, is more interesting for visitors. The five-day **Salmon Festival** (www.salmonfestival.com; ☺mid-Jul) rocks with big-name Canadian bands.

◉ Sights

Mary March Provincial Museum
MUSEUM

(☑709-292-4522; www.therooms.ca/museum; 24 St Catherine St; adult/child $2.50/free; ☺9am-4:45pm Mon-Sat, from noon Sun May-Oct) This

is worth visiting. Exhibits concentrate on the recent and past histories of Aboriginal peoples in the area, including the extinct Beothuk tribe. Take exit 18A south to reach it. Admission includes the loggers' museum.

Loggers' Life Provincial Museum
MUSEUM

(☑709-292-0492; www.therooms.ca/museum; exit 17, Hwy 1; adult/child $2.50/free; ☺9am-4:45pm Mon-Sat, from noon Sun Jun-Sep) Here you can experience the life of a 1920s logging camp – smells and all. Admission includes the provincial museum.

Salmonid Interpretation Centre
PARK

(☑709-489-7350; www.exploitsriver.ca; adult/child $6.50/3; ☺8am-8pm Jun-Sep) Watch Atlantic salmon start their mighty struggle upstream to spawn. Unfortunately, they do so under the pulp mill's shadow. To get there, cross the river south of High St and follow the signs.

⌁ Sleeping & Eating

Hill Road Manor B&B
B&B $$

(☑866-489-5451, 709-489-5451; www.hillroadmanor.com; 1 Hill Rd; r $119-129; 🕾) Elegant furnishings, cushiony beds that will have you gladly oversleeping and a vibrant sunroom combine for a stylish stay. Kids are welcome.

Kelly's Pub & Eatery
BURGERS $

(☑709-489-9893; 18 Hill Rd; mains $8-12; ☺9am-2am) Hidden neatly behind the smoky pub is this great countrified spot. It makes the best burgers in town and the stir-fries are not too shabby either.

❶ Information

Town of Grand Falls-Windsor (www.townofgrandfallswindsor.com)

❶ Getting There & Away

DRL (☑709-263-2171; www.drl-lr.com) has its bus stop at the Highliner Inn on the Hwy 1 service road. The drive to St John's is 430km, to Port aux Basques it's 477km.

Central South Coast

Rte 360 runs 130km through the center of the province to the south coast. It's a long way down to the first settlements at the end of **Bay d'Espoir**, a gentle fjord. Note there is no gas station on the route, so fill up on Hwy 1. **St Alban's** is set on the west side of the fjord. You'll find a few motels with dining rooms and lounges around the end of the bay.

Further south is a concentration of small fishing villages. The scenery along Rte 364 to **Hermitage** is particularly impressive, as is the scenery around **Harbour Breton**. It's the largest town (population 1700) in the region and huddles around the ridge of a gentle inland bay.

Southern Port Hotel (☑709-885-2283; www.southernporthotel.ca; Rte 360, Harbour Breton; r $93-97; ☎) provides spacious, standard-furnished rooms; even-numbered ones have harbor views. Two doors down is **Scott's Snackbar** (☑709-885-2406; mains $7-15; ⏰10:30am-11pm Sun-Thu, to 1am Fri & Sat), serving burgers and home-cooked dishes; it's licensed.

Thornhill Taxi Service (☑866-538-3429, 709-885-2144) connects Harbour Breton with Grand Falls ($40, 2½ hours), leaving at 7:15am. Government passenger ferries serve Hermitage, making the western south-coast outports accessible from here.

NORTHERN PENINSULA

The Northern Peninsula points upward from the body of Newfoundland like an extended index finger, and you almost get the feeling it's wagging at you saying, 'Don't you dare leave this province without coming up here.'

Heed the advice. This area could well be crowned Newfoundland's star attraction. Two of the province's World Heritage–listed sites are here: Gros Morne National Park, with its fjordlike lakes and geological oddities, rests at the peninsula's base, while the sublime, 1000-year-old Viking settlement at L'Anse aux Meadows stares out from the peninsula's tip. Connecting these two famous sites is the **Viking Trail** (www.vikingtrail.org), aka Rte 430, an attraction in its own right that holds close to the sea as it heads resolutely north past the ancient burial grounds of Port au Choix and the ferry jump-off point to big, brooding Labrador.

The region continues to gain in tourism, yet the crowds are nowhere near what you'd get at Yellowstone or Banff, for example. Still, it's wise to book ahead in July and August.

It's a five- to six-hour drive from Deer Lake at the peninsula's southern edge to L'Anse aux Meadows at its northern apex.

Towns and amenities are few and far between so don't wait to fuel up.

Deer Lake

There's little in Deer Lake for the visitor, but it's an excellent place to fly into for trips up the Northern Peninsula and around the west coast.

Those looking for B&B comfort can hunker down at plain-and-simple **Auntie M's Lucas House** (☑709-635-3622; www.lucashousebb.net; 22 Old Bonne Bay Rd; r $65-75; ⏰May-Sep; ☮@☎); it's a five-minute ride from the airport. The biggest show in town is new, 88-room **Holiday Inn Express** (☑709-635-3232; www.ihg.com; 38 Bennett's Ave; r $130-180; ✴@☎☮❄); it's a 10-minute ride from the airport.

The **visitors center** (⏰9am-7pm) and the **DRL** (☑709-263-2171; www.drl-lr.com) bus stop at the Irving gas station sit beside each other on Hwy 1. A taxi from the airport to any of these spots costs about $10.

Deer Lake Airport (YDF; www.deerlakeairport.com) is a stone's throw off Hwy 1. It's a well-equipped little place with ATMs, food, free wi-fi and internet access, and a staffed tourism desk. Flights arrive regularly from St John's, Halifax, Toronto and even London. Avis, Budget and National are among the companies renting cars at the airport.

Gros Morne National Park

This **national park** (☑709-458-2417; www.pc.gc.ca/grosmorne; adult/child/family per day $9.80/4.90/19.60) stepped into the world spotlight in 1987, when Unesco granted it World Heritage designation. To visitors, the park's stunning flat-top mountains and deeply incised waterways are simply supernatural playgrounds. To geologists, this park is a blueprint for the planet and supplies evidence for theories such as plate tectonics. Specifically, the bronze-colored Tablelands are made of rock that comes from deep within the earth's crust. Nowhere in the world is such material as easily accessed as in Gros Morne (it's usually only found at unfathomable ocean depths). Such attributes have earned the park its 'Galapagos of Geology' nickname.

There is enough to do in and around the park to easily fill several days. The hiking, kayaking, camping, wildlife-spotting and boat tours are fantastic.

Several small fishing villages dot the shoreline and provide amenities. Bonne Bay swings in and divides the area: to the south is Rte 431 and the towns of **Glenburnie**, **Woody Point** and **Trout River**; to the north is Rte 430 and **Norris Point**, **Rocky Harbour**, **Sally's Cove** and **Cow Head**. Centrally located Rocky Harbour is the largest village and most popular place to stay. Nearby Norris Point and further-flung Woody Point also make good bases.

◉ Sights

The park is quite widespread – it's 133km from Trout River at the south end to Cow Head in the north – so it takes a while to get from sight to sight. We've listed the following places from south to north. Don't forget to stop in the park's visitors centers, which have interpretive programs and guided walks.

Tablelands   GEOGRAPHIC FEATURE
(Rte 431, near Trout River) Dominating the southwest corner of the park are the unconquerable and eerie Tablelands. This massive flat-topped massif was part of the earth's mantle before tectonics raised it from the depths and planted it squarely on the continent. Its rock is so unusual that plants can't even grow on it. You can view the barren golden phenomenon up close on Rte 431, or catch it from a distance at the stunning **photography lookout** above Norris Point.

West of the Tablelands, dramatic volcanic sea stacks and caves mark the coast at **Green Gardens**.

Bonne Bay Marine Station   AQUARIUM
(📞709-458-2550; www.bonnebay.mun.ca; Rte 430, Norris Point; adult/child/family $6.25/5/15; ⊙9am-5pm Jun-Aug) At the wharf in Norris Point is the Bonne Bay Marine Station, a research facility that's part of Memorial University. Every half-hour there are interactive tours, and the aquariums display the marine ecological habitats in Bonne Bay. For children, there are touch tanks and a rare blue lobster lurking around.

SS Ethie   SHIPWRECK
(Rte 430, past Sally's Cove) Follow the sign off the highway to where waves batter the rusty and tangled remains of the SS *Ethie*. The story of this 1919 wreck, and the subsequent rescue, was inspiration for a famous folk song.

Broom Point Fishing Camp   HISTORIC SITE
(Rte 430, Broom Point; ⊙10am-5:30pm May-Oct) **FREE** This restored fishing camp sits a short distance north of Western Brook Pond. The three Mudge brothers and their families fished here from 1941 until 1975, when they sold the entire camp, including boats, lobster traps and nets, to the national park. Everything has been restored; it's staffed by guides.

Shallow Bay   BEACH
The gentle, safe, sand-duned beach at Shallow Bay seems out of place, as if transported from the Caribbean by some bizarre current. The water, though, provides a chilling dose of reality, rarely getting above 15°C.

The Arches   PARK
These scenic arched rocks on Rte 430 north of Parsons Pond are formed by pounding waves and worth a look-see.

⚡ Activities

Hiking and kayaking can also be done via guided tours.

Hiking
Twenty maintained trails of varying difficulty snake through 100km of the park's most scenic landscapes. The gem is the **James Callahan Gros Morne Trail** (16km) to the peak of Gros Morne, the highest point at 806m. While there are sections with steps and boardwalks, this is a strenuous seven- to eight-hour hike, and includes a steep rock gully that must be climbed to the ridge line of the mountain. Standing on the 600m precipice and staring out over **10 Mile Pond**, a sheer-sided fjord, can only be described as sublime.

Green Gardens Trail (16km) is almost as scenic and challenging. The loop has two trailheads off Rte 431, with each one descending to Green Gardens along its magnificent coastline formed from lava and shaped by the sea. Plan on six to eight hours of hiking or book one of the three backcountry camping areas, all of them on the ocean, and turn the hike into an overnight adventure. A less strenuous day hike (9km) to the beach and back is possible from this trail's Long Pond Trailhead.

Shorter scenic hikes are **Tablelands Trail** (4km), which extends to Winterhouse Brook Canyon; **Lookout Trail** (5km), which starts behind the Discovery Centre and loops to the site of an old fire tower above the tree line; **Lobster Cove Head Trail** (2km), which loops through tidal pools; and Western Brook Pond Trail, the most popular path.

The granddaddies of the trails are the **Long Range Traverse** (35km) and **North Rim Traverse** (27km), serious multiday treks over the mountains. Permits and advice from park rangers are required.

If you plan to do several trails, invest $20 in a copy of the *Gros Morne National Park Trail Guide,* a waterproof map with trail descriptions on the back, which is usually available at the visitors centers.

Western Brook Pond   HIKING

(Rte 430) Park your car in the lot off the highway, then take the 3km easy path inland to Western Brook Pond. 'Pond' is a misnomer, since the body of water is huge. Many people also call it a fjord, which is technically incorrect, since it's freshwater versus saltwater. Here's the thing everyone agrees on: it's flat-out stunning. Western Brook's sheer 700m cliffs plunge to the blue abyss and snake into the mountains. The best way to experience it is on a boat tour (p202).

Kayaking

Kayaking in the shadow of the Tablelands and through the spray of whales is truly something to be experienced. Gros Morne Adventures provides rentals (single/double per day $55/65) for experienced paddlers.

Skiing

Many trails in the park's impressive 55km cross-country ski-trail system were designed by Canadian Olympic champion, Pierre Harvey. Contact the Main Visitor Centre for trail information and reservations for backcountry huts.

☞ Tours

Most tours operate between June and mid-September; book in advance. Kayaking is best in June and July.

Bon Tours   BOAT TOUR

(☎709-458-2016; www.bontours.ca; Ocean View Motel, Main St, Rocky Harbour) Bon runs the phenomenal **Western Brook Pond boat tour** (2hr trip per adult $53-60, child $20-26) every hour between 10am and 5pm. The dock is a 3km walk from Rte 430 via the easy Western

---

THE SEAL HUNT DEBATE

Nothing ignites a more passionate debate than Canada's annual seal hunt, which occurs in March and April off Newfoundland's northeast coast and in the Gulf of St Lawrence around the Îles de la Madeleine and Prince Edward Island.

The debate pits animal rights activists against sealers (typically local fishers who hunt seals in the off-season), and both sides spin rhetoric like a presidential press secretary. The main issues revolve around the following questions.

Are baby seals being killed? Yes and no. Whitecoats are newborn harp seals, and these are the creatures that have been seen in horrifying images. But it's illegal to hunt them and has been for 20 years. However, young harp seals lose their white coats when the seals are about 12 to 14 days old. After that, they're fair game.

Are the animals killed humanely? Sealers say yes, that the guns and/or clubs they use kill the seals humanely. Animal activists dispute this, saying seals are shot or clubbed and left on the ice to suffer until the sealers come back later and finish the job.

Is the seal population sustainable? The Canadian government says yes, and sets the yearly quota based on the total seal population in the area (estimated at 7.3 million). For 2013, the harp seal quota was 400,000. The 2012 quota was the same. Activists say the quotas don't take into account the actual number of seals killed in the hunt, such as those that are 'struck and lost,' or discarded because of pelt damage.

Is the seal hunt really an important part of the local economy? Activists say no, that it represents a fraction of Newfoundland's income. The province disagrees, saying for some sealers it represents up to one-third of their annual income. And in a province with unemployment near 12%, that's significant.

In 2009 the European Union banned the sale of seal products, which hurt the industry considerably. For further details on the two perspectives, see the websites of the **Canadian Sealers Association** (www.sealharvest.ca) and the **Humane Society of the United States** (www.protectseals.org).

Brook Pond Trail. If you haven't purchased a **park pass** ($9.80), you must do so before embarking. Reserve in advance, either on-line or at Bon's office in the Ocean View Hotel. It's about a 25-minute drive from Bon's office to the trailhead.

Bon also runs **Bonne Bay boat tours** (2hr trip per adult/child $40/14) departing from Norris Point wharf, as well as a water taxi (adult/child $14/10 round-trip, foot passengers and bikes only) from Norris Point to Woody Point.

Gros Morne Adventures　　GUIDED TOUR
(☑800-685-4624, 709-458-2722; www.grosmorneadventures.com; Norris Point wharf) It offers daily guided sea-kayak tours (two/three hours $55/65) in Bonne Bay, plus full-day and multiday kayak trips and various hiking tours.

Cycle Solutions　　CYCLING TOUR
(☑866-652-2269, 709-634-7100; www.cyclesolutions.ca; Rte 430, Rocky Harbour) The Corner Brook-based bike shop offers all manner of cycling tours through Gros Morne, from easy half-day rides to hard-core, multiday trips. Prices vary. The office is next to Rocky Harbour's town information center.

Ocean Quest Adventures　　BOAT TOUR
(☑270-326-8687; www.oceanquestadventures.com; Trout River Pond; 1½hr tour $89; ☺Jun-Sep) Offers geologic-themed Zodiac tours from Trout River Pond, as well as kayak rentals and shuttle service to hike the Overfalls Trail (a moderate 5km section of the International Appalachian Trail).

✪ Festivals & Events

Gros Morne Theatre Festival　　THEATER
(☑709-243-2899; www.theatrenewfoundland.com; tickets $15-30; ☺late-May–mid-Sep) Eight productions of Newfoundland plays, staged both indoors and outdoors at various locations throughout the summer.

Writers at Woody Point Festival　　LITERATURE
(☑709-453-2900; www.writersatwoodypoint.com; tickets $30; ☺mid-Aug) Authors from across Newfoundland, Canada and the world converge at the Woody Point Heritage Theatre to do readings.

🛏 Sleeping

Rocky Harbour has the most options. Woody Point and Norris Point are also good bets. Places fill fast in July and August.

Park Campgrounds　　CAMPGROUND $
(☑877-737-3783; www.pccamping.ca; campsites $19-26, reservation fee $11) Four developed campgrounds lie within the park: **Berry Hill** (☺Jun-Sep), the largest, is most central; **Lomond** (☺Jun-Oct) is good and closest to the southern park entrance; **Trout River** (☺Jun-Sep) is average and closest to the Tablelands; and **Shallow Bay** (☺Jun-Sep) has ocean swimming (and mosquitoes). There's also a **primitive campground** (☺year-round) at superb Green Point.

Numerous **backcountry campsites** (campsites $10) are spread along trails; reserve them at the Main Visitor Centre. Berry Hill and Shallow Bay campgrounds also have **oTENTik units** (per night $120), a sort of tent-cabin hybrid equipped with beds and furniture on a raised wooden floor.

Aunt Jane's Place B&B　　B&B $
(☑709-453-2485; www.grosmorne.com/victorianmanor; Water St, Woody Point; d without/with bathroom $75/85; ☺May-Oct; ☻) This historic house oozes character. It sits beachside, so you may be woken early in the morning by the heavy breathing of whales.

Gros Morne Accommodations & Hostel　　HOSTEL $
(☑709-458-3396; www.grosmorneaccommodationsandhostel.com; 8 Kin Pl, Rocky Harbour; dm/r $30/70; ☻🖥) At this small, well-kept, newish hostel, the dorms have pinewood bunk beds, and there's a common area with cable TV and a shared kitchen. Towels are provided for a small fee. Check-in is at the Gros Morne Wildlife Museum at 76 Main St, which is a bit of a walk if you're without a car.

Anchor Down B&B　　B&B $$
(☑800-920-2208, 709-458-2901; www.theanchordown.com; Pond Rd, Rocky Harbour; r $90-100; ☻@) The home and its five rooms are pretty simple, but guests have raved about excellent hospitality and cooking from the friendly hosts.

Middle Brook Cottages　　CABIN $$
(☑709-453-2332; www.middlebrookcottages.com; off Rte 431, Glenburnie; cabins $115-149; ☺Mar-Nov; ☻🖥) These all-pinewood, spick-and-span cottages are both perfectly romantic and perfectly kid-friendly. They have kitchens and TVs, and you can splash around the swimming hole and waterfalls behind the property.

Gros Morne Cabins
CABIN $$

(☑709-458-2020; www.grosmornecabins.com; Main St, Rocky Harbour; cabins $159-199; 🐾) While backed by tarmac, most of these beautiful log cabins are fronted by nothing but ocean (ask when booking to ensure a view). Each has a full kitchen, TV and pullout sofa for children. Bookings can be made next door at Endicott's variety store.

✖ Eating

Rocky Harbour and Woody Point have the most options. There's a good chip van in Sally's Cove.

Earle's
CANADIAN $

(☑709-458-2577; Main St, Rocky Harbour; mains $8-14; ⊘9am-11pm) Earle is an institution in Rocky Harbour. Besides selling groceries and renting DVDs, he has great ice cream, pizza, moose burgers and traditional Newfoundland fare that you can chomp on the patio.

Java Jack's
CAFE $$

(☑709-458-3004; www.javajacks.ca; Main St, Rocky Harbour; mains $9-19; ⊘7:30am-8:30pm Wed-Mon May-Sep; ☑) Art-filled Jack's provides Gros Morne's best coffees, wraps and soups by day. By night, the upstairs dining room fills hungry, post-hike bellies with fine seafood, caribou and vegetarian fare. Greens come fresh from the property's organic garden.

Justin Thyme
CAFE $$

(☑709-458-2326; www.justinthymebeanandbistro. ca; 216 Main St, Norris Point; mains $17-24; ⊘ 9am-9pm, from 5pm Tue) This casual, red-walled bistro serves coffee and baked goods for breakfast, eclectic sandwiches for lunch and lemon-cream cod and pesto mussels among its dinner line-up.

Old Loft Restaurant
SEAFOOD $$

(☑709-453-2294; www.theoldloft.com; Water St, Woody Point; mains $15-21; ⊘11:30am-9pm Jul & Aug, to 7pm May, Jun & Sep) Set on the water in Woody Point, this tiny place is popular for its traditional Newfoundland meals and seafood.

❶ Information

Park admission includes the trails, Discovery Centre and all day-use areas.

Discovery Centre (☑709-453-2490; Rte 431, Woody Point; ⊘9am-6pm May-Oct) Has interactive exhibits and a multimedia theater explaining the area's ecology and geology.

There's also an information desk with maps, daily interpretive activities and a small cafe.

Main Visitor Centre (☑709-458-2066; Rte 430, near Rocky Harbour; ⊘8am-8pm May-Oct) As well as issuing day and backcountry permits, it has maps, books, Viking Trail materials and an impressive interpretive area.

Park Entrance Kiosk (Rte 430; ⊘10am-6pm May-Oct) Near Wiltondale.

Rocky Harbour (www.rockyharbour.ca)

Western Newfoundland Tourism (www. gowesternnewfoundland.com)

❶ Getting There & Around

Deer Lake Airport is 71km south of Rocky Harbour. There are shuttle bus services to Rocky Harbour, Woody Point and Trout River; see Corner Brook for details (p210).

Port au Choix

Port au Choix, dangling on a stark peninsula 13km off the Viking Trail, houses a large fishing fleet, quirky museum and a worthy archaeological site that delves into ancient burial grounds.

◎ Sights

Port au Choix National Historic Site
HISTORIC SITE

(☑709-861-3522; www.pc.gc.ca/portauchoix; Point Riche Rd; adult/child $3.90/1.90; ⊘9am-6pm Jun-Sep) The Port au Choix National Historic Site sits on ancient burial grounds of three different Aboriginal groups, dating back 5500 years. The modern visitors center tells of these groups' creative survival in the area and of one group's unexplained disappearance 3200 years ago. Several good trails around the park let you explore further.

Phillip's Garden, a site with vestiges of Paleo-Eskimo houses, is a highlight. Two trails will take you there. One is the **Phillip's Garden Coastal Trail** (4km), which leaves from Phillip Dr at the end of town. From here you hopscotch your way over the jigsaw of skeletal rock to the site 1km away.

If you continue, it's another 3km to the **Point Riche Lighthouse** (1871). It's also accessible via the visitors center road.

Another way to reach Phillip's Garden is the **Dorset Trail** (8km). It leaves the visitors center and winds across the barrens past stunted trees, passing a Dorset Paleo-Eskimo burial cave before finally reaching the site and linking to the Coastal Trail.

Ben's Studio
GALLERY

(☑709-861-3280; www.bensstudio.ca; 24 Fisher St; ☉9am-5pm Mon-Fri Jun-Sep) **FREE** At the edge of town is Ben Ploughman's capricious studio of folk art. Pieces like *Crucifixion of the Cod* are classic.

🛏 Sleeping & Eating

Jeannie's Sunrise B&B
B&B $$

(☑877-639-2789, 709-861-2254; www.jeanniessunrisebb.com; Fisher St; r $79-99; ❂🛜) Jeannie radiates hospitality through her spacious rooms, bright reading nook and demeanor as sweet as her breakfast muffins. Rooms at the lower end of the price spectrum share a bathroom.

Anchor Cafe
SEAFOOD $$

(☑709-861-3665; Fisher St; mains $12-18; ☉11am-9pm) You can't miss this place – the front half is the bow of a boat – and don't, because it has the best meals in town. The luncheon specials offer good value and the dinner menu has a wide array of seafood.

St Barbe to L'anse aux Meadows

As the Viking Trail nears St Barbe, the waters of the gulf quickly narrow and give visitors their first opportunity to see the desolate shores of Labrador. Ferries take advantage of this convergence and ply the route between St Barbe and the Labrador Straits (p215). At Eddies Cove, the road leaves the coast and heads inland.

As you approach the northern tip of the peninsula, Rte 430 veers off toward St Anthony, and two new roads take over leading to several diminutive fishing villages that provide perfect bases for your visit to L'Anse aux Meadows National Historic Site. Route 436 hugs the eastern shore and passes through (from south to north) St Lunaire-Griquet, Gunners Cove, Straitsview and L'Anse aux Meadows village. Route 437 heads in a more westerly direction through Pistolet Bay, Raleigh and Cape Onion.

🔘 Sights

★ L'Anse aux Meadows National Historic Site
HISTORIC SITE

(☑709-623-2608; www.pc.gc.ca/lanseauxmeadows; Rte 436; adult/child/family $11.70/5.80/29.40; ☉9am-6pm Jun-Sep) Leif Eriksson and his Viking friends lived here circa AD 1000. The remains of their waterside settlement – eight wood-and-sod buildings, now just vague outlines left in the spongy ground – are what visitors can see, plus three replica buildings inhabited by costumed docents. The latter have names such as 'Thora' and 'Bjorn' and simulate Viking chores such as spinning fleece and forging nails. Allow two or three hours to walk around and absorb the ambience.

The premise may seem dull – visiting a bog in the middle of nowhere and staring at the spot where a couple of old sod houses once stood – but somehow this site lying in a forlorn sweep of land turns out to be one of Newfoundland's most stirring attractions.

Be sure to browse the interpretive center and watch the introductory film, which tells the captivating story of Norwegian explorer Helge Ingstad, who rediscoverd the site. Also worthwhile is the 3km trail that winds through the barren terrain and along the coast surrounding the interpretive center.

Norstead
HISTORIC VILLAGE

(☑709-623-2828; www.norstead.com; Rte 436; adult/child/family $10/6.50/30; ☉9:30am-5:30pm Jun-Sep) Can't get enough of the long-bearded Viking lifestyle? Stop by Norstead, just beyond the turnoff to the national historic site. It's a recreation of a Viking village with costumed interpreters (more than at L'Anse aux Meadows) smelting, weaving, baking and telling stories around real fires throughout four buildings. Sounds cheesy, but they pull it off with class. There's also a large-scale replica of a Viking ship on hand.

🛏 Sleeping & Eating

Straitsview, Gunners Cove and St Lunaire-Griquet are all within 12km of the national historic site.

Tickle Inn
B&B $

(☑709-452-4321; www.tickleinn.net; Rte 437, Cape Onion; r with shared bathroom $70-90; ☉Jun-Sep; ❂) This delightful seaside inn, built in 1890, is surrounded by a white picket fence, oodles of grass and your own private beach. Sit in the parlor, feel the warmth of the Franklin woodstove and enjoy great home-cooked meals. The location is wonderfully remote.

Viking Village B&B
B&B $

(☑709-623-2238; www.vikingvillage.ca; Hay Cove, L'Anse aux Meadows village; d $72-78; ❂🛜) A timbered home with ocean views, Viking Village offers comfy, quilted rooms just 1km from

THE VIKINGS

Christopher Columbus gets the credit for 'discovering' North America, but the Vikings were actually the first Europeans to walk upon the continent. Led by Leif Eriksson, they sailed over from Scandinavia and Greenland some 500 years before Columbus and landed at L'Anse aux Meadows. They settled, constructed houses, fed themselves and even smelted iron out of the bog to forge nails, attesting to their ingenuity and fortitude. That it was all accomplished by a group of young-pup 20-somethings is even more impressive.

Norse folklore had mentioned a site called 'Vinland' for centuries. But no one could ever prove its existence – until 1968, when archaeologists found a small cloak pin on the ground at L'Anse aux Meadows. Archaeologists now believe the site was a base camp, and that the Vikings ranged much further along the coast.

the Viking site. Ask for one of the rooms with balcony access and watch the sun rise.

Snorri Cabins CABIN $$
(☑709-623-2241; www.snorricabins.com; Rte 436, Straitsview; cabins $89; ☉ Jun-Sep; ☎) These modern cabins offer simple comfort and great value. They're perfect for families, with a full kitchen, sitting room and a pull-out sofa. There's a convenience store on-site.

Valhalla Lodge B&B B&B $$
(☑709-623-2018, 877-623-2018; www.valhalla-lodge.com; Rte 436, Gunners Cove; r $95-110; ☉May-Sep; ☎☎) Set on a hill overlooking the ocean, the five-room Valhalla is only 8km from the Viking site. Put your feet up on the deck and watch icebergs in comfort. This very view inspired Pulitzer Prize–winning author E Annie Proulx while she wrote *The Shipping News* here.

Daily Catch SEAFOOD $$
(☑709-623-2295; www.thedailycatch.ca; 112 Main St, St Lunaire-Griquet; mains $16-20; ☉11am-9pm) Set on the water overlooking a pretty bay, the Daily Catch is a stylish little restaurant serving finely prepared seafood and wine. The basil-buttered salmon gets kudos. Fish

cakes, crab au gratin and cod burgers also please the palate.

Northern Delight SEAFOOD $$
(☑709-623-2220; Rte 436, Gunners Cove; mains $10-16; ☉8am-9pm) Dine on local favorites such as turbot cheeks and pan-fried cod, fresh lobster and mussels, or just have a 'Newfie Mug-up' (bread, molasses and a strong cup of tea). There's live music on some evenings.

★**Norseman Restaurant & Art Gallery** SEAFOOD $$$
(☑709-623-2018; www.valhalla-lodge.com; Rte 436, L'Anse aux Meadows village; mains $20-38; ☉noon-9pm May-Sep) This casual, waterfront restaurant may be Newfoundland's best. Relish the butternut squash soup, peruse a few vegetarian options or sink your teeth into tender Labrador caribou tenderloin. Norseman chills all its drinks with iceberg ice. Patrons who order lobster hand-pick their dinner by donning rubber boots and heading out front to the ocean, where the freshly caught crustaceans await in crates.

St Anthony

Yeehaw! You've made it to the end of the road, your windshield has helped control the insect population and you have seen two World Heritage sites. After such grandeur, St Anthony may be a little anticlimactic. It's not what you'd call pretty, but it has a rough-hewn charm. And the hiking and whale- and iceberg-watching are inspiring.

Grenfell is a big name around here. Sir Wilfred Grenfell was a local legend and, by all accounts, quite a man. This English-born and educated doctor first came to Newfoundland in 1892 and, for the next 40 years, traveling by dogsled and boat, built hospitals and nursing stations and organized much-needed fishing cooperatives along the coast of Labrador and around St Anthony.

◉ Sights

Grenfell Historic Properties HISTORIC BUILDING
(www.grenfell-properties.com; West St; adult/child/family $10/3/22; ☉8am-5pm Jun-Sep) A number of local sites pertaining to Wilfred Grenfell are subsumed under Grenfell Historic Properties. The **Grenfell Interpretation Centre**, opposite the hospital, is a modern exhibit recounting the historic

and sometimes dramatic life of Grenfell. Its **handicraft shop** has some high-quality carvings and artwork, as well as embroidered parkas made by locals – proceeds go to maintenance of the historic properties.

Grenfell Museum
MUSEUM

(www.grenfell-properties.com; ⏰9am-6pm Jun-Sep) Admission to the Grenfell Historic Properties also includes Grenfell's beautiful mansion, now the Grenfell Museum. It's behind the hospital, about a five-minute walk from the waterfront. Dyed burlap walls and antique furnishings envelop memorabilia, including a polar-bear rug and, if rumors are correct, the ghost of Mrs Grenfell.

Fishing Point Park
PARK

The main road through town ends at Fishing Point Park, where a lighthouse and towering headland cliffs overlook the sea. The **Iceberg Alley Trail** and **Whale Watchers Trail** both lead to clifftop observation platforms – the names say it all.

A **visitors center,cafe** and **craft shop** is also out here; in the side room there's a **polar bear display** (adult/child $3/2). Creatures like this guy have been known to roam St Anthony from time to time as pack ice melts in the spring.

☞ Tours

Northland Discovery Tours
BOAT TOUR

(✆709-454-3092, 877-632-3747; www.discovernorthland.com; 2½hr tour adult/child $58/25; ⏰9am, 1pm & 4pm Jun-Sep) Northland offers

highly recommended cruises for whale- or iceberg-viewing that leave from the dock behind the Grenfell Interpretation Centre on West St. If you tend to get seasick, medicate before this one.

🛏 Sleeping & Eating

Fishing Point B&B
B&B $$

(✆866-454-2009, 709-454-3117; www.bbcanada.com/6529.html; Fishing Point Rd; r $90; ⊕🐾🕸) This tiny place clings to the rocks en route to the lighthouse and offers the best harbor view in St Anthony. Get up early, enjoy a bountiful breakfast and watch the boats head out to sea. The three rooms each have their own bathroom.

Lightkeeper's Seafood Restaurant
SEAFOOD $$

(✆709-454-4900; Fishing Point Park; mains $12-20; ⏰11:30am-8pm Jun-Sep) This little gem of an eatery sits in the shadow of the lighthouse and is often graced by the sight of icebergs and whales. The chowder and scallops are legendary.

❶ Getting There & Away

Flying to St Anthony is technically possible, but the airport is nearly an hour away. **Provincial Airlines** (www.provincialairlines.ca) makes the trip from St John's daily. If you're leaving St Anthony by car, you have two options: backtrack entirely along Rte 430, or take the long way via Rte 432 along the east coast and Hare Bay. This will meet up with Rte 430 near Plum Point, between St Barbe and Port aux Choix.

WORTH A TRIP

ROUTE 432 & THE FRENCH SHORE

Surprises await along lonely Rte 432. First is **Tuckamore Lodge** (✆888-865-6361, 709-865-6361; www.tuckamorelodge.com; r incl breakfast $150-180; ⊕@🕸), a wood-hewn, lakeside retreat with ridiculously comfortable beds and home-cooked meals, located smack in the middle of nowhere. You'll pass about 20 moose on your way out to it. Owner Barb Genge arranges all manner of activities (fishing, birdwatching, hunting, photography classes) with first-rate guides.

The little towns along the coast are known as the **French Shore** (www.frenchshore.com) for the French fishers who lived in the area from 1504 to 1904. Top of the heap is **Conche** with its intriguing gaggle of sights: a **WWII airplane** that crashed in town in 1942, the seaside **Captain Coupelongue walking trail** past old French gravemarkers, and a crazy-huge **tapestry** in the local interpretation center. A woman named Delight runs the sunny **Bits-n-Pieces Cafe** (✆709-622-5400; mains $10-15; ⏰8am-8pm, to 9pm Thu-Sat), ladling out cod cakes, Thai chicken and other fare that's, well, delightful. Two simple rooms above the cafe comprise the **Stage Cove B&B** (r $95; 🕸) if you want to spend the night. It's about 68km from Tuckamore Lodge; take Rte 433 to unpaved Rte 434.

WESTERN NEWFOUNDLAND

Western Newfoundland presents many visitors with their first view of The Rock, thanks to the ferry landing at Port aux Basques. It's big, cliffy, even a bit forbidding with all those wood houses clinging to the jagged shoreline against the roaring wind. From Port aux Basques, poky fishing villages cast lines to the east, while Newfoundland's second-largest town, Corner Brook, raises its wintry head (via its ski mountain) to the northeast.

Corner Brook

POP 19,900

Newfoundland's number-two town is pretty sleepy, though skiers, hikers and anglers will find plenty of action. The handsome Humber Valley, about 10km east, is where it's going on. Centered on the Marble Mountain ski resort, the area experienced a huge development boom until the bottom fell out of the international economy. But now the area is heating up again. The valley offers adventure-sport junkies places to play, while the city itself sprawls with big-box retailers and a smoke-belching pulp and paper mill.

◎ Sights & Activities

Captain James Cook Monument MONUMENT
(Crow Hill Rd) While this clifftop monument is admirable – a tribute to James Cook for his work in surveying the region in the mid-1760s – it's the panoramic view over the Bay of Islands that is the real payoff. Cook's names for many of the islands, ports and waterways you'll see, such as the Humber Arm and Hawke's Bay, remain today.

The site is northwest of downtown via a convoluted route. Ready? Take Caribou Rd to Poplar Rd to Country Rd, then go right on Atlantic Ave, left on Mayfair Ave and follow the signs.

Railway Society of Newfoundland MUSEUM
(☑709-634-2720; Station Rd, off Humber Rd; admission $2; ☺9am-8pm Jun-Aug) Within historic Humbermouth Station, the Railway Society of Newfoundland has a good-looking steam locomotive and some narrow-gauge rolling stock that chugged across the province from 1921 to 1939.

Marble Mountain SKIING
(☑709-637-7616; www.skimarble.com; Hwy 1; day pass adult/child $59/32; ☺10am-4:30pm Sat-Thu, 9am-9:30pm Fri Dec-Apr) Marble Mountain is the lofty reason most visitors come to Corner Brook. With 35 trails, four lifts, a 488m vertical drop and annual snowfall of 5m, it offers Atlantic Canada's best skiing. There are snowboarding and tubing parks, as well as night skiing on Friday, plus there's Oh My Jesus (you'll say it when you see the slope).

When the white stuff has departed, the **Steady Brook Falls Trail** (500m) leads from the ski area's rear parking lot, behind the Tim Hortons, to a cascade of water that tumbles more than 30m.

Marble Zip Tours ZIPLINING
(☑709-632-5463; www.marbleziptours.com; Thistle Dr; 2hr tour adult/child $99/89) It's the highest zip-line in Canada. Strap in near the mountaintop, and zigzag platform to platform down a gorge traversing Steady Brook Falls. It'll take your breath away. Tours depart four to five times daily. The office is past Marble Mountain's lodge, behind the Tim Hortons.

My Newfoundland Adventures ADVENTURE SPORTS
(☑800-686-8900, 709-638-0110; www.mynewfoundland.ca) If skiing doesn't get the adrenaline flowing, you must try snow-kiting (a windsurfing-meets-snowboarding endeavor). Or there's snowshoeing, ice fishing and even ice climbing. Canoeing, salmon fishing and caving all take place in the warmer seasons. There again, pretty much anything is possible with these patient folks; no experience is required. The office is at Marble Mountain's base by the Tim Hortons.

Blow-Me-Down Cross-Country Ski Park SKIING
(☑709-639-2754; www.blowmedown.ca; Lundigran Dr; day pass $13; ☺sunrise-9pm Dec-Apr) It has 50km of groomed trails; ski rentals (per day $12) are available. It's about 6km southwest of downtown.

Cycle Solutions CYCLING
(☑709-634-7100, 866-652-2269; www.cyclesolutions.ca; 35 West St; ☺9am-5:30pm Mon-Thu, to 9pm Fri, to 6pm Sat) This sweet bike shop runs local cycling and caving tours; it's attached to the Brewed Awakening coffee shop.

Corner Brook

🛏 Sleeping & Eating

Brookfield Inn B&B **$**
(☎709-639-3111, 877-339-3111; brookfieldinn@gmail.com; 2 Brookfield Ave; r $60-85; ☻🛜) A cool couple runs this B&B in their white frame house. The homey rooms have hardwood floors and plump beds. In the morning make your own breakfast from the eggs, bacon, cheeses and breads in the well-stocked kitchen. In the evening watch the sun set from the deck. The house dogs will amble up for a scratch if you want.

Glynmill Inn HOTEL **$$**
(☎800-563-4400, 709-634-5181; www.steele-hotels.com; 1 Cobb Lane; r $130-160; ✱@🛜) Lawns, gardens and graciousness surround the Tudor-style Glynmill. It was built originally for the engineers supervising the pulp mill's construction in the 1920s, at that time the largest project in the history of paper making. The inn retains an elegant, if somewhat faded, ambience.

Bell's Inn B&B **$$**
(☎888-634-1150, 709-634-1150; www.bellsinn.ca; 2 Ford's Rd; r $80-120; ☻🛜) Gordon Bell's rambling green house tops a hill that's a 15-minute walk from downtown. The eight smallish, comfy rooms all have pri-

Corner Brook

⊕ Activities, Courses & Tours
1 Cycle Solutions B2

⌂ Sleeping
2 Bell's Inn.. D1
3 Brookfield Inn D3
4 Glynmill Inn B3

⊗ Eating
Brewed Awakening .... (see 1)
5 Gitano's A2
Thistle's Place .... (see 5)

⌂ Shopping
6 Newfoundland Emporium A2

vate bathroom; rooms 1 and 4 have harbor views. Breakfast is a do-it-yourself, continental-style affair.

Thistle's Place CAFE **$**
(☎709-634-4389; www.thistledownflorist.com; Millbrook Mall, Herald Ave; sandwiches $6-11; ☺9am-5pm Mon-Sat; 🛜) Walk through the front flower shop to reach the smoked meat, curried chicken and whole-wheat vegetable wraps at the wee cafe out the back.

Brewed Awakening   COFFEE **$**
(www.brewedawakening.ca; 35 West St; baked
goods $3-7; ⏰7am-9pm Mon-Fri, 8am-9pm Sat &
Sun; 🛜) This small, funky, art-on-the-wall
coffee shop pours fair-trade, organic java
done right. It's attached to the groovy bike
shop Cycle Solutions.

Gitano's   MEDITERRANEAN **$$**
(☎709-634-5000; www.gitanos.ca; Millbrook Mall,
Herald Ave; tapas $8-14, mains $18-32; ⏰11:30am-
2pm Mon-Thu, 5-9pm Sun-Thu, to 10pm Fri & Sat;
🛜) Behind Thistle's Place and owned by the
same family, Gitano's dishes up Spanish-
themed mains such as *estofado* (stewed
sweet potatoes, chickpeas and figs over
couscous) and tapas (try the saltfish cakes)
as well as pastas. Live jazz wafts through
the supper club-esque room on weekends.

🛍 Shopping

Newfoundland Emporium   SOUVENIRS
(☎709-634-9376; 11 Broadway; ⏰10am-5pm
Mon-Sat) It's a trove of local crafts, music,
antiques and books.

ℹ Information

CIBC Bank (☎709-637-1700; 9 Main St)
Post Office (14 Main St)
Visitors Centre (☎709-639-9792; www.
cornerbrook.com; 15 Confederation Dr; ⏰9am-
5pm) Just off Hwy 1 at exit 5. Has a craft shop.

ℹ Getting There & Away

Corner Brook is a major hub for bus services
in Newfoundland. **DRL** (☎709-263-2171; www.
drl-lr.com) stops on the outskirts of town at the
Irving gas station (Confederation Dr), just off
Hwy 1 at exit 5 across from the visitors center.

All other operators use the **bus station**
(☎709-634-2659; Herald Ave) in the Millbrook
Mall building. The following are shuttle vans.
Prices are one way. You must make reservations.

Burgeo Bus (☎709-634-7777) Runs to Burgeo
($38 cash only, two hours) departing at 3pm
Monday through Friday. Leaves Burgeo be-
tween 8am and 9am.

Deer Lake Airport Shuttle (☎709-634-4343)
Picks up from various hotels en route to Deer
Lake Airport ($22, 45 minutes) three to five
times daily.

Eddy's (☎709-643-2134) Travels to/from
Stephenville ($22, 1¼ hours) twice daily on
weekdays, once daily on weekends.

Gateway (☎709-695-9700) Runs to Port aux
Basques ($36, three hours) on weekdays at
3:45pm. Departs Port aux Basques at 7:45am.

Martin's (☎709-458-7845, 709-453-2207)
Operates weekdays, departing for Woody Point
($18, 1½ hours) and Trout River ($20, two
hours) at 4:30pm. Returns from Trout River at
9am.

Pittman's (☎709-458-2486) Runs to Rocky
Harbour ($30, two hours) via Deer Lake on
weekdays at 4:30pm. Departs Rocky Harbour
at noon.

Around Corner Brook

Blomidon Mountains

The Blomidon Mountains (aka Blow Me
Down Mountains), heaved skyward from
a collision with Europe around 500 mil-
lion years ago, run along the south side
of the Humber Arm. They're tantalizing
for hikers, providing many sea vistas and
glimpses of the resident caribou popula-
tion. Some of the trails, especially ones up
on the barrens, are not well marked, so
topographical maps and a compass are es-
sential for all hikers.

Many trails are signposted off Rte 450,
which runs west from Corner Brook along
the water for 60km. One of the easiest and
most popular is **Blow Me Down Brook
Trail** (5km), which begins west of French-
man's Cove at a parking lot. The trail can
be followed for an hour or so; for more avid
hikers it continues well into the mountains,
where it becomes part of the International
Appalachian Trail (IAT). The moderately
difficult **Copper Mine Trail** (7km), by York
Harbour, provides awesome views of the
Bay of Islands and also links to the IAT.

Further on, **Blow Me Down Provincial
Park** (☎709-681-2430; www.nlcamping.ca; Rte
450; campsites $15, per vehicle $5; ⏰Jun-Aug)
has beaches and scenery.

Stephenville

As the drive into town past deserted hang-
ars, piles of rusted pipes and tract housing
portends, Stephenville is in the running
for Newfoundland's least appealing town.
There's not much reason to stop, except for
the **Stephenville Theatre Festival** (www.
stephenvilletheatrefestival.com; ⏰Jul & Aug). It
sweeps into town in summer toting along
the Bard, Broadway and – to stir the pot –
some cutting-edge Newfoundland plays.

Port au Port Peninsula

The large peninsula west of Stephenville is the only French-speaking area of the province, a legacy of the Basque, French and Acadians who settled the coast starting in the 1700s. Today, the culture is strongest along the western shore between **Cape St George** and **Lourdes**. Here children go to French school, preserving their dialect, which is now distinct from the language spoken in either France or Québec.

In **Port au Port West**, near Stephenville, the gorgeous **Gravels Trail** (3km) leads along the shore, passing secluded beach after secluded beach. Nearby in Felix Cove, stop at **Alpacas of Newfoundland** (www.alpacasofnfld.ca; Rte 460; ☺9am-6pm) **FREE** and meet the fluffy namesake critters on a farm tour.

Barachois Pond Provincial Park

This popular **park** (☏709-649-0048; www.nlcamping.ca; Hwy 1; campsites $15, per vehicle $5; ☺May-Sep), sitting just south of Rte 480 on Hwy 1, is one of the few in the province to offer a backcountry experience. From the campground, the **Erin Mountain Trail** (4.5km) winds through the forest and up to the 340m peak, where there are backcountry campsites and excellent views. Allow two hours for the climb.

Not far away are a couple of leisurely nature trails and a nice swimming area.

Port aux Basques

POP 4170

It's all about the ferry in Port aux Basques. Most visitors come here to jump onto the Rock from Nova Scotia, or jump off for the return trip. That doesn't mean the town isn't a perfectly decent place to spend a day or night. Traditional wood houses painted brightly in aqua, scarlet and sea-green clasp the stony hills. Laundry blows on the clotheslines, boats moor in backyard inlets and locals never fail to wave hello to newcomers.

Port aux Basques (occasionally called Channel-Port aux Basques) was named in the early 16th century by Basque fishers and whalers who came to work the waters of the Strait of Belle Isle.

The town is a convenient place to stock up on food, fuel and/or money before journeying onward.

◉ Sights

Several scenic fishing villages lie to the east.

Grand Bay West Beach   BEACH
(Kyle Lane) Located a short distance west of town, the long shore is backed by grassy dunes, which are breeding grounds for the endangered piping plover. The **Grand Bay West Trail** leaves from here and flirts with the coast for 10km.

Scott's Cove Park   PARK
(Caribou Rd) This park, with its restored boardwalk, candy-colored snack shacks and boat-shaped amphitheater, is the place to mingle with townsfolk and listen to live music.

Railway Heritage Centre   MUSEUM
(☏709-695-7560; off Hwy 1; museum $2, railcars $5; ☺10am-8pm Jul & Aug) The center has two things going on. One is a museum stuffed with shipwreck artifacts. Its showpiece is the astrolabe, a striking brass navigational instrument made in Portugal in 1628. The device is in remarkable condition and is one of only about three dozen that exist in the world. Restored railway cars are the center's other facet.

🛏 Sleeping & Eating

With all the ferry traffic, accommodation reservations are a good idea.

ⓘ NEWFOUNDLAND APPALACHIAN

Think the **International Appalachian Trail** ends in Québec just because it runs out of land at Cap Gaspé? Think again. It picks up in Newfoundland, where another 1200km of trail swipes the west coast from Port aux Basques to L'Anse aux Meadows. The province has linked existing trails, logging roads and old rail lines through the Long Range Mountains, part of the Appalachian chain. It's a work in progress, but some of the most complete sections are around Corner Brook and the Blomidon Mountains. See www.iatnl.com for trail details.

Port aux Basques

Port aux Basques

Radio Station B&B
B&B **$$**

(☏709-695-2906; jggillam@hotmail.com; 100 Caribou Rd; r from $89; ⊘May-Oct) Up on the bluff overlooking the harbor, the five-room Radio Station is one of the closest lodgings to the ferry (a 10-minute walk). Three rooms have their own bathroom, the other two share, and there's a kitchen for guest use.

Caribou B&B
B&B **$$**

(☏709-695-3408; www.bbcanada.com/2225. html; 42 Grand Bay Rd; r $90; ⊘May-Sep; ⊜🛜) There's nothing fancy going on here, but the five rooms are clean, bright and carpeted; two of the rooms share a bathroom between them.

St Christopher's Hotel
HOTEL **$$**

(☏800-563-4779, 709-695-3500; www.stchrishotel.com; Caribou Rd; r $93-140; ✳🛜) This is the most professional digs in town, with a small fitness room and a fine seafood restaurant called the Captain's Room (meals $10 to $16, open 7am to 1:30pm and 5pm to 10pm). Odd-numbered rooms have harbor views.

Hotel Port aux Basques HOTEL $$
(☎877-695-2171, 709-695-2171; www.hotelpab.com; 1 Grand Bay Rd; r $85-120, ste $130; ❈�) The closest competition to St Christopher's, this hotel is older but has more character. Kids stay for free.

Harbour Restaurant CANADIAN $
(☎709-695-3238; 121 Caribou Rd; mains $8-15; ☺8am-midnight) While you'll get better food and service elsewhere, you can't beat the harborside view here. Pizzas and *donairs* (spiced beef in pita bread) share the menu with fried chicken. It's licensed, too.

Alma's CANADIAN $
(☎709-695-3813; Mall, Grand Bay Rd; mains $7-13; ☺8am-8pm Mon-Sat) Follow the locals into this no-frills family diner for heaping portions of cod, scallops, fishcakes and berry pies. It serves breakfasts, burgers and sandwiches, too.

Tai Hong CHINESE $
(☎709-695-3116; 77 High St; mains $7-12; ☺11am-10:30pm) Tai Hong stir-fries standard Chinese fare. Vegetarians will find a couple of fried rice options.

ⓘ Information

Bank of Montréal (83 Main St)
Hospital (☎709-695-2175; Grand Bay Rd)
Post Office (3 Main St)
Visitors Centre (☎709-695-2262; www.portauxbasques.ca; Hwy 1; ☺6am-8pm May-Oct) Information on all parts of the province; sometimes open later to accommodate ferry traffic.

ⓘ Getting There & Away

The **Marine Atlantic Ferry** (☎800-341-7981; www.marine-atlantic.ca) connects Port aux Basques with North Sydney in Nova Scotia (adult/child/car $42/20/110). It operates year-round, typically with two sailings daily during winter and three or four sailings between mid-June and mid-September. Crossings take about six hours. The ferry terminal has no ATMs or car rentals.

DRL (☎709-263-2171; www.drl-lr.com) has its stop at the ferry terminal. Buses leave at 8am for Corner Brook ($42, 3½ hours) and St John's ($123, 13½ hours); cash only.

Around Port aux Basques

Cape Ray

Adjacent to John T Cheeseman Provincial Park 14km north of town is Cape Ray.

The coastal scenery is engaging, and the road leads up to the windblown **Cape Ray Lighthouse** (☺8am-8pm Tue-Sun Jul & Aug) FREE. This area is the southernmost known Dorset Paleo-Eskimo site, dating from 400 BC to AD 400. Thousands of artifacts have been found here and some dwelling sites can be seen.

There are also some fine **hikes** in the area. The **Table Mountain Trail** (12km) is more like a rugged road (but don't even think about driving up it) and begins on Hwy 1 opposite the exit to Cape Ray. The hike leads to a 518m plateau, where there are ruins from a secret US radar site and airstrip from WWII. It's not a hard hike, but allow three or four hours.

John T Cheeseman Provincial Park (☎709-695-7222; www.nlcamping.ca; Rte 408; campsites $15-23, per vehicle $5; ☺Jun-Sep) rests next to the beach and has top-notch facilities.

South Coast

Visitors often ignore Rte 470, and that's a shame because it's a beauty. Heading east out of Port aux Basques for 45km and edging along the shore, the road rises and falls over the eroded, windswept terrain, looking as though it's following a glacier that plowed through yesterday.

Isle aux Morts (Island of the Dead) got its label compliments of the many shipwrecks that occurred just offshore over some 400 years. Named for a family famous for daring shipwreck rescues, the **Harvey Trail** (7km) twists along the rugged shore and makes a stirring walk. Look for the signs in town.

Another highlight is the last settlement along the road, **Rose Blanche**, an absolutely splendid, traditional-looking village nestled in a cove with a fine natural harbor – a perfect example of the classic Newfoundland fishing community. From here follow the signs to the restored **Rose Blanche Lighthouse** (www.roseblanchelighthouse.ca; admission $5; ☺9am-9pm May-Oct). Built in 1873, it's the last remaining granite lighthouse on the Atlantic seaboard. If you think it's too pretty to leave, stay the night at **Rose Sea Guest House** (☎709-956-2872; www.roseblanche.ca; r $85-95; ☺Jun-Oct). It offers five rooms in a recently refurbished traditional home right on the water.

SOUTH COAST OUTPORTS

If you have the time and patience, a trip across the south coast with its wee fishing villages – called outports – is the best way to witness Newfoundland's unique culture. These little communities are some of the most remote settlements in North America, reachable only by boat as they cling to the convoluted shore. An anomaly is Burgeo (population 1460), connected by an easy road trip; it has an unspoiled, isolated feel, yet good amenities for travelers. Ramea (population 525) is another uncomplicated option. It's an island just offshore from Burgeo with lodging and activities.

Other outports along the coast include Grey River, François and McCallum. But hurry: the villages are dwindling fast as government pressure and lack of employment force residents to relocate to more accessible areas. The community of Grand Bruit was the latest to call it quits. Down to just 18 residents, they packed up and left for good in 2010.

◉ Sights & Activities

When the sun is out and the sea shimmers between endless inlets and islands, **Burgeo** is a dream. Climb the stairs to **Maiden Tea Hill** and look out in admiration. The 7km of white-sand beaches at **Sandbanks Provincial Park** may be the best in the entire province (at least the piping plover who dawdle there think so).

Author Farley Mowat lived in Burgeo for several years, until he penned *A Whale for the Killing* and irked the locals. The book tells the story of how Burgeo's townsfolk treated an 80-tonne fin whale trapped in a nearby lagoon. Let's just say the whale's outcome was not a happy one. Locals can point out the lagoon and Mowat's old house, though expect to get an earful about it.

The other outports are great areas for remote **camping**, **hiking** and **fishing**; ask locals or at the visitors center in Port aux Basques about arranging a guide. Tiny **François**, surrounded by towering walls of rock, is particularly gorgeous.

🛏 Sleeping & Eating

Ramea Retreat   HOSTEL, B&B $
(☑ 709-625-2522; www.ramea.easternoutdoors.com; 2 Main St, Ramea; dm/r $39/79; ⊘ May-Nov; 🛜) The owners have 10 hostel beds at their lodge, where they arrange kayaking, bird-watching, hiking and fishing tours. In addition, they rent rooms in various vintage clapboard houses scattered around Ramea.

Sandbanks Provincial Park   CAMPGROUND $
(☑ 709-886-2331; www.nlcamping.ca; off Rte 480, Burgeo; campsites $15, per vehicle $5; ⊘ Jun-Sep) Two-thirds of the 25 campsites here are nestled in the forest, while the remainder are in a grassy area. The flies can be brutal.

Burgeo Haven B&B   B&B $$
(☑ 709-886-2544; www.burgeohaven.com; 111 Reach Rd, Burgeo; r $100-110; @ 🛜) Right across from Maiden Tea Hill, this large house backs onto an inlet and offers a serene setting. Some of the five rooms here have views.

Gillett's Motel   MOTEL $$
(☑ 709-886-1284; www.gillettsmotel.ca; 1 Inspiration Rd, Burgeo; r from $99; 🛜) The sole motel in town is, well, motel-like, with all the usual room amenities. It's just fine, as is the on-site Galley Restaurant (meals $8 to $15), where you'll eat cod likely caught that morning.

Joy's Place   CANADIAN $
(☑ 709-886-2569; Reach Rd, Burgeo; mains $6-11; ⊘ 11am-10:30pm) Near Burgeo Haven B&B, Joy whips up fried chicken, Chinese dishes, burgers and pies in addition to her ever-present fish dishes.

❶ Information

Burgeo (www.burgeonl.com) Official town website.

❶ Getting There & Away

Lonely, 148km-long Rte 480 shoots off Hwy 1 south of Corner Brook and then runs straight into Burgeo. Note there is no gas station and barely any civilization, just glacier-cut boulders and ponds and a whole lotta moose.

The Burgeo Bus shuttle van runs between Corner Brook and Burgeo just once per day.

Access to the other towns is by boat only. While the ferries run all year, the routes described here are for mid-May through September. Schedules change, so check with **Provincial Ferry Services** (☑ 709-292-4302; www.tw.gov.nl.ca/ferryservices). Note that the ferries do not take vehicles (except Burgeo to Ramea).

With careful planning a trip through the islands is doable.

Burgeo to Ramea ($4, 1½ hours) Departs twice per day; times do vary but there is usually one at around 11am and another in the evening.

Burgeo to Grey River to François ($8.25, five hours) Goes daily (except Tuesday and Thursday) at 1:45pm.

François to McCallum to Hermitage ($7.50, four hours) Departs on Thursday, but only at 7am.

At Hermitage, you'll have to suss out transportation back to Rte 360. You can then hook up with Thornhill Taxi Service (p200), which runs between Harbour Breton and Grand Falls, and connects with DRL in the latter.

LABRADOR

POP 29,800

It's called the Big Land, and with 293,000 sq km sprawling north toward the Arctic Circle, it's easy to see why. Undulating, rocky, puddled expanses form the sparse, primeval landscape. If you ever wanted to see what the world looked like before humans stepped on it, this is the place to head.

Inuit and Innu have occupied Labrador for thousands of years, and until the 1960s the population was still limited to them and a few longtime European descendants known as 'liveyers.' They eked out an existence by fishing and hunting from their tiny villages that freckled the coast. The interior was virgin wilderness.

Over the past few decades, the economic potential of Labrador's vast natural resources has earned it a new degree of attention. Companies have tapped into the massive iron-ore mines in Wabush and Labrador City and the hydroelectric dam at Churchill Falls. It makes for a boom or bust economy, and right now it's booming big-time.

The simplest way to take a bite of the Big Land is via the Labrador Straits region, which connects to Newfoundland via a daily ferry. From there, a solitary road – the stark, rough Trans-Labrador Hwy – connects the interior's main towns. The aboriginal-influenced northern coast is accessible only by plane or supply ferry.

Labrador is cold, wet and windy, and its bugs are murderous. Facilities are few and far between throughout the behemoth region, so planning ahead is essential.

Labrador Straits

And you thought the Northern Peninsula was commanding? Sail the 28km across the Strait of Belle Isle and behold a landscape even more windswept and black-rocked.

Clouds rip across aqua-and-gray skies, and the water that slaps the shore is so cold it's purplish. Unlike the rest of remote Labrador, the Straits region is easy to reach and exalted with sights such as Red Bay and a slew of great walking trails that meander past shipwreck fragments and old whale bones.

'Labrador Straits' is the colloquial name for the communities that make the southern coastal region of Labrador. Note that your first stop in the area will not actually be in Labrador at all, as the ferry terminal and airport are both in Blanc Sablon, Québec. Once in Labrador, Rte 510 is the road that connects the Straits' communities. South of Red Bay, it is sealed and open all year. From Red Bay north, it's hard-packed gravel but in the process of being paved. Check conditions with the **Department of Transportation & Works** (☑709-729-2300; www.roads.gov.nl.ca).

Blanc Sablon to L'Anse au Clair

After arriving by ferry or plane in Blanc Sablon and driving 6km northeast on Rte 510 you come to Labrador and the gateway town of L'Anse au Clair. Here you will find the Straits' excellent **visitors center** (☑877-931-2013, 709-931-2013; www.labradorcoastaldrive.com; Rte 510, L'Anse au Clair; ⊙9am-5pm Jun-Oct) in an old church that doubles as a small museum. Be sure to pick up hiking trail information for the region.

The town makes a good pre-ferry base. Norm at **Beachside Hospitality Home** (☑709-931-2338; normanletto@nf.sympatico.ca; 9 Lodge Rd; r with shared bathroom $55-65; ☎) plays the accordion for guests in the evening. Quilts await on the beds, while homemade jams await in the kitchen at this three-bedroom, two-bathroom B&B.

The modern, well-kept **Northern Light Inn** (☑800-563-3188, 709-931-2332; www.northernlightinn.com; 56 Main St; r $99-189; ✳☎) is a tour-bus favorite. Even-numbered rooms

> **LABRADOR FAST FACTS**
> ➡ Population: 29,800
> ➡ Area: 294,330 sq km
> ➡ Biggest town: Labrador City
> ➡ Time zones: Labrador Straits are on Newfoundland Time, while the rest of Labrador (starting at Cartwright) is on Atlantic Time, ie 30 minutes behind Newfoundland.

WORTH A TRIP

SCENIC DRIVE: QUÉBEC'S ROUTE 138

This drive is most easily accessed from Québec. Rte 138 (the Québec incarnation of Labrador's Rte 510) runs down the Lower North Shore, the name given to the wild, remote chunk of La Belle Province that extends south of Blanc Sablon. From the ferry landing until the road ends abruptly 65km later at Vieux Fort, Rte 138 makes a beautiful swing past several roadside **waterfalls** and lookouts from which to see the crashing surf and offshore **puffin colonies**.

For those wanting to do more than just drive through the region, **Tourism Lower North Shore** (www.tourismlowernorthshore.com) provides information on attractions and accommodations.

have harbor views. The dining room (mains $12 to $18, open 7am to 9pm Sunday to Thursday, to 10pm Friday and Saturday) here is your best bet for food in town.

The **MV Apollo** (☎866-535-2567, 709-535-0810; www.labradormarine.com; adult/child/car $8.25/6.60/25) sails the two hours between St Barbe in Newfoundland and Blanc Sablon between May and early January. The boat runs one to three times daily between 8am and 6pm. Schedules vary from day to day. In July and August, it's not a bad idea to reserve in advance (though there's a $10 fee). Note that the ferry terminal in Blanc Sablon operates on Newfoundland Time and not Eastern Time (as in the rest of Québec).

Provincial Airlines (www.provincialairlines.ca) has flights to Blanc Sablon from St John's and St Anthony. Just to confuse you, departure times from the airport are on Eastern Time versus Labrador Straits (ie Newfoundland) Time.

Rental cars are available at the airport from **Eagle River Rent-a-Car** (☎709-931-2352, 709-931-3300).

Forteau to Pinware

Continuing northeast on Rte 510 you'll pass Forteau, L'Anse Amour, L'Anse au Loup, West St Modeste and Pinware.

Labrador Adventures (☎709-931-2055; www.tourlabrador.ca; tours $50-210) provides knowledgeable guides for Straits-oriented hikes or day tours by SUV. It also arranges all-inclusive overnight packages. This is a terrific way to see the area, especially if you're short on time or car-less.

In Forteau, the **Overfall Brook Trail** (4km) shadows the coast and ends at a 30m waterfall.

Six houses in total comprise the village of **L'Anse Amour**, but it holds more than its fair share of sights. **L'Anse Amour Burial Mound** (L'Anse Amour Rd), a pile of stones placed here by the Maritime Archaic Aboriginals, is the oldest burial monument in North America. A small roadside plaque marks the 7500-year-old site.

On the same road is **Point Amour Lighthouse** (☎709-927-5825; www.seethesites.ca; L'Anse Amour Rd; adult/child $6/3; ☺9:30am-5pm May-Oct). It is the tallest lighthouse in Atlantic Canada, with 127 steps to climb. When you reach the top, you will be rewarded with a spectacular 360-degree view of the coastline. The lighthouse keeper's house has exhibits on maritime history. The HMS *Raleigh* went aground here in 1922 and was destroyed in 1926. The **Raleigh Trail** (2km) takes you by the site and warship fragments on the beach.

Past L'Anse au Loup is the **Battery Trail** (4km), which meanders through a stunted tuckamore forest to the summit of the Battery, unfurling panoramic sea views.

The road veers inland at Pinware, and skirts along the western side of the Pinware River, until it crosses a one-lane iron bridge, and then runs along the eastern side, high above the rushing white water. This stretch of the Pinware is renowned for its **salmon fishing**. About 10km before reaching Red Bay, the land becomes rocky and barren, except for the superfluity of blueberries and bakeapples (and pickers) in August.

Forteau's **Grenfell Louie A Hall B&B** (☎709-931-2916; www.grenfellbandb.ca; Willow Ave; r $75-85; ☺May-Oct) is in the old nursing station where generations of Labrador Straits folk were born. The five simple rooms (a couple with sea views) share two bathrooms.

The **Seaview Restaurant** (Rte 510; mains $10-20; ☺9am-8pm) is nearby in Forteau. Chow down on the famous fried chicken and tender caribou. A grocery store and jam factory are also on-site.

Up and over the hills in L'Anse au Loup, **Dot's Bakery** (☎709-927-5311; Rte 510; breakfasts $4-6.50, pizzas $23; ☺7am-11pm Mon-Sat) caters to all your needs with her doughnuts, pies, breakfast dishes and pizzas.

Labrador

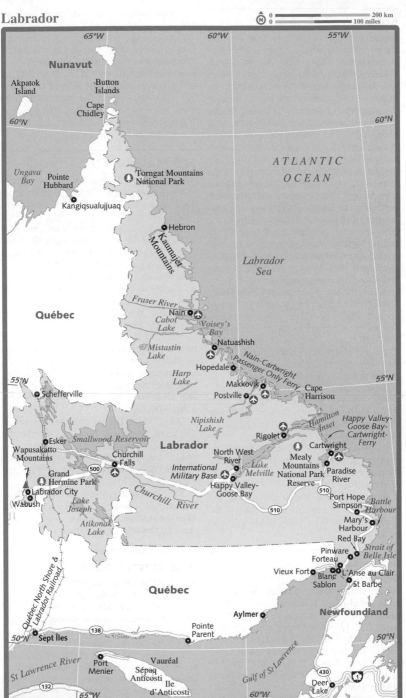

Red Bay

Spread between two venues, **Red Bay National Historic Site** (☑ 709-920-2051; www.pc.gc.ca/redbay; Rte 510; adult/child/family $7.80/3.90/19.60; ☺ 9am-5pm Jun-Sep) – which was declared a Unesco World Heritage site in 2013 – uses different media to chronicle the discovery of three 16th-century Basque whaling galleons on the seabed here. Well preserved in the ice-cold waters, the vestiges of the ships tell a remarkable story of what life was like here some four centuries ago. Red Bay was the largest whaling port in the world, with more than 2000 people residing here. Have a look at the reconstructed *chalupa* (a small Basque dingy used for whale hunting) and some of the other relics in the museum. Then hop in a small boat ($2) to nearby **Saddle Island**, where there is a self-guided interpretive trail around the excavated land sites. Allow at least two or three hours for the museum and island.

Across the bay, the amazing **Boney Shore Trail** (2km) skirts along the coast and passes ancient whale bones (they pretty much look like rocks) scattered along it. The **Tracey Hill Trail** climbs a boardwalk and 670 steps to the top of American Rockyman Hill for a bird's-eye view of the harbor; it takes about 20 minutes each way.

Between the trails and the historic site, a 15m, 400-year-old **North Atlantic right whale skeleton** sprawls through the **Selma Barkham Town Centre** (admission $2; ☺ 9am-5pm Jul-Sep).

Basinview B&B (☑ 709-920-2002; blanchearle@hotmail.com; 145 Main St; r $55-90) is a simple four-room, shared bathroom home right on the water.

Remember, Red Bay is the end of the paved road... for now. Another 200km of the hard-packed gravel is scheduled to be paved by 2015.

Battle Harbour

Sitting on an island in the Labrador Sea is the elaborately restored village and saltfish premises of Battle Harbour. Now a national historic district, it used to be the unofficial 'capital' of Labrador during the early 19th century, when fishing schooners lined its docks. Another claim to fame: this is the place where Robert E Peary gave his first news conference after reaching the North Pole in 1909.

It's accessed by boat from Mary's Harbour (departure at 11am, one hour). Accommodations are spread among various heritage homes and cottages operated by the **Battle Harbour Inn** (☑ 709-921-6325; battleharbour-reservations@gmail.com; r $175; ☺ Jun-Sep). A store and **restaurant** (mains $9-18; ☺ 8am-6pm) are also on-site. At press time, trips were set up as an overnight package deal, but day trips are on the docket. Contact the inn for details.

Mary's Harbour to Cartwright

After departing Mary's Harbour you'll pass through Port Hope Simpson 53km up the road, and then there's nothing for 186km until Cartwright.

Cartwright-based **Experience Labrador** (☑ 709-938-7444; www.experiencelabrador.com; ☺ Jul & Aug) runs adventure trips that range from 2½-hour kayaking jaunts ($50) to day-long boat and hiking tours ($250). The latter go along the Wonderstrands' endless sands that mesmerized the Vikings so long ago.

In 2010, the federal government created the **Mealy Mountains National Park Reserve** from 11,000 sq km of caribou-crossed boreal forest between Cartwright and Happy Valley-Goose Bay. Once the park gets up and running (which is taking place slowly), paddlers, snowshoers, cross-country skiers and hikers will have access to an unblemished wilderness.

Other than that, Cartwright is about the ferry. Passenger boats depart for the remote villages that sprinkle the northern coast. **Labrador Marine** (☑ 866-535-2567, 709-535-0810; www.labradormarine.com) has the schedules.

Rte 510 continues west to Happy Valley-Goose Bay. Contact the **Department of Transportation & Works** (www.roads.gov.nl.ca) for the latest conditions.

Northern Coast

North of Cartwright up to Ungava Bay there are a half-dozen small, semitraditional Inuit communities accessible only by sea or air along the rugged, largely unspoiled mountainous coast. Torngat Mountains National Park is the (literal) high point.

In 1993 on the shores of Voisey's Bay, near Nain, geologists discovered stunningly rich concentrations of copper, cobalt and especially nickel. A giant mine has been built to extract the goods, and it is expected to pump $11 billion into the provincial economy over the next few decades. This is opening up the north – for better or worse.

☉ Sights & Activities

The first port of call on the northern coast is **Makkovik**, an early fur-trading post and a traditional fishing and hunting community. Both new and old-style crafts can be bought.

Further north in **Hopedale** visitors can look at the old wooden Moravian mission church (1782). This **national historic site** (☑709-933-3490; admission $5; ☉8:30am-7pm Jul-Oct) also includes a store, residence, some huts and a museum collection.

Natuashish is a new town that was formed when the troubled village of Utshimassit (Davis Inlet) was relocated to the mainland in 2002. The move was made after a 2000 study showed that 154 of 169 youths surveyed had abused solvents (ie sniffed gasoline) and that 60 of them did it on a daily basis.

The last stop on the ferry is **Nain**, and it's the last town of any size as you go northward. Fishing has historically been the town's main industry, but this is changing due to the Voisey's Bay nickel deposit.

🛏 Sleeping & Eating

Most travelers use the ferry as a floating hotel. For those wishing to get off and wait until the next boat, it usually means winging it for a room, as only Postville, Hopedale and Nain have official lodging.

Atsanik Lodge   HOTEL $$
(☑709-922-2910; atsaniklabrador@msn.com; Sand Banks Rd, Nain; r $150-180; 🛜) This large, 25-room lodge and its restaurant (meals $15 to $22) are your best bet in Nain.

Amaguk Inn   HOTEL $$
(☑709-933-3750; Hopedale; r $140-200; 🛜) This 18-room inn also has a dining room (meals $15 to $20), and a lounge where you can get a cold beer.

ℹ Getting There & Away

Provincial Airlines (www.provincialairlines. ca) serves most of the northern coast's villages from Goose Bay.

The passenger-only MV *Northern Ranger* plies this section of coast from mid-June to mid-November. It leaves once per week, making the three-day (one way) journey between Happy Valley-Goose Bay and Nain, stopping in Mak-

---

TORNGAT MOUNTAINS NATIONAL PARK

From Nain, you can try to arrange boat transportation to otherworldly **Torngat Mountains National Park** (☑709-922-1290; www.pc.gc.ca/torngat) at Labrador's wintry tip. The park headquarters is in town, and staff can direct you to local Inuit guides. The mountains are popular with climbers because of their altitude (some of the highest peaks east of the Rockies) and isolation. The **Kaumajet Mountains**, south of the park, also make for an out-of-this-world hiking experience.

The Inuit-run **Torngat Mountains Base Camp and Research Station** (☑855-867-6428; www.torngatbasecamp. com; ☉Jul & Aug) offers package tours, including air transportation from Happy Valley-Goose Bay. At camp, activities include hiking, boating and flightseeing. An electrified fence keeps out polar bears.

---

kovik, Hopedale and Natuashish along the way. Check with **Labrador Marine** (www.labrador-marine.com) for the ever-evolving schedule and fares.

Central Labrador

Making up the territorial bulk of Labrador, the central portion is an immense, sparsely populated and ancient wilderness. Paradoxically, it also has the largest town in Labrador, **Happy Valley-Goose Bay** (www. happyvalley-goosebay.com), home to a military base. The town (population 7600) has all the usual services, but unless you're an angler or hunter, there isn't much to see or do.

Goose Bay was established during WWII as a staging point for planes on their way to Europe, and has remained an aviation center. The airport is also an official NASA alternate landing site for the space shuttle.

☉ Sights

Northern Lights Building   MUSEUM
(☑709-896-5939; 170 Hamilton River Rd; ☉10am-5:30pm Tue-Sat) FREE The Northern Lights Building hosts a military museum, interesting lifelike nature scenes and simulated northern lights.

Labrador Interpretation Centre   MUSEUM

(☑ 709-497-8566; www.therooms.ca/lic; 2 Portage Rd, North West River; ⊘10am-4pm daily Jul & Aug, 1-4pm Wed-Sun Sep-Jun) **FREE** Officially opened by Queen Elizabeth II in 1997, the Labrador Interpretation Centre is the provincial museum, which holds some of Labrador's finest works of art. It's in North West River, via Rte 520.

🛏 Sleeping & Eating

Everything listed here is in Happy Valley-Goose Bay.

Davis' B&B   B&B $

(☑ 709-896-5077; davisbb@canada.com; 14 Cabot Crescent Rd; r $60-80; 🐾) Family atmosphere and caribou sausages await you at Davis' four-room home. It's near restaurants and amenities.

Royal Inn & Suites   HOTEL $$

(☑ 709-896-2456; www.royalinnandsuites.ca; 5 Royal Ave; d incl breakfast $105-155; ❄🐾) The good-looking Royal has a variety of rooms to choose from; many of them have kitchens. The 'inn' side has wi-fi; the suites side has hard-wired high-speed access.

El Greco   PIZZERIA $$

(☑ 709-896-3473; 133 Hamilton River Rd; pizzas $16-22; ⊘4pm-1am Sun-Wed, to 3am Thu-Sat) This is a decent joint serving pizzas. It's near the Royal Inn.

❶ Getting There & Away

AIR

Air Canada (www.aircanada.com) flies to St John's and Gander. **Provincial Airlines** (www.provincialairlines.ca) flies to St John's, Deer Lake and most towns around Labrador.

BOAT

You can reach Goose Bay by the passenger-only MV *Northern Ranger;* see www.labradorferry.ca.

CAR & MOTORCYCLE

From Happy Valley-Goose Bay you can take gravel (but to be paved by 2015) Rte 500 west to Churchill Falls and then on to Labrador City. The drive to Labrador City takes about 10 hours. There are no services until Churchill Falls, so stock up. The Royal Inn & Suites has free satellite phones you can take on the road (part of a region-wide safety program). Rte 510 is the gravel road heading southeast toward Cartwright (383km) and L'Anse au Clair (623km); parts of it are also being paved. Before leaving, contact the **Department of Transportation & Works** (www.roads.gov.nl.ca) for the latest conditions.

Trucks can be rented at the airport from **National** (☑709-896-5575), but due to road conditions, you cannot buy insurance.

Labrador West

POP 9200

Just 5km apart and 15km from Québec, the twin mining towns of Labrador City (population 7400) and Wabush (population 1800) are referred to collectively as Labrador West, and this is where the western region's population is concentrated. The largest open-pit iron ore mine in the world is in Labrador City, and another mine operates in Wabush. The landscape is massive and the celestial polychromatic artwork can expand throughout the entire night sky.

◉ Sights & Activities

Gateway Labrador   MUSEUM

(☑709-944-5399; ⊘9am-4pm Mon-Fri, 10am-5pm Sat) **FREE** In the same building as the visitors center is Gateway Labrador and its Montague Exhibit Hall, where 3500 years of human history and culture, including the fur trade, are represented with intriguing artifacts and displays.

Grande Hermine Park   PARK

(☑709-282-5369; admission $3; ⊘Jun-Sep) From Wabush, 39km east on Rte 500 is Grande Hermine Park, which has a beach and some fine scenery. The **Menihek hiking trail** (15km) goes through wooded areas with waterfalls and open tundra. Outfitters can take anglers to excellent **fishing** waters.

Wapusakatto Mountains   SKIING

The Wapusakatto Mountains are 5km from town, popping up off the vast landscape interspersed with flat northern tundra. A good, cold dry snow falls from late October to late April, so the ski season here is much longer than anywhere else in Canada. For trail information and fees for world-class cross-country skiing (the Canadian national team trains in the region), check with the **Menihek Nordic Ski Club** (☑709-944-5842; www.meniheknordicski.ca); for alpine skiing, check with the **Smokey Mountain Ski Club** (☑709-944-2129; www.smokeymountain.ca).

⛯ Tours

Mines   MINE TOUR
(☑709-944-7631; tours $10; ⊘1:30pm Wed & Sun
Jul & Aug) If big holes and trucks the size of
apartment buildings make your heart flut-
ter, you can tour the mines; call to make
reservations.

⏚ Sleeping & Eating

Wabush Hotel   HOTEL $$
(☑709-282-3221; www.wabushhotel.com; 9 Gren-
ville Dr, Wabush; r $165-175; ❄☎) Centrally lo-
cated in Wabush, this chalet-style 68-room
hotel has spacious and comfortable rooms.
The dining room (meals $14 to $22, open
6:30am to midnight) has a popular dinner
buffet.

Carol Inn   MOTEL $$
(☑888-799-7736, 709-944-7736; www.carolinn.ca;
215 Drake Ave, Labrador City; d $110-130; ❄☎) All
20 rooms here have a kitchenette. There's
also a fine dining room (meals $20 to $30,
open 5:30pm Tuesday to Saturday) and pub
(meals $11 to $14, open 8am to midnight).

❶ Information

Destination Labrador (www.destination-
labrador.com)
Visitors Centre (☑709-944-5399; www.
labradorwest.com; 1365 Rte 500) Just west of
Labrador City, in the Gateway Labrador
building.

❶ Getting There & Away

AIR

Air Canada (www.aircanada.com), **Provincial
Airlines** (www.provincialairlines.ca) and **Air
Inuit** (www.airinuit.com) fly into the twin cities'
airport (in Wabush).

CAR & MOTORCYCLE

Fifteen kilometers west from Labrador City
along Rte 500 is Fermont, Québec. From there
Rte 389 is mainly paved (with some fine gravel
sections) and continues south 581km to Baie
Comeau. Happy Valley-Goose Bay is a 10-hour
drive east on Rte 500.

Budget (☑709-282-1234) has an office at
the airport; rental cars may not be driven on
Rte 500.

Understand Nova Scotia, New Brunswick & Prince Edward Island

Nova Scotia, New Brunswick & Prince Edward Island Today

Should they stay or should they go? These provinces with their scenic coas tlines, strong family traditions and low cost of living are certainly enticing places to live and raise a family. But are there enough professional opportunities to keep younger generations from moving away? It takes a certain amount of creativity to survive in Atlantic Canada without living the hard and uncertain life of a fisher or taking on newer, and perhaps unsustainable, career choices in the mining industries.

Top Nonfiction

A Whale for the Killing Farley Mowat
Cornwallis, The Violent Birth of Halifax Jon Tattrie
My Cross-Country Checkup Walter Stewart

Good-Read Novels

The Shipping News E Annie Proulx
Mercy among the Children David Adams Richards
Fall on Your Knees Anne-Marie MacDonald
Anne of Green Gables Lucy Maud Montgomery

Films Shot Here

The Shipping News (2001)
Titanic (1997)
The Memory Keeper's Daughter (2008)
Scotland, PA (2001)
The River King (2004)
The Weight of Water (2000)

Hockey Teams

Halifax Mooseheads
Cape Breton Screaming Eagles
PEI Rockets
Moncton Wildcats
Saint John Sea Dogs
Acadie-Bathurst Titans

There's No Place Like Home

Until recently, you could sit down at any dinner table in Atlantic Canada and hear the same thing:

'My ___ [fill in the blank: sister, cousin, neighbor] just left for Alberta to work in the oil fields.'

Outward migration, or 'outmigration,' has been the single biggest issue facing the Atlantic provinces during the past 15 to 25 years, but the region is finally experiencing a small rebound. As the provinces' traditional industries – fishing, logging and mining – continue to fall deeper into decline a glimmer of hope is coming from newer industries, particularly gypsum mining and offshore oil and natural gas.

Although Alberta's oil fields offer high-paying industrial jobs, and plenty of people still leave to make their living where it makes economic sense, the quality of life, low cost of living and hope of finding work closer to home is keeping an increasing number of folks on the Atlantic coasts.

Nova Scotia has been the mover and shaker of the crowd by becoming a hub for Canada's defense and aerospace sector (which also tips into Prince Edward Island). In fact, a surprising 40% of the country's military assets are found in this low-key province. Halifax was also given a massive $25 billion, 30-year military shipbuilding contract in 2011 from the Canadian government; this will theoretically create more than 10,000 jobs during its time span. While some locals complain that most of the jobs go to skilled workers brought in from other provinces, the economic impact of so many paid employees can only be positive on local businesses.

Getting Creative

Despite recent progress, these provinces still have some of the highest unemployment rates in Canada, with Newfoundland leading the pack at around 12%. At present it's a conservative government that's figuring out how to deal with the situation; each of the provinces is led by a center-right party in line with Canada's current federal administration and the area's general conservative leaning.

It's true that many people bemoan the economy and that some expect the government to bail them out, but this is also a region that embraces an independent and entrepreneurial spirit. Plenty of creative folks see it as an opportunity: they refurbish fishing boats into whale-watching boats, or turn mines into attractions that teach about ecology. Meanwhile, the artsy people of Halifax have pushed the city into the fourth-largest film industry in the nation, and small businesses, manufacturing and technology are all growing sectors that are keeping more and more young graduates from the city's universities employed. In other provinces, small-scale businesses add to the ever-plodding-along agricultural economy.

The region's abundant natural resources are still there to be used, but this is taking on new forms: cod fishing may be on its way out, for example, but offshore oil drilling has arrived to take its place. 'Fracking,' a controversial method of mining for natural gas, is happening more, particularly in out-of-the-way areas in Newfoundland and Labrador. While this is great for creating local jobs, environmentalists state that the chemicals used in the process could contaminate the soil, freshwater sources and oceans as well as potentially causing small earthquakes. What remains to be seen is how these resources are developed from now on; whether the region has learned from past mistakes and whether it will move forward responsibly and sustainably. It's this struggle that will loom largest over Atlantic Canada in the coming years.

POPULATION: **2.33 MILLION**

UNEMPLOYMENT: **10.5%**

MEDIAN INCOME: **$61,800**

LIFE EXPECTANCY: **82 YEARS**

ANNUAL MOOSE-VEHICLE COLLISIONS (NFD): **700**

POTATO PRODUCTION PER CAPITA (PEI): **8000KG**

if Atlantic Canada were 100 people

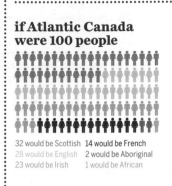

32 would be Scottish · 14 would be French
28 would be English · 2 would be Aboriginal
23 would be Irish · 1 would be African

belief systems
(% of population)

65 Roman Catholic · 13 United Church

9.5 Anglican · 8 Other · 3.5 No religion

population per sq km

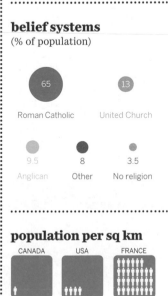

CANADA · USA · FRANCE

� ≈ 4 people

History

Atlantic Canada has always been home to hardy folk whose lives have revolved around the sea. Early Aboriginal people lived on seals and fish, and the first European arrivals could hardly believe their luck when they discovered the plentiful cod stocks. Through the millennia Canadian Aboriginal tribes, the British and the French have all vied for control of the region with the British eventually getting the upper hand, and Canadian Aboriginal people and French-speaking Acadians sticking to the fringes. American Loyalists, including many freed slaves, were taken in after the American Civil War and over time thousands of other immigrants from Europe and around the world have joined the cultural mix. Today, with mine closures and the moratorium on now depleted cod stocks, the region has faced outward migration and economic hard times – yet the natural beauty and quality of life still encourages many to stay put and attracts others.

The First Fishers

First
Nation
Culture
....
Lennox Island,
Price Edward
Island
....
Port au Choix National Historic Site,
Newfoundland
....
Heritage & Cultural
Centre, Bear River,
Nova Scotia
....
First Nation room
at Louisbourg,
Nova Scotia

Atlantic Canada's first inhabitants, the Paleoindians, walked into Labrador 9000 years ago. The harsh, frozen land didn't make life easy or lengthy for these folks. Next came the Maritime Archaic Indians, hunters and gatherers who survived on the sea's bountiful fish-and-seal dinners. They ranged throughout Atlantic Canada, Maine and into parts of Labrador between 7500 and 3500 years ago and are known for their ceremonial burials and other religious and magical practices, evidenced at sites such as Newfoundland's Port au Choix. They mysteriously disappeared around 1000 BC.

The next to tend the land were the Mi'kmaq and Maliseet peoples in the Maritimes and the Beothuk people in Newfoundland – all members of the Algonquin-speaking eastern woodlands tribes. The Mi'kmaq and Maliseet practiced agriculture and lived in fairly permanent settlements. The Beothuk were seminomadic and paddled the area in their birch-bark canoes. It was the Beothuk and their ceremonially ochre-coated faces who were dubbed 'red men' by the arriving Europeans, a name soon applied to all of North America's indigenous groups.

None of these people fared well once Europeans arrived and introduced diseases, land conflict and war to the mix. While the Mi'kmaq

TIMELINE	1000 BC	AD 1000	1492
	After hanging around for a few thousand years eating fish and seals and developing complex ceremonial practices, the Maritime Archaic Indians inexplicably disappear.	Viking Leif Eriksson and crew wash up at L'Anse aux Meadows, create the New World's first European settlements, repair their ships and smelt iron.	Christopher Columbus, under the crown of Spain, stumbles upon the Bahamas and gets credit for 'discovering' America; John Cabot sails five years later and lands on Cape Breton and Newfoundland.

and Maliseet still occupy parts of Atlantic Canada, the last person of Beothuk ethnicity died in 1829, and a unique language and culture was lost forever.

Age of European Discovery

Viking celebrity Leif Eriksson and his tribe of adventurous seafarers from Iceland and Greenland were the first Europeans in North America. Around AD 1000 they poked around the eastern shores of Canada, establishing winter settlements and way stations for repairing ships and restocking supplies, such as at L'Anse aux Meadows in Newfoundland. The local Canadian Aboriginal tribes did not exactly roll out the welcome mat for these intruders, who eventually tired of the hostilities and withdrew.

The action didn't heat up again until after 1492 when Christopher Columbus stumbled upon some small islands in the Bahamas. Other European monarchs, excited by his 'discovery,' quickly sponsored expeditions

HISTORY AGE OF EUROPEAN DISCOVERY

AVAST! PIRATES ON THE HORIZON

Pirates began to ply and plunder Atlantic Canada's waters soon after Europeans arrived to colonize the area.

Peter Easton was one of the region's most famous pirates. He started out as an English naval officer in 1602. But when King James downsized the Royal Navy the next year, stranding Easton and his men in Newfoundland without any money they, perhaps understandably, got pissed off and decided to use the resources at hand (ie boats and a bad attitude) to become pirates. By 1610 Easton was living large in Harbour Grace, commanding a fleet of 40 ships and a crew of 5000 men. The money piled in for several more years, until he eventually retired to France, married a noblewoman and became the Marquis of Savoy.

Black Bart, aka Bartholomew Roberts, was another boatsman who made quite a splash in the local plundering business. He became a pirate after being captured by another, and he took to the lifestyle. Sort of. He liked the booty and the clothing it enabled (crimson waistcoat, scarlet plumed hat, gold necklaces), but he disliked booze and gambling. He also encouraged prayer among his employees. No one mutinied though, because his pirating prowess was legendary. For example, in 1720 he sailed into Newfoundland's Trepassey Bay aboard a 10-gun sloop with a crew of 60 men and they were able to capture 21 merchant ships manned by 1200 sailors.

Halifax put a unique spin on its pirate history when the local government began sponsoring the plunder. The pirates were called privateers, and during the War of 1812 the government sanctioned them to go out and get the goods and then provided them with waterfront warehouses to store it all. You can see where the action took place at the Privateer's Warehouse. The South Shore town of Liverpool commemorates the era by hosting a rollicking Privateer Days festival.

1528
Fishing village of St John's bobs up as North America's first European settlement but belongs to no nation; instead it serves fishing fleets from around the world.

1755
English round up and deport thousands of French Acadians from Bay of Fundy region for not pledging allegiance to the crown. Many move to Louisiana to become known as Cajuns.

EMILY RIDDELL / GETTY IMAGES ©

St John's (p172), Newfoundland

of their own. In 1497 Giovanni Caboto, better known as John Cabot, sailed under a British flag as far west as Newfoundland and Cape Breton. Although there's no evidence of where he first made landfall, the village of Bonavista in eastern Newfoundland usually gets the nod.

Cabot didn't find a passage to China but he did find cod, then a much-coveted commodity in Europe. Soon, hundreds of boats were shuttling between Europe and the fertile new fishing grounds. Several were based at Red Bay in Labrador, which became the world's biggest whaling port during the 16th century.

About this time, French explorer Jacques Cartier also was sniffing around Labrador. He was looking for gold and precious metals, but found only 'stones and horrible rugged rocks,' as he wrote in his journal in 1534. So he moved on to Québec – but not before bestowing Canada with its name. Scholars say it comes from *kanata*, a Huron-Iroquois word for village or settlement, which was written in Cartier's journal and later transformed by mapmakers to Canada.

Settlers Move In

So we've got fish, furs and nice juicy chunks of land – is it any wonder Europe starts salivating?

St John's lays claim to being the oldest town in North America, first settled in 1528. It belonged to no nation; rather it served fishing fleets from all over Europe. By 1583 the British claimed it, and St John's had the distinction of being the first colony of the Empire.

The French weren't just sitting on their butts during this time. In 1604 explorer Samuel de Champlain and his party spent the winter on St Croix Island, a tiny islet in the river on the present international border with Maine. The next year Champlain and his fur-trader patron Sieur de Monts moved their small settlement to Port Royal in the Annapolis Valley, which would soon become an English–French flashpoint.

The French revved up their colonization in 1632 by bringing in a load of immigrants to LaHave on Nova Scotia's south shore. More settlers arrived in 1635, and soon the French had spread throughout the Annapolis Valley and the shores of the Bay of Fundy – a rich farming region they called Acadia.

French & English at War

The French were galling the English, and the English were infuriating the French. Both had claims to the land – hadn't Cabot sailed here first for England? Or was it Cartier for France? – but each wanted regional dominance. They skirmished back and forth in hostilities that

Early European Settler Sites

Highland Village Museum (Scottish), Cape Breton, Nova Scotia

Colony of Avalon Historic Site (British), Ferryland, Newfoundland

Cupids (British), Avalon Peninsula, Newfoundland

Port Royal National Historic Site (French), Annapolis Royal, Nova Scotia

1763	1769	1784	1812
Treaty of Paris boots France out of Canada after France loses the Seven Years' War. France retains St Pierre and Miquelon, however, which remain an overseas French territory to this day.	The colony of Prince Edward Island is created from the larger Nova Scotia and will one day become Canada's smallest province; English is the official language.	New Brunswick is created as a separate province to Nova Scotia in order to appease the huge influx of Loyalists from the USA with the original settlers.	Halifax's local government takes advantage of the War of 1812 by sponsoring 'privateers' to plunder ships then store it all along the city's waterfront.

mirrored those in Europe, where wars raged throughout the first half of the 18th century.

Things came to head in 1713 with the Treaty of Utrecht, which ended Queen Anne's war (1701–13) overseas. Under its provisions the majority of Nova Scotia and Newfoundland went to the British, and Cape Breton Island, Prince Edward Island (PEI) and what is today New Brunswick went to the French. That Acadia was now British was a particularly bitter spoonful for the French; the Brits had even overtaken Port Royal and renamed it Annapolis Royal, after Queen Anne.

The French reorganized and decided to give regional dominance another shot. In 1719 they began construction of a fortress at Louisbourg on Cape Breton Island to protect their interests. Bit by bit the fortified town grew.

The British took note and in 1745 sent out a colonial army from Massachusetts to capture Louisbourg. It fell after a 46-day siege. A treaty a few years later returned it to France.

And so it went, with control of the region ping-ponging, until 1754 when the French and Indian Wars (sometimes called the Seven Years' War) began and ramped up the fighting to a new level.

LOYALIST COLONIES IN THE MARITIMES

Some Acadians returned to Canada but *merde alors*, they hadn't seen the end of English-speaking colonization. Many American colonists who remained loyal to the King of England during the American Revolutionary War fled or were driven out of the USA once the British had been defeated; these families resettled throughout the British Empire, including the Maritime Provinces. Others headed to the British West Indies.

Loyalists were offered free land by the British and their arrival meant a sudden influx of English speakers west and east of Québec. This new division of language and culture divided the country into predominantly British 'Upper Canada' and French 'Lower Canada.' It also led to the division of Nova Scotia into two provinces, modern-day Nova Scotia and New Brunswick.

Meanwhile, many Loyalists from the American south brought their slaves as they were assured by law that their slaves would remain their property. However, there were also freed Black Loyalists who had been granted their freedom by fighting for the British during the Revolution. The government helped these ex-slaves resettle in Canada but they were met far less kindly than their white compatriots.

Ultimately, the influx of Loyalists to Canada helped strengthen ties with Britain and increased antipathy to the United States, which contributed to keeping Canada an independent country in North America.

1840	1864	
Cunard Line shipping company founded in Halifax providing the fastest link to England and boosting the region's economy; immigrants from around Europe and the UK arrive in droves.	Fathers of the Confederation meet in Charlottetown and create the framework for a new country called Canada. The deal is sealed by the *British North America Act* in London three years later.	

Charlottetown (p147), Prince Edward Island

Memo to Acadians: Get Out

The Nova Scotia government maintains a website of all things *Titanic* (http://titanic.gov.ns.ca), including a list of passengers buried in local graveyards and artifacts housed in the local museums.

Charles Lawrence, the security-conscious British governor of Nova Scotia, had had enough. A war was going on and when the French Acadian citizens in his territory refused to swear allegiance to Britain his suspicions mounted to fever pitch. In 1755, he ordered the Acadians to be rounded up and deported.

In a tragic chapter of history known as the Great Expulsion, the British burned villages and forced some 14,000 men, women and children onto ships. (The exact number is unknown.) Grand Pré was the heart of the area from which the Acadians were removed. Many headed for Louisiana and New Orleans; others went to various Maritime points, the Caribbean or back to Europe.

The government gave their lands in the Annapolis Valley to 12,000 New England colonists called 'planters.' After peace was restored, some Acadians chose to return from exile but they were forced to settle on the less favorable 'French Shore' between Yarmouth and Digby.

Ultimately the English won the French and Indian Wars, and the French colonial era in the region ended. At the Treaty of Paris in 1763, France handed Canada over to Britain – except for two small islands off the coast of Newfoundland, named St Pierre and Miquelon, which remain staunchly French to this day.

THE TITANIC'S CORONOR, UNDERTAKER & MOURNER

When *RMS Titanic* sank in April 1912, the rescue and recovery effort started in Halifax, the nearest port city with rail connections. John Snow, owner of JA Snow Funeral Homes, sailed to the disaster site to pull bodies from the ocean, bringing with him 125 coffins, ice, iron, and all the embalming fluid in the city.

Some bodies were buried at sea (the iron ensured the coffins sank) and others were brought back to Snow's funeral home. The building now houses the **Five Fishermen** (1740 Argyle St; ⊙5-9pm Tue-Sat) restaurant; the bodies were stored in today's wine cellar. Snow helped devise a system to match bodies with possessions so they could be identified and returned to their families, or buried with a marked tombstone. Eventually 150 bodies were interred in Halifax, earning the town the grim title of '*Titanic*'s coroner, undertaker and mourner.'

Five years later, the city was struck by another tragedy, known as the Halifax Explosion, when two ships collided in Halifax Harbour. Snow came out of retirement to help Halifax deal with hundreds of bodies, and ensure as many as possible got a proper burial. Snow's Funeral Home still operates out of Halifax (nowadays in the far northwest of town at 339 Lacewood Dr). It unveiled a *Titanic* memorial placard in its front garden in 2012.

By Jon Tattrie, Halifax-based author and journalist

1912
Titanic sinks off the southern coast of Newfoundland and rescue ships are sent from Halifax – most of the recovered bodies are buried in Halifax.

1917
A munitions ship collides with another ship in Halifax Harbour creating the 'Halifax explosion,' the largest man-made explosion before the A-bomb, killing some 1900 people.

ANDREW BAIN / GETTY IMAGES ©

Graves of Titanic victims, Fairview Lawn Cemetery (p45)

A Perfect Union in Prince Edward Island

All through the first half of the 19th century shipbuilding made New Brunswick and Nova Scotia wealthy, and Nova Scotia soon boasted the world's fourth-largest merchant marine. The Cunard Line was founded at Halifax in 1840, and immigration from Scotland and Ireland flourished.

In 1864 Charlottetown on Prince Edward Island served as the birthing room for modern Canada. At the town's Province House, a group of representatives from Nova Scotia, New Brunswick, Prince Edward Island, Ontario and Québec got together and hammered out the framework for a new nation. It took two more meetings – one in Québec City, the other in London – before parliament passed the *British North America Act* in 1867. And so began the modern, self-governing state of Canada. The date the act became official, July 1, is celebrated as Canada's national holiday.

Newfoundland, ever true to its independent spirit, did not join the confederation until 1949.

World Wars

During both world wars Atlantic Canada played a key role as a staging area for the convoys that supplied Britain. The wars also boosted local economies and helped transition the region from an agricultural to an industrial base.

Halifax was the only city in North America to suffer damage during WWI. In December 1917, the *Mont Blanc,* a French munitions ship carrying TNT and highly flammable benzol, collided with the *Imo* in Halifax Harbour. The 'Halifax Explosion' ripped through the city, leveling most of Halifax' north end, injuring 9000 and killing 1900 people.

Newfoundland had the dubious honor of being the only place in North America directly attacked by German forces during WWII. In 1942 just offshore from Bell Island near St John's German U-boats fired on four allied ore carriers sinking them; 69 lives were lost. The Germans fired a torpedo at yet another carrier, but the projectile missed and instead struck inland at Bell Island's loading pier – thus making it the sole spot on the continent to take a straight-on German hit. That same year the Germans also torpedoed a Newfoundland ferry sailing in the Cabot Strait near Port aux Basques; 137 people died.

Loyalist, French & British Holds

Louisbourg (French), Nova Scotia

King's Landing Historical Settlement (Loyalist), Upper St John River Valley, New Brunswick

Quidi Vidi (French & British), Newfoundland

HISTORY A PERFECT UNION IN PRINCE EDWARD ISLAND

1925	**1942**	**1962**	**1969**
Fed up and hungry Cape Breton coal miners stage a 155-day strike and end up with a 7% pay cut. The industry continues to decline from here on.	Bell Island, Newfoundland, torpedoed by German forces and 69 people are killed; this is the only location on the American continent to receive a German hit during WWII.	Trans-Canada Hwy officially opens spanning 7821km from St John's to Victoria, British Columbia, and linking Canada's 13 provinces – it will be completed in 1971.	New Brunswick extends its Equal Opportunity Plan when it passes the *Official Languages Act* making it the only constitutionally bilingual province in Canada.

Modern Times

It wasn't until 1960 that Canada's Aboriginal people were finally granted Canadian citizenship. Even into the late 1960s Aboriginal children were being removed from their families and sent away to residential schools to 'civilize' them; many were abused. Land-rights claims and settlements regarding the schools are still winding their way through Canadian courts, while the damage such policies inflicted continues to haunt the Aboriginal communities.

Meanwhile, in Newfoundland in the 1950s the provincial government also was enforcing a resettlement program. People living in isolated fishing communities (aka outports) were being strongly 'encouraged' to move inland where the government could deliver schools, health care and other services more economically. One method for 'encouraging' villagers was to cut ferry services. Many communities had no road access so this made them inaccessible – people were squeezed out of their ancestral homes in this way.

The later 20th century was particularly harsh to the region's biggest industries: coal mining and fishing. Cape Breton's coal mines started to tank in the 1960s as its product fell out of favor in the marketplace; the mines shut for good in the 1990s. In 1992, the codfishing moratorium was put in place, and many fisherfolk and fish-plant workers – a huge percentage of the population, especially in Newfoundland – lost their livelihoods. The offshore oil and tourism industries have been trying to pick up the slack, but many people are leaving the region to find work elsewhere in Canada.

1992 Cod moratorium imposed and thousands of fisherfolk lose their livelihood. While hoped to be only a temporary measure, the cod stocks do not make a comeback.

2001 Cape Breton's last coal mine shuts down paving the way for outward migration and clean-up of Sydney Tar Ponds, Nova Scotia, North America's largest toxic waste site.

2003 Hurricane Juan hits Halifax passing through central Nova Scotia and Prince Edward Island leaving extensive destruction, eight fatalities and $30 million worth of damage.

2005 Canada legalizes gay marriage throughout the country. Most provinces and territories permitted it anyway, but now hold-out Prince Edward Island has joined the ranks.

Maritimes Music

If Atlantic Canada were a bowl of chowder, music would be the stock in which everything floats. During the winter, fiddle, accordion, piano, vocal harmonies and vivid storytelling keep folks warm and happy; come spring the doors burst open and well-oiled skills are let out in the sunshine. As a visitor you'll run into live performances everywhere, be they called 'ceilidhs' (kay-lees), 'shindigs' or 'kitchen parties;' even if you never gave fiddle music a thought, the festive ambience will make you want to join in, sing along or tap your feet surreptitiously in time.

This region has been mixing cultures since humans have had the technology to cross oceans. It seems that everyone who has come to these shores has brought some sort of instrument, be it a drum, fiddle or bagpipe, along with a bit of rhythm and even more soul. Throughout the centuries music has been a force that has brought these folks from all corners of the globe, and today, everyone from Aboriginal to Scottish and Acadian musicians produce compositions that define the region.

Aboriginal

Aboriginal cultures who populated the Atlantic coast for thousands of years are known to have sung, played music and danced, but details are few. Today, native music has been strongly influenced by the power of the fiddle. The most recent famous Mi'kmaq musician was Lee Cremo (1939–99), whose fiddle-playing talents mixing Mi'kmaq, Scottish and Irish music took him as far as Nashville and Hollywood. It's said that no one played quite like Lee, and he was ranked by many as one of the top 10 fiddle players of his time in North America.

The Mi'kmaq word that most roughly translates into the English word for music is *welta'q*, which literally means 'it sounds good.' This is a wide definition that has come to encompass the poetry of Rita Joe (1932–2007), who is often referred to as the poet laureate of the Mi'kmaq people. Joe's poems are frequently set to music for school performances but even as spoken word are considered to 'sound good' and thus be as agreeable and entertaining as a song. Over her lifetime Joe published seven books of poetry, which can be found online and in bookstores around Nova Scotia.

Your best chance of hearing traditional music is at one of several pow-wows held around the region; for modern aboriginal sounds, head to music festivals that highlight the region's culture, such as Celtic Colours (p236) in Nova Scotia. One of the best acts is the Newfoundland band Tipatshimun, whose lyrics are in the Innu language.

Scottish & Irish

Bagpipes wail mysteriously from a blustery hilltop and a lone fiddler serenades you at lunch. Yes, Scottish music is the dominant influence in the region, particularly in Nova Scotia and Prince Edward Island (PEI). Highland Scots who settled here didn't leave their fiddles at home, and the lively, fun piano-and-fiddle combos were quick to catch on. To this

---

What's On?

Nova Scotia: www. thecoast.ca

Newfoundland: www.thescope.ca

New Brunswick: www.girafecycle. com

Prince Edward Island: www.buz- zon.com

CEILIDHS AND KITCHEN PARTIES

'So what exactly is a ceilidh?' you might ask. Well, in the broadest sense, a ceilidh is a gathering where traditional Gaelic music is played and people can dance – kind of like a rural, family-style disco with an accordion instead of heavy bass. Sometimes it's just a solo fiddle player playing during lunch hours at a restaurant; other times it can be families dressed fully in their clan tartan performing for folks in town halls, or larger, more professional groups playing in front of big audiences. Whatever the size, ceilidhs are always laid-back affairs where the musicians mingle with the audience and hold no airs of being anything more than another local who just happens to play an instrument rather well. There are usually many more locals in the audience than visitors, and everyone goes crazy when, say, Cyril and Betty's seven-year-old son Timmy gets up and step dances – and you'll be into it too because chances are little Timmy is really, really good.

The term 'ceilidh' and 'kitchen party' are often used interchangeably but the latter is a term more likely to be used by Acadians (along with the Acadian French term: *'party de cuisine'*), non-Celtic folks or by anyone on Cape Breton Island in Nova Scotia. A kitchen party is also more likely to actually be at someone's house and to have food and drink, although this is not always the case.

day these folksy sounds define the Atlantic Canadian music scene. Most modern music produced from the music-heavy regions of Cape Breton Island and Halifax still sound quite a bit like the folk music of old, blending the fiddle with some electric guitar but still little percussion. Popular Cape Breton musicians include fiddlers Ashley MacIsaac, Buddy Mac-Master and Natalie MacMaster, and multi-instrumentalist JP Cormier. Banjo-strumming Old Man Luedecke, hailing from Chester, puts on an incredible show and is often touring around the region in summer.

Bagpipes might not often be found in popular music but you will hear them in the area – a lot. Between the College of Piping and Celtic Arts in PEI and the Gaelic College of Celtic Arts and Crafts on Cape Breton, bagpipers are pumped out by the dozen to play at historical sites, busk along the streets of cities and create a mysterious air in some of the most out-of-the-way places, taking you away to the Scottish Highlands.

Up Newfoundland and Labrador way expect to hear more Irish-tinged tunes that move at a faster pace and generally tell a story, with the dialogue dominating the accompaniment – if you've ever listened to the Pogues, you know what we're talking about. This music generally emanates from Irish pubs where accents start to lilt as more beer is consumed. Singer-songwriter Ron Hynes embodies the local style and can be found strumming his guitar in St John's pubs, as does the talented folk group, the Once; the Navigators play driving Celtic tunes; the Novaks evoke Tom Petty with the whoop-ass amped up; Repartee do an excellent job of representing synth pop; and Hey Rosetta are getting uber-popular via their energetic folk rock sounds. But the band that most successfully translates this music to a larger stage is Great Big Sea. They tour throughout the United States and Canada, filling mighty venues with their Celtified rave-ups and kitchen-party enthusiasm. They are a definite must-see.

CHOIR

Men of the Deeps, a choral group of retired coal miners in Nova Scotia, can be found playing around the province and invariably pull a crowd.

Acadian

The Acadians are scattered in small groups throughout Atlantic Canada and were often very remote and isolated before the modern advent of roads; Acadian music has therefore evolved in many different directions. Scottish influences are very apparent in areas such as Cape Breton, and, as you move up the Cabot Trail from Mabou's Scottish fiddling to Chéticamp's Acadian kitchen parties, you'll be struck by how similar the sounds are. Generally, Acadian music is a little more soulful than Scottish music, with more percussion from tricky hand-clapping, foot-tapping and the spoons. The lyrics, of course, are in French.

In southwestern Nova Scotia the local music is far more influenced by rock, bluegrass and country, as well as Cajun styles introduced by descendants of those caught up in the Great Expulsion. The most popular Acadian band today, Blou, is from this region, and they call their sound 'Acadico' – a mix of Acadian, Cajun and Zydeco (an American Creole folk music). The group's accordion-based rock tunes regularly win the East Coast Music Award title for Best Francophone recording of the year. Meanwhile, from the same region, Jacobus et Maleco, which eventually became Radio Radio, was the first Acadian rap group, and internationally renowned Grand Dérangement sings movingly of Acadian reality through its traditional tunes.

Many Acadian groups head to Montréal where there's a much stronger Francophone music scene and it's easier to get recognized. New Brunswick Acadian groups are often very influenced by the traditional Québecois poetic style. Acts from Atlantic Canada that have made names for themselves include Marie-Jo Thério (soothing and lyrical from New Brunswick), Suroît (Cajun and fiddle from the Magdalen Islands), Borlico and Barachois (lively kitchen-party–style duo from PEI), and Felix and Formanger (an accordion-and-guitar group from Newfoundland).

African Influences

Just when you were getting tired of the fiddle, in come more cultures. Many Black Canadians arrived as freed slaves and Loyalists to the British Crown during the American War of Independence. Social inequalities and marginalization (Nova Scotia's racism earned it the moniker 'Mississippi of the North') stopped the black community from making a huge mark in the Maritime music scene in the past, but nowadays it's adding a lot of spice to the region's music scene. The influence had been largely gospel music, but today hip-hop, jazz, blues, R&B, pop and classical music are all holding some cultural sway.

Portia White from Truro, Nova Scotia, was one of the first African-Canadians to make it big in the region when she won a silver cup at the

FOLK & TRADITIONAL PLAYLIST

This playlist will get you in the mood for highland hills, long stretches of Atlantic coastline and perhaps a stop for some step-dancing on the way. These old and new favorites are a little bit folk and a little bit country.

→ *Guysborough Train*, Stan Rogers

→ *The Silver Spear*, Natalie MacMaster

→ *These Roads*, David Gunning

→ *Rant and Roar*, Great Big Sea

→ *Home I'll Be*, Rita MacNeil

→ *Walk With Me*, Pogey

→ *My Nova Scotia Home*, Hank Snow

→ *Wrong Side of the Country*, Old Man Luedecke

→ *Maritime Express*, Eddie LeGere

→ *Maple Sugar*, Don Messer

→ *Snow Bird*, Anne Murray

→ *Sail Away to the Sea*, The Once

PARTYING AT THE PUB

Pubs are by far the best way to experience local music and, fortunately, finding a good one is about as easy as finding a public restroom. With Halifax and St John's vying for the title of most pubs per capita, you'll actually have a harder time finding a nightspot that's not hosting a live gig. The following is a list of our favorites:

➡ **Rare Bird Pub** (p99), Guysborough, Nova Scotia; folk and fiddle

➡ **Red Shoe Pub** (p88), Mabou, Cape Breton, Nova Scotia; folk and fiddle

➡ **Seahorse Tavern** (p53), Halifax, Nova Scotia; indie, punk and metal

➡ **Benevolent Irish Society** (p153), Charlottetown, PEI; Irish

➡ **O'Leary's** (p128), Saint John, New Brunswick; open-mic nights

➡ **Old Cosmo** (700 Main St), Moncton, New Brunswick; punk and rock

➡ **Ship Pub** (p181), St John's, Newfoundland; anything and everything

➡ **Rock House** (p181), St John's, Newfoundland; indie

Nova Scotia Music Festival in 1928 at the age of 17. She went on to become a powerful and well-known contralto classical vocalist and stage presence through the early '40s. In more recent years, Nova Scotian R&B musician Gary Beals placed second in the first season of *Canadian Idol,* and Faith Nolan, a mixed-heritage African, Mik'maq and Irish jazz singer, songwriter and guitarist, has made music with powerful political statements.

Top Festivals

Beyond pubs and concerts, Canada's Atlantic provinces swell with music festivals, especially during the summer. The following are the most renowned:

➡ **Evolve** (p86) Voted best festival in Canada by the listeners of CBC Radio 3 in 2010, this three-day music and awareness festival showcases everything from grassroots music to modern, big-name performers in styles from folk to hip-hop.

➡ **Stan Rogers Folk Festival** (p100) Camp out in remote Canso for three days of live music from fine bluegrass and folk songwriters and performers.

➡ **Celtic Colours International Festival** (www.celtic-colours.com; Cape Breton, Nova Scotia) Watch the trees turn color in several Cape Breton locations while enjoying nine days of Celtic music from around the world.

➡ **Cavendish Beach Music Festival** (www.cavendishbeachmusic.com; Cavendish, PEI) Big names such as Taylor Swift make it to this five-day camp-out, which features a big stage and an audience that pours in from all around Canada and the USA.

➡ **Deep Roots** (www.deeproots.ca; Wolfville, Nova Scotia) Folk and roots music is highlighted at this weekend festival, which also includes music workshops.

➡ **Indian River Festival** (www.indianriverfestival.com; Indian River, New Brunswick) Classical, folk, jazz and world music resonate through the acoustically blessed St Mary's Church.

➡ **Festival 500** (p177) Choirs and beatboxers fill St John's with sound every other year.

➡ **Sound Symposium** (p177) Amazing diversity from jazz, world music and classical musicians; nine days and nights of artistic jamming.

Atlantic Canadian Art

Canada's Atlantic provinces attract artists like kids to cupcakes. That ever-present sea, blend of blues and greens on the horizon, bucolic quiet and low cost of living makes the region a prime place to swipe oil paints on canvas or whittle an old log into something breathtaking. Native Canadians have been taking nature's bounty from porcupine quills to ash wood, and crafting them into beautiful daily objects for thousands of years, but today life is a little easier and most of what's produced by artisans is for art's sake.

The Art Gallery of Nova Scotia has the largest collections with state of the art galleries in both Halifax and Yarmouth. Here you'll find the stars: Alex Colville, Maud Lewis, Arthur Lismer and many more, as well as temporary shows of up and comers and renowned artists 'from away.' But there's an incredible richness to be discovered outside the museum as well. Drive around Cape Breton and it seems that every town has a shop selling arts and crafts, be that outrageous hats, forged iron sculptures, pottery or paintings hanging randomly from trees in a forest. Other regions may not be so thickly dotted with artisans but wherever you go, you'll find a plentiful array of creative folk creating beautiful works. Drive slowly, ask about local artisans at visitor's centres and browse small town galleries and craft shops. If you're looking to buy something special you'll be spoiled for choices.

Art Trails & Resources

www.halifaxart-map.com

www.capebreton-craft.com

www.artsandherit-agepei.com

Aboriginal

Many of Canada's most ancient artistic artifacts hail from the eastern subarctic areas of the country including the Atlantic provinces. The tribes that lived here were nomadic and crafted elaborate head dresses with feathers, sewed patterns of beads and porcupine quills on to

MAUD LEWIS

By far the most well-known and beloved folk artist in Nova Scotia is Maud Lewis. Lewis, born in 1903, was uncommonly small, had almost no chin and suffered from juvenile rheumatoid arthritis. She spent much of her childhood alone and she never traveled beyond Yarmouth and Digby counties. After being left with no money once her parents died in the 1930s, she married Everett Lewis and the couple spent the rest of their lives in a roughly 12ft by 12ft house. But what a house it was! Lewis painted every surface with colorful, happy scenes of the life and community around her, making what many would have considered a place of poverty into a beautiful piece of beguiling art. In 1984, 14 years after Lewis passed away, the house was bought by the province of Nova Scotia as a landmark; it was restored in 1996. Since 2008 the entire house can be seen in the heart-wrenching Maud Lewis Room at the Art Gallery of Nova Scotia. Bring a hanky.

But Maud's artistic endeavors didn't end with her house. She began her career making Christmas cards as a child and as an adult she was an incredibly prolific painter. The small, often 8in by 10in paintings she sold out of her house back in the 1950s for $2 are now sold at auction for up to $22,000. Lewis, who never sold a painting for more than $10, would have hardly believed it.

clothing and wove patterns into their basketware. Art was something that beautified practical objects or for religious purposes. You'll find displays full of these works of refined design at museums large and small throughout the region.

It's been argued that art for art's sake wasn't a concept in native culture until the 20th century. But even then, stereotypes of what aboriginal art should look like (prehistoric) made it difficult for modern-day artists to have their works seen, appreciated or sold. Norval Morrisseau, an Ojibwa from Ontario, has been called the 'Grandfather of Canadian Native Art' for his paintings that capture Ojibwa cultural and spiritual images in a striking, colorful and modern style – his work is simply stunning. Morrisseau and several other artists began to capture the art world from the late 1960s through the 1970s, paving the way for the future.

Today, Native Canadian art is an incredibly rich terrain and in the Eastern provinces inspiration is drawn mostly from Mi'kmaq and Maliseet cultures. Some stand-outs in this region include Ned Bear who carves Pawakan (spirit guide) wooden masks. Recently, Bear has taken to carving living trees throughout New Brunswick – the places aren't advertised but are set up for accidental discovery. Alan Syliboy is one of the better known artists in the region and paints scenes from Mi'kmaq mythology with a striking modern style; prints and note cards of David Brook's stylized animal paintings are found in many native shops; Dozay Christmas specializes in dreamlike paintings of ghostly animal or people in mono-colored natural settings; Ursula Johnson takes traditional basketry to new realms including nonfunctional colorful pieces and incorporating techniques into performance art pieces; high-realism of the natural world is painted by Nova Scotian Leonard Paul; and in Newfoundland Jerry Evans specializes in detailed lithographs.

Big Art Museums

Art Gallery of Nova Scotia, Halifax, Nova Scotia

Art Gallery of Nova Scotia, Yarmouth, Nova Scotia

The Rooms Provincial Art Gallery, St John's, Newfoundland

Beaverbrook Art Gallery, Fredericton, New Brunswick

Confederation Centre of the Arts, PEI

Folk Art

Back when roads were few and budgets were lean, many Canadians in these provinces had limited to no opportunities to visit art museums or learn about art beyond their local sphere. Folk art is the embodiment of what happens when artistic people create works without any influence from the outside world. Today the movement continues with its charming mix of simplicity and sophistication with avant-garde and tradition.

Painters include Joe Norris who depicted classic Maritime scenes of nesting ducks to sailboats in a simple colorful way and Joseph Sleep who uses everything from cardboard to felt tip markers to create, child-like tableaus of animals and plants. The most famous painter of course was Maud Lewis (see the boxed text, p237).

And folk art goes far beyond paint on paper. Well-known wood artists include Ralph Boutilier, known for his lifelike human-sized wood carvings and mechanical wooden birds; Sidney Howard who made more rustic sculptures of polychrome wood of people, fish, birds and animals; Bradford Naugler who has carved life-sized wood sculptures of the Ten Fathers of the Confederation, the Obama family and British royals William and Kate among others; and Collins Eisenhauer who is considered the master of appealing, stylized poultry sculptures.

Marine Inspired Art

Nearly any artist who has spent time in these provinces could be slotted into this category for at least some of their work. And really, how can you paint, sculpt or get creative here without getting inspiration from the surrounding sea that provides jobs, food, briny smells and a never-ending calming swish that rocks your ears to sleep?

Halifax native John O'Brien (1831–91) was one of the best known artists of the region in his generation; he painted detailed, realistic seascapes that have greatly helped historians studying maritime history. Next came Edith Smith, who held the position of Arts Mistress at Halifax Ladies College for nearly 40 years; she was influential in many artists' education, the shaping of the first collections for the Art Gallery of Nova Scotia (AGNS), and most importantly for her masterful realist seascape, landscape and portrait paintings. One of the artists Edith Smith chose for the AGNS collections was Arthur Lismer, another Haligonian who first made his name painting WWI camouflaged naval ships in the harbor; he also sketched the Halifax Explosion of 1917. A few years later Lismer became a part of the 'Group of Seven,' a collaboration of the seven most revered nature artists at that time in Canada who were (contentiously) promoted as Canada's national school of painters.

Other marine artists include HM Rosenberg, who was the principal at the Victoria School of Art and Design (now known as NSCAD University) in Halifax from 1898 to 1910. Rosenberg took a mix of European styles from Gauguin to Sargent to create his own realistic yet stylized approach that's universally appealing. Many of his works can be seen today in the permanent collection at the AGNS.

The Maritime Museum of the Atlantic's art collection focuses on ship-related marine works, but the AGNS has a substantial collection as well.

LOCAL INSIGHTS

How has Atlantic Canada's rich educational terrain influenced the region's art?
Atlantic Realism is perhaps most often associated with Mount Allison University in Sackville, New Brunswick. In fact, the University's School of Fine and Applied Arts was the first to grant a Bachelor's degree of this kind in Canada.

Halifax was home to the country's first art school. In 1887 The Victoria School or Art and Design was founded by Anna Leonowens, then renamed the Nova Scotia College of Art and Design (NSCAD) in 1925 and, over the course of its 125 years, has produced some of the country's brightest artists. From members of the Group of Seven, such as Arthur Lismer, to members of the International art scene, like Gerhard Richter, Nova Scotia and NSCAD have provided a perch from which to fly.

What unique challenges or benefits are artists in this region faced with?
The unique quality of the light here, coupled with the breathtaking and rugged scenery, has long lured artists. Many are drawn to opportunities and rigor that exist in its intellectual centre and the space afforded them in its open spaces. The monetary opportunities are fewer, with smaller cities and longer distances between them. The creative economy, however, is alive and well: galleries and multifaceted businesses that support artists are becoming more in number and more resourceful in how they show artists' work.

What are the best ways to find smaller galleries?
A drive around the provinces will allow you ample opportunities to encounter the rich artistic output. In Nova Scotia, for example, explore from the galleries of Mahone Bay, Lunenberg and Chester, to the artist-run centres of the Annapolis Valley to Antigonish, and Cape Breton is an art-lover's wonderland. The Cape Breton Centre for Craft and Design in Sydney offers a wide range of local artists' work, specializing in craft. It also houses handsome and expansive studios. University galleries across the region house contemporary art exhibitions that showcase work from far and near. Fairs, flea markets and even a walk through the towns will offer a glimpse of artists' handiwork.

Interview with Sarah Fillmore,
Chief Curator of the Art Gallery of Nova Scotia and curator of the Sobey Art Award.

FESTIVALS

Nova Scotia Folk Art Festival (www.nsfolkartfestival.com; Lunenburg; ⊙ early Aug) The festival kicks off with a buffet dinner ($20), commemorative video and a chance to meet the artists. The sale is the following day (entry $5) with an auction and door prize.

Studio Rally (www.studiorally.ca; Nova Scotia; ⊙ early Oct) For more than 20 years, artists all over Nova Scotia have opened their doors to all visitors on this special weekend.

Victoria Park Lantern Festival (http://lanternfest.ca; St John's, Newfoundland; ⊙ last weekend of Jul) A very popular festival where everyone makes lanterns in public workshops. The lanterns are then lit in a public ceremony alongside music, dance and theatrical performances.

Realism

The 20th century was dominated by the realists.

Alex Colville, who's family moved to Amherst, Nova Scotia, from Toronto when he was nine years old, is Atlantic Canada's most famous artist. While Colville is known as a realist, many of his works are reminiscent of the American Precisionist movement of the 1930s and he was greatly influenced by the American realist Edward Hopper. There's a dreamy aspect to Colville's work that make the seemingly innocuous Canadian scenes he painted a shade darker, then they become more enigmatic the longer you examine them. Colville passed away peacefully at the age of 92 in 2013 in Wolfville, Nova Scotia.

Power artist couple (although no longer married) Christopher and Mary Pratt met at Mount Allison University in Sackville, where they both studied under and were influenced by Alex Colville. While Christopher's stark, streamlined landscape pieces are nearly photographic in quality, Mary uses color and design more boldly in her still life, portrait and domestic scenes. Both of the Pratts currently live in Newfoundland and Christopher runs a gallery featuring his works as well as other artists in Bay Roberts.

Another student of Colville's, Tom Forrestall has been called a Magic Realist, a moniker given to many East Coast Canadian artists post-WWII. Forrestall's works are very Maritime in theme (think crab traps on wood docks and ice fields).

Newfoundland painter David Blackwood takes the magic a little farther with star-lit dark images of ghostly people or stormy sea vistas from the shore. In 2003 he was named Honorary Chairman of the Art Gallery of Ontario, although he still maintains a studio in Wesleyville, Newfoundland.

Small-town Artisan Hot Spots

St Ann's Bay, Nova Scotia

Lunenburg, Nova Scotia

St Andrews By-The-Sea, New Brunswick

Fogo Island, Newfoundland

Twillingate Island, Newfoundland

Food & Drink

Until recently, this corner of Canada was noted solely for its seafood rather than the rest of the plentiful bounty on offer. This is changing, particularly in Prince Edward Island (PEI), where Charlottetown's Holland College is churning out more renowned chefs by the year, many interested in making the most of the region's bounty. Even so, for the most part Atlantic Canada's food and drink remains plain and simple; inventive Canadian and international chefs tend to congregate in cities, only occasionally cropping up in remote outposts. A quintessential Atlantic Canadian meal is fish or shellfish, fried or boiled, with a vegie thrown in for good measure, and perhaps a bowl of chowder. Odd local specialties liven up many menus; don't be shy to give them a try.

Bounty from the Sea

The sea defines Atlantic Canada, so it's no surprise that seafood defines the local cuisine.

Cod gets battered and fried and brought to your table as fish and chips; it's the one dish you can trust to be on every menu. The batter itself varies from a rough cornmeal coating to a big, puffy, crispy on the outside and soft on the inside beer batter. Atlantic salmon, cousin of the hotter-known Pacific salmon, usually arrives broiled and sauced, perhaps with dill or hollandaise. 'Nova' is lightly smoked salmon (akin to lox), for which Nova Scotia is deservedly famous.

Nova Scotia, New Brunswick and PEI boil more lobster than you can shake a pat of butter at. Crikey, even McDonald's is in on the action serving a McLobster sandwich at its regional outlets. One of the best places to get down and dirty with the crustacean is at a community-hall lobster supper. Don't eat too much; you'll need to leave room for the bulging fruit pie that'll come your way afterward.

Nova Scotia visitors should also save their appetites for Digby scallops. Those touring PEI will find succulent oysters that grow around the island's shore and have a different flavor depending on when and where they're harvested. Mussels are everywhere although PEI is most famous for them and up Cape Breton and Newfoundland way, look out for sweet and seasonal snow crab. Clams are another great bounty and come primarily from several beaches along Nova Scotia's east coast and Point Prim on PEI. Locals lead clamming trips where you can dig your own mollusks then help prepare them before eating to your heart's content.

The sea doesn't limit itself to meat either – the Maritime provinces harvest seaweeds that are eaten or used for their medicinal properties. Stop by Roland's Sea Vegetables (p124) on Grand Manan Island, New Brunswick, for a bag of dulse to eat as is or to sprinkle on fish; Seaweed Cafe (p168), on the west coast of PEI, for a slice of seaweed pie that's thickened with local carrageen; or to Point Prim, PEI, for Seaweed Secrets (p154), where you collect, learn about and eat the region's vegetables from the sea.

Signature Sea Critters

Mussels, PEI

Digby scallops, Nova Scotia

Malpeque oysters, PEI

Snow crab, everywhere but particularly Newfoundland and Labrador

Lobster, everywhere

DO-IT-YOURSELF SEAFOOD CHOWDER

You've sipped and slurped chowder throughout the region and now you want to do it yourself. The ingredients below await your cooking pot.

Ingredients

➡ 500mL lobster meat

➡ 250mL water

➡ 500g fish fillets

➡ 125mL chopped onions

➡ 50mL butter or margarine

➡ 25mL all-purpose (plain) flour

➡ 1L peeled and diced potatoes

➡ 500g scallops

➡ 1L cream

➡ 750g milk

➡ 5mL salt

➡ pinch of white cayenne pepper

➡ 500g mussels or clams, steamed and shucked.

Method

If frozen, thaw lobster and reserve the water. Remove any bits of shell or cartilage and cut into bite-size pieces. Debone fish fillets and cut into 2.5cm pieces. Set aside.

In a heavy saucepan, sauté onions in butter until tender. Stir in flour and cook for one minute. Add potatoes and enough water to cover, bring to a boil and cook until tender. Add fish and scallops, and simmer for five minutes, stirring once or twice. Add cream, milk, lobster, lobster juice, mussels and seasonings. Heat gently and serve.

Makes 12 servings.

Recipe from Taste of Nova Scotia © 2006 www.tasteofnovascotia.ns.ca

Earthly Delights

Top Foodie Spots

Fleur de Sel,
Lunenburg, Nova
Scotia

Le Caveau, Grand
Pré, Nova Scotia

Lot 30,
Charlottetown, PEI

Chinched,
St John's,
Newfoundland

Rossmount
Inn, St Andrews
By-the-Sea, New
Brunswick

Eastern Canada gets much less fame for its land-based food than for its seafood, but that doesn't mean it can't cook up some tasty non-fish-based dishes. French Acadians in particular have invented several specialties throughout the centuries. In Acadian towns you might see menu items such as rappiepie (also known as *la rapure*), a potato and salted-pork dish. *Tourtière* is a meat pie. *Poutine râpée* is a mixture of grated raw and mashed potatoes wrapped around fresh pork. *Fricot* is a hearty soup or stew.

Newfoundland and Labrador may be boggy, rocky and cruddy for growing most things, but berries flourish here. Thus blueberries, partridgeberries (similar to cranberries) and bakeapples get shoveled into muffins, pies and jams. The best time of year for the harvest is mid-August. PEI rivals Idaho for being the potato capital of North America and it's said the island's tubers have a unique flavor due to the rich, red soil. The Potato Museum (p168) in O'Leary shows off all the things you can do with these hearty treats and you can usually taste samples of tasty potato-based fudge. The Annapolis Valley of Nova Scotia is known for its apples and throws a huge Apple Blossom Festival through the production areas in early June every year. Everywhere in the region you'll find roadside stalls selling strawberries July through August.

Each province also produces its own beef and poultry, and you'll find these very good quality products on menus of better restaurants that promote locally sourced ingredients. Keep an eye out for Cows ice cream, which is produced locally in PEI and is one of the region's best known frozen treats.

Bottoms Up!

Moosehead is the region's best known beer, brewed in Saint John, New Brunswick. In Newfoundland, Quidi Vidi (p175) microbrews flow through the provincial taps; try Eric the Red. Beer lovers will also enjoy Alexander Keith's crisp beer from the eponymous, good-time brewery (p45) in Halifax, but more discerning tastes may prefer the craftier Garrison Brewery (p53) which makes a number of brews including some interesting seasonal flavors such as Sugar Moon Maple. Up and coming craft breweries in Nova Scotia include **Cape Breton's Big Spruce** (www.bigspruce.ca; 64 Yankee Line Rd, Nyanza, near Baddeck, Nova Scotia), which brews an organic and aptly named 'Kitchen Party Pale Ale,' and the **Authentic Seacoast Brewing company** (www.rarebirdpub.com/brewery/; Guysborough, Nova Scotia), which makes a dark and rick coffee stout from beans they roast themselves.

Boutique wineries are also uncorking their bottles in Nova Scotia, mostly in the Annapolis Valley, Bear River area and on the Malagash Peninsula. Domaine de Grand Pré (p76), Blomidon Estate Winery (p76) and Jost Vineyards (p83) are the biggest, and these are the wines that you'll find in many fine restaurants in Nova Scotia and occasionally beyond. Newer wineries to sample include **Benjamin Bridge** (www.benjaminbridge.com), which makes a delicious, crowd-pleasing lightly sparkling white called Nova 7 (do yourself a favor and try some), and Luckett Vineyards (p76), which makes good red, whites and fruit wines – both of these are in the Gaspereaux Valley near Wolfville. **Rossignol Winery** (902-962-4193; Rte 4; 10am-5pm Mon-Sat, 1-5pm Sun) on PEI specializes in delicious and well-respected fruit wines but has begun to focus more on regular wines as well. New on the scene in PEI, Newman Estate (p154) is getting rave reviews for its medium-bodied fruity reds.

The Glenora Distillery (p88) on Cape Breton Island produces a very sip-worthy single-malt whiskey, and a group in Guysborough, Nova Scotia, has plans to open an even bigger distillery on its shores. **Prince Edward Distillery** (902-687-2586; www.princeedwarddistillery.com; Rte 16, Hermanville; 11am-6pm) makes award-winning spirits from, you guessed it, potatoes, as well as a few grain-based beverages. Just around the corner, Myriad View (p155) cooks up a tonsil-searing 'Lightning Shine' that's 75% alcohol and the only legal moonshine in Canada. Newfoundland is famous for its Screech, a brand of rum that's actually made in Jamaica.

A signature Canadian drink worth trying is the Ceasar, a Bloody Mary-ish cocktail made with Clamato (a tomato and clam juice–based beverage), vodka, hot sauce and Worcestershire sauce. It's a good Sunday

Farmers Market Forages

Halifax Seaport Farmers Market, Nova Scotia

Dieppe Market, Moncton, New Brunswick

Boyce Farmers Market, Fredericton, New Brunswick

Old City Market, Saint John, New Brunswick

Charlottetown Farmers Market, Charlottetown, PEI

Bidgood's, Goulds, Newfoundland

WINE FESTIVALS

Nova Scotia Fall Wine Festival (mid-Sep to mid-Oct) Celebrates the grape harvest province-wide with tastings, grape stomping, chef events and food pairings.

New Festival of Wines (www.peiwinefest.com; PEI; late May) The province's largest wine event with two evenings of tastings from vinyards around the world.

Icewine Festival (Nova Scotia; Feb) Ten days of sampling icewines and food pairings at different venues around Halifax.

LOBSTER SUPPERS

You don't need to change out of your jeans or get the kids a babysitter to gorge yourself on the Maritime province's most delicious shellfish. The classic Nova Scotia, New Brunswick and Prince Edward Island (PEI) dining experience is a no-frills lobster supper, held in dining halls, churches and community centers. The lobster is generally unadorned of sauces and fanfare; the suppers are a place to enjoy these critters in the buff (or perhaps with a little melted butter), for their own divine flavors and texture. Kids are not only welcome, they are well-catered for, with half-sized suppers and other menu options such as beef or scallops. Just to make sure no one goes hungry, there is a slew of accompaniments from chowder and mussels to potato salad and oven-fresh rolls. Held daily for dinner from roughly mid-June to mid-October, the most suppers per capita are found on PEI. The cost of dinner depends on the market price of lobster but generally hovers around $31 for an all-inclusive meal with a 1lb crustacean.

morning hair-of-the-dog drink, imbibed on ice in a salt-rimmed glass and garnished with lime and a stalk of celery.

You can get quality coffee, including espresso and cappuccino, in cities. Barring that, the ubiquitous Tim Hortons doughnut shops brew a respectable cup.

Celebrations

Food and drink are a big part of celebrating in Atlantic Canada. Summer's seafood festivals, autumn is Thanksgiving, winter has Christmas get-togethers, and spring's Easter holidays traditionally feature generous family feasts with plenty of meat dishes, salad bowls, giant desserts, beer and wine. A hearty, family-focused Sunday dinner is also a common event.

Several towns throughout the region showcase their special cuisines with annual festivals, including the following:

➜ **Lobster Carnival** (p84) Pictou, Nova Scotia; early July.

➜ **Tyne Valley Oyster Festival** (www.tynevalleyoysterfestival.ca) Tyne Valley, PEI; early August.

➜ **Digby Scallop Days** (www.digbyscallopdays.com) Digby, Nova Scotia; mid-August.

➜ **Fall Flavours** (p150) Charlottetown, PEI; September.

➜ **Roots, Rants & Roars** (www.rootsrantsandroars.ca) Elliston, Newfoundland; September

Where to Eat & Drink

Even the smallest town usually has a midpriced restaurant. In places where this is not the case, your lodging host will likely serve food; for instance, many B&Bs serve meals beyond breakfast for a price and if you prearrange it. Atlantic Canada doesn't feature many fine-dining establishments outside of cities and college towns, but a few do turn up in unexpected, out-of-the-way places. A pub is often the cheapest place to get a good meal.

While there are many variations, most restaurants open for lunch (usually between 11:30am and 2:30pm) and dinner from 5:30pm (some fancy establishments only open for dinner). Midrange and family restaurants often stay open all day. In small towns and rural areas many restaurants close at 8pm but times vary and often depend on how busy the restaurant is that day.

Tipping

Tip around 15% (pretax) in restaurants and bars with good table service but don't tip the full 15% unless the service has been worth it. Also check that a gratuity hasn't been automatically added to your bill – a growing practice.

Budget eateries include takeouts, cafes, markets and basic restaurants where you can fill up for less than $15. At midrange establishments you get full menus, beer and wine lists, and a bill that shouldn't exceed $25 per person for an appetizer, main course and one drink, not including tax and tip. Top-end places are typically gourmet affairs with fussy service and freshly prepared and creative food. At these establishments, main courses alone can cost $25 or more.

Quick Eats

In addition to farmers markets in cities, roadside stands offer enticing seasonal produce in rural areas. Do yourself a favor and pick up a container of strawberries (best in June) or blueberries (August).

The food truck movement is catching on in Halifax. The most popular at the time of research were Food Wolf (internationally inspired comfort food) which tends to linger around the North End, and Nomad Gourmet (burgers, burritos and waffle sandwiches), which is nomadic as you'd guess but announces its whereabouts on its website www.nomadgourmet.com.

Outside the cities, you might come across the occasional roadside van selling fish and chips, and lots of seafood markets serve inexpensive lobster rolls, sandwiches and chowder. *Poutine* (French fries topped with gravy and cheese) isn't as prevalent here as in some other areas of Canada but it is on a few menus. Barring that, well, there's always Tim Hortons.

Vegetarians & Vegans

Vegetarians will be well catered for in the region's principal cities such as Halifax, Fredericton and St John's, but as you move away from urban areas your options become extremely limited. Vegans can expect an even rougher ride. Strict adherents should stick to any vegetarian-only eateries they come across, since 'vegetarian' items in mainstream restaurants may well have been prepared with meat stock or lard. We have marked restaurants that cater particularly well to vegetarians with a vegetarian icon (🖋).

Specialty health food shops are found almost exclusively in the larger cities or hip college towns so you'll want to stock up on supplies before going to more remote regions. Chinese eateries occasionally pop up in remote areas and may be another option. Many fine restaurants (some that pop up in very unexpected rural locations) will nearly always cater to dietary restrictions, as will many B&Bs.

Regional Specialties

Bakeapple, Newfoundland

Fiddleheads, New Brunswick

Oat Cakes, Cape Breton, Nova Scotia

Solomon Gundy, Southshore, Nova Scotia

Dulce, Grand Manan Island, New Brunswick

Éclairs, St-Pierre & Miquelon, Newfoundland

Cod Tongues, Newfoundland

WORTH THE TRIP RESTAURANTS

Some of the best restaurants in these provinces are located in out-of-the-way villages or bucolic areas that make you combine your meal with a road trip. Locals as well as visitors don't seem to find this a hardship, though, as many of these eateries have been open for years and manage to stay full throughout summer (most shut in winter). Our favorites include the following:

➜ **Chanterelle Country Inn** (p94), St Ann's Loop, Nova Scotia

➜ **Bonavista Social Club** (p191), Bonavista, Newfoundland

➜ **Inn at Bay Fortune** (p156), Bay Fortune, PEI

➜ **Shipwright's Cafe** (p165), Margate, PEI

➜ **Wild Caraway** (📞902-392-2889; www.wildcaraway.com; 3721 Hwy 209; lunch mains $6-15, dinner mains $18-24; ⏰11am-8pm Thu-Mon; 📶), Advocate Harbour, Nova Scotia

➜ **Charlotte Lane** (p66), Shelburne, Nova Scotia

TRAVEL YOUR TASTEBUDS

Head-scratching foods you may encounter in Nova Scotia and Prince Edward Island include Solomon Gundy (a pickled-herring and chopped-meat combo) and Lunenburg pudding (pork and spices cooked in the intestines of a pig). Dulce is an edible seaweed; New Brunswick's Grand Manan Island is famous for it. Fiddleheads are a fern's first shoots that are served like vegetables in the region. Figgy duff (a sweet pudding with raisins and molasses) and jig's dinner (meat and vegetables boiled together and eaten with pickles, gravy and figgy duff) are just a few of Newfoundland's colorfully named dishes.

Habits & Customs

Atlantic Canadians follow the tradition of eating morning breakfast, midday lunch and early-evening dinner. Expect the generally high standards of North American restaurant and bar service to apply throughout the region. Table service is common at most pubs, although you can still order at the bar as well. Don't forget to give a tip to your table server, and consider dropping some change in the bar-server's pot if you stick around for a few beers.

All of the Atlantic provinces have adopted widespread smoking bans. Nova Scotia's law is the toughest in the nation, prohibiting smoking at outdoor eating and drinking establishments in addition to all indoor public areas.

Landscape & Wildlife

From unexplored wilderness to dramatic coastlines and phenomenal wildlife, the provinces of Atlantic Canada are a nature-lover's dream. It's a place where you are as likely to see thousands of seabirds resting on a passing iceberg as a moose crossing the road, and, if you're lucky, you may spot feeding blue whales or a wandering polar bear (in Labrador or Newfoundland). This rich and varied landscape is easily explored courtesy of the region's many parks, ranging from the alluring sandy beaches of Prince Edward Island National Park to the soaring fjords of Gros Morne National Park in Newfoundland.

A Geologist's Dream

The spectacular landscapes of Atlantic Canada are both their charm and their challenge. Due to the rugged land and crumpled coastlines, the traditions of isolated villages and homesteads have been preserved to a greater extent than perhaps anywhere else in North America, but the difficulty of coaxing crops from the rocky soil or transporting goods to market keeps much of the region economically depressed to this day.

For geologists this region hides great wealth, not just in rich ore deposits but in the record of earth history preserved by the rocks. This is where two significant geologic provinces converge: Labrador forms the eastern rim of the vast Canadian Shield, the greatest exposure of ancient rocks on the earth's surface; while the other Atlantic provinces perch themselves at the northern tip of the Appalachian Mountains, which is the single most important topographic feature of eastern North America.

Sitting at this great convergence, Atlantic Canada offers a visually dramatic snapshot of more than one billion years of earth history, ranging from the red sandstone cliffs of Northumberland Strait to the famed granite headlands at Peggy's Cove, Nova Scotia. And perhaps even more fascinating for the visitor are the many signs of the massive Pleistocene ice sheet that smothered the region with ice a mile deep as recently as 20,000 years ago: the thrilling fjords of the north, the rounded mounds of Nova Scotia (known locally as drumlins), the tens of thousands of small shallow lakes.

In its simplest form, the geologic story is that Atlantic Canada formed from the fragments and pieces left over after North America and Africa collided and crushed an ocean between them 400 million years ago. In the process of swinging into each other with tremendous force, the two continents compressed and folded seafloor sediments into a giant mountain chain that has eroded over millions of years into the rolling hills we now call the Appalachian Mountains. Mixed into this mélange are the many different pieces of smaller land masses trapped between the colliding continents.

When North America and Africa went their separate ways 180 million years ago, they each left part of their coastline behind. This may be best observed in Newfoundland, for its western third is a remnant of the ancestral North American coastline, its middle third is a slice of ancient seafloor and its eastern third once belonged to northern Africa.

TIME TRAVEL

At the Fundy Geological Museum, 'time travel' with interactive exhibits and visit a lab where dinosaur bones are being cleaned and assembled.

FABULOUS FOSSILS

Kids will be especially intrigued by the region's fossils, many of which are on display in various parks and museums. They include fossil footprints, dinosaur bones, and fossilized creatures that look like they're from outer space. In New Brunswick province, you can see remains of the first life to walk on land in North America (a giant centipede, just in case you're wondering) as well as evidence of the most primitive terrestrial plants. Nova Scotia, however, holds the most accessible fossil viewing at the UNESCO Joggins Fossil Cliffs; you can also search for fossils and semi-precious stones in the low tide flats around Parrsboro in Nova Scotia (but note you can't actually keep the fossils). While in Parrsboro don't miss a stop at Parrsboro Rock & Mineral Shop (p81), where owner Eldon George sells inexpensive copies of his famous discovery of the world's smallest dinosaur footprint.

But geology never stops at the simple story, and for the traveler who's enthusiastic about the subject, this region never runs out of surprises. Even if you don't study rocks or get excited by fossils, you cannot ignore the stunning outcroppings and rock types visible at nearly every stage of your journey. There are, for example, sea stacks, drowned coastlines, glacial grooves and erratics everywhere – what more could you ask for?

Critters of the Great North

Whether you come for a glimpse of caribou, whales or moose, Atlantic Canada's wildlife can be elusive but it is plentiful. Many people travel to the region to see the incredible numbers of seabirds and whales that can be spotted from coastal bluffs or on whale-watch trips, and these sightings are nearly guaranteed. Polar Bears, however quintessentially Canadian they may be, are only present in the far north of this region.

The plants and animals of Atlantic Canada are even more amazing when you realize that the entire region was completely buried in ice only 20,000 years ago and was not accessible for life until about 10,000 years ago. Where all these critters came from and how they got here so quickly is anybody's guess!

Animals

If you needed one single reason to visit Atlantic Canada, it might be the world-class encounters with whales that gather in these food-rich waters. Around 22 species of whale and porpoise can be seen on whale-watch tours, which are offered from countless coastal harbors. Leaping and diving humpback whales are most common throughout the region, but you might also catch a glimpse of the highly endangered North Atlantic right whale or even the largest leviathan of all, the blue whale.

Closer to shore or hauled out on the ice, it is common to see seals, including in winter the snowy white young of the harp seal. Harbor and gray seals are easily observed, though in winter they seek out the edges of the pack ice.

Land animals are also a powerful draw. Fox, bear and otter are widespread throughout the region. Rabbits are everywhere. On Newfoundland there are more than 100,000 moose and there are many more on Cape Breton Island, although they do stick to the woods so unless you're a hiker, the highest likelihood of seeing them is on the road – a very good reminder to drive slow (hitting a moose often does more damage to the car and driver than it does the moose). As you travel north the animals become even more exotic. From Newfoundland north you will find polar bear, Arctic fox, wolf, lynx and musk oxen. Labrador has the largest herd of caribou in the world, as well as wolves that follow the long lines of migrating caribou.

POLAR BEARS

The white hairs on a polar bear are hollow and trap sunlight to help keep the animal warm in frigid temperatures.

Birds

Seabirds are the primary wildlife attraction in Atlantic Canada, and rightly so. There are few places in North America where it's easier to see outstanding numbers of seabirds such as razorbill, Atlantic puffin, common murre and northern gannet. Huge nesting colonies on rocky islands and promontories may contain more than a million birds, but these merely hint at the numbers that once nested here before market hunters slaughtered uncounted millions of birds.

Mudflats and shorelines, especially along the Bay of Fundy, are famous for the tremendous quantities of shorebirds they attract during the May and August migration. Upwards of two million birds stop here annually. On nearby beaches, the endangered piping plover tries to hold its own against the trespass of invading sunbathers and beach walkers – please respect signs that warn you of this bird's home.

On Cape Breton Island and in Newfoundland and Labrador you're very likely to see bald eagles, Canada's largest bird of prey and the only eagle exclusive to North America. The birds can weigh up to 6.8kg (females are larger than males) and the wing span is around 2m. Besides their sheer size, you'll know them when you see them thanks to their distinctive white heads and brown bodies. Keep an eye out for their massive nests, often high in the trees along the coast, that weigh around 2 tons.

Fish

More than any other animal, fish have placed Atlantic Canada on the map, in particular the northern cod. With the collapse of the great cod fishery, other species such as halibut, mackerel, haddock and herring have grown in economic importance. In the region's many lakes and rivers, fisherfolk seek out trout, bass, salmon and river herring (with the quaint name alewives).

Insects

Although it is easy to focus on the region's showiest animals, we cannot ignore the one that is smallest but not least in Atlantic Canada. It has been said that the diminutive black fly has single-handedly maintained the wild splendor of Labrador. This may sound like an exaggeration until you step foot onto the shore in midsummer and are blanketed in insects against which you are defenseless. Second only to the black fly are prolific mosquitoes. If it's any consolation, every animal from ant to moose is tormented equally by these creatures, so they're not picking on you.

But what can be most troubling to those unaccustomed to them are North American Leeches (also called freshwater leeches or medicinal leeches) found in many freshwater lakes, slow moving streams and

World Heritage Sites

Gros Morne National Park, Newfoundland

L'Anse aux Meadows National Historic Site, Newfoundland

Old Town Lunenburg, Nova Scotia

Joggins Fossil Cliffs, Nova Scotia

The Landscapes of Grand Pré, Nova Scotia

LANDSCAPE & WILDLIFE CRITTERS OF THE GREAT NORTH

THE GRAND BANKS

Banks are a funny name for a shallow area, but in the case of the Grand Banks off Newfoundland's southeast coast it's no laughing matter. Until recently this was considered the greatest site in the world for ocean fish and the animals that came to feed on them. Even today, with the fish nearly hunted out, millions of seabirds and uncounted whales come to feed in the rich waters. This area is incredibly productive because the continental shelf off the coast of Newfoundland sticks out like a thumb to intercept the south-flowing waters of the frigid Labrador Current right at the point where they mingle with the warm north-flowing waters of the Gulf Stream. The mix of warmth and nutrient-rich Arctic waters creates an explosion of plankton that feeds everything from the smallest fish to the biggest whale. And because the shallow waters allow sunlight to penetrate to the ocean floor, the food chain is active at all depths.

NATIONAL & PROVINCIAL PARKS

Atlantic Canada has taken its park systems seriously and many important sites are protected within both national and provincial parks. Nova Scotia alone has more than 120 parks, but even Newfoundland and Labrador, which are so sparsely settled as to be parks in their own right, have a total of 34 parks.

Not all parks are set up for camping, but they are all worthy of a visit. In a few parks it is possible to plan extended hiking and camping trips, but all of them offer splendid opportunities for activities ranging from picnicking to beachcombing to kayaking and cycling. Those that are open in the winter are favored by cross-country skiers and snowshoers.

marshes. These 2in-long parasites usually spend their days chilling out under rocks or leaves in the cool, mucky bottoms, but water disturbances (such as a splash of diving in or stepping out into the water for a swim), are a bit akin to a dinner bell and out they swim looking for grub. While it can be very disturbing being a meal for a leech, the bites are painless and the critters carry no diseases. If you do get bitten, you can opt either to let the leech eat its fill and drop off, or try to release it's suction with a fingernail or sharp flat object before gently pulling it off. Salt or insect repellent can work to suffocate the leech.

Plants

Although Atlantic Canada presents some tree diversity in its southern reaches with a mix of birch, maple and ash, vast areas of forest are completely dominated by spruce as you head north. And at some point even those homogenous forests give way to soggy tundra that stretches to the Arctic. Surprisingly the area can be rich with abundant wildflowers during the short growing season.

The yellow dandelion-like flowers of the coltsfoot may be the first ones to come out each spring, but far more attention is given to the region's delightful midsummer orchid displays, including showy lady's slipper, which may carpet entire boggy areas. Blue lupines seem to bloom everywhere, and many other varieties and colors can be found.

The most common shrubs, especially in Newfoundland and Labrador, are those in the heath family, including blueberries, cranberries and other delicious berries that grow in profusion in August. Wild roses bloom along the coasts from late June through August.

Perhaps the most curious plant is the odd lichen called caribou moss. Growing in such a dense spongy carpet that other plants cannot get a toehold, this pale greenish moss may be the most dominant plant in the northern forests. It is an important food source for caribou, hence its name, and is often mixed with seal meat to vary the diets of sled dogs.

Environmental Issues

Early Europeans explorers were dumbfounded by the apparently inexhaustible numbers of animals they encountered in Atlantic Canada. It was a scene of such incredible abundance that they thought it would never end, so they bent their will toward exploiting and profiting from the natural wealth in every way possible. The result is only too predictable and sad: animals lost forever include the mythical great auk, the Labrador duck and the sea mink. Today Atlantic Canada is facing the horrifying prospect that the greatest fishery in the world, the uncounted millions of cod that sustained their provincial livelihood for 400 years, may have come to an end when cod were listed as endangered in 2003.

Even with fishing limitations the recovery of stocks is hindered by the proliferation of species cod and other predator fish once fed on, such as herring and snow crab, which eat fish eggs making it even more difficult for the fish to make a comeback. In the end, not only has the environment suffered great damage, but so have the villages and traditions that needed the fish for their survival.

Unfortunately resource exploitation continues unabated on several other fronts. Some $3 billion a year is generated from logging, with half of the production coming from New Brunswick. Vast ore deposits are being explored and developed all the time, with huge areas stripped of their forest and soil cover to access coal, iron, nickel and other mineral resources.

ATLANTIC CANADA'S TOP NATURAL AREAS

PARK	FEATURES	ACTIVITIES	BEST TIME TO VISIT
Nova Scotia			
Cape Chignecto Provincial Park	largest and newest park in province, rugged wilderness, old growth forest, deer, moose, eagles	hiking and back-country camping	Jun–Oct
Kejimkujik National Park	pristine wilderness, network of glacial lakes; otter, loon, bald eagles	canoeing, camping, hiking	late Sep–early Oct
Cape Breton Highlands National Park	dramatic oceanside cliffs, world-famous scenic drive; whales, bald eagles, seabirds, bear, moose, wild orchids	hiking, camping, sightseeing, whale watching	May–Oct
New Brunswick			
Fundy National Park	sandstone cliffs, extensive beach, dramatic tides; bear, moose, beaver, peregrine falcons	mountain biking, birdwatching, hiking	year-round
Kouchibouguac National Park	lagoons, white-sand beaches; moose, deer, bear	strolling, clam digging, bicycling, skiing, kayaking, birdwatching	year-round
Prince Edward Island			
Prince Edward Island National Park	red sandstone bluffs, dunes, beaches; red foxes, piping plover, sandpipers	birdwatching, beach walking, swimming, picnicking	May–Sep
Newfoundland			
Cape St Mary's Ecological Reserve	rugged ocean cliffs; one of the most accessible seabird colonies in North America, nesting gannets, whales	birdwatching	Mar–Aug
Terra Nova National Park	craggy cliffs and many sheltered inlets; lakes, bogs; moose, beaver, bald eagles, whales	kayaking, fishing, camping	mid-May–mid-Oct
Witless Bay Ecological Reserve	offshore islands; more than one million breeding seabirds, feeding whales, icebergs	birdwatching, whale watching	Jun–Aug

The newest threat to the environment yet perk for jobs and suffering local economies is hydraulic fracturing for natural gas exploration (often called 'fracking'). The technique involves drilling into shale or coal bed deposits and injecting a water and chemical fracking fluid filled with ceramic beads into the holes. The beads hold open the cracks allowing natural gas to rise to the surface and be collected. The environmental risks here are many, including a huge use of valuable fresh water and the risk of fracking chemicals to leak into the water table and ocean. Fracking rigs also emit large amounts of greenhouse gases into the atmosphere. In 2013 there were fracking wells in or planned to be open in every province covered in this book. What is particularly troubling is how much exploitation occurs in seldom-visited parts of Labrador, where there is little public scrutiny or attention.

Survival Guide

Directory A–Z

Accommodations

In this part of Canada, you'll be choosing from a wide range of B&Bs, chain motels, hotels and hostels. Provincial tourist offices publish comprehensive directories of accommodations and take bookings online or from visitor information centers. The budget category includes camping, hostels and simple B&Bs and hotels where you'll likely share a bathroom. Midrange accommodations, including most B&Bs, inns, motels and some hotels, generally offer the most for your money; expect a good-sized comfortable room with attached bathroom and TV. Top-end choices offer an international standard of amenities which often include a fitness and business center and other upmarket facilities.

Seasons

➡ Peak season is summer, from mid-June to early September, when prices are highest.

➡ It's best to book ahead during summer and during holidays and major events when rooms can be scarce.

Amenities

➡ Most properties offer in-room wi-fi. It's typically free in budget and midrange lodgings, while top-end hotels often charge a fee.

➡ Many smaller properties, especially B&Bs, ban smoking. Marriott and Westin brand hotels are 100% smoke free. Other properties may have rooms set aside for smokers.

➡ Air-conditioning is not a standard amenity at most budget and midrange places. If you want it, be sure to ask about it when you book.

Discounts

➡ In winter, prices can plummet by as much as 50%.

➡ Membership in the American Automobile Association (AAA) or an affiliated automobile association, American Association of Retired Persons (AARP) or other organizations also yield modest savings (usually 10%).

➡ Check the hotel websites listed throughout this guide for special online rates. The usual suspects also offer discounted room prices throughout Canada:

Priceline (www.priceline.com)

Hotwire (www.hotwire.com)

Expedia (www.expedia.com)

Travelocity (www.travelocity.com)

Tripadvisor (www.tripadvisor.com)

B&Bs

➡ **Bed & Breakfast Online** (www.bbcanada.com) is the main booking agency for properties nationwide.

➡ In Canada B&Bs, known as *gîtes* in French, are essentially converted private homes whose owners live on-site. People who like privacy may find B&Bs too intimate, as walls are rarely soundproof and it's usual to mingle with your hosts and other guests.

➡ Standards vary widely, sometimes even within a single B&B. The cheapest rooms tend to be small with few amenities and a shared bathroom. Nicer ones have added features such as a balcony, a fireplace and an ensuite bathroom. Breakfast is always included in the rates (though it might be continental instead of a full cooked affair).

➡ Not all B&Bs accept children, while others cater to them.

BOOK YOUR STAY ONLINE

For more accommodations reviews by Lonely Planet authors, check out http://hotels.lonelyplanet.com. You'll find independent reviews, as well as recommendations on the best places to stay. Best of all, you can book online.

➡ Minimum stays (usually two nights) are common, and many B&Bs are only open seasonally.

Camping

Canada's Maritime and Atlantic provinces are filled with campgrounds – some federal or provincial, others privately owned. Private campgrounds sometimes cater only to trailers (caravans) and recreational vehicles (RVs), and may feature convenience stores, playgrounds and swimming pools. It is a good idea to phone ahead to make sure the size of sites and the services provided at a particular campground are suitable for your vehicle.

Season Varies by location but most campgrounds are open from May to September. Some campgrounds remain open for maintenance year-round and may let you camp at a reduced rate in the off-season. This can be great in late autumn or early spring when there's hardly a soul tramping about. Winter camping, though, is only for the hardy.

Facilities Vary widely. Backcountry campgrounds offer little more than pit toilets and fire rings, and have no potable water. Unserviced (tent) campgrounds come with access to drinking water and a washroom with toilets and sometimes showers. The best-equipped grounds feature flush toilets and hot showers and water, electrical and sewer hookups for RVs.

Fees In national and provincial parks range from about $20 to $35 for tents up to $39 for full hookup sites per night; fire permits often cost a few dollars extra. Backcountry camping costs about $14 per night. Private campgrounds tend to be a bit pricier.

Availability On a first-come first-served basis at most government-run campgrounds. Sites fill up quickly, especially in July and August. Several national parks

> ## PRICES
> ....
> Prices listed in this guide are for peak-season travel and, unless stated otherwise, do not include taxes (which can be up to 17%). If breakfast is included and/or a bathroom is shared, that information is included in our listing.
>
> **$** less than $100
>
> **$$** $100–$180
>
> **$$$** more than $180

participate in Parks Canada's **camping reservation program** (📞877-737-3783; www.pccamping.ca; reservation fee $11), which is a convenient way to make sure you get a spot.

Homestays & Holiday Rentals

How do you feel about staying on the couch of a perfect stranger? If it's not a problem, consider joining an organization that arranges homestays. The following groups charge no fees to become a member, and the stay itself is also free:

Couch Surfing (www.couch-surfing.org)

Hospitality Club (www.hospitalityclub.org)

Another option is a holiday rental where individuals rent out anything from a room in their house to private cabins or even their whole house. Locations are equally variable – you can find an apartment in Halifax to cottages deep in the woods of New Brunswick. Great bargains can be found and this can be a fantastic option for families in particular. The following sites offer the most listings in the region:

Airbnb (www.airbnb.com)

VRBO (www.vrbo.com)

Hostels

Canada has independent hostels as well as those affiliated with Hostelling International (HI). All have dorms ($25 to $35 per person on average), which can sleep from two to

10 people, and many have private rooms (from $60) for couples and families. Rooms in HI hostels are gender segregated, and alcohol and smoking are prohibited; nonmembers pay a surcharge of about $4 per night.

Bathrooms are usually shared and facilities include a kitchen, lockers, internet access, laundry room and common TV room. Most hostels, especially those in big cities, are open 24 hours. If not, ask if you can make special arrangements if you're arriving late.

For additional information and online reservations:

Backpackers Hostels Canada (www.backpackers.ca) Independent hostels.

Hostelling International Canada (www.hihostels.ca)

Hostels.com (www.hostels.com) Includes independent and HI hostels.

Hotels & Motels

Most hotels are part of international chains, and the newer ones are designed for either the luxury market or businesspeople. Hotels have cable TV and wi-fi; other facilities may include swimming pools and fitness and business centers. Rooms with two double or queen-sized beds sleep up to four people, although there is usually a small surcharge for the third and fourth person. Many places advertise that 'kids stay free' but sometimes you have to pay extra for a crib or a rollaway (portable bed).

THE CHAIN GANG

Budget

Days Inn (800-329-7466; www.daysinn.com)

Econo Lodge (877-424-6423; www.econolodge.com)

Super 8 (800-800-8000; www.super8.com)

Midrange

Best Western (800-780-7234; www.bestwestern.com)

Comfort Inn (877-424-6423; www.comfortinn.com)

Fairfield Inn (800-228-2800; www.fairfieldinn.com)

Hampton Inn (800-426-7866; www.hamptoninn.com)

Holiday Inn (888-465-4329; www.holidayinn.com)

Howard Johnson (800-446-4656; www.hojo.com)

Quality Inn & Suites (877-424-6423; www.qualityinn.com)

Travelodge/Thriftlodge (800-578-7878; www.travelodge.ca)

Top End

Delta (877-814-7706; www.deltahotels.com)

Fairmont (800-257-7544; www.fairmont.com)

Hilton (800-445-8667; www.hilton.com)

Hyatt (888-591-1234; www.hyatt.com)

Marriott (888-236-2427; www.marriott.com)

Radisson (888-201-1718; www.radisson.com)

Ramada (800-272-6232; www.ramada.com)

Sheraton (800-325-3535; www.sheraton.com)

Westin (800-937-8461; www.westin.com)

In Canada, like the US (both lands of the automobile), motels are ubiquitous. They dot the highways and cluster in groups on the outskirts of towns and cities. Although most motel rooms won't win any style awards, they're usually clean and comfortable and offer good value for travelers. Many regional motels remain your typical 'mom and pop' operations, but plenty of North American chains have also opened up around the region.

University Accommodations

In the lecture-free summer months some universities and colleges rent beds in their student dormitories to travelers of all ages. Most rooms are quite basic, but with rates ranging from $30 to $80 a night, often including breakfast, you know you're not getting the Ritz. Students usually qualify for small discounts.

Activities

Some resources:

Parks Canada (www.pc.gc.ca) National park action.

Canada Trails (www.canadatrails.ca) Hiking, biking, cross-country skiing.

Canadian Ski Council (www.skicanada.org) Skiing and snowboarding.

Paddling Canada (www.paddlingcanada.com) Kayaking and canoeing.

Alpine Club of Canada (www.alpineclubofcanada.ca) Climbing and mountaineering.

See also our chapter on outdoor activities in the region (p28).

Customs Regulations

The **Canada Border Services Agency** (CBSA; www.cbsa.gc.ca) has the customs lowdown. A few regulations to note:

Alcohol You can bring in 1.5L of wine, 1.14L of liquor or 24 355mL beers duty free.

Gifts You can bring in gifts totaling up to $60.

Money You can bring in/take out up to $10,000; larger amounts must be reported to customs.

Personal effects Camping gear, sports equipment, cameras and laptop computers can be brought in without much trouble. Declaring these to customs as you cross the border might save you some hassle when you leave, especially if you'll be crossing the US–Canadian border multiple times.

Pets You must carry a signed and dated certificate from a veterinarian to prove your dog or cat has had a rabies shot in the past 36 months.

Prescription drugs You can bring in/take out a 90-day supply for personal use (though if you're bringing it to the USA, know it's technically illegal, but overlooked for individuals).

Tobacco You can bring in 200 cigarettes, 50 cigars, 200g of tobacco and 200 tobacco sticks duty free.

Discount Cards

Discounts are commonly offered for seniors, children, families and people with disabilities, though no cards are issued (you get the savings on-site when you pay). AAA and other automobile association members also receive various travel-related discounts. Many cities have discount cards for local attractions.

International Student Identity Card (ISIC; www.isic.org) Provides students with discounts on travel insurance and admission to museums and other sights. There are also cards for those who are under 26 but not students and for full-time teachers.

Parks Canada Discovery Pass (www.pc.gc.ca/ar-sr/lpac-ppri/ced-ndp.aspx; adult/child/family $68/33/136) Gives access to over national parks and historic sites for a year around Canada. Can pay for itself in as few as seven visits over daily entry fees; also provides quicker entry into sites.

Electricity

120V/60Hz

120V/60Hz

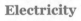

Embassies & Consulates

All countries have their embassies in Ottawa, although a few maintain consulates in Nova Scotia, New Brunswick and/or Newfoundland.

Ottawa

Australian High Commission (☑613-236-0841; www.canada.embassy.gov.au; Suite 710, 50 O'Connor St)

British High Commission (☑613-237-2008; www.gov.uk/government/world/canada; 80 Elgin St)

New Zealand High Commission (☑613-238-5991; www.nzembassy.com/canada; Suite 727, 99 Bank St)

Nova Scotia

German Honorary Consulate (☑902-420-1599; achapman@coxandpalmer.com; 1100 Purdy's Wharf Tower 1, 1959 Upper Water St, Halifax)

Italian Consulate (☑902-494-3934; itconsul@netcom.ca; 1959 Upper Water St, Suite 1800, Halifax)

Japanese Consulate (☑902-421-1723; 1894 Barrington St, Halifax)

Mexican Consulate (☑902-466-3678; gcarrera@ns.sympatico.ca; 130 Lakeshore Park Tce, Dartmouth)

Netherlands Honorary Consulate (☑902-422-1485; halifax@nlconsulate.com; 1181 Hollis St, Halifax)

US Consulate (☑902-429-2480; http://halifax.usconsulate.gov; Purdy's Tower II, suite 904, 1969 Upper Water St, Halifax)

New Brunswick

French Consulate (☑506-857-4191; www.consulfrance-moncton.org; 777 Main St suite 100, Moncton)

Netherlands Consulate (☑506-453-7771; Cox & Palmer, 371 Queen St, Fredericton)

Newfoundland

German Consulate (☑709-739-9727; 2 Winter Pl, St John's)

Irish Consulate (☑709-738-6280; 95 Water St, 2nd fl, St John's)

Italian Honorary Consulate (☑709-368-8800; delcontracting@nl.rogers.com; 8 Circular Rd, St John's)

Japanese Consulate (☑709-722-4166; viciyoung@hotmail.com; 9 Primrose Pl, St John's)

Gay & Lesbian Travelers

Canada is tolerant when it comes to gays and lesbians, though this outlook is more common in the big cities than in rural areas. Same-sex marriage is legal throughout the country (Canada is one of a growing number of nations that permits this).

Halifax is by far this region's gayest city, with a humming nightlife scene, publications, and lots of associations and support groups. It has a sizeable pride celebration, too, which attracts big crowds.

While very low-key, Prince Edward Island also has a

decent-sized gay population and has a small pride event in July.

The following are good resources for gay travel; they include Canadian information, though not all are exclusive to the region.

Damron (www.damron.com) Publishes several travel guides, including *Men's Travel Guide, Women's Traveller* and *Damron Accommodations;* gay-friendly tour operators are listed on the website, too.

Gay Canada (www.gaycanada.com) Search by province or city to find businesses and resources that are queer-friendly.

Lesbian & Gay Hospitality Exchange International (LGHEI; www.lghei.org) A network of gay and lesbians who host travelers in their homes or offer hospitality to visitors.

Out Traveler (www.outtraveler.com) Gay travel magazine.

Purple Roofs (www.purpleroofs.com) Website listing queer accommodations, travel agencies and tours worldwide.

Queer Canada (www.queercanada.ca) A general resource.

Xtra (www.xtra.ca) Source for gay and lesbian news nationwide.

Health

Before You Go
INSURANCE
Canada offers some of the finest health care in the world. The problem is that, unless you are a Canadian citizen, it can be prohibitively expensive. It's essential to purchase travel health insurance if your regular policy doesn't cover you when you're abroad. Check www.lonelyplanet.com/travel_services for supplemental insurance information.

Bring medications you may need clearly labeled in their original containers. A signed, dated letter from your physician that describes your medical conditions and medications, including generic names, is also a good idea.

RECOMMENDED VACCINATIONS
No special vaccines are required or recommended for travel to Canada. All travelers should be up to date on routine immunizations, listed in the table below.

MEDICAL CHECKLIST
➡ acetaminophen (eg Tylenol) or aspirin

➡ anti-inflammatory drugs (eg ibuprofen)

➡ antihistamines (for hay fever and allergic reactions)

➡ antibacterial ointment (eg Neosporin) for cuts and abrasions

➡ steroid cream or cortisone (for poison ivy and other allergic rashes)

➡ bandages, gauze, gauze rolls

➡ adhesive or paper tape

➡ safety pins, tweezers

➡ thermometer

➡ DEET-containing insect repellent for the skin

➡ permethrin-containing insect spray for clothing, tents and bed nets

➡ sunblock

➡ motion-sickness medication

WEBSITES
Canadian resources:
Public Health Agency of Canada (www.phac-aspc.gc.ca)

General resources:
MD Travel Health (www.mdtravelhealth.com)
World Health Organization (www.who.int)

Government travel health websites:
Australia (www.smarttraveller.gov.au)
United Kingdom (www.nhs.uk/healthcareabroad)
United States (www.cdc.gov/travel/)

IMMUNIZE YOURSELF

VACCINE	RECOMMENDED FOR	DOSAGE	SIDE EFFECTS
chickenpox	travelers who've never had chickenpox	two doses one month apart	fever, mild case of chickenpox
influenza	all travelers during flu season (November through March)	one dose	soreness at the injection site, fever
measles	travelers born after 1956 who've had only one measles vaccination	one dose	fever, rash, joint pains, allergic reactions
tetanus-diphtheria	all travelers who haven't had booster within 10 years	one dose lasts 10 years	soreness at injection site

In Canada

AVAILABILITY & COST OF HEALTH CARE

Medical services are widely available. For emergencies, the best bet is to find the nearest hospital and go to its emergency room. If the problem isn't urgent, call a nearby hospital and ask for a referral to a local physician, which is usually cheaper than a trip to the emergency room (where costs can be $500 or so before any treatment).

Pharmacies are abundant, but prescriptions can be expensive without insurance. However, Americans may find Canadian prescription drugs to be cheaper than drugs at home. You're allowed to take out a 90-day supply for personal use (though know it's technically illegal to bring them into the USA, but overlooked for individuals).

INFECTIOUS DISEASES

Most are acquired by mosquito or tick bites, or environmental exposure. The **Public Health Agency of Canada** (www.phac-aspc.gc.ca) has details on all listed below.

Giardiasis Intestinal infection. Avoid drinking directly from lakes, ponds, streams and rivers.

Lyme Disease Occurs mostly in southern Canada. Transmitted by deer ticks in late spring and summer. Perform a tick check after you've been outdoors.

Severe Acute Respiratory Syndrome (SARS) At the time of writing, SARS has been brought under control in Canada.

West Nile Virus Mosquito-transmitted in late summer and early fall. Prevent by keeping covered (wear long sleeves, long pants, hats, and shoes rather than sandals) and apply a good insect repellent, preferably one containing DEET, to exposed skin and clothing.

ENVIRONMENTAL HAZARDS

Cold exposure This can be a significant problem, especially in the northern regions. Keep all body surfaces covered, including the head and neck. Watch out for the 'Umbles' – stumbles, mumbles, fumbles and grumbles – which are signs of impending hypothermia.

Heat exhaustion Dehydration is the main contributor. Symptoms include feeling weak, headache, nausea and sweaty skin. Lay the victim flat with their legs raised, apply cool, wet cloths to the skin, and rehydrate.

Insurance

Make sure you have adequate travel insurance, whatever the length of your trip. At a minimum, you need coverage for medical emergencies and treatment, including hospital stays and an emergency flight home. Medical treatment for non-Canadians is very expensive.

Also consider insurance for luggage theft or loss. If you already have a homeowners' or renters' policy, check what it will cover and only get supplemental insurance to protect against the rest. If you have prepaid a large portion of your vacation, trip cancellation insurance is worthwhile.

Worldwide travel insurance is available at www.lonelyplanet.com/travel_services. You can buy, extend and claim online at anytime – even if you're already on the road. Also check the following providers.

Insure.com (www.insure.com)

Travelex (www.travelex.com)

Travel Guard (www.travelguard.com)

Internet Access

It's easy to find internet access. Libraries, schools and community agencies in practically every town provide free high-speed internet terminals for public use, travelers included. The only downsides are that usage time is limited (usually 30 minutes), facilities have erratic hours and you may not be able to upload photos (it depends on the facility). The government's **Community Access Program** (http://www.ic.gc.ca/eic/site/cap-pac.nsf/eng/home) provides the services.

Internet cafes are limited to the main tourist areas, and access generally costs from $2 per hour.

Wi-fi is widely available. Most lodgings have it (in-room, with good speed), as do many urban coffee shops and bars. We've identified sleeping, eating and drinking listings that have wi-fi with a 📶. We've denoted lodgings that offer internet terminals for guest use with a @.

Legal Matters

Police

If you're arrested or charged with an offense, you have the right to keep your mouth shut and to hire any lawyer you wish (contact your embassy for a referral, if necessary). If you cannot afford one, be sure to ask to be represented by public counsel. There is a presumption of innocence.

Drugs & Alcohol

The blood-alcohol limit is 0.08% and driving cars, motorcycles, boats and snowmobiles while drunk is a criminal offense. If you are caught, you may face stiff fines, license suspension and other nasty consequences.

Consuming alcohol anywhere other than at a residence or licensed premises is also a no-no, which puts parks, beaches and the rest of the great outdoors off-limits, at least officially.

Avoid illegal drugs, as penalties may entail heavy fines and possible jail time,

LEGAL AGE

➡ Driving a car: 16

➡ Smoking tobacco: 19

➡ Homosexual consent (for males): 18

➡ Consent for other sexual activity: 16

➡ Voting in an election: 18

➡ Drinking alcoholic beverages: 19

as well as a criminal record. The only exception is the use of marijuana for medical purposes, which became legal in 2001. Meanwhile, the decriminalization of pot possession for personal use remains a subject of ongoing debate among the general public and in the parliament.

Other Legalities

➡ Abortion is legal.

➡ Travelers should note that they can be prosecuted under the law of their home country regarding age of consent, even when abroad.

Maps

Most tourist offices distribute free provincial road maps.

For extended hikes or multiday backcountry treks, it's a good idea to carry a topographic map. The best are the series of 1:50,000 scale maps published by the government's **Centre for Topographic Information** (www.nrcan.gc.ca). These are sold by around 900 map dealers around the country; check the website for vendors.

You can also download and print maps from **GeoBase** (www.geobase.ca).

Money

All prices quoted throughout this guide are in Canadian dollars ($), unless stated otherwise.

Canadian coins come in 5¢ (nickel), 10¢ (dime), 25¢ (quarter), $1 (loonie) and $2 (toonie or twoonie) denominations. The gold-colored loonie features the loon, a common Canadian water bird, while the two-toned toonie is decorated with a polar bear.

Paper currency comes in $5 (blue), $10 (purple), $20 (green) and $50 (red) denominations. The $100 (brown) and larger bills are less common and tough to change.

The Canadian dollar has seen fluctuations during the past decade, though since 2007 it has tracked quite closely to the US dollar.

For changing money in the larger cities, currency exchange offices may offer better rates than banks.

ATMs

Many grocery and convenience stores, airports, and bus, train and ferry stations have ATMs. Most are linked to international networks, the most common being Cirrus, Plus, Star and Maestro.

Most ATMs also spit out cash if you use a major credit card. This method tends to be more expensive because, in addition to a service fee, you'll be charged interest immediately (in other words, there's no interest-free period as there is with purchases). For exact fees, check with your bank or credit card company.

Visitors heading to Canada's more remote regions (such as in Newfoundland) won't find an abundance of ATMs, so it is wise to cash up beforehand.

Scotiabank, common throughout Canada, is part of the Global ATM Alliance. If your home bank is a member, fees may be less if you withdraw from Scotiabank ATMs.

Cash

Most Canadians don't carry large amounts of cash for everyday use, relying instead on credit and debit cards. Still, carrying some cash, say $100 or less, comes in handy when making small purchases. In some cases, cash is necessary to pay for rural B&Bs and shuttle vans; inquire in advance to avoid surprises. Note that shops and businesses rarely accept personal checks.

Credit Cards

Major credit cards such as MasterCard, Visa and American Express are widely accepted in Canada, except in remote, rural communities where cash is king. You'll find it hard or impossible to rent a car, book a room or order tickets over the phone without having a piece of plastic. Note that some credit card companies charge a transaction fee (which is around 3% of whatever you purchased); ensure you check with your provider to avoid surprises.

For lost or stolen cards, these numbers operate 24 hours:

American Express (☎866-296-5198; www.americanexpress.com)

MasterCard (☎800-307-7309; www.mastercard.com)

Visa (☎800-847-2911; www.visa.com)

Taxes & Refunds

Canada's federal goods and services tax (GST), variously known as the 'gouge and screw' or 'grab and steal' tax, adds 5% to just about every transaction. Most provinces also charge a provincial sales tax (PST) on top of that. Several provinces have combined the GST and PST into a harmonized sales tax (HST). Whatever the methodology, expect to pay 10% to 15% extra on all transactions. Unless otherwise stated, taxes are not included in prices given.

You might be eligible for a rebate on some of the taxes. If you've booked your accommodations in conjunction with a rental car, plane ticket or other service (ie if it all appears on the same bill from a 'tour operator'), you should be eligible to get 50% of the tax refunded from your accommodations. Fill out the GST/HST Refund Application for Tour Packages form available from the **Canada Revenue Agency** (☑800-668-4748, 902-432-5608; www. cra-arc.gc.ca/E/pbg/gf/gst115).

LOCATION	TAX RATE (GST + PST)
New Brunswick*	13%
Newfoundland*	13%
Nova Scotia*	15%
Prince Edward Island	14%

*has a combined HST

Tipping

Tipping is standard practice. Below are some general rates.

SERVICE	TIPPING RATES
Restaurant waitstaff	15% to 20%
Bar staff	$1 per drink
Hotel bellhop	$1 to $2 per bag
Hotel room cleaners	$2 per day
Taxis	10% to 15%

Traveler's Checks

Traveler's checks are becoming obsolete in the age of ATMs. Traveler's checks issued in Canadian dollars are generally treated like cash by businesses. Traveler's checks in most other currencies must be exchanged for Canadian dollars at a bank or foreign currency office. The most common issuers:

American Express (www.americanexpress.com)

MasterCard (www.mastercard.com)

Visa (www.visa.com)

Opening Hours

The following list provides 'normal' opening hours for businesses. Reviews throughout this guide show specific hours only if they vary from these standards. Note, too, that hours can vary by season. The listings in this guide are for peak season operating times.

Banks 10am to 5pm Monday to Friday; some open 9am to noon Saturday

General office hours 9am to 5pm Monday to Friday

Museums 10am to 5pm daily, sometimes closed on Monday

Restaurants Breakfast 8am to 11am, lunch 11:30am to 2:30pm Monday to Friday, dinner 5pm to 9:30pm daily; some open for brunch 8am to 1pm Saturday to Sunday

Bars 5pm to 2am daily

Clubs 9pm to 2am Wednesday to Saturday

Shops 10am to 6pm Monday to Saturday, noon to 5pm Sunday, some open to 8pm or 9pm Thursday and/or Friday

Supermarkets 9am to 8pm, some open 24 hours

Post

Canada's national postal service, **Canada Post/ Postes Canada** (www.canadapost.ca), is neither quick nor cheap, but it is reliable. Stamps are available at post offices, drugstores, convenience stores and hotels.

Postcards or standard letters cost 63¢ within Canada, $1.10 to the USA and $1.85 to all other countries. Travelers often find they have to pay high duties on items sent to them while in Canada, so beware.

Postal abbreviations:

New Brunswick NB

Newfoundland & Labrador NL

Nova Scotia NS

Prince Edward Island PE

Public Holidays

Canada observes 10 national public holidays a year and more at the provincial level. Banks, schools and government offices close on these days.

National Holidays

New Year's Day January 1

Good Friday March or April

Easter Monday March or April

Victoria Day Monday before May 25

Canada Day July 1; called Memorial Day in Newfoundland

Labour Day First Monday of September

Thanksgiving Second Monday of October

Remembrance Day November 11

Christmas Day December 25

Boxing Day December 26

Provincial Holidays

Some provinces also observe local holidays, with Newfoundland leading the pack.

St Patrick's Day Monday nearest March 17

St George's Day Monday nearest April 23

National Day Monday nearest June 24 in Newfoundland

Orangemen's Day Monday nearest July 12 in Newfoundland

Civic Holiday First Monday of August; applies everywhere *except* Newfoundland and PEI

School Holidays

Children break for summer holidays in late June and don't return to school until early September. University students get even more time off, usually from May to early or mid-September. Most people take their big annual vacation during these months.

UNIQUELY CANADIAN CELEBRATIONS

National Flag Day (⊘Feb 15) Commemorates the first time the maple-leaf flag was raised above Parliament Hill in Ottawa, at the stroke of noon on February 15 1965.

Victoria Day (⊘late May) This day was established in 1845 to observe the birthday of Queen Victoria and now celebrates the birthday of the British sovereign who's still Canada's titular head of state. Victoria Day marks the official beginning of the summer season (which ends with Labour Day on the first Monday of September). Some communities hold fireworks.

National Aboriginal Day (⊘Jun 21) Created in 1996, it celebrates the contributions of Aboriginal peoples to Canada. Coinciding with the summer solstice, festivities are organized locally and may include traditional dancing, singing and drumming, storytelling, arts and crafts shows, canoe races and lots more.

Canada Day (☑613-239-5000; www.canadascapital.gc.ca/canadaday; ⊘Jul 1) Known as Dominion Day until 1982, Canada Day was created in 1869 to commemorate the creation of Canada two years earlier. All over the country, people celebrate with barbecues, parades, concerts and fireworks.

Thanksgiving Day (⊘mid-Oct) First celebrated in 1578 in what is now Newfoundland by explorer Martin Frobisher to give thanks for surviving his Atlantic crossing, Thanksgiving became an official Canadian holiday in 1872 to celebrate the recovery of the Prince of Wales from a long illness. These days, it's essentially a harvest festival involving a special family dinner of roast turkey and pumpkin, very much as it is practised in the US.

Telephone

Canada's phone system is almost identical to the USA's system.

Domestic & International Dialing

Canadian phone numbers consist of a three-digit area code followed by a seven-digit local number. In many parts of Canada, you must dial all 10 digits preceded by 1, even if you're calling across the street. In other parts of the country, when you're calling within the same area code, you can dial the seven-digit number only, but this is slowly changing. The pay phone or phone book where you are should make it clear which system is used.

For direct international calls, dial ☑011 + country code + area code + local phone number. The country code for Canada is 1 (which is the same as for the USA, although international rates still apply for all calls made between the two countries).

Toll-free numbers begin with 800, 877 or 866 and must be preceded by 1. Some of these numbers are good throughout Canada and the USA, others only work within Canada, and some work in just one province.

Emergency Numbers

Dial ☑911. Note it is *not* the emergency number in the Yukon, Northwest Territories or Nunavut.

Cell Phones

Local SIM cards can be used in European and Australian phones. Other phones must be set to roaming.

If you have a European, Australian or other type of unlocked GSM phone, buy a SIM card from local providers such as **Telus** (www.telus. com), **Rogers** (www.rogers. com) or **Bell** (www.bell.ca).

US residents can often upgrade their domestic cell phone plan to extend to Canada. **Verizon** (www. verizonwireless.com) provides good results.

Reception is poor in rural areas no matter who your service provider is.

Public Phones

Coin-operated public pay phones are fairly plentiful. Local calls cost 50¢; many phones also accept prepaid phonecards and credit cards. Dialing the operator (0) or directory assistance (411 for local calls, 1 + area code + 555-1212 for long-distance calls) is free of charge from public phones; it may incur a charge from private phones.

Phonecards

Prepaid phonecards usually offer the best per-minute rates for long-distance and international calling. They come in denominations of $5, $10 and $20 and are widely sold in drugstores, supermarkets and convenience stores. Beware of cards with hidden charges such as 'activation fees' or a per-call connection fee. A surcharge ranging from 30¢ to 85¢ for calls made from public pay phones is common.

Time

Canada spans six of the world's 24 time zones. The Eastern zone in Newfoundland is unusual in that it's only 30 minutes different from the adjacent zone. The time difference from coast to coast is 4½ hours.

Canada observes daylight saving time, which comes into effect on the second Sunday in March, when clocks are put forward one hour, and ends on the first Sunday in November.

Occasionally and especially in francophone areas, times for shop hours, train schedules, film screenings etc are usually indicated by the 24-hour clock.

CITY	TIME
Vancouver	3pm
New York City	6pm
Halifax, Fredericton & Charlottetown	7pm
Newfoundland	7:30pm
London	11pm

Tourist Information

The **Canadian Tourism Commission** (www.canada.travel) is loaded with general information, packages and links.

All provincial tourist offices maintain comprehensive websites packed with information helpful in planning your trip. Staff also field telephone inquiries and, upon request, will mail out free maps and directories about accommodations, attractions and events. Some offices can also help with making hotel, tour or other reservations.

For detailed information about a specific area, contact the local tourist office, aka visitors center. Just about every city and town has at least a seasonal branch with helpful staff,

racks of free pamphlets, and books and maps for sale.

Provincial tourist offices include the following:

Tourism New Brunswick (📞800-561-0123; www.tourismnewbrunswick.ca)

Newfoundland & Labrador Tourism (www.newfoundlandlabrador.com)

Tourism Nova Scotia (📞800-565-0000; www.novascotia.com)

Prince Edward Island Tourism (📞800-463-4734; www.peiplay.com)

Travelers with Disabilities

Canada is making progress when it comes to easing the everyday challenges facing people with disabilities, especially the mobility impaired.

Many public buildings, including museums, tourist offices, train stations, shopping malls and cinemas, have access ramps and/or lifts. Most public restrooms feature extra-wide stalls equipped with hand rails. Many pedestrian crossings have sloping curbs.

Newer and recently remodeled hotels, especially chain hotels, have rooms with extra-wide doors and spacious bathrooms.

Interpretive centers at national and provincial parks are usually accessible, and many parks have trails that can be navigated in wheelchairs.

Car rental agencies offer hand-controlled vehicles and vans with wheelchair lifts at no additional charge, but you must reserve them well in advance.

For accessible air, bus, rail and ferry transportation check **Access to Travel** (www.accesstotravel.gc.ca), the federal government's website. In general, most transportation agencies can accommodate people with disabilities if you make your needs known when booking.

Other organizations specializing in the needs of travelers with disabilities:

Access-Able Travel Source (www.access-able.com) Lists accessible lodging, transport, attractions and equipment rental by province.

Mobility International (www.miusa.org) Advises travelers with disabilities on mobility issues and runs an educational exchange program.

Society for Accessible Travel & Hospitality (www.sath.org) Travelers with disabilities share tips and blogs.

Visas

Citizens of dozens of countries – including the USA, most Western European nations, Australia, New Zealand, Japan and South Korea – do not need visas to enter Canada for stays of up to 180 days. US permanent residents are also exempt. **Citizenship & Immigration Canada** (www.cic.gc.ca) has the details.

Nationals of other countries – including China, India and South Africa – must apply to the Canadian visa office in their home country for a temporary resident visa (TRV). A separate visa is required if you plan to study or work in Canada.

Single-entry TRVs ($75) are usually valid for a maximum stay of six months from the date of your arrival in Canada. Multiple-entry TRVs ($150) allow you to enter Canada from all other countries multiple times while the visa is valid (usually two or three years), provided no single stay exceeds six months.

Visa extensions ($75) need to be filed with the **CIC Visitor Case Processing Centre** (📞888-242-2100; ⊘8am-4pm Mon-Fri) in Alberta at least one month before your current visa expires.

PRACTICALITIES

Newspapers & Magazines

The most widely available newspaper is the Toronto-based *Globe and Mail* and *Maclean's* (www.macleans.ca) is Canada's weekly news magazine. Regional principal dailies:

➜ *Chronicle Herald* in Halifax

➜ *New Brunswick Telegraph Journal* in Saint John

➜ *Guardian* in Charlottetown

➜ *Telegram* in St John's

Television

The Canadian Broadcasting Corporation (CBC) is the dominant nationwide network for both radio and TV. The Canadian TV Network (CTN) is the major competition.

Measurements

Canada officially uses the metric system, but imperial measurements are used for many day-to-day purposes.

Smoking

Smoking is banned in all restaurants, bars and other public venues nationwide.

polar bear and other wildlife research.

Earthwatch (www.earth-watch.org) Help scientists track whales off the coast of British Columbia, track moose and deer in Nova Scotia, and monitor climate change in Churchill, Manitoba or the Mackenzie Mountains of the Northwest Territories. Trips last from seven to 14 days and cost from $2250 to $5050.

Volunteers for Peace (www.vfp.org) Offers tutoring stints in Aboriginal communities in Canada's far north, as well as projects in Québec.

World-Wide Opportunities on Organic Farms (www.wwoof.ca; application fee $50) Work on an organic farm, usually in exchange for free room and board; check the website for locations throughout Canada.

Visiting the USA

Admission requirements are subject to rapid change. The **US State Department** (www.travel.state.gov) has the latest information, or check with a US consulate in your home country.

Under the US visa-waiver program, visas are not required for citizens of 36 countries – including most EU members, Australia and New Zealand – for visits of up to 90 days (no extensions allowed), as long as you can present a machine-readable passport and are approved under the **Electronic System for Travel Authorization** (ESTA; www.cbp.gov/esta). Note you must register at least 72 hours before arrival and there's a $14 fee for processing and authorization.

Canadians do not need visas, though they do need a passport or document approved by the **Western Hemisphere Travel Initiative** (www.getyouhome.gov). Citizens of all other countries need to apply for a US visa

in their home country before arriving in Canada.

All visitors, regardless of their country of origin, are subject to a US$6 entry fee at land border crossings. Note that you don't need a Canadian multiple-entry TRV for repeated entries into Canada from the USA, unless you have visited a third country.

Volunteering

Volunteering provides the opportunity to interact with local folks and the land in ways you never would just passing through. Many organizations charge a fee, which varies depending on the program's length and the type of food and lodging it provides. The fees usually do not cover travel to Canada. Groups that use volunteers:

Churchill Northern Studies Centre (www.churchillscience.ca) Volunteer for six hours per day (anything from stringing wires to cleaning) and get free room and board at this center for

Women Travelers

Canada is generally a safe place for women to travel, even alone and even in the cities. Simply use the same common sense as you would at home.

In bars and nightclubs, solo women are likely to attract a lot of attention, but if you don't want company, most men will respect a firm 'no thank you.' If you feel threatened, protesting loudly will often make the offender slink away – or will at least spur other people to come to your defense. Note that carrying mace or pepper spray is illegal in Canada.

Physical attack is unlikely, but if you are assaulted, call the police immediately (☎911 except in the Yukon, Northwest Territories and Nunavut) or contact a rape crisis center. A complete list is available from the **Canadian Association of Sexual Assault Centres** (☎604-876-2622; www.casac.ca). It has hotlines in some of the cities:

Halifax (☎902-425-0122)
St John's (☎800-726-2743)

Fredericton (📞506-454-0437)
Charlottetown (📞800-289-5656)

Resources

Journeywoman (www.journeywoman.com)

Her Own Way (www.travel.gc.ca/travelling/publications/her-own-way) Published by the Canadian government for Canadian travelers, but contains a great deal of general advice.

Women Welcome Women Worldwide (5W; www.womenwelcomewomen.uk.org; membership fee UK£35) A member's network of women to meet, greet and welcome those from abroad.

Work

Permits

In almost all cases, you need a valid work permit to work in Canada. Obtaining one may be difficult, as employment opportunities go to Canadians first. Before you can even apply, you need a specific job offer from an employer who in turn must have been granted permission from the government to give the position to a foreign national. Applications must be filed at a visa office of a Canadian embassy or consulate in your home country. Some jobs are exempt from the permit requirement. For full details, check with **Citizenship & Immigration Canada** (www.cic.gc.ca).

Employers hiring temporary service workers (such as hotels, bars, restaurants or resorts) and construction, farm or forestry workers sometimes don't ask for a permit. If you get caught, however, you can kiss Canada goodbye.

Finding Work

Students aged 18 to 30 from over a dozen countries, including the USA, UK, Australia, New Zealand, Ireland and South Africa, are eligible to apply for a spot in the **Student Work Abroad Program** (SWAP; www.swap.ca). If successful, you get a six-month to one-year, non-extendable visa that allows you to work anywhere in Canada in any job you can get. Most 'SWAPpers' find work in the service industry as waiters or bartenders.

Even if you're not a student, you may be able to spend up to a year in Canada on a 'working holiday program' with **International Experience Canada** (www.international.gc.ca/experience). The Canadian government has an arrangement with several countries for people aged 18 to 30 to come over and get a job; check the website for participants. The Canadian embassy in each country runs the program, but basically there are quotas and spaces are filled on a first-come first-served basis.

Transportation

GETTING THERE & AWAY

Flights, tours and rail tickets can be booked online at www.lonelyplanet.com/bookings.

Entering the Country

Entering Canada is pretty straightforward. First, you will have to show your passport (and your visa if you need one). The border officer will ask you a few questions about the purpose and length of your visit. After that, you'll go through customs. See **Going to Canada** (www.goingtocanada.gc.ca) for details.

Note that questioning may be more intense at land border crossings and your car may be searched.

For updates (particularly regarding land-border crossing rules), check the websites for the **US State Department** (www.travel.state.gov) and **Citizenship & Immigration Canada** (www.cic.gc.ca).

Having a criminal record of any kind, including a DUI (driving under the influence) charge, may keep you out of Canada. If this affects you, you should apply for a 'waiver of exclusion' at a Canadian consulate in your country. The process costs $200 and takes several weeks.

Passport

Most international visitors require a passport to enter Canada. US citizens at land and sea borders have other options besides using a passport, such as an enhanced driver's license or passport card. See the **Western Hemisphere Travel Initiative** (www.getyouhome.gov) for approved identification documents.

Visitors from selected countries also require a visa to enter Canada.

Air

Airports

Halifax has the region's largest airport and it's the only one so far to have US pre-clearance privileges (ie nonstop passengers to the US are processed through customs prior to departure, thus ensuring a no-fuss arrival on the US side). Moncton is also busy and may offer lower fares than Halifax. For visitors heading to Newfoundland, Deer Lake is a great option if you are centering your travels on the west coast.

Atlantic Canada's main airports:

Charlottetown, Prince Edward Island (YYG; ☎902-566-7997; www.flypei.com)

Deer Lake, Newfoundland (YDF; www.deerlakeairport.com)

Fredericton, New Brunswick (YFC; www.yfcmobile.ca)

Halifax, Nova Scotia (YHZ; www.hiaa.ca)

CLIMATE CHANGE & TRAVEL

Every form of transport that relies on carbon-based fuel generates CO_2, the main cause of human-induced climate change. Modern travel is dependent on airplanes, which might use less fuel per kilometer per person than most cars but travel much greater distances. The altitude at which aircraft emit gases (including CO_2) and particles also contributes to their climate change impact. Many websites offer 'carbon calculators' that allow people to estimate the carbon emissions generated by their journey and, for those who wish to do so, to offset the impact of the greenhouse gases emitted with contributions to portfolios of climate-friendly initiatives throughout the world. Lonely Planet offsets the carbon footprint of all staff and author travel.

Moncton, New Brunswick (YQM; www.gmia.ca)

St John's, Newfoundland (YYT; www.stjohnsairport.com)

Sydney, Nova Scotia (YQY; ☎902-564-7720)

Airlines

The region is not particularly well serviced, and flight and airline choices are limited. Many visitors will need to fly into Montréal, Toronto, or a US hub city such as New York, and then connect with another flight to reach their destination in Atlantic Canada. Most flights are via the national flagship carrier **Air Canada** (AC; ☎888-247-2262; www. aircanada.com); it's one of the world's safest airlines, though locals often gripe about its stiff prices. Subsidiary **Air Canada Jazz** operates the majority of flights to and within the Atlantic region.

Other companies that are based in Canada and are serving international destinations are the charter airline Air Transat and discount airline WestJet. There are numerous US airlines that also serve Atlantic Canada, which are worth researching.

Airlines operating to/from the region:

Air St-Pierre (PJ; ☎877-277-7765, 902-873-3566; www. airsaintpierre.com)

Air Transat (TS; ☎866-847-1919; www.airtransat.com)

Condor (www.condor.com)

Cubana Airlines (www. cubana.cu)

Delta Airlines (DL ; ☎800-241-4141; www.delta.com)

Iceland Air (www.icelandair. com)

Porter Airlines (PD; ☎888-619-8622; www.flyporter.com)

Provincial Airlines (www. provincialairlines.com)

Sunwing (www.sunwing.ca)

United Airlines (UA; ☎800-241-6522; www.united.ca)

US Airways (US; ☎800-428-4322; www.usairways.com)

WestJet (WS; ☎888-937-8538; www.westjet.com)

Land

Border Crossings

The three major border crossings into Atlantic Canada are between Maine, USA, and New Brunswick at Calais/St Stephen, Madawaska/Edmundston and Houlton/Woodstock. The website for the **Canadian Border Services Agency** (www.cbsa-asfc.gc.ca/bwt-taf/menu-eng.html) has details on estimated wait times. In general, waits rarely exceed 30 minutes, except during the peak summer season and holidays.

When returning to the USA, check the website for the **US Department for Homeland Security** (http://apps.cbp.gov/bwt) for border wait times.

Bus

Maritime Bus (☎902-429-2029; www.maritimebus.com) plies the roads from Saint John, New Brunswick, as far as Riviere-du-Loup in Quebec, up through Charlottetown, Price Edward Island (PEI) and to Nova Scotia as far as Halifax and up to Cape Breton Island to North Sydney (for ferry connections to Newfoundland). From Riviere-du-Loup, you can connect onto the **Orleans Express** (www. orleansexpress.com) to head farther afield into Quebec. The changeover is pretty seamless.

At the time of writing there was no public bus to get to destinations south of Saint John or to Maine in the US. You're best bet until someone fills this niche is with a shuttle bus company like **Eastlink** (www. eastlinkshuttle.com), which offers door to door service from Calais in Maine to many destinations throughout New Brunswick, PEI and Nova Scotia. From Calais in Maine you can take Greyhound buses to other destinations in the US.

Car & Motorcycle

The USA's extensive highway network connects directly with the Canadian system at numerous key points along the border. These Canadian highways then go on to meet up with the east–west Trans-Canada Hwy, an excellent way to traverse the country.

If you're driving into Canada, you'll need the vehicle's registration papers, proof of liability insurance and your home driver's license. Cars rented in the USA usually can be driven into Canada and back, but make sure your rental agreement says so. If you're driving a car registered in someone else's name, bring a letter from the owner authorizing use of the vehicle in Canada.

Train

Via Rail (☎888-842-7733; www.viarail.ca), Canada's national rail line, offers one service to the Atlantic region: a Montréal to Halifax train (advance purchase adult/child two to 11 years $151/76, 21 hours) that runs daily except Tuesday, and includes several stops in New Brunswick and Nova Scotia. It leaves Montréal at 6:30pm, and arrives in Halifax at 4:20pm the next day.

Visitors coming from the USA can hop aboard America's national rail line, **Amtrak** (www.amtrak.com), and its daily service connecting New York City with Montréal.

Sea

Ferry

Various ferry routes connect Atlantic Canada to the USA and even France:

NOVA SCOTIA

The Yarmouth/Maine Ferry was not running at the time of writing but it's possible it may start running again with a new boat. The ferry previously ran from the towns of Bar Harbor and Portland, Maine, and it's likely that those ports would be used for the service again.

NEW BRUNSWICK

East Coast Ferries (506-747-2159, 877-747-2159; www.eastcoastferries.nb.ca) Links Deer Island to Eastport, Maine.

NEWFOUNDLAND

From the Burin Peninsula, you can reach the French territory of St-Pierre & Miquelon.

GETTING AROUND

Air

Airlines in Nova Scotia, New Brunswick & Prince Edward Island

Most regional flights within the Maritimes are operated by Air Canada's subsidiary, Air Canada Jazz. Small provincial airlines fly out to the more remote portions of the region. Fares in such noncompetitive markets can be high.

The following are the main carriers flying within Atlantic Canada:

Air Canada & Air Canada Jazz (AC; 888-247-2262; www.aircanada.com) Flights throughout the region.

Air Labrador (800-563-3042; www.airlabrador.com) Flies mostly within Labrador.

Air St-Pierre (PJ; 877-277-7765, 902-873-3566; www.airsaintpierre.com) Flights from the French island of St Pierre to St John's, Halifax, Sydney and Moncton.

Provincial Airlines (800-563-2800; www.provincialairlines.ca) St John's–based airline with service throughout Newfoundland and to Labrador.

WestJet (WS; 888-937-8538; www.westjet.com) Nationwide discount carrier with a route between St John's and Halifax.

Air Passes

Star Alliance (www.staralliance.com) members Air Canada, United Airlines and US Airways have teamed up to offer the North American Airpass, which is available to anyone not residing in the USA, Canada, Mexico, Bermuda or the Caribbean. It's sold only in conjunction with an international flight operated by any Star Alliance–member airline. You can buy as few as three coupons or as many as 10. Prices start at around C$800 for three flights.

Bicycle

The Maritime provinces, particularly Prince Edward Island, are ideal for bicycle touring.

Transportation

➡ By air: most airlines will carry bikes as checked luggage without charge on international flights, as long as they're in a box. On domestic flights they usually charge between $30 and $65. Always check details before you buy the ticket.

➡ By bus: **Maritime Bus** (902-429-2029; www.maritimebus.com) only charges $5 per bikes and also offers boxes ($6.50) or bags ($5.65) to pack them in. Bikes only travel on the same bus as the passenger if there's enough space. To ensure that yours arrives at the same time as (or before) you do, ship it a day early.

➡ By train: **VIA Rail** (888-842-7733; www.viarail.ca) will transport your bicycle for $25. There are no trains with bike racks that run through this part of Canada so you'll have to dismantle and pack your bike to put on as baggage.

Rental

Outfitters renting bicycles exist in most tourist towns; many are listed throughout this guide. Rentals cost around $15 per day for touring bikes and $25 per day for mountain bikes. The price usually includes a helmet and lock. Most companies require a security deposit of $20 to $200.

Purchase

Buying a bike is easy, as is reselling it before you leave. Specialist bike shops have the best selection and advice, but general sporting-goods stores may have lower prices. Some bicycle stores and rental outfitters also sell used bicycles. To sniff out the best bargains, scour flea markets, garage sales and thrift shops, or check the notice boards in hostels and universities. These are also the best places to sell your bike.

CYCLING RULES & RESOURCES

➡ Cyclists must follow the same rules of the road as vehicles, but don't expect drivers to always respect your right of way.

➡ Helmets are mandatory for all cyclists in British Columbia, New Brunswick, Prince Edward Island and Nova Scotia, as well as for anyone under 18 in Alberta and Ontario.

➡ The **Better World Club** (866-238-1137; www.betterworldclub.com) provides emergency roadside assistance. Membership costs $40 per year, plus a $12 enrollment fee, and entitles you to two free pick-ups and transport to the nearest repair shop or home, within a 50km radius of where you're picked up.

Boat

The watery region hosts an extensive ferry system. Walk-ons and cyclists should be OK anytime, but call ahead for vehicle reservations or if you require a cabin berth. This is especially important during peak season (July and August). Main operators are listed below:

Bay Ferries (☑888-249-7245; www.bayferries.com) Year-round service operating between Saint John, New Brunswick, and Digby, Nova Scotia.

Coastal Transport (☑506-662-3724; www.coastaltransport.ca) Ferry from Blacks Harbour to Grand Manan in the Fundy Isles, New Brunswick.

CTMA Ferries (☑418-986-3278, 888-986-3278; www.ctma.ca) Daily ferries to Québec's Îles de la Madeleine from Souris, PEI.

East Coast Ferries (☑506-747-2159, 877-747-2159; www.eastcoastferries.nb.ca) Connects Deer Island to Campobello Island, both in the Fundy Isles, New Brunswick.

Labrador Marine (☑709-535-0810, 866-535-2567; www.labradormarine.com) Connects Newfoundland to Labrador.

Marine Atlantic (☑800-341-7981; www.marine-atlantic.ca) Connects Port aux Basques and Argentia in Newfoundland with North Sydney, Nova Scotia.

Northumberland Ferries (☑902-566-3838, 888-249-7245; www.peiferry.com) Connects Wood Islands, PEI and Caribou, Nova Scotia.

Provincial Ferry Services (www.gov.nl.ca/ferryservices) Operates a coastal ferry service throughout Newfoundland.

Bus

Greyhound Canada does not operate within the Atlantic provinces. The main bus lines in the region:

Maritime Bus (☑902-429-2029; www.maritimebus.com) For New Brunswick, PEI and Nova Scotia.

DRL Coachlines (☑709-263-2171; www.drl-lr.com) Service throughout Newfoundland.

Bus frequency ranges from one to two buses per day along most routes. Buses generally are clean, comfortable and reliable. They usually have onboard toilets, air-conditioning (bring a sweater), reclining seats and onboard movies.

A series of small, regional shuttle vans comprises the rest of bus service in the area.

Bus Passes

Neither Maritime nor DRL offer any special discount passes.

Costs

Bus travel is cheaper than other means of transportation. Advance purchases (four, seven or 14 days) save quite a bit, too.

Sample fares on Maritime:

➡ Halifax to North Sydney ($68.50, seven hours)

➡ Halifax to Charlottetown ($58.25, 5½ hours)

➡ Charlottetown to Moncton ($33.75, 3½ hours)

Sample fares on DRL Coachlines:

➡ St John's to Corner Brook ($101, 10½ hours)

➡ St John's to Port aux Basques ($124, 13½ hours).

Reservations

Tickets can be bought online or at bus terminals for Maritime and on the bus (cash) for DRL; there are no phone or online sales. Show up at least 30 to 45 minutes prior to departure.

Car & Motorcycle

Automobile Associations

Auto-club membership is a handy thing to have in Canada. Try the following:

Better World Club (☑866-238-1137; www.betterworldclub.com) Donates 1% of its annual revenue to environmental cleanup efforts. It offers service throughout the USA and Canada, and also has a roadside-assistance program for bicycles.

Canadian Automobile Association (CAA; ☑800-268-3750; www.caa.ca) Offers services, including 24-hour emergency roadside assistance, to members of international affiliates such as AAA in the USA, AA in the UK and ADAC in Germany. The club also offers trip-planning advice, free maps, travel-agency services and a range of discounts on hotels, car rentals etc.

Bring Your Own Vehicle

There's minimal hassle driving into Canada from the USA as long as you have your vehicle's registration papers, proof of liability insurance and your home driver's license.

Driver's License

In most provinces visitors can legally drive for up to three months with their home driver's license. In some, such as British Columbia, this is extended to six months.

If you're spending considerable time in Canada, think about getting an international driving permit (IDP), which is valid for one year. Your automobile association at home can issue one for a small fee. Always carry your home license together with the IDP.

Fuel & Spare Parts

➡ gas is sold in liters

➡ at the time of writing, the average for midgrade fuel

was $1.35 per liter (about C$5 per US gallon)

➡ prices are higher in remote areas

➡ fuel prices in Canada are usually higher than in the USA, so fill up south of the border

➡ most gas stations are self-service

➡ finding a gas station is generally easy except in sparsely populated areas such as Labrador and Newfoundland's South Coast

➡ finding spare parts can be difficult far from big cities

➡ when traveling in remote regions always bring some tools and at least a spare tire

Insurance

Canadian law requires liability insurance for all vehicles, to cover you for damage caused to property and people.

The minimum requirement is $200,000 in all provinces except Québec, where it is $50,000.

Americans traveling to Canada in their own car should ask their insurance company for a nonresident interprovince motor vehicle liability insurance card (commonly known as a 'yellow card'), which is accepted as evidence of financial responsibility anywhere in Canada. Although not mandatory, it may come in handy in an accident.

Car-rental agencies offer liability insurance. Collision damage waivers (CDW) reduce or eliminate the amount you'll have to reimburse the rental company if there's damage to the car

itself. Some credit cards cover CDW for a certain rental period, if you use the card to pay for the rental, and decline the policy offered by the rental company. Always check with your card issuer to see what coverage they offer in Canada.

Personal accident insurance (PAI) covers you and any passengers for medical costs incurred as a result of an accident. If your travel insurance or your health insurance policy at home does this as well (and most do, but check), then this is one expense you can do without.

Rental

CAR

To rent a car in Canada you generally need to:

➡ be at least 25 years old (though some companies will rent to drivers between the ages of 21 and 24 for an additional charge.)

➡ hold a valid driver's license (an international one may be required if you're not from an English- or French-speaking country)

➡ have a major credit card

You should be able to get an economy-sized vehicle for about $25 to $65 per day. Child safety seats are compulsory (reserve them when you book) and cost about $13 per day.

Car-rental prices can double in July and August, and it's essential to book ahead in prime tourist spots such as Charlottetown or St John's, as there often just aren't enough cars to go around.

International car-rental companies usually have branches at airports and in city centers; note that ferry terminals often do not have branches.

Avis (☎800-437-0358; www.avis.com)

Budget (☎800-268-8900; www.budget.com)

Dollar (☎800-800-4000; www.dollar.com)

Enterprise (☎800-261-7331; www.enterprise.ca)

Hertz (☎800-263-0600; www.hertz.com)

National (☎877-222-9058; www.nationalcar.ca)

Thrifty (☎800-847-4389; www.thrifty.com)

In Canada, on-the-spot rentals often are more expensive than pre-booked packages (ie rental cars booked online or with your flight).

MOTORCYCLE

Nova Scotia's tourism office produces a free **motorcycle guide** (☎800-565-0000; www.novascotia.com/ride); take a look at **Motorcycle Tour Guide Nova Scotia** (www.motorcycletourguide.com) for online information. Unfortunately there are no Harley rentals available in this region, the nearest are in Montréal, Québec, and Bangor, Maine.

Northeastern Motorcycle Tours (www.motorcycletours.com) runs tours along the Cabot Trail from Maine, USA.

RECREATIONAL VEHICLES

Rentals cost roughly $160 to $265 per day in high season for midsize vehicles, although insurance, fees and taxes add a hefty chunk. Diesel-fueled RVs have considerably lower running costs.

Cruise Canada (☎800-671-8042; www.cruisecanada.com) Offers three sizes of RVs. Locations in Halifax, central and western Canada; offers one-way rentals.

TRAVELING WITH CHILDREN?

Single parents, grandparents or guardians traveling with anyone under the age of 18 should carry proof of legal custody, or a notarized letter from the nonaccompanying parent authorizing the trip. Unaccompanied children will also need a notarized letter of consent from both parents or legal guardians. This is in addition to their passport and/or proof of citizenship.

Islander RV (✆709-364-7368, 888-848-2267; www.islanderrv.com) Rentals from St John's.

Road Conditions & Hazards

Road conditions are generally good, but keep the following in mind:

➡ Fierce winters can leave potholes the size of landmine craters. Be prepared to swerve. Winter travel in general can be hazardous due to heavy snow and ice, which may cause roads and bridges to close periodically. **Transport Canada** (✆800-387-4999; www.tc.gc.ca/road) provides links to road conditions and construction zones for each province.

➡ If you're driving in winter or in remote areas, make sure your vehicle is equipped with four-seasonal radial or snow tires, and emergency supplies in case you're stranded.

➡ Distances between services can be long in sparsely populated areas so keep your gas topped up whenever possible.

➡ Moose, deer and elk are common on rural roadways, especially at night. There's no contest between a 534kg bull moose and a Subaru, so keep your eyes peeled.

Road Rules

➡ Canadians drive on the right-hand side of the road.

➡ Seat-belt use is compulsory. Children under 18kg must be strapped in child-booster seats, except infants who must be in a rear-facing safety seat.

➡ Motorcyclists must wear helmets and drive with their headlights on.

➡ Distances and speed limits are posted in kilometres. The speed limit is generally 40km/h to 50km/h in cities and 90km/h to 110km/h outside town.

➡ Slow down to 60km/h when passing emergency vehicles (such as police cars and ambulances) stopped on the roadside with their lights flashing.

➡ Turning right at red lights after coming to a full stop is permitted in all provinces.

➡ Driving while using a hand-held cell phone is illegal in Newfoundland, Nova Scotia and Prince Edward Island.

➡ Radar detectors are not allowed. If you're caught driving with a radar detector, even one that isn't being operated, you could receive a fine of $1000 and your device may be confiscated.

➡ The blood-alcohol limit for drivers is 0.08%. Driving while drunk is a criminal offense.

Hitchhiking

Hitchhiking is never entirely safe in any country and we don't recommend it. That said, in remote and rural areas in Canada it is not uncommon to see people thumbing for a ride.

➡ If you do decide to hitch, understand that you are taking a small but potentially serious risk. Remember that it's safer to travel in pairs and let someone know where you are planning to go.

➡ Hitchhiking is illegal on some highways and in the provinces of Nova Scotia and New Brunswick although you'll see people hitchhiking there anyway.

Ride Sharing

Many hostels have ride-share boards that can be a boon if you're traveling without a car.
Digihitch (www.canada.digi-hitch.com) A decent, if dated, resource.

Liftsurfer (www.liftsurfer.com) Caters to backpackers looking for ride-shares across Canada and the US.

Local Transportation

Bicycle

Cycling is more of a recreational activity than a means of local transportation in Atlantic Canada. City bike paths are not common. Still, most public transportation allows bicycles to be brought on at certain times of day.

Bus

The only cities in the region with municipal bus services are Fredericton, Saint John, Moncton, Halifax, Sydney and St John's. The Annapolis Valley has an excellent regional bus service between Wolfville and Bridgetown. Elsewhere the private car is king.

Taxi

Taxis usually are metered, with a flag-fall fee of $2.70 and a per-kilometer charge around $1.75. Drivers expect a tip of between 10% and 15%. Taxis can be flagged down or ordered by phone.

Tours

Group travel can be an enjoyable way to go, especially if you're traveling solo. Try to pick a tour that will suit you in terms of age, interest and activity level.
Arctic Odysseys (✆20 6-325-1977, 800-574-3021; www.arcticodysseys.com) Arctic-oriented company with yacht trips up the Newfoundland and Labrador coast.

Backroads (✆800-462-2848, 510-527-1555; www.backroads.com) Guided and self-guided bicycle tours worldwide, including Nova Scotia.

Road Scholar (✆800-454-5768; www.roadscholar.org) Run by nonprofit organization Elderhostel, offering study tours for active people over 55 years old, including bus and walking tours in Atlantic Canada.

Freewheeling Adventures (☑800-672-0775, 902-857-3600; www.freewheeling. ca) Nova Scotia–based company with bicycle and walking tours throughout Atlantic Canada, including bike-and-yoga getaways.

Routes to Learning (☑613-530-2222, 866-745-1690; www. routestolearning.ca) From walking in the steps of Newfoundland's Vikings to exploring New Brunswick's Acadians or Nova Scotia's lighthouses, this nonprofit group has dozens of educational tours throughout Canada.

Salty Bear Adventure Tours (☑902-202-3636; www. saltybear.ca) Backpacker-oriented van tours through the Maritimes with jump-on/ jump-off flexibility. There's a three-day circuit around Cape Breton, Nova Scotia, and a five-day route that goes into PEI.

Train

Train travel is limited within the region. PEI and Newfoundland have no train services. Nova Scotia and New Brunswick are served along the **VIA Rail** (☑888-842-7245; www.viarail.ca)

Montréal–Halifax route. For a train schedule, check the website. Most stations have left-luggage offices.

Western Labrador is also accessible by train with the Quebec Northshore & Labrador Railway. There are twice weekly services from Sept Îles, Québec, to Labrador City. There is no website so you'll have to call for current prices and information.

Train buffs should also check out **Canada by Rail** (www.canadabyrail.ca), an excellent portal packed with information on regional excursion trains, railroad museums and historical train stations.

Classes

There are four main classes:

➡ Economy Class buys you a fairly basic, if indeed quite comfortable, reclining seat with a headrest. Blankets and pillows are provided for overnight travel.

➡ Sleeper Class is available on shorter overnight routes. You can choose from compartments with upper or lower pullout berths, and private single, double or triple roomettes, all with a bathroom.

➡ Touring Class is available on long-distance routes and includes Sleeper Class accommodations

plus meals, access to the sightseeing car and sometimes a tour guide.

➡ Business Class provides access to a business lounge with spacious seats, free nonalcoholic beverages, high-speed wi-fi and more.

Costs

Taking the train is more expensive than the bus, but most people find it a more comfortable way to travel. June to mid-October is peak season, when prices are about 40% higher. Buying tickets in advance (even just five days before) can yield significant savings.

Reservations

Tickets and train passes are available for purchase online, by phone, at VIA Rail stations and from many travel agents. Seat reservations are highly recommended, especially in summer and for sleeper cars.

Train Passes

VIA Rail offers the Canrailpass-System, good for seven trips on any train during a 21-day period. All seats are in Economy Class; upgrades are not permitted. You must book each leg at least three days in advance (doable online). It costs from $1008/630 in high/low season.

Language

English and French are the official languages of Canada. You'll see both on highway signs, maps, tourist brochures, packaging etc.

New Brunswick is Canada's only officially bilingual province, although only about one third of the population speaks both French and English. French is widely spoken, particularly in the north and east of the province. Nova Scotia also has a significant French-speaking population. The strongest French Acadian ancestry on Prince Edward Island is found in Région Évangéline, where some 6000 residents still speak French as their first language.

You'll find that the French spoken in Canada is essentially the same as in France, and locals will have no problem understanding more formal French.

French pronunciation is pretty straightforward for English speakers, as the sounds can almost all be found in English. The exceptions are nasal vowels (represented in our coloured pronunciation guides by o or u followed by an almost inaudible nasal consonant sound m, n or ng), the 'funny' u (ew in our guides) and the deep-in-the-throat r. Bearing this in mind and reading the pronunciation guides in this chapter as if they were English, you shouldn't have problems being understood. Syllables in French words are, for the most part, equally stressed. English speakers tend to stress the first syllable, which is unusual in French, so try adding a light stress on the final syllable to compensate.

WANT MORE?

For in-depth language information and handy phrases, check out Lonely Planet's *French Phrasebook*. You'll find it at **shop.lonelyplanet.com**, or you can buy Lonely Planet's iPhone phrasebooks at the Apple App Store.

BASICS

Hello.	*Bonjour.*	bon·zhoor
Goodbye.	*Au revoir.*	o·rer·vwa
Excuse me.	*Excusez-moi.*	ek·skew·zay·mwa
Sorry.	*Pardon.*	par·don
Yes./No.	*Oui./Non.*	wee/non
Please.	*S'il vous plaît.*	seel voo play
Thank you.	*Merci.*	mair·see
You're welcome.	*De rien.*	der ree·en

How are you?
Comment allez-vous? ko·mon ta·lay·voo

Fine, and you?
Bien, merci. Et vous? byun mair·see ay voo

My name is ...
Je m'appelle ... zher ma·pel ...

What's your name?
Comment vous appelez-vous? ko·mon voo· za·play voo

Do you speak English?
Parlez-vous anglais? par·lay·voo ong·glay

I don't understand.
Je ne comprends pas. zher ner kom·pron pa

ACCOMMODATIONS

Do you have any rooms available?
Est-ce que vous avez des chambres libres? es·ker voo za·vay day shom·brer lee·brer

How much is it per night/person?
Quel est le prix par nuit/personne? kel ay ler pree par nwee/per·son

Is breakfast included?
Est-ce que le petit déjeuner est inclus? es·ker ler per·tee day·zher·nay ayt en·klew

a ... room	*une chambre ...*	ewn shom·brer ...
single	*à un lit*	a un lee
double	*avec un grand lit*	a·vek un gron lee

air-con	*climatiseur*	klee·ma·tee·zer
bathroom	*salle de bains*	sal der bun
campsite	*camping*	kom·peeng
dorm	*dortoir*	dor·twar
guesthouse	*pension*	pon·syon
hotel	*hôtel*	o·tel
window	*fenêtre*	fer·nay·trer
youth hostel	*auberge de jeunesse*	o·berzh der zher·nes

DIRECTIONS

Where's ...?
Où est ...?   oo ay ...

What's the address?
Quelle est l'adresse?   kel ay la·dres

Could you write the address, please?
Est-ce que vous pourriez écrire l'adresse, s'il vous plaît?   es·ker voo poo·ryay ay·kreer la·dres seel voo play

Can you show me (on the map)?
Pouvez-vous m'indiquer (sur la carte)?   poo·vay·voo mun·dee·kay (sewr la kart)

at the corner	*au coin*	o kwun
at the traffic lights	*aux feux*	o fer
behind	*derrière*	dair·ryair
in front of ...	*devant ...*	der·von ...
far (from ...)	*loin (de ...)*	lwun (der ...)
left	*gauche*	gosh
near (to ...)	*près (de ...)*	pray (der ...)
next to ...	*à côté de ...*	a ko·tay der...
opposite ...	*en face de ...*	on fas der ...
right	*droite*	drwat
straight ahead	*tout droit*	too drwa

EATING & DRINKING

A table for (two), please.
Une table pour (deux), s'il vous plaît.   ewn ta·bler poor (der) seel voo play

What would you recommend?
Qu'est-ce que vous conseillez?   kes·ker voo kon·say·yay

What's in that dish?
Quels sont les ingrédients?   kel son lay zun·gray·dyon

I'm a vegetarian.
Je suis végétarien/ végétarienne.   zher swee vay·zhay·ta·ryun/ vay·zhay·ta·ryen (m/f)

I don't eat ...
Je ne mange pas ...   zher ner monzh pa ...

KEY PATTERNS

To get by in French, mix and match these simple patterns with words of your choice:

Where's (the entry)?
Où est (l'entrée)?   oo ay (lon·tray)

Where can I (buy a ticket)?
Où est-ce que je peux (acheter un billet)?   oo es·ker zher per (ash·tay un bee·yay)

When's (the next train)?
Quand est (le prochain train)?   kon ay (ler pro·shun trun)

How much is (a room)?
C'est combien pour (une chambre)?   say kom·buyn poor (ewn shom·brer)

Do you have (a map)?
Avez-vous (une carte)?   a·vay voo (ewn kart)

Is there (a toilet)?
Y a-t-il (des toilettes)?   ee a teel (day twa·let)

I'd like (to book a room).
Je voudrais (réserver une chambre).   zher voo·dray (ray·ser·vay ewn shom·brer)

Can I (enter)?
Puis-je (entrer)?   pweezh (on·tray)

Could you please (help)?
Pouvez-vous (m'aider), s'il vous plaît?   poo·vay voo (may·day) seel voo play

Do I have to (book a seat)?
Faut-il (réserver une place)?   fo·teel (ray·ser·vay ewn plas)

Cheers!
Santé!   son·tay

That was delicious.
C'était délicieux!   say·tay day·lee·syer

Please bring the bill.
Apportez-moi l'addition, s'il vous plaît.   a·por·tay·mwa la·dee·syon seel voo play

Key Words

appetiser	*entrée*	on·tray
bottle	*bouteille*	boo·tay
breakfast	*déjeuner*	day·zher·nay
children's menu	*menu pour enfants*	mer·new poor on·fon
cold	*froid*	frwa
delicatessen	*traiteur*	tray·ter
dinner	*souper*	soo·pay
dish	*plat*	pla

food	nourriture	noo·ree·tewr
fork	fourchette	foor·shet
glass	verre	vair
grocery store	épicerie	ay·pees·ree
highchair	chaise haute	shay zot
hot	chaud	sho
knife	couteau	koo·to
local speciality	spécialité locale	spay·sya·lee·tay lo·kal
lunch	dîner	dee·nay
main course	plat principal	pla prun·see·pal
market	marché	mar·shay
menu (in English)	carte (en anglais)	kart (on ong·glay)
plate	assiette	a·syet
spoon	cuillère	kwee·yair
wine list	carte des vins	kart day vun
with	avec	a·vek
without	sans	son

Meat & Fish

beef	bœuf	berf
chicken	poulet	poo·lay
fish	poisson	pwa·son
lamb	agneau	a·nyo
pork	porc	por
turkey	dinde	dund
veal	veau	vo

Fruit & Vegetables

apple	pomme	pom
apricot	abricot	ab·ree·ko
asparagus	asperge	a·spairzh
beans	haricots	a·ree·ko
beetroot	betterave	be·trav
cabbage	chou	shoo
celery	céleri	sel·ree
cherry	cerise	ser·reez
corn	maïs	ma·ees
cucumber	concombre	kong·kom·brer
gherkin (pickle)	cornichon	kor·nee·shon
grape	raisin	ray·zun
leek	poireau	pwa·ro
lemon	citron	see·tron
lettuce	laitue	lay·tew
mushroom	champignon	shom·pee·nyon
peach	pêche	pesh
peas	petit pois	per·tee pwa

(red/green) pepper	poivron (rouge/vert)	pwa·vron (roozh/vair)
pineapple	ananas	a·na·nas
plum	prune	prewn
potato	pomme de terre	pom der tair
prune	pruneau	prew·no
pumpkin	citrouille	see·troo·yer
shallot	échalote	eh·sha·lot
spinach	épinards	eh·pee·nar
strawberry	fraise	frez
tomato	tomate	to·mat
turnip	navet	na·vay
vegetable	légume	lay·gewm

Other

bread	pain	pun
butter	beurre	ber
cheese	fromage	fro·mazh
egg	œuf	erf
honey	miel	myel
jam	confiture	kon·fee·tewr
lentils	lentilles	lon·tee·yer
oil	huile	weel
pasta/noodles	pâtes	pat
pepper	poivre	pwa·vrer
rice	riz	ree
salt	sel	sel
sugar	sucre	sew·krer
vinegar	vinaigre	vee·nay·grer

Drinks

beer	bière	bee·yair
coffee	café	ka·fay
(orange) juice	jus (d'orange)	zhew (do·ronzh)
milk	lait	lay
red wine	vin rouge	vun roozh

Signs	
Entrée	Entrance
Femmes	Women
Fermé	Closed
Hommes	Men
Interdit	Prohibited
Ouvert	Open
Renseignements	Information
Sortie	Exit
Toilettes/WC	Toilets

tea	*thé*	tay
(mineral) water	*eau (minérale)*	o (mee·nay·ral)
white wine	*vin blanc*	vun blong

EMERGENCIES

Help!
Au secours! — o skoor

I'm lost.
Je suis perdu/perdue. — zhe swee pair·dew (m/f)

Leave me alone!
Fichez-moi la paix! — fee·shay·mwa la pay

There's been an accident.
Il y a eu un accident. — eel ya ew un ak·see·don

Call a doctor.
Appelez un médecin. — a·play un mayd·sun

Call the police.
Appelez la police. — a·play la po·lees

I'm ill.
Je suis malade. — zher swee ma·lad

It hurts here.
J'ai une douleur ici. — zhay ewn doo·ler ee·see

I'm allergic to ...
Je suis allergique ... — zher swee za·lair·zheek ...

Where are the toilets?
Où sont les toilettes? — oo son lay twa·let

SHOPPING & SERVICES

I'd like to buy ...
Je voudrais acheter ... — zher voo·dray ash·tay ...

May I look at it?
Est-ce que je peux le voir? — es·ker zher per ler vwar

I'm just looking.
Je regarde. — zher rer·gard

I don't like it.
Cela ne me plaît pas. — ser·la ner mer play pa

How much is it?
C'est combien? — say kom·byun

It's too expensive.
C'est trop cher. — say tro shair

Can you lower the price?
Vous pouvez baisser le prix? — voo poo·vay bay·say ler pree

Question Words

How?	*Comment?*	ko·mon
What?	*Quoi?*	kwa
When?	*Quand?*	kon
Where?	*Où?*	oo
Who?	*Qui?*	kee
Why?	*Pourquoi?*	poor·kwa

There's a mistake in the bill.
Il y a une erreur dans la note. — eel ya ewn ay·rer don la not

ATM	*guichet automatique de banque*	gee·shay o·to·ma·teek der bonk
credit card	*carte de crédit*	kart der kray·dee
internet cafe	*cybercafé*	see·bair·ka·fay
post office	*bureau de poste*	bew·ro der post
tourist office	*office de tourisme*	o·fees der too·rees·mer

TIME & DATES

What time is it?
Quelle heure est-il? — kel er ay til

It's (eight) o'clock.
Il est (huit) heures. — il ay (weet) er

It's half past (10).
Il est (dix) heures et demie. — il ay (deez) er ay day·mee

morning	*matin*	ma·tun
afternoon	*après-midi*	a·pray·mee·dee
evening	*soir*	swar

yesterday	*hier*	yair
today	*aujourd'hui*	o·zhoor·dwee
tomorrow	*demain*	der·mun

Monday	*lundi*	lun·dee
Tuesday	*mardi*	mar·dee
Wednesday	*mercredi*	mair·krer·dee
Thursday	*jeudi*	zher·dee
Friday	*vendredi*	von·drer·dee
Saturday	*samedi*	sam·dee
Sunday	*dimanche*	dee·monsh

January	*janvier*	zhon·vyay
February	*février*	fayv·ryay
March	*mars*	mars
April	*avril*	a·vreel
May	*mai*	may
June	*juin*	zhwun
July	*juillet*	zhwee·yay
August	*août*	oot
September	*septembre*	sep·tom·brer
October	*octobre*	ok·to·brer
November	*novembre*	no·vom·brer
December	*décembre*	day·som·brer

TRANSPORTATION

Public Transportation

boat	*bateau*	ba·to
bus	*bus*	bews
plane	*avion*	a·vyon
train	*train*	trun

I want to go to ...
Je voudrais aller à ... — zher voo·dray a·lay a ...

Does it stop at ...?
Est-ce qu'il s'arrête à ...? — es·kil sa·ret a ...

At what time does it leave/arrive?
À quelle heure est-ce — a kel er es
qu'il part/arrive? — kil par/a·reev

Can you tell me when we get to ...?
Pouvez-vous me — poo·vay·voo mer
dire quand — deer kon
nous arrivons à ...? — noo za·ree·von a ...

I want to get off here.
Je veux descendre — zher ver day·son·drer
ici. — ee·see

first	*premier*	prer·myay
last	*dernier*	dair·nyay
next	*prochain*	pro·shun

a ... ticket	*un billet ...*	un bee·yay ...
1st-class	*de première classe*	der prem·yair klas
2nd-class	*de deuxième classe*	der der·zyem las
one-way	*simple*	sum·pler
return	*aller et retour*	a·lay ay rer·toor

aisle seat	*côté couloir*	ko·tay kool·war
cancelled	*annulé*	a·new·lay
delayed	*en retard*	on rer·tar
platform	*quai*	kay
ticket office	*guichet*	gee·shay
timetable	*horaire*	o·rair
train station	*gare*	gar
window seat	*côté fenêtre*	ko·tay fe·ne·trer

Driving & Cycling

I'd like to hire a ...	*Je voudrais louer ...*	zher voo·dray loo·way ...
car	*une voiture*	ewn vwa·tewr
bicycle	*un vélo*	un vay·lo
motorcycle	*une moto*	ewn mo·to

Numbers

1	*un*	un
2	*deux*	der
3	*trois*	trwa
4	*quatre*	ka·trer
5	*cinq*	sungk
6	*six*	sees
7	*sept*	set
8	*huit*	weet
9	*neuf*	nerf
10	*dix*	dees
20	*vingt*	vung
30	*trente*	tront
40	*quarante*	ka·ront
50	*cinquante*	sung·kont
60	*soixante*	swa·sont
70	*soixante-dix*	swa·son·dees
80	*quatre-vingts*	ka·trer·vung
90	*quatre-vingt-dix*	ka·trer·vung·dees
100	*cent*	son
1000	*mille*	meel

child seat	*siège-enfant*	syezh·on·fon
diesel	*diesel*	dyay·zel
helmet	*casque*	kask
mechanic	*mécanicien*	may·ka·nee·syun
petrol/gas	*essence*	ay·sons
service station	*station-service*	sta·syon·ser·vees

Is this the road to ...?
C'est la route pour ...? — say la root poor ...

(How long) Can I park here?
(Combien de temps) — (kom·byun der tom)
Est-ce que je peux — es·ker zher per
stationner ici? — sta·syo·nay ee·see

The car/motorbike has broken down (at ...).
La voiture/moto est — la vwa·tewr/mo·to ay
tombée en panne (à ...). — tom·bay on pan (a ...)

I have a flat tyre.
Mon pneu est à plat. — mom pner ay ta pla

I've run out of petrol.
Je suis en panne — zher swee zon pan
d'essence. — day·sons

I've lost my car keys.
J'ai perdu les clés de — zhay per·dew lay klay der
ma voiture. — ma vwa·tewr

Where can I have my bicycle repaired?
Où est-ce que je peux — oo es ker zher per
faire réparer mon vélo? — fair ray·pa·ray mon vay·lo

Behind the Scenes

SEND US YOUR FEEDBACK

We love to hear from travelers – your comments keep us on our toes and help make our books better. Our well-traveled team reads every word on what you loved or loathed about this book. Although we cannot reply individually to postal submissions, we always guarantee that your feedback goes straight to the appropriate authors, in time for the next edition. Each person who sends us information is thanked in the next edition – the most useful submissions are rewarded with a selection of digital PDF chapters.

Visit **lonelyplanet.com/contact** to submit your updates and suggestions or to ask for help. Our award-winning website also features inspirational travel stories, news and discussions.

Note: We may edit, reproduce and incorporate your comments in Lonely Planet products such as guidebooks, websites and digital products, so let us know if you don't want your comments reproduced or your name acknowledged. For a copy of our privacy policy visit lonelyplanet.com/privacy.

OUR READERS

Many thanks to the travelers who used the last edition and wrote to us with helpful hints, useful advice and interesting anecdotes: Amy Goben, Carmen Stanley, Chad Stewart, David Drake, Gisela Broderick, Helen Tyson, Herman Goellnitz, Lynette Olfert, Meike Ferrari, Michael Duffey, Nigel Rayner, Rob McCleave, Sarah Hayter, Sebastian Cool, Semin Poonja, Sheree and Carl Lovell, Tarini Casinader and Terrie Phillips.

AUTHOR THANKS

Celeste Brash

Thanks to Andrea Young at Destination Halifax and Isabel MacDougall with PEI Tourism, to the good folks of Digby Backpackers, Bear on the River and Kiwi Kaboodle, John Tattrie, everyone at Authentic Seacoast in Guysburough, Coastal Adventures Sea Kayaking, Kate Prest and Doug in Pictou, Isaac in Mabou, Sandra in Creignish, Beartown Baskets, Juana in North Sydney and Brian and Al in Wolfville. I wish I could work with Karla Zimmerman on every book. Biggest thanks as always to my family.

Caroline Sieg

Thanks to everyone who shared their tips with me and for the friendly conversations at all the local watering holes, where (thankfully) few things change.

Karla Zimmerman

Thanks to St John's gurus Bryan Curtis, Sarah Mathieson and their compadres. Huge gratitude to Lisa Beran for woman'ing the wheel once again. Kudos to fellow scribes Celeste and Caroline for awesome work. Thanks most to Eric Markowitz, the world's best partner for life.

ACKNOWLEDGMENTS

Climate map data adapted from Peel MC, Finlayson BL & McMahon TA (2007) 'Updated World Map of the Köppen-Geiger Climate Classification', *Hydrology and Earth System Sciences*, 11, 163344.

Cover photograph: Peggy's Cove Lighthouse, Nova Scotia, Beverley Lu/Alamy.

THIS BOOK

This 3rd edition of Lonely Planet's *Nova Scotia, New Brunswick & Prince Edward Island* was commissioned in Lonely Planet's Oakland office, and produced by the following:

Commissioning Editor Korina Miller

Coordinating Editors Kate Mathews, Amanda Williamson

Senior Cartographer Mark Griffiths

Book Designer Katherine Marsh

Assisting Editor Kristin Odijk

Assisting Book Designer Virginia Moreno

Cover & Internal Image Research Naomi Parker

Thanks to Samantha Forge, Briohny Hooper, Indra Kilfoyle, Trent Paton, Tracy Whitmey

Index

Map Legend

Sights

- Beach
- Bird Sanctuary
- Buddhist
- Castle/Palace
- Christian
- Confucian
- Hindu
- Islamic
- Jain
- Jewish
- Monument
- Museum/Gallery/Historic Building
- Ruin
- Sento Hot Baths/Onsen
- Shinto
- Sikh
- Taoist
- Winery/Vineyard
- Zoo/Wildlife Sanctuary
- Other Sight

Activities, Courses & Tours

- Bodysurfing
- Diving
- Canoeing/Kayaking
- Course/Tour
- Skiing
- Snorkeling
- Surfing
- Swimming/Pool
- Walking
- Windsurfing
- Other Activity

Sleeping

- Sleeping
- Camping

Eating

- Eating

Drinking & Nightlife

- Drinking & Nightlife
- Cafe

Entertainment

- Entertainment

Shopping

- Shopping

Information

- Bank
- Embassy/Consulate
- Hospital/Medical
- Internet
- Police
- Post Office
- Telephone
- Toilet
- Tourist Information
- Other Information

Geographic

- Beach
- Hut/Shelter
- Lighthouse
- Lookout
- Mountain/Volcano
- Oasis
- Park
- Pass
- Picnic Area
- Waterfall

Population

- Capital (National)
- Capital (State/Province)
- City/Large Town
- Town/Village

Transport

- Airport
- BART station
- Border crossing
- Boston T station
- Bus
- Cable car/Funicular
- Cycling
- Ferry
- Metro/Muni station
- Monorail
- Parking
- Petrol station
- Subway/SkyTrain station
- Taxi
- Train station/Railway
- Tram
- Underground station
- Other Transport

Note: Not all symbols displayed above appear on the maps in this book

Routes

- Tollway
- Freeway
- Primary
- Secondary
- Tertiary
- Lane
- Unsealed road
- Road under construction
- Plaza/Mall
- Steps
- Tunnel
- Pedestrian overpass
- Walking Tour
- Walking Tour detour
- Path/Walking Trail

Boundaries

- International
- State/Province
- Disputed
- Regional/Suburb
- Marine Park
- Cliff
- Wall

Hydrography

- River, Creek
- Intermittent River
- Canal
- Water
- Dry/Salt/Intermittent Lake
- Reef

Areas

- Airport/Runway
- Beach/Desert
- Cemetery (Christian)
- Cemetery (Other)
- Glacier
- Mudflat
- Park/Forest
- Sight (Building)
- Sportsground
- Swamp/Mangrove

OUR STORY

A beat-up old car, a few dollars in the pocket and a sense of adventure. In 1972 that's all Tony and Maureen Wheeler needed for the trip of a lifetime – across Europe and Asia overland to Australia. It took several months, and at the end – broke but inspired – they sat at their kitchen table writing and stapling together their first travel guide, *Across Asia on the Cheap*. Within a week they'd sold 1500 copies. Lonely Planet was born. Today, Lonely Planet has offices in Melbourne, London and Oakland, with more than 600 staff and writers. We share Tony's belief that 'a great guidebook should do three things: inform, educate and amuse'.

OUR WRITERS

Celeste Brash

Coordinating Author, Nova Scotia, Prince Edward Island Trading Dungeness crab for lobster was no hardship on this, Celeste's fourth grand tour of the Maritimes. Over the years she's rafted the Fundy tidal bore, watched eagles nest, got stuck in a 'moose jam,' and climbed more lighthouses than she can count and yet, these provinces come up with new surprises on each visit. Celeste has written around 50 Lonely Planet guides. Find out more about Celeste and her writing at www.celestebrash.com.

Read more about Celeste at:
lonelyplanet.com/members/celestebrash

Caroline Sieg

New Brunswick Caroline Sieg is a half-Swiss, half-American writer. Her relationship with New Brunswick started when she first lived in Boston and she began heading up to Canada to see the crazy high tides everyone told her about. She was delighted to return for Lonely Planet.

Read more about Caroline at:
lonelyplanet.com/members/carolinesieg

Karla Zimmerman

Newfoundland & Labrador Karla has covered Canada coast to coast for Lonely Planet. Newfoundland is her current beat, and over the years she has paddled by icebergs, come nose-to-beak with puffins, hiked in polar bear territory and driven by most of Newfoundland's 120,000 moose. She's visited Dildo, Come by Chance and Heart's Delight, and intends to get to Jerry's Nose one day soon. Karla writes travel features for books, magazines and online outlets. She has authored or co-authored several Lonely Planet guides to the USA, Canada, Caribbean and Europe. Follow her at twitter.com/karlazimmerman.

Read more about Karla at:
lonelyplanet.com/members/karlazimmerman

Published by Lonely Planet Publications Pty Ltd
ABN 36 005 607 983
3rd edition – Apr 2014
ISBN 978 1 74220 294 5
© Lonely Planet 2014   Photographs © as indicated 2014
10 9 8 7 6 5 4 3 2 1
Printed in China